21st January, 1984 33p

CW00456886

KEEGAN

Dream goal

KEVIN KEEGAN really proved he was king of Newcastle yesterday when he celebrated his debut with a dream goal.

And the Geordie fans reckon that their 1-0 Second Division win over QPR is just the start of a lucky streak for the start of a lucky team.

The goal came on the hour — soon after the 36,185 crowd saw a streaker dash on to the field wearing nothing but the socks and a black-and-white scarf as the teams got ready for the second half.

The man whipped off the scarf presented it to King Kev — before into the arms of the poli—

Then £100,000 K—

He began i—
Varadi—
go—

■ Kevin Keegan (centre) didn't expect his new club's strip to be like this.

65 'derby' arrests

By Neil McKay

YOUNG police-
oman was in
ospital last night—
n early victim of the
w soccer season.

She was taken to Sunderland General Hospital and detained overnight with head cuts and shock.

Police made 65 arrests at the "friendly" derby at Roker Park between Sunderland and Newcastle

Published by jLj publishing in December 2009
First Edition
Copyright©Mick Edmondson 2009

jLj publishing

c/o The Back Page
56, St Andrews Street
Newcastle upon Tyne NE1 5SF
email: jljpublishing@live.com

ISBN 978-0-9564410-0-3

Pictures and images supplied with the kind permission of NCJ Media, Newcastle upon Tyne, Julian Brannigan, Danny Brannigan, Stephen Brennan, Paul Bell, Paul Joannou and Chris Bell.

Research: Mick Edmondson & Kev Drew
Design: Gary Henderson (city-printers.com) & Mick Edmondson
Cover Design: Mark Moore (Printing.com) & Mick Edmondson
Printed in North East England by city-printers.com ltd.

The author wishes to express that the views of the contributors do not always represent the views of himself. Only fact and relevant information has been added to each contributor's anecdote. It is told, as it was by those who were there.

Black & White Daft

Following Newcastle United in the 1980's
1979 - 1984

by Mick Edmondson

Acknowledgements

I wish to acknowledge the following people for their time, help and kind cooperation; My beautiful wife Nichola for all her patience, help, support and understanding, without whom, the book wouldn't have been possible. The hundreds of fellow lifelong Newcastle United supporters (You know who you are) who have helped and supported this project for the past 30 years, without whose loyalty, passion and unconditional support for Newcastle United, through thick and thin, would have made this book impossible to write. A big thank you too every single contributor whom I've met, whilst on my travels following Newcastle United, up and down the country and around Europe. I apologise to those whose names have slipped my mind, mainly due to a few too many beers, as most tales have come from conversations in the pubs.

Special thanks to NCJ Media Editor Paul Robertson and work colleague Ann Dixon for their tremendous help and friendly cooperation. A big mention to Gary Henderson who has helped push the publication over the final few hurdles, nothing was a problem. Cheers to John & Charlie and all at Beyond Bar, Newcastle. Thanks also to Cass Pennant, Andrew Clarke, Andy Rivers and Paul Joannou for their guidance, kind words and advice. Cheers to my mate Kev Drew who ate all the cakes and pastries, whilst feeding me with vital material – the perfect sub when my head was about to explode. Newcastle John (Allen) for allowing me into his office! Newcastle City Library yet another reason, why were so very proud to be Geordies. Not forgetting Mark Hannen, Pete McParlin, Ken Waugh and Mark Moore and everybody else who has helped in whatever small way – you know who you are – thank you.

To my late Grandad and my late Dad for taking me and introducing me to Newcastle United and to my Mam who still holds a season ticket to this day. Apologies to any one I may have missed out.

Bibliography

A Complete Record 1882-1990 by Paul Joannou (Breedon Books- 1990)
Black 'n' White Alphabet by Paul Joannou (Polar Publishing 1996)
Fortress St James by Paul Joannou (Ballast 2000)
Geordie Passion by Mark Hannen (Keepdate Publishing 1996)
Standing in the Corner (Pete McParlin)
Newcastle Evening Chronicle, Newcastle Journal, The Sunday Sun, Daily Mirror & Football Pink.

Contents

The author

Mick Edmondson a lifelong Newcastle United fan was born in Newcastle upon Tyne in 1965 on the day Newcastle United lost at Anfield (the writing was on the wall). Raised in Walker in the city's East End he spent the first 4 years of his life living on the 11th floor of a block of flats in Pottery Bank. From the window he could see the River Tyne below, the Tyne Bridge and St.James Park floodlights, a perfect start to his Geordie life.

At a young age he spent Sunday mornings copying the First Division league table from the Football Pink – the only difference is that he would make sure Newcastle United were top. His Grandad, Mam and Dad were all Newcastle fans and would take him as often as they could, his first match was with his Grandad to see Supermac's home league debut v Liverpool in 1971. Before that his Dad had taken him to welcome the triumphant Fairs Cup team arrive back from Budapest in 1969 and his Mam and him had chased Bobby Moncur around Fenwick's in 1970, so that he could have his autograph. By the time Mick started school he had moved a few blocks away to a house near 'The County' pub, where his Mam still lives to this day.

At 7 years old he was playing for the under-11 school team at St Anthony's (A protestant school on Pottery Bank). Then at 9 years old Mick was playing for Newcastle Boys under-11's and went on to captain them for the next 6 years. He loved football, and was just as happy watching it as he was playing it. Sometimes though playing clashed with watching Newcastle and this was a nightmare scenario, especially in 1976 when he was on tour with Newcastle boys and he had to give up his League Cup Final ticket, which his Dad had got for him. Eventually though he would unfortunately have to choose between watching and participating. Mick's school football career was a huge success as he went onto captain Walker School to the County Cup twice in 4 years, as well as numerous league titles and City Cups. Throughout this period he would stand and watch Newcastle United from the Leazes End until it was knocked down in 1978. He then stood in the Gallowgate End 'Scoreboard' before moving to 'The Corner.' Mick was amazed by the noise, passion and repertoire of songs and would spend as much time watching the crowd as he would the match. Mick represented Northumberland and was close to an England call up along with fellow team mates Neil McDonald and Andy Sinton but suffered a really bad ankle injury.

Throughout his teens Mick enjoyed training at various league clubs and represented Newcastle United, Middlesbrough, Ipswich and West Brom at youth level whilst on trial. He played at St James Park twice, Roker Park, Sheilfield Park, Brunton Park and Tynecastle. Mick enjoyed training under Bobby Robson at Ipswich on numerous occasions and watched the Royal Wedding with England's Paul Mariner. He also played at Wallsend Boys club for 6 seasons which meant that he played at least 2 games every weekend for years. Mick absolutely loved his schoolboy football career, but when he played for West Brom youth team on Saturday 24th April 1982 against Coventry City, he actually walked away forever from playing on a Saturday. That afternoon West Brom first team lost at home to Sunderland and Mick had the misfortune to have to travel back on the Sunderland bus with all their team, wearing his Red Harrington jacket with the NUFC club crest sewn on.

The reason for telling you about his successful school football career is to try and explain what following Newcastle United means to him. Mick left school in the summer of 1982 and has never once played football on a Saturday since, as he made the choice that he would follow Newcastle United around the country instead of pursuing his playing career. The following season 1982/83, Mick never missed a single match home or away including friendlies and would spend the next twenty odd years travelling to over 120 different grounds to watch Newcastle United all over Europe. He has sold the programme, scored an own goal at the Leazes End, been a ball boy, edited the fanzine Toon Army News, seen Newcastle play in 15 different countries. But still awaits that first trophy!

But Mick confesses not to being their best fan as there are many others who actually spend their whole lives breathing NUFC. But he has been so lucky to meet so many genuine supporters, some great characters from all walks of life, so many happy memories, some sad, some happy, some crazy. Micks business and career still revolve around Newcastle United.

Dedicated to Nichola, Joe, Lucy and Jessica.

Introduction

1979-1984

Although this period saw European football dominated by English clubs as Nottingham Forest, Aston Villa and Liverpool all lifted the the European Cup the game itself was in trouble back home. The national side had failed to qualify for the World Cup between 1970 and 1982, whilst the game was apparently being ruined by football hooligans as this new social disease made many football supporters turn their backs on our national game. As a result crowds were falling dramatically and the game was heading for financial ruin. The country itself was in a huge mess under 'Thatcher Tory Rule' as over 3 million were unemployed and the North East suffered badly as the Shipyards, the Pits and most of our industry started to disappear.

Unfortunately on Tyneside our beloved football team Newcastle United was also in a terrible mess after years of good work by Joe Harvey had been quickly undone by a succession of inept managers; Gordon Lee, Richard Dinnis and Bill McGarry. Geordies needed their football on a Saturday afternoon more than ever to lift their spirits,but Second Division Newcastle weren't exactly the perfect answer. But we still turned up and hoped.

Hope you enjoy the read, if you have any anicdotes, photos of your
own that you would like to be considered for the next edition,
Black & White Daft... following Newcastle United in the 1980's...1984 to 1990
which will be published September 2010, then please email the publishers
at jljpublishing@live.com

WITHE, SHOULDER, MARTIN & HARDWICK!
WE'RE GONNA WIN THE LEAGUE
HAPPY NEW YEAR / PETROL BOMBS / WE HATE SUNDERLAND

1979-80 Season

Since last winning promotion from the Second Division as champions in 1965, we had spent the following 13 seasons in the First Division. Sadly this was to be our second season outside the top flight since being relegated back to the Second Division at the end of the 1977-78 season. And after the previous 1978-79 season, things had to improve and quickly. But if the summer was anything to go by, then the signs weren't good. In the past 12 months we had lost the services of John Blackley, Colin Suggett and Mark McGhee as well as a few fringe players such as Robinson, Barker, Mulgrove, Manners, Parkinson and Scott. And we had already accepted that Irving Nattrass our talented right back would be leaving soon on freedom of contract after 9 years at the club. He was the first player to leave the club in this way when he eventually signed for Middlesbrough on August 16th for £375,000, a then record amount received by Newcastle United. His transfer took a while and the fee was decided by a league tribunal. So our squad was thin and in typical Newcastle United style we only signed 3 players over the summer. Ian Davies a left back arrived from Norwich City for £150,000. He was joined by midfielder Peter Cartwright a local lad from non-league side North Shields. Also arriving at Gallowgate was Keith Armstrong, 22, from West Denton, who was formerly with Sunderland. One for the future - he would never, ever play for us! We weren't exactly competing with the likes of Real Madrid in the transfer market, nor did we expect too. But we seemed to be taking an all too familiar further step back. As we embarked on our mini pre-season tour of the West Country Eire international Mick Martin was promoted to captain. He had already experienced promotion from the Second Division twice before with different clubs. Once with Manchester United in 1974-75, then again with West Bromwich Albion, the following season. Off the field the 'Newcastle

United Supporters Club' formed in 1955 was celebrating its Silver Jubilee. It was also 25 years ago since we last won a domestic trophy - the FA Cup. Our priority was promotion. Could we also be celebrating come May?

v BATH CITY	**THUR 26TH JULY 1979**
TWERTON PARK	**FRIENDLY**
ATT; 2,146	**DREW 1-1**

I had a nightmare train journey through the night as the train seemed to break down on about three occasions but at least I made the kick-off. The West Country minnows were just about to embark on their first season in the Alliance Premier League and put up a good show. I eventually got home on the Friday just after 2pm.

Cliffy Ahmed
South Shields, Tyneside

Our most expensive new summer signing Ian Davies started with a nightmare against his part time non-league opponent. The left back allowed his winger to get away from him a few times and admitted, "I'm sometimes caught out by the long ball. This is because I like going forward but it's something I'm working on." Bill McGarry thought he had picked up a bargain! It was going to be a long season. If I ever saw the useless twat in the Dolce Vita I'd catch him out alright and I'd give him something to work on.

Matty Taylor
Wallsend, Tyneside

"We are all raring to go, really looking forward to the new season. The enthusiasm of Alan Shoulder and the patter of the two Irish lads Tommy Cassidy and Mick Martin does wonders for the boys off the field. Our morale is sky high."

David 'Dick' Barton
Newcastle United Player

v PLYMOUTH ARGYLE	**SUN 29TH JULY 1979**
HOME PARK	**FRIENDLY**
ATT; 2,397	**WON 3-0**

In the summer of 1979 Newcastle United went on a pre-season tour of the West Country. I was assistant secretary of the Newcastle United Supporters' Club at the time and as I was going to the games I had been designated to get the match programmes for the club shop which resided in Prudhoe Place in the Haymarket. I was staying with some friends in Taunton and duly drove to Plymouth and parked right beside the ground at about 2.30pm. Strangely there was hardly a soul about, so I ventured into the ground only to be told by some elderly gentleman that kick-off was at 7pm and not as I'd assumed 3pm - fabulous. The weather wasn't particularly great, so I made myself known at the Plymouth Club Office and they duly gave me 50 (fifty) programmes to bring home. I left my car in the parking bay and got the bus into the centre of Plymouth and ended up at the 'Pictures' watching 'The Champ' starring Jon Voight Ricky Schroder and Faye Dunaway!!! The match saw new team captain Mick Martin score with our first shot and lead United in the long grass to a good win. Newcastle fans were well represented in the crowd on a damp and misty night.

Bob Day
Heaton, Newcastle

I hadn't planned on making the longest journey in English football for a friendly but was out the night before and got tanked up, so as you do me and Davy Bolton got the midnight bus down to London. We then got the train from Paddington to Plymouth which seemed longer than the trip from Newcastle to the capitol. After a few beers we made our way to the ground and ended up having a game of football in the car park but were surprised to see Bill McGarry getting off the team coach at about 2.30pm so close to kick-off. He like us was under the impression that it was a standard 3pm kick-off, but we were all amazed when we were informed that it was actually a 7pm start! So that meant we had a few hours to kill (Pubs shut) and we had little choice but to spend the night in Plymouth as we couldn't get back to London. After the match we ended up playing pool with the Plymouth Chairman's son and had a great night.

Fink
The Sad Mad Ground Hopper

v TORQUAY UNITED	WED 1ST AUGUST 1979
PLAINMOOR	FRIENDLY
ATT; 2,450	WON 3-2

I, like loads of other Geordies had decided to spend my hollies in Torquay and take in our pre-season match on the west coast, at a ground which at the time happened to be the second longest trip in English league football. On a lovely sunny evening one squad from Newcastle turned up in fancy dress which included amongst their ranks an 'Asterix the Gaul' (stripy shirt and horny hat), one Viking (complete with another horny hat, leather studded belt and sword - plastic obviously), one fairy (pink silk dress, wings and a wand) and another 3 or 4 very drunk kids (I just can't remember their costumes) who decided to go around the ground to "attack" the Torquay mob at half time. This was to the tune of D-I-S-C-O or A-G-G-R-O as they improvised, demonstrating good spelling ability I thought. All were wearing Doc Martens and to be fair they put up a decent fight considering they were outnumbered - even if not out dressed. As a result of the battle they lost most of the fancier bits of their costumes which were littered across the pitch throughout the second half, as they themselves were either arrested or ejected. I wonder what Bill McGarry thought of it all?

Marty Taylor,
Newcastle

Newcastle United's first ever visit to Plainmoor and in my capacity of Newcastle United Supporters Club representative I duly did my job of getting the programmes for back home and then went into the ground. To my amazement the bloke and his son who sat next to me in the East Stand at St James' was in the front row of the seats. An amusing coincidence-he was down there on holiday and just turned up to watch the game-as you do.

Bob Day
Heaton, Newcastle

v EXETER CITY	FRI 3RD AUGUST 1979
ST JAMES PARK	FRIENDLY
ATT; 1,829	LOST 2-3

I made myself known to their club office to collect the match programmes. However this time instead of just being given them and ushered on my way I was treated like royalty and chatted to by some commercial manager or someone who mistakenly thought I was part of the official Newcastle United party!! I did not disillusion him. The Exeter supporters were well up for this match and I was a bit peeved at losing as this woman had a rattle and cranked it up the more the game went on, and she obviously enjoyed the victory over more illustrious opponents as they scored a last minute winner with a fierce free kick.

Bob Day
Heaton, Newcastle

Whilst Newcastle were losing to Third Division Exeter City a more significant result was taking place at Feethams, where Darlington were playing host to Carlisle United. A youngster by the name of Peter Beardsley who'd played the previous season for Wallsend Boys Club under 18's had been on trial at Newcastle all week, but McGarry had never seen him so an offer wasn't made. Instead Carlisle scout Brian Watson, himself a Geordie, drove Beardsley down to Darlington where he signed for Carlisle United. Newcastle later said that they

Back Row (left to right): John Connolly, Steve Hardwick, Kevin Carr, Peter Manners, David Barton.
Middle Row: John Brownlie, Gary Nicholson, Tommy Cassidy, Colin Suggett, Jamie Scott, Kenny Mitchell, Jim Pearson, Keith Mulgrove, Stuart Robinson, Ian Davies, Alan Shoulder, John Bird.
Front Row: Peter Cartwright, Mick Martin (Captain), Peter Withe, Nigel Walker, Bill McGarry (Manager), Terry Hibbitt, Irving Nattrass (now Middlesbrough F.C.), Kenny Wharton.

were ready to offer terms, but Carlisle caught them on the hop acting quickly.

Mick Edmondson
Walker, Newcastle

v BLYTH SPARTANS
CROFT PARK
ATT; 2,398

THURS 9TH AUGUST 1979
FRIENDLY
DREW 1-1

Five days earlier the sad news reached us that former Newcastle United goal scoring legend Malcolm 'Supermac' MacDonald had announced his premature retirement due to injury. He had struggled over the previous 18 months with a nagging knee injury and as he attempted to make his latest comeback he broke down in training on Arsenal's tour of Germany. Our latest goal scoring machine Alan Shoulder was returning to his former club and duly scored our goal in a dour affair which attracted a lot more than the 2,398 recorded for this fixture. One thing about Croft Park is that the floodlights seem to light up the whole town and even when you are about a mile away you would think that you were actually over the road!! Oh and we noticed quite a few glue sniffers also.

Mick Edmondson
Walker, Newcastle

Just twelve months after Giant Killers Blyth Spartans had unfairly been totally robbed of a place in the 6th Round (last 8) of the FA Cup against Arsenal, Newcastle travelled the few miles to play the heroes. In the 1977/78 season Blyth were beating Wrexham in the 5th Round down in Wales when in injury time a Wrexham corner which was caught by the Spartans keeper had to be mysteriously retaken. For some strange reason the referee decided that because the corner had been taken whilst the corner flag was lying on the ground that it should be taken again? If anything this was a disadvantage to Blyth and an advantage to Wrexham as the kicker had more room to take his kick. So instead of winning the match, Blyth were robbed when instead of their keeper hoofing the ball up field and the final whistle going, the corner was retaken and the welsh side equalized!! The replay was played at St James' Park and thousands were locked out as 42,167 inside witnessed a narrow 1-2 defeat. Since then we had signed their goal scorer Alan Shoulder and would later pinch Steve Carney from them. The summer had seen the departure of Irving Nattrass who was solid, steady, consistent, underrated and as good as a centre back as he was at full back. But what were his folks thinking when they named him? He sounds like a disease or a broken bed! He had more teeth than the modern parents out of the Viz Comic! Most important of all though was the fact that Peter Withe had remained at the club, his sweat bands spawned a thousand school yard copies. As a teenager I would also roll over the top of my footy shorts over for games so I could look like a pro.

Tommy Knox
Fenham, Newcastle

v SPARTA ROTTERDAM
ST JAMES' PARK
ATT; 7,596

SAT 11TH AUGUST 1979
FRIENDLY
LOST 0-1

After our West Country tour it was welcome back to St James' Park for a game against the oldest club in the Dutch First Division, Sparta Rotterdam who included Dutch super striker Ruudy Geels and Louis Van Gaal in their side. We were actually the better side although the Dutch technique and skills on display were slightly different to what we were used to. Their veteran keeper 35 year old Pim Doesburg pulled off at least 8 top class saves. Our visitors were returning the compliment as we played against them over in Holland in 1977 drawing 2-2. The admission prices had been announced for the coming season with a 50% increase! The club said that the increased admission costs were necessary so that the club would have the finances available to make the return to the First Division a realistic possibility. The club also said that General inflation, overheads and especially transfer fees had influenced the new levels of entrance fees! If anything the admission prices should have been reduced as the total cost of our summer signings Ian Davies, Keith Armstrong and Peter Cartwright was only £177,000, yet we recouped a huge £375,000 just from the sale of one player, Irving Nattrass, a profit of £198,000. Keith Armstrong came for a month's trial but was given a 1 year deal instead! Some things never change.

Mick Edmondson
Walker, Newcastle

v OLDHAM ATHLETIC
ST JAMES' PARK
ATT; 19,099

SAT 18TH AUGUST 1979
SECOND DIVISION
WON 3-2

"We All Agree Alan Shoulder Is Magic... Is Magic, Not Tragic" The previous season which was his first as a professional, the little Geordie striker signed from cup heroes Blyth Spartans had scored a very impressive 11 goals in 24 appearances, an ever present since his switch from the pits. Along with Peter Withe he was our new hero and we were hoping that the little and large partnership would propel us back into the First Division. Although Shoulder netted a penalty and made the other for Withe, the team got off to a shaky start as Oldham also netted twice, as 4 goals were scored in the opening 15 minutes. In fact we needed a hotly disputed penalty in the sixth minute of injury time to win the game. And it was thanks once again to Shoulder as we beat an Oldham side who'd won at Roker Park in the Anglo Scottish Cup the previous week. That night we went around the town and as a gesture to Alan Shoulder we drank

6

in pubs whose first letter spelt out his name. We started in the Adelaide at 5.30pm, and then continued in order as follows; Lowther, Adelphi, Newcastle Arms, Strawberry, Hotspur, Oscars, Urton, Lord Collingwood, Darn Crook, Eldon and finished off in the Rose & Crown twelve pints later. Now you probably haven't heard of the Urton, as we had to cheat a little bit. We went to the Burton on Croft Street and after borrowing a pair of ladders from the Portland pub we proceeded to cover the letter 'B' on the signage with a coat before any of us could enter. From that night on we always gave it our adopted name and would often call in when we stepped off the number 12 bus for our first pint right up until it sadly closed. We were all in our forties at the time, young and daft I suppose. A canny pub was the Urton.

Eddie Gittens
Byker, Newcastle

v PRESTON NORTH END
DEEPDALE
ATT; 12,707

TUES 21ST AUGUST 1979
SECOND DIVISION
LOST 0-1

With little early season optimism two pals Geordie, Gus and I caught the train via Carlisle for an evening at Deepdale. John Bird played against his former club with a broken nose and gave away a dubious last minute penalty which dwarf Eric Potts converted. In goal for them was Roy Tunks who'd been on trial at SJP months earlier. After the defeat which kept Preston top, we decided to hang back and go for a quick pint and let the angry Geordie army head off, and then catch the next train up to Carlisle for a planned night-club visit. Leaving the pub, Gus spotted a young local following the group, noting that the lad had clearly overheard our accents. Action was taken immediately which resulted in the youngster running off. Unfortunately when we reached the station the youngster reappeared and shouted across the road to a 60 strong group of Preston lads. Before we knew it, it was time to curl up into a ball. A steel comb was used in self-defence but not much else, as we were battered until the police came out of the station. They intervened and in very Anglo-Saxon words told us to get off the ground and head back to Newcastle. When we arrived at Carlisle station my hand was up like a balloon and it was decided that I needed hospital treatment and the lads decided that I needed company so they tossed a coin to decide who would accompany me. Geordie lost, so sat in the hospital disgruntled about missing the night out and muttering that a big club should not have to play against Preston anyway, whilst I was diagnosed with a badly-broken hand along with some bruises, and left in plaster. Meanwhile Gus joined the group of Newcastle skinheads we had met on the train and thoroughly enjoyed himself in the Nightclub.

Brian Hall
Heaton, Newcastle

v CHARLTON ATHLETIC
THE VALLEY
ATT; 6,849

SAT 25TH AUGUST 1979
SECOND DIVISION
DREW 1-1

On the Friday night I met up with a couple of mates at about 6pm and we drank around the Central Station, making sure we were well tanked up for the overnight train journey to London. At roughly 8pm we bumped into one of our neighbours in the 'Geordie Pride' pub, a right character called Dishy Donnelly who looked as though he had been drinking non stop for a week. When the pubs closed we went to catch our midnight train along with our new pal 'Dishy Donnelly' who refused to pay the full fare to London, instead purchasing a return ticket to Durham! It was in the early hours when he eventually woke from his drunken sleep, about half an hour from Kings Cross. He didn't look too pleased as he enquired, "Where the fuck are we?" "Just outside London," I replied. "London you're taking the piss, I've never been out of Rowland's Gill before apart from the Toon! Wor lass will kill me." Although he wasn't interested in football he decided to stick with us for the weekend, even though he had no money. This problem was soon solved when we entered the first bar. He walked into the toilets and kicked the Blob machine off the wall, scoring for a bag full of 50p coins. He seemed to enjoy his weekend and a 1-1 draw as Peter Cartwright made his league debut coming on as a sub in South London. Not many Charlton fans turned up in a ground that not long ago held 70,000. Dishy was quiet on the way home, as he dodged the ticket inspector and awaited the fire work display on his return!

Martin
Rowland's Gill, Tyneside

v SUNDERLAND
ROKER PARK
ATT; 27,746

WED 29TH AUGUST 1979
LEAGUE CUP 2ND RND 1ST LEG
DREW 2-2

A midweek trip south to Sunderland as they were known then, (Can't ever recall them being known as the Mackem's back then) for my first ever local derby. We boarded one of the 'Football Specials' which was jam packed and soon we arrived at Seaburn station, where we were met by the police. The fashion at the time was dungarees and black hats (Dexy's style) and as we left the station we were all whistling and singing the chorus to the 'Geno' song. I loved the police escort or should I say police containment operation, as what seemed like hundreds of coppers dozens with dogs, some on horseback worked tirelessly to stop any of the Geordie army from escaping down the side streets. We were to play them both home and away in the newly formatted League Cup which for the first time consisted of two legs at the second round stage. Our hatred of the Wearsider's was to be rekindled as it meant that we would play them a total of 4 times over the season, which considering that we had only played 2 matches against them in the previous 10 seasons, was pretty exciting/nerve racking. I mean 'Supermac' never ever got the chance to run them ragged as they'd spent years playing at their true level in the Second Division whilst we'd been in the top flight. Newcastle outplayed Sunderland for long periods with some lovely one touch football and passing movement, yet we were trailing 0-2 with only 15 minutes remaining. We pulled one back through Ian Davies before ex-North Shield's player and Philatelist Peter Cartwright came on as a sub and put a far post header past the hapless Barry Siddall (Basil Fawlty). The life long stamp collecting Newcastle supporter sent the travelling masses into ecstasy and put us in an ideal situation for the second leg.

Dave Drape
Walker, Newcastle

19 fans arrested after derby battles

A Police superintendent and a police horse were injured by flying bricks as clashes between rival fans marred last nights Sunderland - Newcastle derby match. In other incidents around Roker Park, a police officer was assaulted and a 16 year old youth taken to hospital with facial injuries. Sunderland police said today that 19 arrests were made in and around Roker Park during the match and 21 fans were ejected from the ground. The youth taken to Sunderland General Hospital was detained for observation. The police horse, ridden by Insp. Oswald Burt, was treated for a deep cut to a hind leg. Supt. David Lander, of Washington police was hit on the side of the face by a brick but did not require treatment.

My first visit to Roker Park, the tension was huge, even for such a fairly low key game and I had first hand experience of 'life in enemy territory' as we were chased through gardens after the game on the way back to our Armstrong Galley coach, parked on the Seaburn front. It was an added bonus that a lad from North Shields, Peter Cartwright, scored our equaliser in a 2-2 draw. I was now getting to a few away games and what a laugh they used to be, the lack of entertainment on the pitch often made up by the antics and banter from the terraces.

Anth Nicholson
North Shields, Tyneside

At the end of the match Terry Hibbitt led the whole Newcastle team to the Roker End to applaud the thousands of travelling Geordies, who had given them such great vocal support throughout. Over the years it has really annoyed me when our players have ignored the travelling fans and just disappeared down the tunnel. It's the height of ignorance as we always travel in huge numbers giving support second to none. All we ever ask is players whose wages we pay to show a little bit of respect. When I look back matches like this one were worth twenty of todays.

Mick Edmondson
Walker, Newcastle

I asked my sister Liz to get a couple of tickets for the cup match at Roker Park, as I was at work. She duly got the tickets and the on the night of the match my mate and I queued up at the Roker End with fellow Newcastle fans. When we got to the turnstile we were refused entry as our tickets were for the Fulwell End! Confused, we argued our case, but were still refused entry. So we had little choice but to watch in silence from the Sunderland End. When I eventually arrived home and pulled my sister and asked how she ended up with tickets for the Sunderland End, she replied: "I don't know, the wife at the Roker Park ticket office, just gave me them." That's women for you.

John Allen
Shiremoor, Newcastle

v CHELSEA　　　　　　　　　　　　　　　**SAT 1ST SEPTEMBER 1979**
ST JAMES' PARK　　　　　　　　　　　　　　**SECOND DIVISION**
ATT; 25,047　　　　　　　　　　　　　　　　　　　**WON 2-1**

Hooligans must pay £2,480

Newcastle magistrates are to step up their campaign against football hooligans, according to one city bench chairman. Mr Robert Owen has warned: "We think behaviuor like this cannot go on. People should be able to go into town on Saturday free from worry. The city of Newcastle is not going to tolerate this sort of behavior." The warning came when 12 North-East youths and two others were fined a total of £2,340 with £140 costs after incidents at the Newcastle-Chelsea football match.

I remember this match as Peter Withe and Chelsea's big ugly giant centre-half Micky Droy nearly came to blows at one point, a fight that would have been interesting. Droy tried to contain Withe, but the Newcastle number nine went onto win the match for us scoring two headers. Stuart Boam had a very encouraging debut after his recent £140,000 move from Middlesbrough. The Pensioners', who'd recently been relegated, were hot favourites for promotion and an immediate return to the top flight. The London outfit wore an all yellow second strip instead of their famous all blue strip for no apparent reason, football was definitely changing. I'd always prefer to see visiting sides wearing their official club colours where at all possible. Your loyalty for turning up today was an opportunity to buy a ticket for the forthcoming League Cup tie at home to local rivals Sunderland on the following Wednesday, available from the turnstile operator as you entered the ground. This was to save supporters from making an additional trip to St James' Park for the all ticket affair with tickets on sale until 2pm, Wednesday the day of the match. Starting on the front of today's match programme was a 'Star Face' competition with prizes totaling £195, which was split into four separate prizes of £100, £50, £25 and £20 respectively. Inkerman Publications Limited ran this competition for the whole season. To stand a chance of winning you had to scratch out with a coin the silver adhesive circle on the front cover of your programme, where a player's face would appear. If you won you had to claim your prize within 30 minutes of the final whistle at the clubs lottery offices. Typically a Chelsea fan actually won one of the first prizes.

Mick Edmondson
Walker, Newcastle

Fan arrested at match

A process worker made indecent hand signals and swore at rival Chelsea fans. Steven Robinson of Bowburn, was seen standing towards the rear of the New Stand Paddock when he was arrested as he pushed a large group of supporters down the terraces. In his defence he said: "We were assembled at the back and I went to the shop for a pie and when I returned there was a disturbance at the front of the crowd. A policeman went down to the front and on his way back up he came to where I was and said I was under arrest." I said "Why am I being arrested? I haven't done anything."

v SUNDERLAND
ST JAMES' PARK
ATT; 30,533

WED 5TH SEPTEMBER 1979
LEAGUE CUP 2ND RND 2ND LEG
DREW 2-2 (LOST 6-7 PENS)

What it's like to be a Newcastle fan can be summed up by this match. It's filled with expectation, tension, agony and ecstasy, with a few laughs but more often than not a kick in the teeth at the end. Here we had great expectations after coming from two down to draw the first leg at Roker Park. Then there was tension as the game stayed goalless till late on. Agony; Alan Brown scores for them, then ecstasy as Alan Shoulder equalises then incredibly Stuart Boam puts us ahead. More agony, Brown equalises with the last kick of normal time. Then there's the tension of a goalless extra time period, then penalties. They score, we score again and again. Their penalties are crap, unfortunately the laughs are provided by our keeper Steve Hardwick, whose idea of attempting a penalty save seemed to consist of him falling backwards on his arse and slapping his knees as the ball trickles past him. They lead 7-6 and the final agony is left to Jim Pearson, not a bad penalty but Siddall saves it. Last minute equaliser followed by a penalty defeat the ultimate kick in the teeth. Afterwards outside there was bovver amongst our own. The mood waiting for the bus as you'd expect was pretty ugly. You had to keep your wits about you as you had a feeling something would kick off. There was something about the two blokes who pushed into the front of a long queue which told you it was probably not a good idea to point out the error of their ways. One lad who was with his lass didn't share that view and told them to get to the back of the queue. The blokes looked at each other, said nowt but walked towards the lad, then picked him up and threw him through the window of the bus shelter before returning to the front of the queue. This time nobody said anything!

Chris Ramshaw
West Denton, Newcastle

I can still see their fans sneaking out as they were heading for defeat just before full time. Most of them missed a last gasp Alan Brown equalizer which sent the game into extra time resulting in penalties. I have never needed a pint after a match so much and I couldn't get one as the bars closed at 10.30pm in those days and it was too late to drown our sorrows as it was 10.20pm when Jim Pearson stepped up.

Mike Pollard
Wallsend, Tyneside

Fact; we have never ever been any good at penalty shoot outs. We lost our first ever game which went to penalties against Pecsi Dozsa in Budapest, Hungary in November 1970. That night Bryan Pop Robson missed for us hitting the Hungarian woodwork with our first (We missed the next two also), yet unbelievably tonight nine years later he scored the first one for Sunderland against us! You couldn't make it up. With five penalties taken each after 210 minutes of Cup football it was still level as all ten pens had been converted. Shoulder, Withe, Martin, Davies and Brownlie scoring at the Gallowgate End for us. The twelve yard lottery was now to be competed Russian roulette style. Surprise, surprise Steve Hardwick never saved one and after Barton converted poor Jim Pearson failed to convert number seven as Siddell saved. Unlucky Jim Pearson wasn't even fully fit and shouldn't have even played. He only played because Tommy Cassidy was injured. Surprisingly Terry Hibbitt and Peter Cartwright never volunteered allowing 3 defenders go before them. The only other player not to take one was Stuart Boam who was actually to blame for Brown's match saving last minute effort, when he lost the ball outside of our area! For some fans the agony of defeat at the hands of Sunderland was made worse when they realized that they had been the target of gangs of pick pockets who apparently made a killing at the game.

Mick Edmondson
Walker, Newcastle

Sunderland's stay away supporters were rapped by the clubs manager Ken Knighton who was very disappointed with the red-and-white turn out at St James' Park. Only 3,500 Roker fans made the trip to Newcastle and Knighton said; "That disappointed me. I thought there would have been a lot more than that." I expected to see a lot more red-and-white scarves than I did." A mixture of reasons were suggested for their lack of support which included: Fans being worried about their safety, fans thinking they were already beaten and the wearsiders having far inferior support than Newcastle.

Ken Knighton, Sunderland Manager

v LEYTON ORIENT   **SAT 8TH SEPTEMBER 1979**
BRISBANE ROAD   **SECOND DIVISION**
ATT; 5,700   **WON 4-1**

Our first away win of the season which moved us in to the top three wasn't as straight forward as the score line suggests, as Orient had twelve corners compared to our one!! The lowest crowd to watch us in the 1979-80 season, also saw Orient miss a penalty whilst Terry Hibbitt scored his first Newcastle goal since our Texaco Cup match against Aberdeen in 1974. His last league goal was our winner at Highbury on New Year's Day the same year. We travelled with the Newcastle United Supporters Club at a cost of £5.90 and we were dropped off at Kings Cross after the match so we could celebrate our first ever league win at Brisbane Road and a valuable two points, in London's West End before being picked up at 11pm, followed by a drunken sleep back up the A1, arriving home in the early hours.

Tommy B
Walker, Newcastle

v LEICESTER CITY
ST JAMES' PARK
ATT; 26,443

SAT 15TH SEPTEMBER 1979
SECOND DIVISION
WON 3-2

Outside the Gallowgate End turnstiles before every home match there used to be a bloke selling large tin badges from a board. Now these basic badges although printed were definitely homemade jobbies, with black ink on various coloured backgrounds including lime green, bright orange and cream. They were ideal to put on your woolly Black-and-White scarf with lyrics like 'Jesus saves, but Alan Shoulder puts in the rebound,' and 'John Connolly walks on water.' Two pens from Alan Shoulder and a Peter Cartwright goal was enough to put us top of the league. *"Were Gonna Win The League, Were Gonna Win The League, And Now You're Gonna Believe Us, Were Gonna Win The League."*

Mick Edmondson
Walker, Newcastle

v WREXHAM
ST JAMES' PARK
ATT; 27,904

SAT 22ND SEPTEMBER 1979
SECOND DIVISION
WON 1-0

Only one defeat in our opening six league games! These were exciting times indeed as we sat proudly on top of the old Second Division and welcomed BBC's 'Match of the Day' cameras for a very rare visit. With the old Leazes End gone the season before last, the Gallowgate was the new home for the Geordie Choir who congregated in the centre section of this open terrace behind the goal, known to all as the 'Scoreboard.' Even though we were off to a good start our football still didn't match the entertainment that was provided by the Geordies on the packed terraces. My hero at this time wasn't Alan Shoulder who scored the games only goal (already his sixth league penalty of the season), but a living legend who was known to all as the Geordie Hulk. Each home match he would appear from nowhere and climb up onto one of the concrete barriers towards the back of the terrace, about 20 metres in front of the scoreboard - which actually looked more like a Pigeon Cree. He would then respond to the cheers by removing his top, whilst clenching his fists inwards towards his big fat belly which used to hang over the top of his jeans. He would then take a big deep breath before turning purple in colour whilst making a massive growling noise - aaaaarrrrrrgghhhh!! This ritual would last for a few minutes until his blood pressure was at boiling point. He then spent the next ten minutes with his back to the pitch as a cheerleader going through a medley of classic Geordie terrace chants. That night at home as I excitedly watched 'Match of the Day' we were the second match of only two shown, in the days when all matches in the football league were played at 3pm on a Saturday afternoon (unless of course Tranmere were at home on a Friday). They didn't even show the goals from any of the other matches played that day; we were on centre stage and guess who made his T.V. debut that night? Yes as the cameras panned the crowd they zoomed in on the Geordie Hulk who was half naked on the barrier in the middle of his act. Just a pity it was in the days before video machines! A living legend we called 'The Geordie Hulk.'

Mick Edmondson
Walker, Newcastle

A mundane game settled by a hotly disputed Alan Shoulder penalty and a rare appearance on BBC Match of the Day. We stayed top as the nation witnessed our fourth consecutive league win. The commentator was Des Lynam. The talking point at school on Monday was not the match but Lynam's half time report covered on Grandstand. The camera had apparently spent the whole report focussed on a lad standing on a barrier in the Gallowgate End doing an impression of the Incredible Hulk complete with Hulk mask. "That wasn't Des Lynam" said host Frank Bough when they returned to the studio. It turned out The Hulk was a lad who had left our school in the summer.

Chris Ramshaw
West Denton, Newcastle

v BIRMINGHAM CITY	SAT 29TH SEPTEMBER 1979
ST ANDREWS	SECOND DIVISION
ATT; 19,967	DREW 0-0

A journey down to the Midlands, to play what was our 3,000th league match. The 'Blues' had just been relegated last season and were amongst the favourites to be promoted. We had utilised over 600 different players since our first ever league match at Woolwich Arsenal back in September 1893. The team which played out a boring scoreless draw was Hardwick, Brownlie, Barton, Boam, Davies, Martin, Cassidy, Hibbitt, Shoulder, Withe, Cartwright with Nigel Walker as an unused sub. Steve Hardwick and Stuart Boam were our top players as we defended well against a decent Birmingham side. After four wins and a draw in the league in September our boss Bill McGarry was named 'The Second Division

Bells Manager of the Month.' The other awards went to First Division Terry Venables (Crystal Palace), Third Division Harry Haslam (Sheffield United) and Fourth Division George Kirby (Halifax Town).

Mick Edmondson
Walker, Newcastle

A few of us got the train down and ended up in the Birmingham City supporters club for a few beers. I got talking to the brother of Tommy Cassidy's who was playing for us at the time. There was a good mixture of both sets of fans who were being entertained by this singer who was absolutely shite. So I got up on stage and took the microphone off him and started my own repertoire of songs. The atmosphere was starting to change and eventually all mayhem broke loose when I stupidedly sang: *"Down In Birmingham In The Sun, The Pakis Outnumbered 10 To 1, Some Are Black Some Are Tanned, Some From Jamaica Some From Pakistan."* I wasn't able to get the rest of the song out when I was being attacked by a group of big black lads. I defended myself with the microphone stand swinging it around my head. One lad Piper, got put on his arse and ended up with splinters of glass in his buttocks. Eventually the coppers restored order and I was pointed out by Birmingham fans. Luckily for me though a lad we knew as Coventry John who followed Newcastle was in the room and he explained in his Midlands accent that I was innocent. The coppers took me outside where there was a large mob waiting for me, they were going off it. I shouted towards them "Ye not hard enough," from behind the safety of the police. After the match I went to an Off-license to get some drink for the train. Then as I crossed the road towards New Street Train Station there was the mob from earlier. I was well and truly punched and kicked around the street. I practically crawled into the station and onto the train. Unfortunately my cans were badly dented but I still managed to have a night out in Sheffield.

Black Horse Tony
Low Fell, Tyneside

Before the match we went for a quiet drink in their supporters club near the ground but ended up in a full scale riot as glasses were smashed, tables and chairs were thrown. I was fined £180 as a result of being in the wrong place at the wrong time.

Deka
Gateshead, Tyneside

v WEST HAM UNITED
UPTON PARK
ATT; 23,206

SAT 6TH OCTOBER 1979
SECOND DIVISION
DREW 1-1

Left Morden Street at 7am on the old Supporters Club coaches, can't remember what number coach we were on but it definitely wasn't number one as that was 'Fatty Mullen's' coach for all his cronies. We had only lost one of our opening eight league games and were sitting on top of the league as we made our way down to East London and to a proper football ground. We were half expecting some bother as we'd been to Orient a few weeks earlier and a few West Ham had showed up before the match for a bit of a ruck. I remember it was a red hot day but that hadn't stopped us wearing the then obligatory Donkey Jacket! Only aged 16 it was one of the biggest matches we had been to and thanks to the driver we ended up hopelessly lost and didn't arrive outside the 'Boleyn Arms' pub until 2.45pm. For those of you not familiar with this bar imagine the scenario if a bus load of cockneys had got off their bus outside The Strawberry' 15 minutes before kick-off in the late seventies. Well the inevitable happened and as we were totally outnumbered and carrying passengers we got absolutely battered before the Bizzies eventually managed to get us into the away section. In those days we didn't take the huge numbers we were to take in the near future, so there were just over a thousand Mags in our end as well as a load of their mob mingling in, fights were going off left, right and centre. We got a free-kick ten yards from their goal after Phil Parkes was adjudged to have caught the ball with an upraised foot by World Cup referee Clive Thomas. West Ham had 9 men on the goal line with Parkes in front of them. This was a great chance to take the lead, with everyone thinking the same thing - if this goes in then there will be hell on. The ball got tapped to Peter Withe who buried into the bottom corner, 'GOAL.' Cue mayhem in our end with loads getting dragged out, being bairns we were shitting ourselves as there seemed to be as many of them as us in our end. I remember being almost pleased when they equalized and after being kept in the ground for what seemed like ages we were escorted to our bus and reunited with our driver-Stevie Wonder. That afternoon made a big impression on us as most had never been to or seen anything like that before, so to all the lads and lasses who now roam the streets around Upton Park wearing their Black 'n' White shirts trust me you couldn't do that in 1979.

Paul Wardle
Wallsend, Tyneside

My son and I made the journey by coach to West Ham - but never again. When Newcastle equalized one great lout of a so called West Ham supporter crashed his fist into my sons face knocking him flying down the terraces. We spent half an hour in the ambulance room and after the match hundreds of their supporters were battling with police trying to get at our fans. Some cars were strewn across the road and one van had all its windows broken. The police had one youth handcuffed to a lamp-post and had a terrible job on their hands escorting us to our coaches. My son and I breathed a sigh of relief when escorted by the police; we drove out of West Ham.

T. McNaughton
Wallsend, Tyneside

v PRESTON NORTH END   **WED 10TH OCTOBER 1979**
ST JAMES' PARK   **SECOND DIVISION**
ATT; 25,154   **DREW 0-0**

There was nothing like a classic encounter under the floodlights at St James' Park in the late seventies and this was nothing like a classic encounter under the floodlights at St James' Park in the late seventies!! A decent midweek crowd turned up to witness a terrible game, our third consecutive draw as we met

Preston Knob End for the second time even though we'd only played ten league matches, (Computers will never take off). Our only defeat so far had been at Deepdale and now they'd taken a total of 3 points off us, although we still remained top. We had started the season quite aggressively and had picked up twenty bookings already with Peter Cartwright the only regular outfield player yet to pick up a caution.

Mick Edmondson
Walker, Newcastle

v SHREWSBURY TOWN	**SAT 13TH OCTOBER 1979**
ST JAMES' PARK	**SECOND DIVISION**
ATT; 21,603	**WON 1-0**

One of our favourite pre-match haunts in the late seventies/early eighties was the Hofbrauhaus down by the old cattle market which used to have strippers entertaining until just after 3pm on Saturdays. This led to many either being late for the game, or, in the case of Benji and a couple of the other lads from Shiney Row just staying until the bitter, or rather entertaining end, and getting a bus back home instead. They didn't miss much. The Sunday Sun headlines the next morning read 'United play badly and win, Roker play well and lose.' This was the first time in our history we'd played Shrewsbury in the League.

Brian Hall
Heaton, Newcastle

v WATFORD	**SAT 20TH OCTOBER 1979**
VICARAGE ROAD	**SECOND DIVISION**
ATT; 17,715	**LOST 0-2**

We were only 18 years old and travelled down to Watford in my mates Dad's car a new Ford Escort. What we didn't tell him was that there were seven of us and none of us had a clue on how to get to Watford. It was a long journey but a right laugh, scarves hanging out the windows and beeping every time other Toon fans passed us (as you do) and hiding every time we saw any coppers. We eventually managed to get there although it actually took us eight hours, due to bad navigation, too much weight and needing to stretch our legs and bodies constantly. But we still had time for a few pints after parking the car in a side street near the ground. The match was terrible as we dropped from top down to third being replaced by the 'Hornets' neighbours Luton. Watford chairman Elton John was the lucky one as he was on tour in the USA so missed this stinker - at least his side won though. We headed back to the car only to find that it wasn't there. For some unknown reason we started roaming the surrounding streets looking for it, as though somebody had pushed it around the corner! It had been nicked, what could we do? Bry had to get in touch with his Dad to break the news and ask his advice but as his Mam and Dad didn't have a phone it wasn't easy. Three of us decided to stick around whilst the other four made their way to the motorway to start hitching, as the police wouldn't be over the moon with seven of us in an Escort! After all of our details were taken the Police gave us a lift to the railway station where we then started the journey home. We managed to escape paying, eventually arriving home just after midnight. The others got split up, two of them ended up nearly freezing to death sleeping rough near Doncaster, the remaining two ended up getting a taxi from Leeds. As for the car it was found a few days later, burnt out. The car saga wasn't over though as Bry's dad went berserk when he received a parking ticket a few weeks later for a car he was never to see again.

Dave Thompson
Killingworth, Newcastle

v CAMBRIDGE UNITED **ST JAMES' PARK** **ATT; 24,104**	**SAT 27TH OCTOBER 1979** **SECOND DIVISION** **WON 2-0**

Must we pay the price of prettiness?

The recent decision of the City planners to refuse the Club permission to build the new North Stand – before completing the East Stand corner section – is totally unacceptable to Newcastle United.

The Club's argument is one of simple commercial viability. Would any going concern invest £1.45m, to achieve an annual return of £58,000, BEFORE investing £1.85m, to achieve income of £134,000 over the same period?

When the Club signed a new ninety nine year lease in 1971, it undertook, within ten years, to spend one million pounds (or its equivalent in terms of costs prevailing at that time), on the re-development of St. James' Park.

We have already spent considerably in excess of £1m, with the new East Stand, and the first phase of the North Stand, representing the major part of that investment. We are now poised to spend again to build this new stand, an investment which will more than satisfy the terms of our lease.

What we cannot accept is that before then, we must spend almost one and a half million pounds, literally "bridging the gap," and then have to strive for a considerable number of years raising vast sums of money to build what we really need now – a new stand.

The Planners rejection is based on aesthetic grounds. So no-one in this Club is going to argue that cantilever football stands are necessarily pretty things. But if visual acceptability is to be put before sound commercial judgement, must we be expected to pay the price?

THE DIRECTORS
Newcastle United Football Co. Ltd.

This victory meant that we remained unbeaten at home in the league with a pleasing 13 points out of a possible 14, lying second in the table. Making his debut was our new striker Billy Rafferty signed from Wolverhampton Wanderers for £175,000. He originally made his first ever league appearance of his career as a Coventry City player against Newcastle United way back in April 1970. We managed to beat Birmingham City and Derby County for the services of the striker. We hoped that he would give us that extra something up front; you could say that he succeeded as he was definitely something different! He was bloody different alright. If Newcastle were playing away and you weren't travelling then many teenagers would usually spend Saturday afternoons in town hanging around the Record shops, like HMV which was small back then and was located at the bottom of Northumberland Street where Scotts/La Coste is now. There was also Volume, Virgin, Windows and Callers which even had their own Northern Soul chart. Other popular haunts included the Kard Bar located in the Handyside (Hippy) arcade where the Sham Army/Elswick Mafia Boys (EMB & an eye tattooed on the back of their necks), L.B.A.B. and the likes used to clash or just chin the hippies.

Mick Edmondson
Walker, Newcastle

United fan knifed
FOUR HURT IN BATTLE ON THE TERRACES

A Newcastle United fan was stabbed and four other people were hurt when rival fans ran riot yesterday! Before United's match at Oldham fighting broke out in a town centre pub. The Newcastle fan injured was Donald Irwin, 21, of Woodhorn Villas, Ashington. He was taken to hospital with an arm injury. Four other fans received treatment at Oldham Royal Infirmary after battles on the terraces. Oldham Athletic goalkeeper Peter McDonnell had a lucky escape when bricks were thrown at him from the stands. United's fans were massed behind him in the second half and police had to wade in several times to break up fighting. McDonnell said later: "It was a little hair-raising at times; things were thrown down and were flying about my ears including a couple of half bricks. "It was a bit off-putting, especially as we were under a fair bit of pressure." Last night Oldham police said that 23 people were arrested at the match and a further 43 were thrown out. They are to appear in court charged under the Public orders act. A man has also been charged in connection with the wounding of Mr Irwin. Oldham Royal Infirmary refused to reveal his condition last night. But Insp. Barry Own of Oldham Police said: "We've had a lot of trouble with United fans today. They have run riot." "We had to move in to separate them at the match and some of my men have gone home hurt, although not seriously." "They had to fight to keep the fans apart." "There is no doubt that Newcastle gave us most aggro today." There was also trouble on the train before the match as United fans smashed bottles.

v OLDHAM ATHLETIC
BOUNDARY PARK
ATT; 11,486

SAT 3RD NOVEMBER 1979
SECOND DIVISION
LOST 0-1

On a cold and damp day we got beat at Oldham, which at the time was classed as Lancashire and not Greater Manchester. I usually travelled with the Supporters Club on an Armstrong Galley coach, a fine and reliable service, memberships and photographs taken on a Tuesday night, upstairs in 'The Bridge.' Stuart Boam led the side at the centre of defence, though could do nothing about a scrappy goal. Almost half the crowd were from Newcastle and we stood on old concrete terracing behind one goal, behind which was grass banking then fencing near the turnstiles. For some reason, perhaps security, the local vendors decided it may be best to sell their wares from outside the fence, rather than inside the away enclosure. Hot food, drinks and programmes were all available via the fence. At half-time as people in their droves headed for warm food and drink, someone decided it would be fun to receive your order then just walk/run away, leaving the vendors grasping and pleading for their cash. Incredibly, they continued to serve for most of half time, as people just wandered away without paying. By the time the Police eventually arrived all the evidence was gone, warming the bellies of the away support. The defeat meant that we dropped out of a promotion place down to fourth.

Anth Nicholson
North Shields, Tyneside

This match down in Lancashire was well supported by the huge Geordie following, but also resulted in serious disturbances as Newcastle fans rampaged through the town before the match. All afternoon fighting also erupted on numerous occasions on the terraces. The police were stretched all afternoon but the worst incident inside the ground was when bricks were thrown at the

Oldham keeper Peter McDonnell. The concrete was widely available around your feet as the dilapidated terracing just crumbled with ease. Missile throwing was becoming increasingly common which questioned the mentality of some supporters. Newcastle Captain Mick Martin was furious claiming that the players had been distracted by the actions and that "No club wants to be tainted by the antics of these sort of people." The Newcastle United Supporters Club - having been founded just before the 1955 FA Cup final - was just about to celebrate it's Silver Jubilee Year. Although membership was high the vast majority of travelling fans were not members. Only 20% of the fans who made the trip to Oldham had travelled with the Supporters Club.

Mick Edmondson
Walker, Newcastle

This was a day that brought shame on Newcastle United football club and football in general. One man stabbed, 26 arrests and a further 43 thrown out of the ground. Magistrates at Oldham imposed fines between £50 and £200 on Newcastle United fans, one accused of assault on a copper and another shouted "Lets get them" as he headed a group of Newcastle fans who charged Oldham fans. He told a court he had been provoked when someone called him a Geordie bastard and hit him in the mouth. He said he had now stopped going to matches.

v CARDIFF CITY
ST JAMES' PARK
ATT; 22,867

SAT 10TH NOVEMBER 1979
SECOND DIVISION
WON 1-0

The almost non-existent support from the South of Wales didn't really help, but nevertheless this was a healthy Second Division crowd. Less than 30 supporters had travelled from the Welsh capitol and they looked lost standing on the away terrace which could house up to 1,000 when full. The Soul-less Crew. But credit to the handful who bothered. The win meant United went second within a solitary point of leaders QPR. As United were starting to get it right on the field everything they did off it seemed to get on my tits. One of my moans is that they would constantly play the same 4 records at half-time every bloody week. "Some girls will, some girls won't......." Why they didn't buy some new records?

Phil Anderson
West Denton, Newcastle

What a weekend! Friday night went to see 'The Specials, Madness and The Selector' at the Mayfair all for £2.50. Then paid 80p to stand on the Gallowgate End and watched Alan Shoulder get the winner to put Newcastle second in the league. You could just about manage to buy a pint now with £3.30. Just too round things off I met my future wife in 'The Lowther' at last orders. Dare not say what gave me the greatest buzz that weekend.

George Curtis
Lemington, Newcastle

Ken McGowan a Newcastle newsagent did not have much faith in Newcastle

United's ability to win promotion back into the First Division. In fact he thought so little of their chances of climbing back within the next five years that he tried to bet on it. Ken of Kingston Park, asked Ladbrokes to give him odds for a £200 bet that United would not get into the First Division in the next five seasons - but they wouldn't take it. "Mr McGowan's bet would have to lie on the counter for five years before anyone knew the outcome. This is an unusually long time for any piece of paper to remain in a betting office."

Newspaper Article

v MANCHESTER CITY
ST JAMES' PARK
ATT; 14,955

TUES 13TH NOVEMBER 1979
IAM McFAUL TESTIMONIAL
WON 4-1

Born William Stewart McFaul in Coleraine, 1st October 1943 he made 354 appearances between the sticks for 'The Magpies' between 1967 and 1975, before coaching the reserves and then the first team, eventually becoming manager himself at a later date. He won six Northern Ireland caps but would have won dozens more if it hadn't of been for the fact that his fellow countryman Pat Jennings was one of the world's best all-time keepers. In typical Newcastle fashion he was signed by them after he conceded seven goals in a friendly!! United arranged to play a friendly against Linfield so that Joe Harvey and the late Stan Seymour could have a another look at the keeper as on the two previous occasions they'd watched him he'd had nothing to do. His club honours include: a European Fairs Cup winners medal, two Texaco Cup winners medals, as well as an Anglo Italian winners medal. He played 24 games in Europe for Newcastle and played in the 1974 FA Cup Final. He was currently a coach which would eventually lead to the gaffers desk. As I prepared to make my way across the town for the match the headlines on the front page of the Chronicle caught my eye: Ripper badge of shame. It continued - Sunderland football club officials are trying to find out who is producing a badge which reads: John Hawley strikes faster than the ripper. Det Supt. Peter Docherty, in charge of the Wearside hunt for the killer said: "It is absolutely disgusting and totally irresponsible." A supporter reported the badge after seeing a 13 year old girl wearing it. The police would have been better off looking for the Wearside hoaxer never mind the Wearside badge seller. John Hawley by the way didn't strike at all, never mind as quickly as the badge insinuated.

Mick Edmondson
Walker, Newcastle

"I've always said that nothing surprises me up here, but I was pleasantly surprised by the size of the crowd for tonight's match."

Bill McGarry,
Newcastle Manager

v BRISTOL ROVERS   **SAT 17TH NOVEMBER 1979**
EASTVILLE   **SECOND DIVISION**
ATT; 7,626   **DREW 1-1**

What a shithole this place was. Without doubt the worst ground I've ever visited. After 13 seasons of visiting the likes of Highbury, Anfield, Old Trafford and Maine Road it had now come to this. The previous season our first in this division since our relegation was a bit of a novelty as it gave us a chance to visit pastures new, plus we hoped that we would bounce straight back. Eastville or Amityville as we call it, was in an area that you could drop a bomb on and if it totally flattened a square mile with Eastville at the epicentre there would be no loss of life and about £76 worth of damage. Littered with Gas Tanks, empty builders yards, waste ground and disused factories the surrounding area was so bleak and miserable - especially after a long journey. No pubs and no taxis or public transport anywhere to be seen to enable us to find a pint. Then once in the ground I was hit on the head by a missile thrown from the North Stand. The object which hit me was later found to be a spark plug! Total Tramps. Never again.

Chris Reid
Wallsend, Tyneside

A group of six of us made what was our first visit to the City of Bristol. So we weren't familiar with the place and accidently ended up in a couple of pubs in the St. Pauls area, where riots had taken place in recent months. It wasn't a good move but luckily we survived. As we made our way towards the ground we were suddenly approached by a nasty looking group of locals who had guessed our identity as they started winding us up with chants of "Sunderland, Sunderland." One of them looked like a right mental case with his mohican style haircut. Then just as we were about to face the music, the cavalry arrived in the shape of two police vans who dispersed the crowd. Eventually we took our places amongst our fellow supporters of which 700 or so had made the long journey south. Just when we thought we were safe a nutter ran onto the pitch ten minutes into the game from the far end, we couldn't beleive our eyes when we realised it was the mohican from earlier. He was sprinting towards our end on a one man sucide mission as play continued, as he approached our penalty area a copper rugby tackled him to the ground and play was stopped.

Ray Baptist
Cochrane Park, Newcastle

v SWANSEA CITY
VETCH FIELD
ATT; 15,442

SAT 24TH NOVEMBER 1979
SECOND DIVISION
WON 3-2

We went clubbing to Madison's nightclub on the Friday night before travelling down by van to South Wales arriving first thing Saturday morning. Whilst in Madison's we had met a lad we knew and he had got in our van probably thinking he was getting a lift home as he was totally drunk. You should have seen his face when he woke up to the sound of seagulls as we parked up in Swansea, not remembering a thing from the night before. He eventually got home on Monday which didn't go down to well. Meanwhile Bill McGarry predicts there will be a great many unemployed footballers at the end of the season due to the prevailing economic climate of the game.

Deka
Wallsend, Tyneside

Gang Terror Spills into City

Soccer stadium terror is spilling over into Newcastle City centre. Gangs are hunting like packs of animals, hell-bent on trouble, warns the City police commander. Many of the trouble makers and bully boys aren't bothering to travel away with United for their Saturday afternoon aggro. They are spreading fear in a permanent home fixture-either at St James' Park or the city centre shops and streets. Chief Supt. Frank Smith said: "These gangs of youths are roaming the shops when Newcastle United are away. "They are hell-bent on causing public disorder. They have nothing better to do when their team is away." Eldon Square shopping centre is a major target. Manager Gordon Allanson says: "Several gangs have converged on the centre on Saturdays. "They have fights and create a nuisance. There is certainly a risk of someone being injured." Chief Supt. Smith said: "We know how these gangs operate. It is the same as on the football match terraces. "They create a disturbance purely and simply to attract the attention of a couple of police officers. Then the gang immediately turns on them. An officer maybe loses his helmet and collects a broken nose. "They hunt like packs of animals. They invite an officer to chase them. The elderly and the infirm are frightened out of their wits"

v FULHAM
ST JAMES' PARK
ATT; 23,485

SAT 1ST DECEMBER 1979
SECOND DIVISION
WON 2-0

Former Blyth Spartans cup hero Steve Carney made his Newcastle debut. This meant that 3 of our starting line-up were playing in the Northern League the previous season, the other two being Peter Cartwright and Alan Shoulder. Meanwhile, elsewhere Tottenham Hotspur had two new Argentinean signings in their team who'd won the World Cup the previous year!! Yet Westwood the Pirate and his cronies thought they were sailing our ship in the right direction, but in the real world it was sinking. The victory put us joint top with Chelsea and QPR although only one point separated the top six which also included Luton, Birmingham and Leicester City. Jimmy Hill suggested to the national media that at least two of every team's eleven on the pitch should consist of at least two players born within 20 miles of the ground. He also thought that if you have a player sent off then the other side would take a penalty from 18 yards out, but this was soon squashed as it could cause crowd trouble. Jimmy Hill was a mad bloke with a pervert's beard who probably ate liver.

Mick Edmondson,
Walker, Newcastle

23

Newcastle and Sunderland football clubs have been rapped by a councillor for their attitude towards disabled supporters. Councillor Tom Bell, chairman of South Tyneside social services committee claims both clubs show a "lack of consideration" towards the disabled. He is writing to both of them to reconsider their present policies. "Sunderland AFC does not allow any wheelchairs into their ground at all and I think this is disgraceful. Newcastle does allow access for a limited number but they have to queue with everyone else even though it is extremely difficult for them to do so." Disabled people should not be debarred from watching football matches just because they are handicapped." A spokesperson for Newcastle United denied that disabled supporters had to queue with everyone else. He said the ground had facilities for 30 wheelchair spectators who were provided with a separate gate. And the car parking facilities were only about 75 yards from the pitch. A spokesman for Sunderland football club could not be contacted.

..... (Maybe he would disagree and argue that the Sunderland players on the pitch were disabled?)

v NORTH SHIELDS	**MON 3RD DECEMBER 1979**
APPLEBY PARK	**FRIENDLY**
ATT; 1,100	**WON 4-1**

A match arranged to help celebrate North Shields FC, 50th Anniversary. Their Chairman, Len Murphy apologised to Newcastle officials for the poor turn-out. Unbelievably both sides had a Billy Rafferty. Furthermore they both scored. *"Two Billy Rafferty's, There's Only Two Billy Rafferty's,"* sang the crowd. The problem was you couldn't tell which one was the professional! A very strong squad of players travelled down, almost the entire first team squad as the likes of Peter Withe even played.

Mick Edmondson
Walker, Newcastle

My mate Bill originally from North Shields travelled all the way back home from Australia to witness his local town play this friendly against his beloved Newcastle United. He only stayed a few days before travelling back. "Aye, I've only come back for the match and some proper fish & chips." A long way to travel, too see Billy Rafferty get a brace. I just got the ferry across.

Cliffy Amhed
South Shields, Tyneside

v LUTON TOWN	**SAT 8TH DECEMBER 1979**
KENILWORTH ROAD	**SECOND DIVISION**
ATT; 14,845	**DREW 1-1**

I was still recovering from 'The Jam' concert at the City Hall a couple of nights earlier. The Setting Sons tour hit Newcastle and we went on a 3 day bender and it was hard work travelling down the A1 at dawn on the Saturday. From their opening number 'Girl on the Phone' right through to their 'Tube Station and Eton

Rifles finale, the packed crowd were bouncing. We listened to Jam cassettes all the way down and all the way back. We still had our boating blazers on at the match. A draw was enough to put us back on top. Great days.

Phil
Gateshead, Tyneside

Fans skull fractured in attack

A Newcastle soccer fan was in hospital with a fractured skull last night after Luton Supporters hurled bricks at a mini-bus. A dozen United fans had just boarded the Dormobile after the match at Luton when they were ambushed. They were surrounded by about 100 youths, police said last night. The angry mob of rival fans rained bricks on the bus, smashing most of the windows and badly injuring 22 year old Karl Aidla. He was rushed to Luton and Dunstable hospital where surgeons prepared to carry out an emergency operation. Late last night, Karl, of Stainforth, Doncaster, a lifelong United supporter who used to live in Ryton, was said to be comfortable. Two of his friends were also hurt in the attack and needed hospital treatment, but were later released. Last night Karl's stepfather, Mr John Robson, said from their home in Church Road: "Karl has always been a Newcastle fan, ever since he was a lad." He added "We moved from Ryton when he was only nine, but he has continued to support United. The whole family does. By late last night police had notched up 40 arrests after a series of incidents throughout the town. Police took away the wrecked van and it was kept at the station while enquiries continued.

I remember this match for two reasons neither of which is Billy Rafferty, although the record books will show he gave us a half-time lead. As we were heading to the ground a mid-size furniture van on hire from 'Purvis Van Hire' (remember them) pulled up, the driver got out, opened up the rear door and about thirty Newcastle fans piled out - all looking the worse for wear. Then my next recollection is actually getting into the away end which at the time meant walking through what appeared to once upon a time be someone's front room as we entered through the middle of a row of terraced houses. This was the only way to gain access to the turnstile. A draw was enough to take us top although the large following from Newcastle saw Mick Martin pick up a serious knee injury which would need an operation followed by sometime in plaster, which kept him out of action for the rest of the season.

Mike Pollard
Wallsend, Tyneside

v QUEENS PARK RANGERS
ST JAMES' PARK
ATT; 25,027

SAT 15TH DECEMBER 1979
SECOND DIVISION
WON 4-2

This was one of my favourite Newcastle matches from the late seventies. Glen Roeder and Paul Goddard gave QPR a half-time lead in this top of the table clash cancelling out a perfect early lob from Alan Shoulder. With our inspirational captain Mick Martin out for the season after his injury the previous weekend we looked to have lost our way that is until a Black-and-White Collie Dog entered the proceedings wandering all over the pitch in the second half. Then it happened Peter Withe launched himself diving full length in the box at the Gallowgate End pouncing on the dog which he caught before it struggled free and two Coppers managed to pick it up and remove it from the pitch. Terry Hibbitt and Tommy Cassidy then ran the show for United. From an immediate free kick swung over from the right, Withe headed an equaliser, before Cassidy volleyed us in front then Withe rounded off an excellent afternoon with his second. QPR who were promotion favourites and had stuffed Burnley 7-0 were well and truly beaten in the second half where Terry Hibbitt was class. Ranger's boss was the famous ex-Man Utd manager Tommy Docherty and he got loads of stick and abuse from the Gallowgate End choir over his affair which resulted in his sacking from Old Trafford in July 1977. He had just won the FA Cup against Liverpool at Wembley and shaken hands on a new four year contract when it emerged that he had been having an affair with Mary Brown, wife of Laurie Brown, the 'Red Devils' physio. Docherty married with four children was sacked and his career hit the skids. The Gallowgate reminded him throughout the match singing, *"Who's Up Mary Brown, Who's Up Mary Brown, Tommy Tommy Docherty, Tommy Tommy Docherty."*

Mick Edmondson
Walker, Newcastle

v NOTTS COUNTY
MEADOW LANE
ATT; 11,224

SAT 22ND DECEMBER 1979
SECOND DIVISION
DREW 2-2

I hate Notts County in a similar way to which I hate Exeter City. Whilst Exeter play their home games at St James Park, Notts County have the nickname 'The Magpies!' This is the match when I first had doubts about promotion when we failed to beat a poor struggling side whose only two real chances were the penalties that they scored. Luck was definitely going against us when Peter Withe got injured early on and would miss two crucial games over the holiday programme. The highlight of our trip was Withe's replacement John Connolly's equalising diving header just before the break and our Christmas night out in Wakefield on the way back where more than half of our transit van managed to pull, which was quite amazing considering the number of Donkey Jackets donned.

Dave Jackson
Tynemouth, Tyneside

Whenever in Nottingham we used to drink in a pub called the Trent Navigation pub near the ground which was a Courage Tavern boozer. Once inside the ground we noticed a huge advert hanging from one of the stands which read; 'Courage Tavern…it's what your right arm is for.' The lads who had the dirty mags stuck to our van windows on the way down weren't so sure I can tell you.

Matty Anderson
Heaton, Newcastle

v BURNLEY
TURF MOOR
ATT; 16,443

WED 26TH DECEMBER 1979
SECOND DIVISION
LOST 2-3

I remember the excitement in the weeks leading up to this Boxing Day fixture as it was my first ever away match. I remember on the morning of the game everyone had been making logistical arrangements calling on each other. Most of the lads never told their parents where they were off, just making various alibis. During the match I can account for us being packed in along the side and having almost half the crowd. After the match, I can remember Geordies seemingly just swarming the place and it seemed to us that we had taken over the place. There was total mayhem and I can remember seeing all the glass broken in every bus shelter. All the trouble didn't help us young kids in our quest to find our coach which wasn't where we'd disembarked it earlier. With about 30 coaches outside and ours nowhere to be seen, half of the passengers off our coach had been left behind including 5 of our group all aged 15. When parents were alerted there was hell on as you can imagine and with getting home impossible, the local Police station waiting area was used for the night. We were top they were bottom yet we lost. My first away game and the writing was on the wall.

Dave Drape
Walker, Newcastle

The National Express bus was packed as it left Gallowgate bus station, every passenger bound for our Boxing Day visit to Turf Moor - not a normal traveller in sight. 'Victoria Wines' must have sold out of stock as every alcoholic drink was well represented on board. After persuading the driver to do a couple of piss stops en-route, he eventually announced that there would be no more stopping until we reached our destination. Later on he did however succumb to our threats by amazingly opening the door whilst driving down the motorway, to enable us to 'piss into the wind.' Imagine doing that these days? Although it could be argued that we've all spent the last 30 years 'pissing in the wind' following Newcastle United.

John Cooper
Walker, Newcastle

v CHARLTON ATHLETIC
ST JAMES' PARK
ATT; 26,225

SAT 29TH DECEMBER 1979
SECOND DIVISION
WON 2-0

Our last match of the 1970's produced 2 points which was enough to put us back at the top of the table after the disappointing defeat at Burnley on Boxing Day. In a week when Kevin Keegan was named 'European Footballer of the Year' for the second consecutive time, Alan Shoulder scored his 15th league goal of the season, on a day when I bought a new florescent photo-copied tin badge which exclaimed 'Alan Shoulder bends more balls than Jeremy Thorpe!' It didn't go down too well at school I seem to remember!

Hendy
Kenton, Newcastle

v SUNDERLAND
ST JAMES' PARK
ATT; 38,784

TUES 1ST JANUARY 1980
SECOND DIVISION
WON 3-1

Police set for Trouble

Police chiefs are planning a major campaign to prevent violence at the New Year football derby between Newcastle United and Sunderland. Rest days for officers covering Newcastle's St James' Park have been cancelled and all uniformed personnel will be on duty in the city centre, it was revealed last night. Bus, rail and coach stations will be heavily guarded and a plan to separate rival fans inside the ground will be in operation. "We want to make sure properties as well as people are protected," said Chief Supt. Frank Smith. More than 50 arrests were made following last season's derby match back in February, when trouble erupted between rampaging fans in Newcastle. Following that game Chief Supt. Smith said he thought the violence had been organised after Newcastle fans were found carrying leaflets urging them to attack Sunderland supporters.

Let's go into the 80's in style with a derby match to savour. Let us take the fear out of football - and I don't mean fear on the field. I mean on the terraces. My strong belief is that fear, even more than the drop in the playing standards of both Newcastle and Sunderland, have ruined Tyne-Wear derby gates in recent times. No longer will dad risk his son, or even himself, in the presence of the thugs who abuse our national sport, using it as an excuse for gang warfare. Obscenities and physical violence have violated the very core of football, and until all stadiums are dominated by seats rather than terracing, I suppose our present-day society is going to continue to put the honest supporter at risk. Once upon a time Tyne-Wear derbies meant capacity gates with tickets more precious than gold. There were only 27,746 at Roker earlier in the season. Perhaps Sheffield has already shown us the way. If we suffer in any shape or form from the hooligan element today, then I suggest we follow the example of the steel city in the future. The derby between Wednesday and United at Hillsborough on Boxing Day was switched from the afternoon to an 11am start, quite deliberately to avoid trouble. The outcome: the biggest crowd in the history of the Third Division 49,302, paying all-time record receipts for that division of £70,000, and not one solitary arrest! A total of 549 police were on duty, yet not one was called upon to do anything bar wish punters the compliment of the season.

John Gibson (Man with vision)
Evening Chronicle, Newcastle

What did you do for your 18th birthday? Can you remember? Maybe you had a party at the social club with a pickled onion infested Buffet? Or you went clubbing to Reflections, Tiffany's, Madison's, Julies, The Stage Door or the Tuxedo Princess? New Years Day 1980, a match against the great unwashed the day of my 18th Birthday!! What a way to spend your 18th Birthday eh. I seem to remember we won 3-1 and an absolute carthorse called Peter Cartwright scored for Newcastle we really were dreadful back then. I had just started working at Tuxedo Junction the Christmas before and the Tottie ohmmeter was on overload. I had arranged to meet a lass I had met a couple of days earlier at Tux, later that day after the match. Unfortunately I got mortal drunk and forgot to turn up, but found out later my mate Kev Murray had bumped into her in town and consequently gave her one all night!! Happy Birthday!!! Happy New Year!!! The first day of the 1980's and what a day it was.

Rob Scott
Walker, Newcastle

Man went after fans with a knife

A dispute with a group of Sunderland supporters led to a Consett man going after them armed with a knife. When stopped by the police he told them: "I've even sharpened it. I'm going to get them." Before Durham crown court was Kenneth White (36), of Consett who pleaded guilty to possessing an offensive weapon. Mr Ewan Duff, prosecuting, said White was eventually persuaded by police to hand over the knife, but he asked them: "You'll still let me get them?" He was jailed for 12 months, suspended for two years.

This was indeed a happy New Year, as we beat Sunderland, Tommy Cassidy scoring a screamer, with "one of those shots" that normally ended up nearer the floodlight. My other memory of this game was when Alan Shoulder made it 2-1, someone discarded a tab end, which landed in the hair of an unsuspecting hippy type, standing near to the tunnel. His head smouldered for about two minutes, to the amusement of many, then his mate informed him and he raked the tab end from his smoking locks.

Anth Nicholson
North Shields, Tyneside

"Hark Now Hear The Geordies Sing The Sunderland Ran Away, And We Will Fight Forever More Because Of New Years Day." When you are 15 there are three things important in life; football, girls and music. After getting my ticket in the middle of December I counted down the days till the match even though Christmas and New Years Eve happened before. During the build-up I lapped up every article, television and radio report about the game. We had been top since September and although Cummins gave Sunderland the lead - Cartwright, a Shoulder pen and a Tommy Cass special gave us the win. I never slept much that night and had a smile on my face permanently for the next couple of days. *"Happy New Year, Happy New Year, Hello Hello."*

Chris Ramshaw
West Denton, Newcastle

New Years Day 1980 was the last time I can remember using the old trains from Wallsend station which was the only pubic transport to get you into town that day. A 3pm kick-off and I remember the atmosphere at home games was always consistently good. But this game the atmosphere was exceptional with the performance and result obviously helping.

Dave Drape
Walker, Newcastle

A friend of mine was always predicting that Newcastle would win 3-1 and of course after this result he was beside himself. He kept on saying 3-1, 3-1 and kicking his leg as though kicking a ball and when he saw what looked like a piece of paper on the ground he decided to give it a whack. Unfortunately for him it wasn't a piece of paper but a metal object!!! The curses that came from his mouth cannot be repeated but needless to say I had a good laugh at his expense. Mind we both carried on saying 3-1, 3-1.

Bob Day
Heaton, Newcastle

V Sign costs Fan £160

A triumphant Newcastle United fan who made an abusive sign to the opposing team's supporters was fined £100 with £60 costs by Newcastle magistrates. Duncan Donnelly (17), from Jarrow denied causing a breach of the peace at St James' Park after the match between Newcastle and Sunderland. "Donnelly enraged Sunderland fans by running on to the pitch, kissing his black-and-white scarf and indicating the score with his fingers," said Mr J. Ferguson, prosecuting. Donnelly told magistrates: "I only indicated the score to friends in the crowd. I have nothing against Sunderland supporters."

While sitting around a dinner table having Christmas lunch we were all asked to name a song that meant a lot to us, I picked 'Take A Chance On Me' by Abba.....all of the women thought that my choice was really romantic and was something to do with an ex-girlfriend..........then the shock came........don't be stupid I said, the reason it means a lot to me is because it's the last song they played on the tannoy at St James' Park on New Years Day 1980 before we stuffed Sunderland 3-1!!

Julian Brannigan
Gosforth, Newcastle

After a late night of 'first footing' and gate crashing house parties all over Walker we made our way to Town on foot as there was no public transport, for what was the 104th Tyne & Wear derby. With 37 wins each and 30 draws, things were perfectly balanced. Also there was the added spice that if we had of beaten Brighton on the final game of the previous season then Sunderland would have already been playing in the top flight. Now we were sitting top of the league all set for promotion, Sunderland in 5th place. Shoulder had already scored 16 league goals and Withe had 9 to his name. The hatred between the two sets of fans reached new heights as we played each other 4 times during the season. The battle of Bath Lane took place after the match as Newcastle fans ambushed and attacked Sunderland fans being escorted to the ground for the second consecutive year. Sunderland's record £320,000 Argentine signing Claudio Marangoni was totally and contemptuously outplayed and outstripped by our former non-league player Peter Cartwright. We sang in the Gallowgate End to the tune of Yankee Doodle: *"Ken Knighton Rode In To Town, Riding On A Pony. He Bought A Load Of Foreign Shite And Called Him Marangoni."*

Mick Edmondson
Walker, Newcastle

v CHESTER CITY
ST JAMES PARK
ATT; 24,548

SAT 5TH JANUARY 1980
FA CUP 3RD ROUND
LOST 0-2

A life-long supporter of Third Division Chester City by the early seventies I'd moved from my native home to the North East. The Chester supporters train had been delayed so I was one of only a few Chester fans in the ground at kick-off time. When Chester scored after 3 minutes I will always remember being an almost lone celebrator of the goal as I danced amongst empty seats whilst Black-and-White zebras shouted and sung *"You're Going Get Your Fucking Head Kicked In."* By the time Ian Rush scored our second goal I'd been joined by the rest of the Chester contingent, a lovely day I will always remember.

Andy
Gateshead, Tyneside

Typical Newcastle United. Stay top of the league with an emphatic victory over our auld enemy Sunderland on New Year's Day then 4 days later get stuffed and knocked out the FA Cup by Third Division Chester City! Near the end Terry Hibbitt was replaced which didn't go down to well with the midfielder. As he walked towards the tunnel he made a V-sign with both hands towards Bill McGarry on the bench before disappearing for the changing rooms.

Mick Edmondson
Walker, Newcastle

v CHELSEA
STAMFORD BRIDGE
ATT; 32,281

SAT 12TH JANUARY 1980
SECOND DIVISION
LOST 0-4

Chelsea wasn't a nice place to visit in the late seventies and twelve days into a new decade things hadn't obviously had time to improve and wouldn't for many a season. It just wasn't their Cockney bullshit, arrogance and large hooligan element but also the ground which was more hideously misshaped than ours, which wasn't helped by the wide open spaces behind the goals between the pitch and terracing. Like Coventry City they had a line of 'Sky Blue, One Seated Invalid Chariots' along the touchline as well as an Ice Cream van next to the pitch by the 'Infamous Shed End!' Our centre half David 'Dick' Barton had recently said that if he could meet anyone in the whole world then it would be Raquel Welch! "And I would just sit and look at her." Not shag her eh David? She must have been playing up front for Chelsea as along with the rest of the team he definitely wasn't moving. After our excellent result on New Year's Day the year was quickly turning into a nightmare as Chelsea replaced us at the top and to add insult to injury, elsewhere Alan Brown scored a hat-trick as Sunderland won 4-2. The large away following on the freezing open terrace knew we had problems and were missing the influential Mick Martin and our luck was running out as they defiantly sang the doom and gloom anthem *"We'll Support You Ever More, We'll Support You Ever More, Newcastle, Newcastle…We'll Support You Ever More."*

Tommy Scott
Blakelaw, Newcastle

Segregation was still in its infancy down at 'The Bridge' as Chelsea fans were able to quite easily infiltrate our end during the game. This led to sporadic fighting throughout. The Coppers kept us locked in for what must have been an hour after the match as Chelsea hooligans still tried to get at us. We eventually got put on a non-stop tube from Fulham Broadway, only for it to kick-off again at Kings Cross.

Piper
Felling, Tyneside

v HUDDERSFIELD RESERVES
ST JAMES' PARK
ATT; 1,700

SAT 12TH JANUARY 1980
CENTRAL LEAGUE
WON 1-0

Throughout the late 70's and early 80's I was a regular at the reserve matches attending with my mate Beefy. Back then St James' Park was used as the home venue for the stiffs and matches would be played on a Saturday afternoon when the first team were away, with the odd game on a Wednesday night. We got free entry because his fatha' had two season tickets we could use for free (and I was addicted to football). Walking up to that relic of an old stand with the grey shell and huge letters of "NEWCASTLE UNITED" painted on the back to watch the likes of Man Utd, Everton and Liverpool's second string in the old Central league. Climbing the rickety wooden stairs and taking our seats, before deciding to switch to another seat at the other end of the stand 5 minutes later. A Saturday afternoon spent sitting among the auld blokes, with their flat caps and big woollen coats, huddled together in twos and threes, with the distinct smell of tobacco and Bovril, the West Stand being the only side of the ground in use. Buying those boiled sweets with the chocolate centres (You could only get them at the Toon, Lord Westwood must have got a job lot!) with my pocket money at the shop and getting a cup of scalding hot tea - served by some old Wifey' in an overall with a mouth as dangerous as her produce - with four sugars as my mother wasn't there to give me grief! Every now and then some auld bloke with an out of tune transistor radio would mutter the latest scores, to those in ear shot, which were then relayed within seconds to all four corners of the stand. Newcastle's score down at Stamford Bridge was continually met with groans as news filtered through of another Chelsea goal. Some weeks if you were lucky you would see some big name players for the opposition if they were either returning from injury or currently out of favour. That's how it was then and should be today instead of the team being full of youth players. We regularly had first team players playing, the likes of Bird, Walker, Suggett, Nicholson, Kelly, Halliday and Mitchell as well as fringe players Carr and Wharton. This match was only our second win in thirteen at home as Wearsider Brian Ferguson got the winner, but as usual Nigel Walker was man of the match.

Tom Knox
Fenham, Newcastle

v LEYTON ORIENT	SAT 19TH JANUARY 1980
ST JAMES' PARK	SECOND DIVISION
ATT; 20,954	WON 2-0

Although a target of the St James' Park boo boys, facts and figures tell that Steve Hardwick was the best keeper in the division! After our recent blip we were back to winning ways and back on top of the table against an Orient side with Cockney veterans Mervyn Day, Ralph Coates, Billy Jennings and Tommy Taylor unbeaten on their travels in three months. After completing the double over them we headed down to the auld Black 'n' White Pub as we always got an early unofficial drink in there straight after the match. Later on we would get a broom shank and move the pointers on the clock back just in case our lock-in was raided by the Police, our excuse we'd just say that the clock must be slow. What a cracking pub it was.

Fink
The Mad Sad Groundhopper

v LEICESTER CITY	SAT 2ND FEBRUARY 1980
FILBERT STREET	SECOND DIVISION
ATT; 24,549	LOST 0-1

Leicester knocked us off the top after this top of the table clash, replacing us as we slipped to second. I always found it difficult to find a pub near the ground but a lot easier to get a fight if you were that way inclined. There was trouble all afternoon. The start of the second half was delayed for a few minutes after Steve

Fans fined £13,40 for trouble after match

Six Newcastle United fans appeared before Leicester magistrates for offences at the Leicester football ground and in the city streets on February 2nd. They were fined a total of £1,340. Three Leicester fans were fined a total of £750. Desmond Hedley (19) of Washington admitted causing actually bodily harm after the match and was fined £250. He was also ordered to compensate the fan for £15 worth of damage to his clothing. Chief Insp. Peter Baker, prosecuting said fighting broke out as Newcastle fans, being escorted by police back to their coaches, passed Leicester supporters who were waiting at a bus stop. Hedley punched one of the Leicester youths in the mouth and kicked him causing cuts and bruises. He told the police: "I got carried away in the heat of the moment. These Leicester fans were shouting abuse." Most of the violence occurred in the streets around the ground as rival fans shouted and abused each other. Andrew Lawson (19) from Jarrow was caught swearing and with his fist clenched he ran towards a barrier separating the rival fans and shouted at the Leicester fans, "Come on over and we'll sort you out!" Martin Hogg (19) a welder from Darlington admitted threatening behaviour at the ground by throwing an object towards the Leicester fans and was fined £250. When asked what he had thrown he told an officer, "I'm not telling you." said the Chief Inspector.

Hardwick was hit on the head by a missile thrown from the Leicester crowd behind his goal. The Newcastle keeper went down on his knees. Referee Ashley spoke to several police officers and picked up a couple of objects from the pitch, before restarting the game. Filbert Street was a proper old English football ground with roofs on all four sides and surrounded by street upon street of terraced houses. I miss this type of ground so much as the new stadiums are totally boring lacking any individual character, usually stuck on retail parks miles out of town. The new Walkers Stadium is actually quite close to the old Filbert Street ground but is just like any other modern cheap flat pack stadium. Three days earlier a certain Chris Waddle had played for Sunderland at Gateshead in a friendly. But the Geordie from Heworth was now at St James' Park for talks as Bill McGarry had agreed terms with the teenagers club Tow Law.

Mick Edmondson
Walker, Newcastle

I have some fond memories of regularly travelling away with the supporter's club buses. After the match when we were all sitting on the coach listening to Sports Report on Radio 2, you could bet your bottom dollar that if you looked towards the front seats, there would be 'Fatty Mullen' munching away on a wagon wheel.

Geordie Brown
Stanley, Durham

v WREXHAM
RACECOURSE GROUND
ATT; 13,299

SAT 9TH FEBRUARY 1980
SECOND DIVISION
LOST 0-1

Four of us travelled down, having decided at 9pm the previous night whilst supping at the Rosehill Social Club in Wallsend. Our driver picked us up in the very, very early hours of Saturday morning and away we went to Wales. While going down through the night, our driver suddenly went right back in his seat and luckily did an emergency stop, as the pin at the back of his seat had snapped. The next hour was taken up with four mad Geordies searching around the all night garages for bloody Araldite adhesive to see if we could fix the seat! We eventually managed to get some and applied it to the seat. We sat around for what seemed an eternity waiting for the Araldite to work. Eventually...success and away we went happy as a team who had just beaten Sunderland 10 - 0, until disaster struck again...yes the bloody seat pin snapped again! So after some quick thinking one of the lads had to sit with his knees up in the back seat supporting the driver's seat. We finally parked up and made the long walk to the ground. We thought that was the end of our worries until we got to the turnstiles. I reached in to my pocket for money to buy a programme and there were my darts...you see we had all been playing a local darts league match the night before. I asked two of the lads (the driver did not play darts) to look in their pockets and lo and behold there were their darts also! Now how the hell were we going to get past the Police body searches? We decided to go over and speak to a Police Officer with pips on his shoulders and tell him what had happened. When I told him, he said "Are you sure you did not just bring them to throw in the ground?" To which I replied with "No way, you see we play in a Darts League and we have just forgotten to leave them at home." The Officer then got one of his men over and asked what he thought but before he could answer one of our group, Joe whipped out his Willington Quay darts league fixture book and after looking at it the officer laughed and said "Okay boys, just leave them with my officer here and you can pick them up after the game!" We lost 1-0, picked up our darts and the journey home was a very long one but even longer for poor Tony as he was selected to prop the driver's seat up with his knees!

Bill Gibbs
Wallsend, Tyneside

The 1980's saw me start the decade in my late teens and my team in the old Second Division. Some lads had passed their driving tests and ventured to away trips in vehicles barely road worthy to get around the streets of Tyneside, let alone travel around the country. But travel we did and the 1980's brought about new and different ways to travel. My clothes had never been as clean (though I still could not afford the designer gear) when Persil launched their "Persil train travel" offer. It basically meant you could collect tokens and get cut price travel by rail. It was always amusing to see loads of fans on trains clutching their Persil vouchers, heading for some obscure places such as Wrexham. I have never forgiven them for our FA Cup exit, as well as the dodgy corner flag decision in 1978 which unfairly prevented Blyth Spartans from a FA Cup 6th Round tie with Arsenal. And the name Dixie McNeil still knocks me sick. Alex Cropley on loan from champions elect Aston Villa couldn't even help prevent what was our fourth successive away defeat. I really hated Wrexham.

Anth Nicholson
North Shields, Tyneside

One of the biggest hidings following Newcastle occurred outside the ground. Only about 800 Newcastle fans had made the journey, outside the ground we were totally outnumbered but stood and took it on the chin next to the river, odds weren't good.

Tess Mann
Longbenton, Newcastle

We made our way to Newcastle and met up with a group of lads we vaguely knew from the match. Our plan was to drive down to watch the match, then to stop off at Blackpool on the way back up, for the night. However on the way down we had to pull in at Wetherby because the wheel studs on our mini-bus were shearing. Once we eventually got going again we estimated that we wouldn't get to Wrexham until after half-time. So we took a vote and decided to head straight for Blackpool. On our way I noticed that 2 of the lads - who were friends of friends - had hammers in their overnight bags! They were nutters and when we got to Blackpool they wanted to fight everybody. Probably a good job that we didn't get to Wales!

Kenny
Amble, Northumberland

v DUNDEE	**FRI 15TH FEBRUARY 1980**
DENS PARK	**FRIENDLY**
ATT; 3,596	**WON 3-1**

I got the train up via Edinburgh and stayed overnight in Dundee at a bed and breakfast which was like going on holiday for me. About 1,000 Geordies cheered the lads on as Mitchell, Withe and Rafferty got the goals.

Cliffy Ahmed
South Shields, Tyneside

v BIRMINGHAM CITY	**WED 2OTH FEBRUARY 1980**
ST JAMES' PARK	**SECOND DIVISION**
ATT; 27,069	**DREW 0-0**

Unbelievably we had taken an amazing 26 points from a possible 28 at home, but another blank sheet meant that since beating the unwashed on New Year's Day we had failed to score in 5 of our last 6 matches. Alex Cropley on loan from Aston Villa made his home debut but ended up being subbed as Jim Smith's Birmingham side, which included the likes of Frank Worthington, Archie Gemmill, Colin Todd, Willie Johnston and Alan Curbishley, gained a valuable point. In the week leading up to the match the sad news that both Jim Pearson and Peter Kelly had been forced to hang up their boots due to very similar bad knee injuries, didn't exactly help our promotion hopes.

Mick Edmondson
Walker, Newcastle

v SHREWSBURY TOWN	**SAT 23RD FEBRUARY 1980**
GAY MEADOW	**SECOND DIVISION**
ATT; 10,833	**LOST 1-3**

We all had nicknames but one of the lads had a really good one; 'Bronco Billy Anderson' from the Fossway in Walker, who went to more away games than most of the lads at the time! It helped if your father was into football and travelled away as well, so Billy was a bit lucky in that respect. So as you can imagine, at school the first day back after any game we used to get all the stories if you had not travelled away yourself. On the Monday we weren't really interested in hearing about on loan flop Alex Cropley's last appearance before being sent packing back to Villa, but more interested in his trip. He didn't let us down as he told us that at this particular match the lads had for some reason had an argument with the programme seller and decided to nick all his programmes and then throw him in the river adjacent to the ground!

Dave
Walker, Newcastle

After the match four of us got the train back stopping off in Manchester for a night out. After a canny night we arrived at Victoria station at 11.30pm to get on the last train home only to find out that it actually left from Piccadilly Station. We legged it across Manchester but missed the train so were left stranded. Muzz came up with the idea to get a taxi home but this was to expensive, so we paid £32 to get a taxi to York instead and got the 4am train arriving back in Newcastle early Sunday morning totally knackered.

Paul Younger
Dunston, Tyneside

My first visit to Shrewsbury's Gay Meadow and anybody who went to that ground knows that the top of the away terrace roof is very low, as I found out to my cost when I jumped up when we scored our consolation goal, splitting my head open on the low beam, much too every fuckers amusement!!!! I wonder how many who laughed were among the 44 Newcastle fans who were stranded for 4 hours after the match when their coach failed to turn up.

Archie
Wallsend, Tyneside

v WATFORD	**SAT 1ST MARCH 1980**
ST JAMES' PARK	**SECOND DIVISION**
ATT; 23,091	**LOST 0-2**

Our fifth game without a win included a 'Dick' Barton own goal as Elton John's club did the double over us. While we were slipping down the table - now down to sixth place - West Ham had collected 13 points from their last 14, whilst Birmingham City had obtained 11 points. Ironically we were still only 2 points behind the leaders Chelsea. The frustration was growing on the terraces as the team were in free fall and two fans in particular made their feelings be known when they ran on to the pitch, stomped on their scarves and gestured towards the Directors box. It was around this time that we used to go to Campbell's bakery on Nun's Moor Road in Fenham, where the players used to go for scran after training at Benwell, dressed in their sky blue Bukta tracksuits and driving their Ford Capri's. Great memories of speaking with the players and meeting Alan Shoulder when I was 12 and being taller than him!

Tom Knox
Fenham, Newcastle

On this very day Everton legend Dixie Dean hailed as the greatest centre forward of all time died at his beloved Goodison Park whilst incongruously watching the Merseyside derby v Liverpool. Meanwhile on Tyneside this defeat ended our impressive unbeaten home record in the league and stretched or winless run to five games.

Mick Edmondson
Walker, Newcastle

v CAMBRIDGE UNITED
ABBEY STADIUM
ATT; 6,908

SAT 8TH MARCH 1980
SECOND DIVISION
DREW 0-0

We arrived at 8am, after travelling through the night. We had a few cans before finding a bar at about 10am which wasn't locked yet it seemed to be closed to the public. We had little option but to help ourselves to a few beers before heading off to the next bar. I'd obviously never been to this town before. Either it seemed had the driver as we had been dropped off near Cambridge City's ground and we didn't' realise until just before kick-off. We eventually got to the correct ground but not surprisingly I can't remember much about the match. Missed nowt as John Bird was recalled and Bobby Shinton a £175,000 signing from Man City made his Newcastle debut.

Derek
Gateshead, Tyneside

v WEST HAM UNITED
ST JAMES' PARK
ATT; 25,474

SAT 15TH MARCH 1980
SECOND DIVISION
DREW 0-0

Word had reached Tyneside that the Hammers hooligan hard core were coming up to take the town and give the Geordies hell. Few realise there was also some political element involved, as many of them were allegedly National front. The impact of the news of this impending visit led to the emergence of some pretty wild locals in town, some joining the wild locals already ensconced in the majority of the now open Leazes End, which was home to those who liked to be

next to the away end, the North-East Leazes corner. West Ham had almost filled this section which housed 1,000 fans sandwiched between irate Geordies, and the cockney skinheads tried to shelter from deluges of stones, bricks and snooker balls raining down on them from both the Leazes to their right and from the East Stand paddock and seats above on their left. Some overshot, and thus Newcastle fans managed to hit Newcastle fans. The worst moment though came in the form of a petrol bomb, which fortunately did not inflict too much damage on the Hammers, although a couple did end up in hospital. The behaviour of the Newcastle fans was not and cannot be condoned, but most of the cockneys had arrived in Newcastle looking for trouble. The song says it all: *"He's Only A Poor Little Hammer, His Clothes Are All Tattered And Torn, He Came For A Fight, So We Set Him Alight, And Now He Won't Come Anymore."* The areas near the ground were later spray-painted with slogans such as 'Free The Bomber' and 'Petrol Is Dear, But Cheap Enough To Burn The Hammers.'

Brian Hall
Heaton, Newcastle

I was at the match and looked over and saw the flames and thought it was a scarf on fire that is until the West Ham fans panicked and scattered everywhere. The next day former Newcastle United player Terry McDermott now at Anfield was named Footballer of the Year.

Jimmy King
North Shields, Tyneside

To quote Shaun James aged 14 (and a half).....March 6th 1980... "We have signed Bobby Shinton...that's great....had R.E. Exam....that's shite. Sat 15th March......Played West Ham about 1000 came up...I was in the scoreboard....a petrol bomb got thrown at them...lots of fighting after match....Boots and RS McColl's windows got smashed....gobstopper machine got smashed and they were all over......felt sick had about 20."

Shaun James
Byker, Newcastle

West Hams infamous ICF (Inter City Firm) had caused havoc in recent months at little towns and sleepy outposts but there was no way on earth that they were ever going to take Newcastle. Hours before kick-off Geordie gangs roamed, patrolling the city streets in eager anticipation of a good battle against one of footballs finest. West Ham 750 strong arrived by train and were marched through the town with a huge police protection operation which managed to get them up to St James' and into the ground without any major injuries, although they were repeatedly attacked throughout en-route by Geordie mobs that had to resort to throwing missiles when unable to get close enough to physically attack. One of the biggest flashpoints came beside the Waterloo pub when a large Newcastle mob managed to get close as Police tried to get West Ham across the West Road. Missiles rained down on the cockneys. As well as football thugs the Geordie bikers in the area seemed to enjoy getting involved. Once inside the ground the air was full of hatred and no matter what you've read elsewhere I can guarantee you that West Ham's finest had turned up yet never had a look in and although claim to have been giving it the big one, in reality they were shiting themselves from the moment they were greeted at the station right up until they escaped with police protection back across the river by train. I've never heard 1,000 football supporters be so quiet in a

PETROL BOMB ATTACK ON FANS

MP demands major inquiry

An exploding petrol bomb brought terror to the terraces at St James' Park, Newcastle yesterday. Fans screamed in horror as the home-made missile burst into flames in the middle of a packed section of the visiting crowd. It was hurled at West Ham supporters, penned into the Leazes End of the ground. And last night a senior police officer put the blame on Newcastle United fans in the adjoining East Stand. One Londoner was taken to the city's Royal Victoria Infirmary after the bomb made from a milk bottle filled with petrol - set fire to his clothes. Anthony Short aged 20, from Essex was treated for shock and burns at the hospital, but was later allowed to return south. Throughout the game police had to dodge flying beer cans, bottles, coins and bricks thrown between rival fans. At least one supporter was hit by a missile and a policeman had his neck gashed. After the game, fans staged a series of battles while leaving the ground. Police with dogs moved in and surrounded the West Ham supporters while United fans stopped and rained bottles and stones on them. Twice police had to wade in and force them back. Last night Newcastle North MP Sir Williams Elliott condemned the incident and promised some immediate action. Sir William said: "I shall be raising this with the home secretary, Mr Whitelaw. "I am appalled and horrified by this incident - I never thought I'd see the day when this happened at a football fixture." He also urged Newcastle United FC the Football league and Northumbria Police to hold full inquiries into what he called a "dreadful display of hooliganism." Sir William added: This must never be allowed to happen again. I am amazed that a bomb was smuggled in to the ground. The incident reinforces my belief that football thugs should be dealt with very severely. They should be fined at least £1,000 and given sharp and tough prison sentences. The final arrest toll came to 32, most of them Newcastle supporters. Dozens more fans were ejected from the ground. And late last night the bomb thrower had still not been found.

football ground before or since that day as they were tortured to over 2 hours of abuse, attacks and missiles such as bricks, stones, coins, even a salt cellar, raining down on them not forgetting a petrol bomb thrown from the paddocks which exploded in their packed terrace shooting flames 30 foot in the air. The majority of the ground cheered as though a goal had been scored, how times have changed, eh.

Kevin
Elswick, Newcastle

41

I THREW THE SOCCER BOMB

An 18-year old Newcastle United supporter decided he was going to put Newcastle on the map by throwing a petrol bomb, Newcastle Crown Court was told today. He was sick of them being in the Second Division, said Mr John Milford, prosecuting, and to put them on the map he was going to throw the petrol bomb inside the ground. This he did when Newcastle United played West Ham in a vital match. Andrew Smith of Buddle Road, Newcastle a labourer in a metal spinning factory admitted throwing a destructive substance with intent. Mr Milford said about 25,500 people were at the match, 855 of them West Ham supporters at the Leazes End of the ground. They were tightly packed together. One of the West Ham supporters Brian Short aged 20 was in this section. After 15 to 20 minutes objects were being thrown at the West Ham supporters by the Newcastle fans. A petrol bomb was seen to come from the adjoining area and to fly through the air. It must have travelled 15-20 yards from the hand of Smith to the place where it actually hit the ground said Mr Milford. As it shattered on the ground the petrol vapour exploded and flames shot 15 to 20 feet in the air. Brian Shorts trousers were engulfed in flames, his legs were burning and flames were going higher up his body. He or one of his friends pulled his trousers down and extinguished the flames. He was taken to the St John Ambulance Brigade hut and from there to hospital where his legs were bandaged. "But as a measure of his enthusiasm he went back to the ground and watched the remainder of the game," said Mr Milford. He was still having treatment for the first degree burns 6 weeks later. The trousers of schoolboy Michael Wright also caught alight, but the flames were smothered. Mr Milford said: "Another man, Nigel Jones saw the petrol bomb coming over but it exploded in front of a boy called Cunningham. He was taken to hospital and had to have his legs bandaged." He added that the petrol bomb caused panic on the terraces as people were running around in every direction to escape. Police had to control fights in the ground and later in the city. Pieces of the milk bottle were later recovered on the terraces. Mr Milford said that on the night of the incident Smith said to his girlfriend: "Have you read the papers? I threw a petrol bomb at the cockneys. You will see when you read the papers." When interviewed Smith told a police officer that he threw the bomb "because it hadn't been done before. I wanted to put Newcastle on the map. I'm sick of them being in the Second Division. What Manchester can do with darts we can do with a petrol bomb." When asked whether he intended to hurt or injure anyone, he said: "I suppose so. I did it because I hate those Cockney bastards. I also did it to put Newcastle on the map. I shouted when I threw the bomb: "You Cockney bastards." Smith said he had been a Newcastle supporter for 3 years and went to all the home and away games. He also said that he had tried to make bombs before but didn't want to get picked up for the offence to early. Before Smith threw the bomb he lit the wick and held it until it caught alight properly before letting it fly. He then dived into the crowd. He was eventually jailed for three years.

Coins and Bricks Flew at Match

Sharpened coins and bricks flew through the air during disturbances at the Newcastle v West Ham match. It led to soccer fans from both sides appearing before Newcastle magistrates. A Newcastle fan from Longbenton was sent to Crown Court for sentence to Borstal training. He was seen to throw 3 pieces of building brick at rival fans. Another Newcastle fan was fined for throwing a tomato at West Ham fans. A West Ham fan was fined for throwing a stone at Newcastle fans. He said that he had only retaliated as they were being bombarded with bricks and coins all afternoon.

Soccer Fan swore at Police

A policeman on duty at Newcastle Central Station who went to the aid of a football supporter was met by abuse, city magistrates were told. Apprentice plater Paul Bradwell, (17) of Wallsend, denied a charge of a breach of the peace but was found guilty and fined £50 with £15 costs. The court was told that when the officer approached Bradwell who was kneeling with his hands on his face in the entrance of the station after the match against West Ham. "I asked him if he was alright and he shouted, "It's one of you black bastards who hit me." Then pointing to some West Ham supporters he added, "I'll get those others as well." Bradwell said he had gone to the station to buy a travel card when he had been punched by a constable.

There was pure hell on the whole game. In the 'Gallowgate Scoreboard' I saw some West Ham fans in an escort go up past the Strawberry Pub into Death Alley, as bottles and allsorts rained down on them, even thrown from inside the ground and over the wall. During the match loads of non-stop pushing and shoving with police cordons trying to keep the masses apart, then, what seemed to be a burning rag hurled into the away enclosure which just went up and from memory I think the ref just let play continue with a bonfire on the terraces in the background!

Ginger
Gateshead, Tyneside

This was the first match I had taken our Joe - my son, to see, the infamous game with West Ham, when a Molotov cocktail was thrown in the Leazes corner. We were in the Gallowgate east corner and at half-time I sat our Joe on one of the concrete barriers that were there in those days. He was quite happy and I set off to the kiosk for two Bovril's. In those days there was an exit/entrance between the East Stand and the 'Gallowgate Corner' and I went out that way and turned right down the ramp to the very south-east corner fence where there was a kiosk. I stood in the queue for most of the break, got my two Bovril's and set off again up the ramp. As I turned left towards the pitch there was a bit of a melee and the crowd were chanting "Tommy is our leader!" Some guy called Tommy apparently well known in the Gallowgate was getting turfed out and there was a rumpus in the Gallowgate which had effected the entrance. Undaunted I ploughed on and after a bit of pushing and shoving (usual for those days) I came out the other side towards where our Joe was sitting. I could see he was laughing his head off and realised why when I looked down. Although I had managed to hold on to the two cups there was only about a third of liquid left in each and the rest was in two brown stains in a line down my chest on my light coloured bomber jacket. I had to see the funny side which was Joe's highlight in a drab 0-0 game which meant no goals for his first ever visit.

Kevin Haigh
Whickham, Newcastle

As I watched from the scoreboard a big bang was followed by flames shooting 30 foot in the air. Although quite horrific, many fans in the ground seemed to celebrate. Quite a mental moment - to say the least. Legend has it that both Tony Cottee and John Cornwall were amongst the West Ham fans in the away section when the petrol bomb landed near their feet. Both would become footballers and play top flight league football. Cornwall would eventually sign for Newcastle and marry a Geordie lass called Sandra having his wedding evening reception in the Harvey suite at SJP, with Tony Cottee as his best man. After retiring he would eventually settle in the north east.

Mick Edmondson
Walker, Newcastle

v CARDIFF CITY
NINIAN PARK
ATT; 9,304

SAT 22ND MARCH 1980
SECOND DIVISION
DREW 1-1

As we got on the Newcastle United Supporters Club bus at the Haymarket we had our Steel Cap Boots taken off us, and they were put in the hold and stayed there until we got back. Our eighth consecutive match without a win and we got some strange looks from the Welsh as we watched it in our socks. We never travelled with them again. NUSC that is not the socks!!

C.T
Cochrane Park, Newcastle

We asked a lad who wasn't a football fan to take us to Cardiff. Three times on the way down, he took wrong turns which were making us really late. Three of us were drinking on the way down and we were all in a deep sleep when the Driver's voice boomed out, "Howay lads we are here and although I am not a football fan I must say the Cardiff City ground is fantastic!" We all looked out the windows whilst rubbing our eyes and I said "This is bloody Cardiff Arms Park the National Rugby Stadium!! With the time at 3.20pm, we were not best pleased and after another ten minutes he eventually got us to Ninian Park. The police officer on the other side of the turnstiles smirked at us and said we were 0-1 down but as soon as we took up our places in the ground Bobby Shinton equalised! One other thing which I remember about this game, is that the famous *"He's Only A Poor Little Hammer!"* song was first sang at this game.

Bill Gibbs
Wallsend, Tyneside

v BRISTOL ROVERS
ST JAMES' PARK
ATT; 18,975

SAT 29TH MARCH 1980
SECOND DIVISION
WON 3-1

A day earlier English League Clubs agreed at a meeting that they wish to display shirt advertising. The BBC and ITV say that they are against the idea. A Peter Withe brace which were his last goals for the club gave us our first win in nine and helped us move up into fifth. With only seven games to play the promotion battle was between us, Sunderland, Chelsea and firm favourites Birmingham and Leicester City. Meanwhile my mate won a small fortune on backing the winner in the Grand National. His horse Ben Nevis won at 40-1. I can still see his face to this day, dancing with the girls in Robinson's pub in the 'Bigg Market' thinking he was Rockefella. Even though we won, we still had a mountain to climb to try and pinch a promotion place.

Chris Scott
Killingworth, Newcastle

v NOTTS COUNTY
ST JAMES' PARK
ATT; 22,005

WED 2ND APRIL 1980
SECOND DIVISION
DREW 2-2

Things I remember about these days include the Geordie Hulk who used to provide the half-time entertainment in the Gallowgate End by standing on a barrier with no top on doing impersonations of the Hulk. He would just stand up above everyone snarling with his fists clenched! Everyone thought he was hilarious! Even though I was a kid I still remember cringing at some of the songs being sung in that era. The worst by far - sung to the same tune as (*You're Going To Get Your Fucking Heads Kicked In*) was - "*The Fonz Is Cool But Geordies Are Cooler!*" I just remember putting my little head in my hands and thinking to myself - Oh for fucks sake! In those days as long as we won on a Saturday that was enough for me, I was happy. I knew we were never going to win the league or anything else. I was just happy to win a match and then watch Starsky & Hutch & Match of the Day on a Saturday night. I enjoyed watching Peter Withe. Sure he was no Supermac, but he came from the then Champions Forest and we were a struggling Second Division side. He won everything in the air and I always remember him running away both arms aloft, fists clenched showing off his white arm bands. He also looked like a Werewolf!! My Grandad Joe Graham was the Groundsman at St James in those days, he got me and my dad Danny in for free for years, and he'd be turning in his Grave if he knew we were paying nearly £700 these days!

Hendy
Kenton, Newcastle

v SUNDERLAND
ROKER PARK
ATT; 41,752

SAT 5TH APRIL 1980
SECOND DIVISION
LOST 0-1

Police in Strength at Derby

Police were out in force this afternoon as supporters travelled to the Newcastle and Sunderland derby football game. British Transport Police were manning local rail services as well as five soccer specials taking fans to and from Seaburn for the match at Roker Park. Insp. Stephen Chapman said dog handlers were to be on duty at stations along the line. A capacity crowd was expected at the football ground. Plans were laid last week for strict shepherding of Tyneside supporters between the stations and the stadium. Youths were being searched for weapons and missiles, and police were to form a barrier between rival groups during the game.

Sunderland became the first club in the country to sell match tickets in supermarkets! This new plan was first implemented for this match. The novel plan was explained and arranged quite proudly by promotions manager Corny O'Donnell. The tickets went on sale at 11 supermarkets and it was hoped that it would become a regular practice. "It means that our supporters will not have to make two journeys to Roker Park. Instead of going to the ground to buy a ticket and then going again for the match, they can get a ticket from their local high street." Tickets were on sale at 9 Presto Supermarkets - Ashington, Bedlington, Blyth, Cramlington, Jarrow, Doxford Park, Wrekenton, Ryhope and North Shields. And at 2 Lipton's at Consett and Stanley. "A loaf of bread, a tub of butter, a box of corn flakes and a ticket for Roker Park! Oh that reminds me, I must pick up some Bog Roll." Sunderland always the smaller club.

Mick Edmondson
Walker, Newcastle

The atmosphere in Newcastle Central Station was electric from midday as the sun shone through the glass roof onto thousands of men aged between 16 and 45, most of whom were pissed, as they queued before continually squeezing onto the numerous crammed carriages which resembled cattle trucks. *"Sunderland, Sunderland Here We Come"* rang around the station as some who couldn't wait to reach Wearside wrestled with Coppers who were having a hard day at the office already. The fashions were brilliant as the majority were dressed for battle - not a trainer in sight - instead a mixture of the regular 'boot boy' shoes such as Brogues, Doc Martins, Riders & Dealers not forgetting the odd monkey boot. Jeans and Sta- Press were complimented with braces, skinhead haircuts and a black n' white scarf either tied around your neck or wrist. No mob anywhere could have stopped Newcastle's army of followers today as it seemed every nutter from Tyneside was Sunderland bound. As our train pulled into Seaburn station the battle cry went up as the waiting police struggled to contain the Geordies who managed to break free and chase every Sunderland fan in sight. I lost all my mates as we battled and chased Sunderland all the way to the ground down side streets, attacking pubs, cars and anybody who got in the way. The match was best forgotten as we went down 1-0 to a Stan Cummins goal our first defeat at Roker since 1967. And it would take another 28 years for Newcastle United to lose another football match in Sunderland. No police cameras in those days, just £10 fines and scrubs and a good kicking in the back of the Black Mariah, no wonder there was hell on week in week out. After the match I was involved in a mass battle outside the ground and was lifted for the first time ever, my Dad went mental and he had every right as I was only 15 and he thought I was playing football in the Park. That's the way it was then and at the time I was young and daft and I loved it, but now I have kids of my own I think what an idiot.

Ian W.
Walker, Newcastle

Easter Saturday and surprisingly we were still in with a chance of promotion as we packed into and filled the 'Roker End, as well as hundreds getting into the home ends, mainly the Fulwell and the Clock Stand as usual. Played the twats off the park but couldn't put any of our chances away and in the end lost to a goal from a poncy dwarf in white boots called Stan Cummins, who netted at the Fulwell End. At the time the defeat was hard to take as not only was it against the enemy but it also basically ended any hope we had of promotion as we dropped to seventh not to mention putting them in a very strong position as they remained in the top three. One of my all time lows as a Newcastle United fan but it would be the last time they'd ever beat us at that dump.

Paul Wardle
Wallsend, Tyneside

I was in the Police escort between Seaburn Station and Joker Park and we were being walked along the wide pavement with the coppers on the road. I was pushed off the kerb and onto the road where a copper approached me and shouted angrily "Fuck off, back on to the pavement!" to which I replied "You Fuck off." I was immediately arrested and thrown in to the back of a Black Mariah, stone cold sober at 1pm (only had a couple in Yates opposite the central) and kept in the cells until 9am Sunday when the duty sergeant informed me that he'd only come in on his day off to charge Newcastle fans! I was therefore charged and later fined £160 for Drunk and Disorderly? Aggressive behaviour? And swearing at an officer of the law, okay I hold my hands up to the final charge, but only after the cheeky horrible bastard had sworn at me.

Deka
Gateshead, Tyneside

I remember fondly the escorts we used to get from Seaburn Station to the ground and back and Geordies trying to break out and run after Sunderland (they weren't known as the Mackem's then!) and the Football Special train used to stop at old Gateshead train station on the way back!

Dave Drape
Walker, Newcastle

How the fortunes of the sides had changed since the previous game on New Year's Day. We had been clear at the top of the League then but had only beaten Orient in January and Bristol Rovers in March (when it has to be said only because future Mag Martin Thomas got injured). They were on a roll and were looking as though it would be them not us who would go up. Newcastle actually played well but Cummins got the only goal. On the Sunday I was talking to a neighbour who like a lot of people at the time was having to go abroad to find work. "Well son, the only good thing about yesterday is I can go away, knowing I'm not going to miss us going up." Being young and still full of hope I replied "We still have a chance you know, if we can beat blah blah and blah blah beat blah blah we could still do it." He gave me a sympathetic laugh and added "I hope your right son, I hope your right"

Chris Ramshaw
West Denton, Newcastle

86 Arrests in Big Game
But most fans keep their cool

Eighty-six Fans arrested - but no serious injuries. That was the tally last night after the North East's big soccer derby. And fans damaged two coaches on rail specials to Sunderland. Three windows were smashed, two toilets damaged and dozens of light bulbs taken. But the general feeling of both police and British Rail was that it could have been a lot worse. Problems started long before the kick-off at Roker Park where Sunderland met Newcastle United in a Division Two promotion clash. United fans shouted and chanted as they marched to catch the specials at Newcastle station. Some set off fireworks. During the game - which Sunderland won by a single goal - sporadic fighting broke out on the terraces. Police some with dogs waded into the crowd to stop the trouble. Last night police were on the alert for further isolated outbreaks of violence. Most of the arrested - 50 were Newcastle supporters, 36 Sunderland - were for threatening words and behaviour. But a British Rail spokesman said: "The vast majority of the fans behaved themselves. It could have been a lot worse." Last night it was not clear how many of those arrested would actually face charges in court.

I had just been given a suspended sentence prior to this local derby for hitting two coppers, so was doing my best to stay out of trouble. As I knocked on my mate who lived in Winlaton 'the Asylum on the hill,' his Mam was polishing his boots. A group of us got 4 taxis to the Grey Horse pub in Whitburn, Sunderland. Although we had a game mob we planned to keep ourselves to ourselves as we stood outside the pub in the boiling hot sun. A few drinks and we were starting to attract the attention of passing Sunderland fans. A group of about 10 of them were mouthing off but wouldn't come across the road. So after a while of listening to abuse we charged them, one of our lads got knocked on his arse, I hit a kid and put his nose all over his face and as they ran we chased them. I couldn't catch the main mouthpiece but he was hit on the back of the head by one of the numerous flying bottles. I was duly pointed out to police to whom I announced "Looks like I'm off to the big house." The Sunderland fan said that he could feel the blood running through his hands from his head wound to which I asked "Are you sure it was blood and not Brown Ale?" This didn't go down to well and didn't help my defence - whatsoever. Trying to stay out of trouble resulted in a 12 month sentence for me.

Black Horse Tony
Low Fell, Tyneside

v BURNLEY   **MON 7TH APRIL 1980**
ST JAMES' PARK   **SECOND DIVISION**
ATT; 18,863   **DREW 2-2**

Our season was now definitely over as already relegated Burnley added another point to the two they took us off us at Turf Moor on Boxing Day. Brian Ferguson who joined us on a free transfer from Mansfield in January 1979 made his debut when he came on as a sub for Peter Withe! I just wanted the season to end quickly. We'd come down with the Christmas decorations.

Mick Edmondson
Walker, Newcastle

v FULHAM   **SAT 12TH APRIL 1980**
CRAVEN COTTAGE   **SECOND DIVISION**
ATT; 7,152   **LOST 0-1**

It had been a busy month since the Petrol bomb incident against West Ham with away matches at Cardiff then Sunderland, Newcastle getting good results off the pitch at both. This was a potential nightmare as we were back in the capitol for the first time and were public enemy number one down there, and although not well organised we still showed and had a tremendous mob for a normally very low key fixture. Many of us didn't even go into the match and just hung around the ground but West Ham never showed. It was a long journey just to drink flat overpriced piss.

Unknown
Newcastle

I hitched a lift to Birmingham in the early hours. Then I spotted a day trip bus so asked for a lift & was given the only spare seat. I was half pissed so was soon asleep. The next thing I remember is I had somebody licking my cheek. I awoke to find it was an Afghan Dog. The coach was full of old biddies and their dogs going to a dog show. A disgraceful performance and result against a team already doomed to the Third Division.

Piper,
Felling, Tyneside

v SWANSEA CITY
ST JAMES' PARK
ATT; 14,314

SAT 19TH APRIL 1980
SECOND DIVISION
LOST 1-3

One of the real characters from the terraces used to be a bloke known to everybody as 'Auld Tommy.' I have fond memories of listening to auld Tommy in front of the scoreboard in the Gallowgate End, when he used to climb on the concrete barrier with his back towards the pitch, singing his favourite song, 'Little White Bull' - the old Tommy Steele ditty. Always dressed in an oversized 'Suit Jacket' with a single vent in the back, a dress shirt underneath always half open, plain trousers hanging off his arse and he always looked as though he'd just woken up. He'd sing in a mumbled voice, *"Once Upon A Time There Was A Little White Bull"* the crowd would then chant *"A Little White Bull"* and so on. He would sometimes piss in to the crowd below whilst standing on the barrier. The crowd would chant "Tommy is weh leada." His real name I believe was Tommy Crane and he used to work in and around the Grainger and Green markets, a proper Character known and strangely loved by all.

Tommy Knox
Fenham, Newcastle

A couple of days earlier on Wednesday 16th April 1980, Her Majesty Queen Elizabeth the Queen Mother opened the Newcastle 900 celebrations with the immortal words; "Who does not listen on a Saturday night to hear the fortunes of Newcastle United?" You can just imagine her sitting with tea and cakes in Buckingham Palace watching Frank Bough on Final Score, Grandstand with the corgi's running around her feet. "Oh no, dear me, that's five games without a win now for Newcarsil. Think I'll have an Indians later."

Mick Edmondson
Walker, Newcastle

v QUEENS PARK RANGERS
LOFTUS ROAD
ATT; 11,245

SAT 26TH APRIL 1980
SECOND DIVISION
LOST 1-2

The last away game of that season was my first away game in London and even with nothing to play for, a huge number turned up at Loftus Road, to cheer on 'The Mags.' We got beat, again, 2-1, though I do recall that the QPR scorers that day were Glen Roeder and David McCreery, both of whom who went on to play for us later in the eighties under the Keegan revolution. Our scorer that day was a certain Brian Ferguson, remember him? No didn't think so.

Anth Nicholson
North Shields, Tyneside

Outside after the match it kicked off as we walked back towards the White City for our buses. It was quite dodgy especially with nobody quite knowing who was who! Once back at the coaches the rumour was that it was West Ham who had started it to avenge the petrol bomb and the reception they had received at

St James' Park a few weeks earlier. I've since read in a hooligan book that West Ham reckon that the Geordies were up for the fight until the shout of 'fight West Ham' went up! Well I was there and the reality of it was that the Newcastle football fans who didn't want to fight got out the way while the Geordies who wanted to know got stuck in, and although seemingly outnumbered didn't do to badly. It was just another day at the office, but not really worth writing about in the first place.

Paul
Gateshead, Tyneside

v LUTON TOWN **ST JAMES' PARK** **ATT; 13,765**	**SAT 3RD MAY 1980** **SECOND DIVISION** **DREW 2-2**

This was our lowest home gate of the season which was amazingly and sadly 25,019 down on our home crowd against Sunderland four months earlier. Peter Withe played his last match before signing for Aston Villa for £500,000, a team he would help win the First Division title followed by the European Cup within two seasons. He will always be remembered on Gallowgate for his commitment and effort during his two year stay in which he scored 27 goals in 83 games. Also making his last appearance was Brian Ferguson, who scored once in four games and would eventually sign for Hull City the following December.

Mick Edmondson
Walker, Newcastle

As a bairn I entered a competition in the match programme where you had to nominate your favourite Magpie player for the 79-80 season and then using no more than 30 words, describe why he was your choice. I nominated John Brownlie and wrote, "Every run I see him make, ends in defenders wanting to shake." Aye, not quite Shakespeare, but nevertheless good enough to finish third out of over 400 entrants! The match programme for our final home game against Luton had a full page colour photo of the winner Mark Scott with John Brownlie. He got to present Brownlie with a 'My favourite Magpie' silver tankard and himself received a £10 note and a ball signed by all the United players, as well as free admission to the game against Swansea.

Tom Knox
Fenham, Newcastle

1979-80 Season Summary

After a slightly indifferent first few matches, United soon put a run together and looked quite comfortable in the league without playing that well. Losing to Sunderland at the first hurdle in the League Cup hurt. But by News Years Day it was a distant memory, as we hammered the Wearsider's, whilst cementing our position at the top of the Second Division. Our front two were on fire, Alan Shoulder had scored 16 league goals and Peter Withe a respectable 9 goals. We were favourites for promotion and had been drawn at home to Third Division Chester City in the FA Cup. But in true Newcastle United style, 'little' Chester knocked us out and we fell to pieces, winning only 2 of our remaining 18 matches! We couldn't sustain our early season form and more importantly our results. To think we only needed 18 points from a possible 54, to be promoted & 21 points to be champions. It was absolutely soul destroying. After our win on New Year's Day we only collected a mere 13 points, sliding down the table to ninth place! If things weren't bad enough, just to rub salt in our wounds, Sunderland, unbelievably snatched promotion on the final day of what was their centenary season. Their last match was at home to West Ham which had previously been postponed twice, once for bad weather then again for the Hammers involvement in the FA Cup. They actually lifted the cup as John Lyall's side beat Terry Neil's Arsenal, who were current holders and were making their 3rd consecutive appearance in the final (a record).

SECOND DIVISION	FINAL TABLE 1979-80						
Leicester City	42	21	13	8	58	38	55
Sunderland	42	21	12	9	69	42	54
Birmingham City	42	21	11	10	58	38	53
Chelsea	42	23	7	12	66	52	53
QPR	42	18	13	11	75	53	49
Luton Town	42	16	17	9	66	45	49
West Ham	42	20	7	15	54	43	47
Cambridge	42	14	16	12	61	53	44
Newcastle United	**42**	**15**	**14**	**13**	**53**	**49**	**44**
Preston	42	12	19	11	56	52	43
Oldham Athletic	42	16	11	15	49	53	43
Swansea City	42	17	9	16	48	53	43
Shrewsbury Town	42	18	5	19	60	53	41
Orient	42	12	17	13	48	54	41
Cardiff City	42	16	8	18	41	48	40
Wrexham	42	16	6	20	40	49	38
Notts County	42	11	15	16	51	52	37
Watford	42	12	13	17	39	46	37
Bristol Rovers	42	11	13	18	50	64	35
Fulham	42	11	7	24	42	74	29
Burnley	42	6	15	21	39	73	27
Charlton Athletic	42	6	10	26	39	78	22

The promotion decider wasn't actually played until a few days after the Cup Final, long after all of their promotion rivals had already completed their fixtures. A draw would have been good enough, but a 2-0 win against a half hearted West Ham put them 2nd, only 1 point above 4th. They were promoted along with Leicester and Birmingham. Ken Knighton's red and white bastards. Still top at the end of January we had failed to score in 8 of our last 16 games, winning only once. We had fallen so low that even Cambridge United finished above us in the league. In fact if we hadn't of started the season off so well, then we could have easily been relegated. So where did it all go wrong? The injury which ruled out our skipper, Mick Martin, from early December didn't help our cause, and was a major factor. We relied on certain players and when Shoulder and Withe's goals dried up we were knackered. We were found wanting all over the pitch as we lacked strength in depth. The team also had no pace, partly due to the average age. Bill McGarry who took all the plaudits before Christmas must also take the majority of the blame. We had failed miserably in a poor Second Division, it was well below par. This was proved when only 3 clubs out of the 13 Second Division sides who were at home in the third round of the FA Cup progressed, as Chelsea lost to Fourth Division Wigan and non-league Harlow knocked Leicester out. When the end of season accolades were handed out Peter Withe was our only representative in the Second Division side. The big question was could we hold on to Peter Withe over the summer. It goes without saying that it's so important to hold on to your best players, as not only do they improve your side, but they also help attract other quality players. In the past we had let our better players leave to easily. A prime example was former Newcastle player Terry McDermott (Liverpool) who was named English Footballs Player of the Year 1979-80. Meanwhile Peter Withe's former club Nottingham Forest managed by a certain Brian Clough won the European Cup for the second year in succession, beating Kevin Keegan's side SV Hamburg. The thing is Forest were and still are as relatively small club compared to us, which made the whole situation worse. Another question being asked was would money be made available to strengthen the ageing squad. But if so was McGarry the right man to spend it? It was now 25 years since we'd last won a domestic trophy. This was a big summer ahead for Newcastle United and its long suffering fans.

Typical representative team for the season:
Steve Hardwick, John Brownlie, Ian Davies, David Barton, Stuart Boam, Tommy Cassidy, Peter Cartwright, Terry Hibbitt, Mick Martin/Billy Rafferty, Alan Shoulder & Peter Withe

Total Appearances: (League, FA Cup & League Cup) - 45 matches played
Hardwick, Shoulder (44), Brownlie (41), Boam, Davies, Withe (40), Cartwright (39), Hibbitt (37), Barton (35), Cassidy (32), Rafferty (25), Martin (21), Connolly (16), Walker (13), Carney (11), Bird, Shinton (10), Mitchell (6), Ferguson (5), Nicholson (4), Cropley, Pearson (3), Carr, Wharton (1). *Includes all sub appearances.

Total Goals: (League, FA Cup & League Cup) Total Scored 57.
Shoulder (21), Withe (11), Cassidy (6), Cartwright, Rafferty (4), Barton, Connolly, Davies, Hibbitt (2), Boam, Ferguson, Shinton (1), plus Opp Own Goals (0).

1979/80 SELECTION OF ITEMS FROM NUSC SHOP

ALAN SHOULDER SCARF	£2.10
TARTAN SCARF	£1.15
BOB HAT AWAY COLOURS	£1.40
BOWLER HAT	£1.90
MIRROR 22"x 14	£9.50
LARGE WING PATCH BADGE	£1.45
MAGPIE TIE	£3.90
FINGER RING	70p
STAINLESS STEAL NECKLET	£1.30
N/C BALL PEN	30p
TABLE LAMP	£4.50
APRON	£2.30
FLASK	£2.90
CIRCULAR TRAY	£1.20
MATCHBOX LIGHTER	£3.00

Sadie - Everybody loved Aunty Sadie who worked in the supporters shop.

BLUE STAR / CRUYFF FROM BRIGHTON / TRANSFER RECORDS
BURY & EXETER / SHINTON, CLARKE & RAFFERTY
TEAMS WHO SHOULDN'T & GOALSCORERS WHO COULDN'T

1980-81 SEASON

Somehow Bill McGarry managed to keep his job over the summer, but unfortunately wasn't able to keep our star player Peter Withe who understandably needed top flight football. He left for Aston Villa on freedom of contract and within a year he would help them to lift the First Division title, (just as he had done at Nottingham Forest months prior to his arrival at Gallowgate). Then 12 months later he scored the winner for Villa in the European Cup final. We sold him for a club record fee £500,000 to go with the £30,000 we received from Burnley for Tommy Cassidy. Northern Ireland international Cassidy had spent just 2 months short of 10 years at St James' Park. Also departing on free transfers were John Bird (Hartlepool), John Connolly (Hibernian) and Brian Ferguson (Hull City). We also lost Jim Pearson who retired from the professional game due to injury. We also secured our first ever shirt sponsorship deal with our Barrack Road neighbours Scottish & Newcastle Breweries. The deal which was worth £100,000 over 2 years was in return for us wearing the famous blue star on our shirts, whenever possible. (TV companies wouldn't allow shirt sponsorship when the games were televised). Even though we had banked a healthy sum over the summer, we apparently couldn't afford to sign any quality players? Our greedy directors wouldn't spend big, in fact wouldn't spend at all. They paid local non-league side Tow Law £500 for the services of Chris Waddle, with the promise of another £500 when he broke into first team. Waddle was paid £70 a week! We also signed Ray Clarke who had played for Sparta Rotterdam, Ajax and Club Brugge. He was hailed by some as the next Johan Cruyff!! He came from Brighton for £80,000! Another bargain basement deal saw Frans Koenen arrive on loan. We had only spent £80,500 on 2 new signings, yet lost 6 players and received £530,000 as well as the revenue from the breweries and cash from season ticket sales. Our squad which was already small and weak, desperately in need of reinforcements, was now even smaller and weaker. Long term absentee and skipper, Mick Martin was still out injured, heaven help us if we had any more injuries. If we didn't get off to a flyer then McGarry was history. The writing was on the wall. As the season drew closer it was reported that Newcastle United needed 30,000 fans through the turnstiles to break even and that the directors were exploring other ways to raise funds. The report continued; the fact that they are in the Second Division doesn't help and the fact that last season visiting clubs took £89,794 away from Gallowgate as their share of the gates. United had to hand over 30p per adult and 15p for children and OAPS to their visitors. The directors are constantly exploring new avenues of raising cash. That's why the sound of music could soon be coming out of SJP. The possibility of Pop Concerts in the near future, are currently being considered. The last balance sheet revealed that United were over half a million pounds in the red at the bank. Club secretary Russell Cushing says "We are cutting as far back as we can in every direction without dropping our standards. "A computer will soon be installed at our offices to help improve efficiency and help spell out just where the money goes." As well as concerts United hoped to stage super star competitions! Cut backs include United travelling to every game by coach. In the past, United have travelled on a private carriage, on a London train with their own chef. Now the chef on the coach is the player who happens to be nearest to the packed lunches! Work on the new North stand behind the Leazes End has been suspended because a lack of money. United's total income last season was £880,000. Players gobbled up 40% of this. The balance sheet showed that 6 employees earned over £20,000 last season. It was going to be a long winter!

1980-81 TOUR OF SWEDEN   MON 20th - MON 28th JULY 1980

A low-key pre-season tour against mediocre opposition in Sweden saw United play five matches and win only twice. It was very much a 'get fit' and 'bonding' session in Scandinavia with the forward pairing of Bobby Shinton and Billy Rafferty the Magpies' big promotion hope for the new season. It was a plan doomed to failure, while tours abroad were soon to change into high-profile occasions when United brought a certain Kevin Keegan into the camp.

20TH JULY	v SOLVESBORGS	0-0	ATT; 1,500
22ND JULY	v OSKARASHAMS ATK	3-0	ATT; 2,000
24TH JULY	v TRELLEBORGS FF	1-1	ATT; 1,000
26TH JULY	v HOOR IS	1-2	ATT; 1,000
28TH JULY	v TORMELILLIA	3-0	ATT; 2,000

Paul Joannou
Club Historian

v HEARTS
TYNECASTLE
ATT; 3,334

MON 4TH AUGUST 1980
FRIENDLY
DREW 1-1

In the school holidays a few of us got the train up to Edinburgh to watch this friendly. There was a good 800 plus from Newcastle up there against Bobby Moncur's side. After the match we were leaving the ground and were greeted by loads of young Hearts fans that had come to have a pop at us. There just seemed to be us youngsters in the street and we were totally outnumbered so had to back off. Then from behind us our older lads appeared and one in particular growled at them at the top of his voice, which sent them all scattering. We managed to walk back to the station without any hassle and get the last train home. Our first outing of the season produced our first pre-season casualty as John Brownlie last seasons 'Player of the Year' hobbled off his leg ending up in plaster as he damaged Knee ligaments similar to Mick Martin's injury. He would miss six months of the coming season! New £180,000 striker Ray 'Cruyff' Clarke had failed to score in 4 of the 5 friendly's but was quite adamant that the goals would come: "I'll get goals for Newcastle United." Meanwhile McGarry

watched the match between Peterborough & Barnsley at the weekend as he was allegedly looking at home striker Billy Kellock and Barnsley's Ronnie Glavin. Kellock was injured so didn't play. And in all the years watching Newcastle I have never known a supposed Newcastle target mentioned in the Chronicle, half as much as Ronnie Glavin was. It was tedious and he obviously never ever signed for us. Good job really as he was shit. As for Billy Kellock he went on to win 356 caps for Brazil and was named as European footballer of the year whilst playing for Barcelona………or maybe I've never heard of him since.

Dave
Walker, Newcastle

v LEEDS UNITED
ST JAMES' PARK
ATT; 7,448

SAT 9TH AUGUST 1980
FRIENDLY
DREW 2-2

The visit of First Division giants Leeds United (five years earlier they were beaten finalists in the European Cup Final) for our first match at St James' Park, a week before the season's opener. I was one of the first to sit in the new East Stand Paddock seating area (more commonly known as 'The Benches') as the old standing terracing was replaced (built on) with wooden benches and open for the first time. There was a new ticket kiosk in the East Stand where you had to purchase your tickets from for this area if you were under 16 priced £1.50. For

many, the start of a whole new era. Meanwhile we got our first glimpse of young Dutch trialist Frans Koenen who the Evening Chronicle had earlier in the week called Kasma Koenen. All double-dutch to me.

Mick Edmondson
Walker, Newcastle

v SHEFFIELD WEDNESDAY
HILLSBOROUGH
ATT; 26,164

SAT 16TH AUGUST 1980
SECOND DIVISION
LOST 0-2

6000 in Soccer Invasion

At least 6,000 Newcastle fans were on their way to Hillsborough today for the first match of the season v Sheffield Wednesday. A spokesman for Sheffield police said they had slightly more officers on duty than usual, mainly because of Wednesday's promotion to the second division, but they weren't expecting any trouble. More than 3,000 supporters travelled by coach alone.

A massive turnout as thousands travelled down to the steel city for the season's opener. League debuts for summer signings Frans Koenen and Ray Clarke on what was a very hot day. Koenen (Fransiscus Leonarious Albertus Koenan) had arrived from Dutch club NEC Nijmegan signing after a loan period for £60,000. Clarke had also played on the continent with Ajax, Club Brugge, and Sparta Rotterdam as well as in England for Swindon, Mansfield and Brighton - whom we paid £180,000 for his services. Steve Carney was sent off which didn't go down to well with the travelling hordes. My memory of the trip though isn't of any players but is of the crazy scenes as we left the stands and terracing at full time as the police tried to keep the Newcastle fans in the ground whilst Geordies attempted to smash their way through the fencing adjacent to the turnstiles as mass fighting took place in the streets outside. In all the melee on top of what seemed like a supporters shop hut a Police woman was being pushed about and stripped of her clothes in full view of all, which at first seemed like harmless fun and she seemed to be laughing going along with it, but things got totally out of hand and it was pretty horrific. Reported later in the press as 'Distasteful Crowd Trouble!'

Craig Colquhoun
Wallsend, Tyneside

Fans Saves Policewoman

Fourteen police officers were hurt on the first day of the league soccer season as Newcastle United fans went on the rampage. Last night two of the officers were still in hospital-one of them a policewoman with a crushed abdomen. A total of 41 people were arrested after United's away game against Sheffield Wednesday. A police spokesman said all but one of them were from Newcastle. And last night the yobs were still brawling and in the streets and pubs of Sheffield. A senior police officer said: "They're animals. "This was the worst day of soccer violence this city has ever seen. "It is evident that the violence was associated with drink." A number of men will appear before magistrates in Sheffield tomorrow in connection with these incidents. Violence erupted long before United's game with newly promoted Wednesday. The senior police officer said: "They were causing trouble from early in the day." The "animals" left a trail of destruction. They smashed windows in Rotherham on the way to the match. They ran riot through the fox Hotel at Brotherton on the A1 in Yorkshire. And they attacked innocent passers-by after their team had lost 2-0. At the match itself trouble erupted after the referee sent off Newcastle's Steve Carney when the score was 0-0. An eye witness said that six policeman trying to control more than 6,000 Geordie fans were mocked and jeered at. He said: Their helmets were thrown into the air and they were pushed about. "Then all of a sudden a big cheer went up from the rest of the crowd as at least 30 policemen waded in to sort out the trouble and rescue their mates." After the game, the senior police officer said that the fans hurled bricks at a double-decker bus and smashed most of its windows.

A good squad of us was travelling down in a furniture van and we'd only just stopped for a piss so I was surprised when Paul pulled open the shutters at the back? There were Boro fans having a piss break themselves on the lay-by and sure enough we poured out and got stuck into them and a mass battle ensued-much to the disgust of a 'caravanner' who'd pulled in for a tea break with his missus. The smog monsters were admittedly game and whilst the fighting continued and the 'caravanner' loudly berated us, Paul who was very posh but also stone mad broke it up before the police arrived suggesting that we could meet up on the way back! Middlesbrough were away to Man Utd that day. After our match there was hell on as two coppers tried to hold back the whole away end which contained thousands, one was a WPC and she nearly had her whole kit ripped off..........not good.

Jim
North Shields, Tyneside

I wouldn't have believed it if I hadn't of witnessed with my own eyes. After the match we were walking back up that massive hill where the massive convoy of coaches were parked when I decided to pop into this small baker's type shop for a can of pop. There were a few already in the shop, so I was waiting my turn when all of a sudden in came a police horse, the copper ducking as they came through the door. As he shouted to us all to get a move on and get on our buses the horse was busy scoffing a cream cake on the counter!

Paul
Gateshead, Tyneside

After the match as we tried to leave the terracing we were unable to move as the Police had locked the gates to prevent the huge travelling army from spilling onto the streets. The ones who had already managed to get out were already causing mayhem battling with locals. I and many others got stuck in the now notorious tunnel under the stand at the Leppings Lane End which joined the courtyard - situated just inside the turnstiles - to the terraces. Luckily there were no fences so we were able to spill over onto the pitch.

Piper
Felling, Tyneside

Soccer Fans Face Trial

A judge ordered a retrial for two Newcastle football fans accused of assaulting police after a jury at Leeds Crown court failed to reach a verdict. The assaults were alleged to have happened at the Sheffield Wednesday-Newcastle United match at Hillsborough. Both fans were granted bail pending the retrial.

Highlights of this match were shown on TV on the Sunday at 4.35pm. Football was in the doldrums and this was certainly the case as BBC1 broadcast Match of the Day on a Sunday tea-time. ITV had the right to the popular and regular Saturday night slot, so Tyne Tees television broadcast 'Shoot' with anchorman George Taylor.

Mick Edmondson
Walker, Newcastle

v NOTTS COUNTY
ST JAMES' PARK
ATT; 17,272

WED 20TH AUGUST 1980
SECOND DIVISION
DREW 1-1

The Club Editorial in the match day programme, referring to the disturbing and disgraceful crowd trouble at Hillsborough days earlier read: "If we as a club or Bill McGarry as an individual had of wanted a Black-and-White army we would have introduced conscription." Even though thousands had travelled to Hillsborough, this was our lowest post-war crowd for an opening home fixture at Gallowgate. The fact that it was on a Wednesday night obviously didn't help, but our lack of activity in the transfer market and state of the club were bigger factors.

Mick Edmondson
Walker, Newcastle

Graffiti pair each fined £50

A pair of punk painters were spotted by a police patrol when making their daubed green graffiti on a Newcastle United stadium. And their illegal artwork earned them each a £50 fine, 12 hours at an attendance centre and £10.35 compensation. Christopher Patrick Allan and Paul Mark Mowbray, both aged 18 and both from Newminster Road, Fenham, admitted at Newcastle Magistrates Court damaging gates at St James' Park and stealing a pot of paint. Insp. Eric Green, prosecuting said the slogans "Punk" and "N.U.F.C" were found daubed on the stadium gates. They admitted stealing the paint from a contractor who had been working at a Newcastle hotel.

v BOLTON WANDERERS
BURNDEN PARK
ATT; 11,835

SAT 23RD AUGUST 1980
SECOND DIVISION
LOST 0-4

We slipped to our lowest placing in our 86 year history. Bottom of the league and humiliated by a team which although played in last season's First Division would eventually just miss out on relegation by two points. Brian Kidd got a hat-trick although one of his shots went in off Billy Rafferty's arse, as ex-mag and veteran Alan Gowling ran the show. The travelling hordes decided enough was enough and held a mass sit down protest on the concrete terraces. Disgruntled fans chanted throughout the game, *"Sack McGarry, Sack McGarry"* and *"Sack The Board, Sack The Board, Sack The Board"* The only cheer of the afternoon was when at half-time it was announced that Sunderland were losing against Southampton. We were a club in crisis and tempers were rife as the Newcastle fans showed their disgust. Many just walked out in silence before the end. Back on Tyneside the plight of our club was obvious as our reserve side entertained Man City second string. After the game both the home and visitors players' lounges were closed, with no refreshments available. When probed club secretary Russell Cushing commented, "We have to economise, it's as simple as that."

Mick Edmondson
Walker, Newcastle

v BURY
ST JAMES' PARK
ATT; 9,073

WED 27TH AUGUST 1980
LEAGUE CUP 2ND RND 1ST LEG
WON 3-2

Newcastle old boys Pat Howard and Keith Kennedy (Alan's Brother) arrived with the Fourth Division side managed by another former Magpie Jim Iley. Billy Rafferty - the goalscorer who couldn't - did! Twice! A lovely move involving Shoulder and Koenon for his first, but it wasn't enough to save Bill McGarry's job as he was sacked two days later. In his last match in charge he gave youngster Phil Leaver his only ever appearance. The next morning John Connolly announced that "he didn't get on with McGarry! "My abiding memory of Newcastle will be the fans" he said. "They have been great and I'm sorry to leave them but, frankly I haven't got a choice under the circumstances. I could have sat on my backside and picked up my wages for another year, but I wanted first team football and it was obvious that it wasn't going to happen at Newcastle. So I'd prefer to go out and look for a club." He soon returned north of the border and signed on a free for Hibs.

Mick Edmondson
Walker, Newcastle

v LUTON TOWN
ST JAMES' PARK
ATT; 13,175

SAT 30TH AUGUST 1980
SECOND DIVISION
WON 2-1

A month into the new season and our situation was desperate. Bill McGarry was sacked as manager the day before after we failed to win any of our first 3 league matches giving him a dismal record of winning only 3 league matches out of 22 in 1980 (Who would believe that in exactly two years to the day McGarry was fired we would all be in dream land hung over reading the Sunday papers reporting Kevin Keegan's Newcastle debut!!)   Newcastle United legend Joe Harvey aged 62 was appointed Caretaker Manager and without doubt helped inspire a rare league victory as Frans Koenan got his only ever Newcastle goal which turned out to be the winner.

Mick Edmondson
Walker, Newcastle

Racial taunts fans are fined Nazi salute given at the match

The Nazi salute and chants of Sieg heil were used to insult coloured footballers when Luton Town played Newcastle United at St James' Park. Coloured Luton players Ricky Hill and Brian Stein were subjected to a barrage of obscenities and racial taunts, Newcastle magistrates were told. Police moved in and arrested several Newcastle fans who had upset both home and visiting supporters by their obscene remarks and   racial abuse, said Mr. Neil Robson, prosecuting. Five Newcastle fans were each fined £150 with £10 costs when they admitted behavior likely to cause a breach of the peace. Mr. Robson said the coloured players were subjected to abuse during the match and when the fans ran onto the pitch at the final whistle.

United Fans Provoked Visitors

Newcastle fan Stephen Wilson got over-excited when United went 2-1 up against Luton. Wilson (23), of South View, Lesbury, Northumberland, climbed on to a crash barrier, held a black-and-white scarf in the air and then made V-signs at visiting supporters, city magistrates were told. "He then started to jump up and down on the barrier, still making V-signs, in time with the chants of Newcastle supporters around him," said Mr. Gerald Chalk, prosecuting. Wilson, unemployed admitted a breach of the peace. He was fined £150 and bound over to keep the peace for a year in the sum of £100.

As we look from the North East corner, this is how the Directors envisaged the all new St James' Park Stadium would look. More or less a mirror image of the East Stand. It was never to be as lack of funds meant that the club couldn't afford to complete the corner section first as instructed by the city Council. So the Leazes End, the home of the Geordie Choir, which had been demolished in 1978 would stay a shadow of its former self for years to come.

v BURY
GIGG LANE
ATT; 4,348

TUES 2ND SEPTEMBER 1980
LEAGUE CUP 2ND RND 2ND LEG
LOST 0-1 (Agg 3-3 lost on away goals)

Unfortunately Joe Harvey couldn't work the magic again as we were embarrassingly dumped out of the League Cup by Fourth Division minnows Bury, before the schools went back. Bury won on the away goal rule meaning that we had fallen at the first hurdle in this competition four years in succession. Listening on the radio back home on Tyneside must have been hard but actually being there in the humble surroundings, a typical small town football ground in Lancashire, was bloody awful. I had seen Newcastle play here four times in the league in the early sixties and never seen them lose; in fact we put 7 past them in 1961. Yet in typical Newcastle fashion we lost all four league games against them at St James' Park!! Since we lost 2-7 at Old Trafford in 1977 we hadn't progressed in this competition.

Eddie Thompson
Washington

v CARDIFF CITY
ST JAMES' PARK
ATT; 15,787

SAT 6TH SEPTEMBER 1980
SECOND DIVISION
WON 2-1

Joe Harvey continued his magic in the league as the Evening Chronicle announced earlier in the week that Brian Clough was rumoured to be on his way to St James' Park. However by the Thursday the club had announced that our new manager was in fact Arthur Cox and he would join us on the following Monday. Cardiff only brought thirty fans (Soul Crew must have still been on holiday?) Anybody who attended the matches back then will remember the Police station in the corner of the ground opposite the Strawberry Pub. Well believe it or not there used to be a gate next to the Cop Shop and for years this was the easiest way to get into the match as the lad would always take a small bribe never more than £1 to gain entry.

Peter Shaw
Westerhope, Newcastle

Can I Swear at the Goalie? asked fan

Painter and decorator Peter Redhead had a brush with the law at St James' Park. He only went to the soccer match to give Newcastle United goalkeeper Steve Hardwick some stick, the city magistrates were told. But he paid the penalty when he was fined £150 for behaviour likely to cause a breach of the peace. He asked a crowd-control policeman if he would be arrested for swearing at the Magpie goalie during the game against Cardiff City, said prosecutor Miss Helen Ferguson. He was told to move away and behave himself, the court was told. But, Miss Ferguson said, he replied: "Go on, just a little swear. I only come here to give him some stick. He is useless. The visiting team attacked on the pitch-and the shot went narrowly wide. The policeman saw Redhead shouting abuse and waving his fists at the goalkeeper. Other supporters were becoming upset, Miss Ferguson said. Redhead (24), of Garth Six, Killingworth, Newcastle, pleaded guilty and was ordered to pay £10 costs. He said: "I did not say anything to the police officer before I was swearing." He later agreed he later swore but said he did not know it was an offence. Earlier, the court ordered a supporter to attend a Saturday afternoon attendance centre. Paul McGowan (18), of Hedgehope Road, Newcastle, admitted behaviour likely to cause a breach of the peace. He was told to pay £10 costs and ordered to attend for a total of 24 hours, starting at 2pm on Saturday October 4th.

v QUEENS PARK RANGERS
LOFTUS ROAD
ATT; 10,865

SAT 13TH SEPTEMBER 1980
SECOND DIVISION
WON 2-1

I was about 15 years old and definitely too young to drink in London. The Supporters Club bus would leave about midnight on a Friday from the Haymarket, so I would always try my luck in the Farmers Rest pub beforehand but always had to rely on somebody older to get them in! After a few pints off we went, looking forward to the next six hours of no sleep and no toilet eventually arriving at Kings Cross at about 6am, with everybody a bit excited. Then it was a case of milling around burger bars before taking part in the expected shoplifting spree (only nicking total crap cockney memorabilia). By opening time, the older lads disappeared into the bars, leaving us younger ones to fend for ourselves. This is when the fun used to begin as we got closer to Loftus Road, although all of a sudden, I didn't feel so big and clever! Inside the ground (can't remember much of the game) all the big lads turn up, half pissed and this is where my bravado comes back. After the game, we made our way back to Kings Cross (mob handed until the big 'uns headed back to the pubs). Bearing in mind the returning bus wasn't leaving until midnight, it was a case of being in the middle of a potential war zone with every squad who had been playing in London all congregated in this small area. The inevitable happened, with us young 'uns taking a few minor slaps off numerous different mobs (Arsenal was definitely one of them). A bit later, about 6 of us were standing on the street corner when from nowhere, a gang of Chelsea fans (seemed about 100 but probably about 20-30) came running straight towards us. We obviously were straight on our toes (good job we were young n' fit) up one of the side streets, then disappeared into a block of flats, with the basement at pavement level where we see a load of Doctor Martins and Steel Cap boots marching past, with us trying not to breathe as not to make the slightest sound! After staying in the flats basement for about half an hour, we decided to brave it out and head back towards the war zone (Kings Cross) where thankfully the older, bigger lads had returned in dribs and drabs so the inevitable bravado returns to the point of us Young 'uns giving out a few slaps of our own to whoever was still about... This was one of my first trips to London and at the time I thought that it would be my last.

Steve (REG)
Longbenton, Newcastle

The Newcastle Evening Chronicle reported that rumours suggested that twice European Cup winning legendary manager Brian Clough was on his way to the St James' Park hot seat!! We ended up with Arthur Cox on a four year deal from third Division Chesterfield!! Even worse he'd coached Sunderland to their FA Cup victory in 1973 and had to work with the remnants of the previous three managers. Even so he seemed positive and honest "You can command wonderful support if you are prepared to be honest, straightforward and hardworking as the men, women and children who pay at the turnstiles. "The top flight is where Newcastle belongs and that has to be my target." The 'Match of the Day' cameras dropped down a division and were there to capture a rare

Newcastle away win as Cox got off to a flyer as we recorded our third consecutive 2-1 league victory. Stuart Boam had put us in front at the interval then QPR equalized, but I remember Terry Hibbitt got the winner whilst his number was being held up to be substituted. Peter Cartwright still replaced him as the referee had already noticed his number go up but was just waiting for the ball to go out of play. Meanwhile football was in trouble as attendances for the first four weeks of the new season were down by 140,000. This was the amount of fans missing from the same period who watched football matches up and down the country the previous season. The media were saying that it was all down to the aggro boys, that they had frightened and chased away the fans. It was hard to argue against the fact after numerous riots and one fan dying. There were calls for Sunday football as fans and hooligans wouldn't mix with shoppers. But Graham Kelly secretary of the football league was completely against Sunday football. "It is absolute nonsense to suggest playing our league games on Sunday. "People still like Sunday as a day of rest. Playing football on a Sunday would have no effect on soccer violence." And to think he was one of the main idiots running our national game for years!

Mick Edmondson
Walker, Newcastle

v OLDHAM ATHLETIC
ST JAMES' PARK
ATT; 19,786

SAT 2OTH SEPTEMBER 1980
SECOND DIVISION
DREW 0-0

After three consecutive league wins Arthur Cox's first home match as our new manager ended in a disappointing draw. Cox was being labelled the wrong man for the job. "Why haven't Bob Paisley, Lawrie McMenemy, Bobby Robson or myself as successful managers not been asked to tackle the job?"

Brian Clough
Nottingham Forest Manager

In response to Brian Clough's comments, "I'll make him eat his words." But the new manager was full of praise for the Newcastle fans and paid tribute to them, "It's our responsibility to give them more to shout about."

Arthur Cox
Newcastle United Manager

It was the Thursday night leading up to this match I will forever remember. As a 14 year old I watched Madness on 'Top of the Pops' before catching the number 12 bus with my 17 year old mate, over the town, as my favourite band were playing the Mayfair. I originally went over - dressed in my Black & White dogtooth check Harrington, Loafers, Fred Perry and 2-Tone strides - to enjoy the atmosphere and check out the fashions. Terry Hall and the Specials were in town and I was 'much too young' to get into the Mayfair. I'd only ever once been inside, aged 6 to receive my 25 yard swimming award. I was gutted, but thought that watching the over 18's queuing outside, was better than watching Question-time with my Mam & Dad. I'd never seen so many skinheads before, it was class. Eventually the crowds disappeared inside, and we were alone in the adjacent back lane when out of the blue a bloke gave us a ticket for nix. We approached the bouncers who had noticed what had happened. We both expected the knock back, but we couldn't believe it when he beckoned us towards the door asking: "Do you both want to go in?" Not only had my 'bum fluff tache' fooled the doorman, but I'd saved £3 into the bargain. Down the stairs, turn to the right, a few more stairs then a quick purchase at the merchandise stall, before walking into the electric atmosphere. I watched from the balcony as thousands of skinheads battled to stay on their feet as the crowd swayed all over the place down below. Many were on their mate's shoulders chanting Newcastle football songs, as the crowd relished the forthcoming visit of West Ham. It was like the match, but with a roof. When Terry Hall and the band took to the stage, it was bedlam. The Bouncers were at the side opposed to the front hosing the crowd with water. After a few songs the stage became packed with nutters and when Terry Hall shouted; "I thought this was the Newcastle Mayfair not Newcastle St James' Park" many in the crowd turned on the Coventry band, as chaos broke out. Missiles were thrown towards Man Utd fan Terry Hall the lead singer. A flying beer glass hit Jerry Dammers on the chest which was the final straw, as the band ran for the safety of backstage. After a few more encores, it would be another 29 years until the band returned. But both gigs go down without doubt as the best ever-and I've been to hundreds over the years- Terry Hall may be a glory hunting Man U twat, but in the world of music he is a god to many. *"You're Wondering Now"*

Mick Edmondson
Walker, Newcastle

Skinhead Invasion Halts Show!

Chanting skinheads occupied the stage during a concert at the Newcastle Mayfair last night. The show had to be stopped and started several times while the band tried to clear about 50 youths who crowded on to the stage. Some of the skinheads threw beer glasses. One hit a singer in the chest. They spat and climbed on to the platform during the encores. The group, The Specials, traded abuse with them and managed to clear the stage several times. At one stage they stopped mid-song and walked off. By the end of the show they were completing their encores from the back of the small stage while the youth's lept around on the front. Microphones and instruments were knocked to the ground. While other members of the audience taunted those on stage, the skinheads were chanting: *"Newcastle, Newcastle."* One of The Specials shouted back: "I thought this was the Newcastle Mayfair, not St James' Park."

<table>
<tr><td>

v BRISTOL ROVERS
ASHTON GATE
ATT; 5,171

</td><td>

SAT 27TH SEPTEMBER 1980
SECOND DIVISIOND
DREW 0-0

</td></tr>
</table>

As a result of a huge fire on 17th August 1980 in the South Grandstand at their ground Eastville, Rovers had to play their home games at their neighbours Bristol City's ground, Ashton Gate. We were the sixth and final visitors before they returned to their home ground. Amazingly we were due back at Ashton Gate to play City two weeks later.

Mick Edmondson
Walker, Newcastle

v WEST HAM UNITED
ST JAMES' PARK
ATT; 24,866

SAT 4TH OCTOBER 1980
SECOND DIVISION
DREW 0-0

Newcastle United matches against West Ham would never be the same again ever since the petrol bomb incident a few months earlier. Our highest home crowds always seemed to be against clubs with hooligan firms like Chelsea and West Ham as everybody would turn out. The Hammers had to play their European Cup Winners Cup game against Castilla three days earlier at Upton Park behind closed doors due to previous incidents. British

Soccer Fans Fighting Talk

Newcastle United supporter Robert Gray called on West Ham fans to fight as they were being escorted to the Central Station after the match at St James' Park magistrates heard. He was one of 150 Newcastle fans shouting, threatening and throwing things at supporters of the London team in Marlborough Crescent. Gray admitted causing a breach of the peace and was bound over for two years in the sum of £200.

Rail slapped a booze ban on soccer specials from today involving all future Newcastle United home and away matches. The same applied to all of Sunderland's matches also. There was also an alcohol ban on two scheduled trains stopping at Newcastle as it travelled from Kings Cross to Edinburgh. As well as the bans police would patrol all stations and stop anyone boarding with bottles or cans. The police would also ride the soccer specials to deal with outbreaks of violence or vandalism. Even non-football supporters would be unable to purchase alcohol on certain scheduled trains. This was all part of the on-going crack down on football violence. As for the match this was our third consecutive goalless draw in the league as we failed yet again to beat the FA Cup holders who were also our bogey team. But, Newcastle United were still unbeaten at any level since Arthur Cox had joined the club.

Mick Edmondson
Walker, Newcastle

Six minute muddle as 60 fans arrested

Sixty arrests - that was the toll last night after Newcastle United's home game with West Ham, which ran over time by a remarkable six minutes! But it could have been a lot worse - that was the verdict after the second division clash that many feared would prompt serious clashes between rival supporters. At the Magpies home game last season against the Londoners, one Hammers fan was hurt by a blazing petrol bomb, hurled by a Newcastle fan. But yesterday the vast majority of people arrested were to be charged with threatening words or behaviour and drunkenness. Another 50 fans were ejected from St James' Park, a police spokesman said. "But all in all we are satisfied that we kept any trouble down to a minimum." he added. A young policeman was injured however. He was treated for bruising after a kick in the face. He did not have to go to hospital. Crowd trouble at the game first erupted when the match referee George Nolan had to go off the field with a back injury. Mr Nolan swapped jobs with linesman Norman Wilson for the remainder of the first half. But Mr Wilson added on another six minutes. After the game he would not explain why. At half-time Mr Nolan went off the pitch altogether and his place was taken by Morpeth linesman Bill Holian. When the final whistle went mounted police were ready outside the ground to escort hundreds of West ham fans to catch their special train back to London. They were quickly joined by police with dogs who managed to keep the rival factions apart on the march through the town to the Central Station.

v PRESTON NORTH END
DEEPDALE
ATT; 5,301

TUES 7TH OCTOBER 1980
SECOND DIVISION
WON 3-2

Mick Martin returned from his long injury lay-off. A much needed first win at Deepdale in three attempts since being relegated was more of a fluke than owt else. Unbelievably we were two up at half-time but as expected all level and heading for a draw as we approached full time, with one of their goals coming from former Magpie Alex Bruce - looked and played like a girl with his shirt constantly hanging over his shorts-maybe it was a dress? Just as it looked like we'd thrown it away our lethal strike partnership combined like no other partnerships could or have done since as Rafferty going for a rare hat-trick miss kicked only for the wayward shot to hit off the oblivious Shinton and go in! "To tell the truth the ball just hit me" admitted Shinton. Keeper Kevin Carr hoisted a long kick down the middle and when Billy Rafferty flicked the ball through it struck Shinton, completely wrong-footed the Preston keeper and looped into the net.

Mick Edmondson
Walker, Newcastle

v BRISTOL CITY
ASHTON GATE
ATT; 10,539

SAT 11TH OCTOBER 1980
SECOND DIVISION
LOST 0-2

This must be some sort of football league record as we played our second league match at Ashton Gate in a fortnight against two different sides? After an all-day session and our usual away defeat, a coach load of us headed into Bristol for a night out. There were some dodgy characters on the bus and anything that wasn't nailed down seemed to be pinched that night (Young, daft and stupid). When we got back on our bus at the end of the night the police arrived and warned us that the coach wasn't going anywhere until some plaques from a nearby pub were returned. Nobody owned up and to my horror they were actually found under my seat! I later found out that somebody had kicked them there. As a result I was lifted and locked up in the cells wearing a black leather jacket which I'd actually obtained as a result of the shoplifting spree. I was eventually released along with many others at 3am still wearing my new leather jacket which the police didn't even question and jumped on the coach which had waited to pick us all up.

Deka
Gateshead, Tyneside

We drank pre-match in a village on the outskirts of Bristol, the first time I had ever tasted Scrumpy Jack Cider. Of all the places I have ever visited watching Newcastle without doubt Bristol is definitely one of the roughest and they are definitely underestimated as a mob. We spent the majority of the 90 minutes avoiding missiles inside the ground and the locals were well up for it outside both before and after.

Les
Newbiggin Hall, Newcastle

v SWANSEA CITY	**SAT 18TH OCTOBER 1980**
ST JAMES' PARK	**SECOND DIVISION**
ATT; 16,278	**LOST 1-2**

Not the ideal way to celebrate a centenary of football at St James' Park as Chris Waddle's relative Alan Waddle, a 22 year old Newcastle fan scored the winner for 'The Jack's.' Peter Kelly wore the Black-and-White shirt for the final time, eventually retiring at the end of the season due to injury after 38 appearances in six years. A poor crowd by our customary high standards watched as Cox lost his first Newcastle home match as manager. Little did we know that crowds would drop further.

Mick Edmondson
Walker, Newcastle

v SHREWSBURY TOWN	**WED 22ND OCTOBER 1980**
ST JAMES' PARK	**SECOND DIVISION**
ATT; 11,985	**WON 1-0**

The fact that we were actually entertaining teams like Shrewsbury said it all. No team has the divine right to be a successful top flight side, but if tradition and support have anything to do with it; we would be in the top three in the country permanently. A single goal victory put us back up to mid-table but the attendance was an embarrassment to the name of Newcastle United and a clear sign that both on and off the field the club was in a parlous state. The team that represented United that night was probably the worst team I have had the misfortune to see. Clearly there have been rank bad players in every era at the club and you could easily pick a worst ever United team from all of those players, but collectively, and for the number of second rate players all playing together at once, you'd be hard pushed to beat this lot. I will list them for the sake of posterity: Kevin Carr – Would only ever be a Second Division keeper, Steve Carney – came from the Northern league and should have stayed there, Chris Withe – Hopelessly out of his depth, Mick Martin – A mystery as to how he ever got an Irish international cap, Stuart Boam – Did okay for Boro but over the hill, Kenny Mitchell – A failed centre forward and now a failed centre half, Bobby Shinton – Possibly the worst striker ever to wear the Black & White shirt, Kenny Wharton – I'll let him off, Chris Waddle – making his debut, therefore exonerated from blame, Billy Rafferty – see Shinton, Terry Hibbitt – Great servant to the club in the 1970's but past his sell-by date, Sub Nigel Walker – A useful player actually but either too nice or too lazy to succeed. Manager Bill McGarry - sacked two months earlier but it was still 'his' team. The 11 listed above were backed up by the likes of Frans Koenan (a poor man's Arnold Muhren), Ray Clarke (almost as fat as Micky Quinn but with none of his goal scoring ability) and last but not least Peter Johnson (so bad I can barely even remember him).

Mark Hannen
Ponteland, Newcastle

Two youngsters made their Newcastle United league debut's on this wet, cold and windy night. Chris Withe was the brother of the former Newcastle favourite - Peter Withe - who was now helping Aston Villa win the First Division title. Chris Waddle was a local lad who'd joined us from Tow Law. He'd also worked for a sausage seasoning company. He couldn't drive so he still had to catch 2 buses everyday from Wardley to get to the Benwell training ground.

Mick Edmondson
Walker, Newcastle

The match had been played on a dismal wet and foggy night - "The football was often as bleak as the weather."

John Donoghue
Journalist, Daily Express

v CHELSEA   **SAT 25TH OCTOBER 1980**
STAMFORD BRIDGE   **SECOND DIVISION**
ATT; 22,916   **LOST 0-6**

The previous season we had lost 4-0 so when the fourth went in the thousands of pissed off travelling Geordies sarcastically sang "We want five, we want five", even cheering when it came. Then "We want six, we want six" which soon came, to be greeted by more cheers from the away terraces. As well as the self abuse the support was exceptional under the circumstances and this was noticed by Chelsea officials as the Electronic Scoreboard behind us read "Newcastle fans you are a credit to your team, pity your team isn't a credit to you." This was our heaviest defeat since we lost by the same score at Anfield, way back in 1967.

"We'll Support You Ever More, We'll Support You Ever More, Newcastle, Newcastle We'll Support You Ever More."

Derek
Gateshead, Tyneside

Former apprentice Bruce Halliday's debut, Chris Waddle and Chris Withe's second game, Rafferty and Shinton up front and John Motson and the 'Match of the Day' cameras watching us go in three down at half time! We were up against it!!! It was also our first visit to Stamford Bridge since the petrol bombing incident against West Ham on Tyneside and we were now enemy number one in London. Apparently it was going off all over West London all day. This wasn't one of the better days to be a Newcastle fan as we got hammered for the second consecutive year; as yet again we were absolutely shocking. Halliday the hapless Wearside born centre-half remarked "If I never got picked again it would be a nightmare!" - Not for us it wouldn't mate. Waddle who had worn the number nine shirt in his first two appearances was immediately thrown back into the reserves and Chris Withe was never to appear for us again. Chelsea boss and former England World Cup hat trick hero Geoff Hurst had experienced some great moments in football as a player and was now quite enjoying management. The most embarrassing moment came in the 81st minute when Chelsea's John Bumstead came off injured with us trailing 0-5. As Chelsea had already used their sub he wasn't replaced and the 10 men went on to grab a sixth! This was a low point in my times as a Newcastle fan. The present state of the club was a shambles and the future looked even bleaker. The sky blue one-seater Invalid Chariots which were parked pitch side near the Shed, could have easily been our players sponsored club cars.

Mick Edmondson
Walker, Newcastle

v WATFORD
ST JAMES' PARK
ATT; 14,590

SAT 1ST NOVEMBER 1980
SECOND DIVISION
WON 2-1

In recent years every time there is a crisis at the club a mixture of rent a quote characters and kids gurning for the camera turn up much to the bemusement of most Newcastle fans. I share that view about those who should really know better but I am more sympathetic to the kids, because I used to be one. Having a Saturday job meant I didn't get to many games that season, so with a rare Saturday off I decided to treat myself to a place on one of the benches in the East Stand paddocks. The match, which saw Peter Johnson a £60,000 signing from Boro make his debut, was shown on ITV's Shoot. On the programme just as the late great Terry Hibbitt was about to take a throw you could clearly see Mark, Brucie and yours truly bouncing up and down behind Terry waving and pulling faces . Later on, when Watford's Malcolm Poskett was taking a throw you could see us making more faces and directing hand signals at him. Kids eh?

Chris Ramshaw
West Denton, Newcastle

v CAMBRIDGE UNITED
ABBEY STADIUM
ATT; 5,684

Cambridge had lost their previous match 6-0 and although Bobby Shinton scored against his former club we were beaten by a team which we should never have been playing league football against in the first place. This was the first time Cambridge United had beaten us as their lanky plank up front George Reilly dominated in the air. There was a lad who used to travel away at the time called 'Bronco Billy Anderson' and he went to my school - and he got caught up with some home fans and told them "Kick me but leave my new leather jacket alone!" How a fellow Walker lad could afford a leather jacket always puzzled me.

Davey
Walker, Newcastle

v NOTTS COUNTY
MEADOW LANE
ATT; 8,093

Half day from work and we were on our way down the A1, four of us with me the youngster and unfortunately at the wheel sober and already wishing that I'd never volunteered to drive my brother in-law and his mates. The drunker and louder they became as the journey progressed and I was getting really pissed off as they took the piss and flicked my ears and threw things at the back of my head calling me a puff continuously. Eventually enough was enough so when my brother in-law asked; "Have you ever shagged anybody up the arse?" I replied "Aye funnily enough I have - your sister!!" The rest of the journey was rather quiet.

Graham K
Walker, Newcastle

We got down there sharp and ended up in a boozer near the ground. The pub was quite busy and full of Newcastle fans. After a while my mate was approached by a bloke who asked him: "Are you with the Midlands NUSC?" To which my mate replied quite seriously: "Nah mate, I'm with the TSB."

Kenny Smith
Amble, Northumberland

v SHEFFIELD WEDNESDAY
ST JAMES' PARK
ATT; 19,145

"A total of 29 arrests were made as fans clashed on the terraces as fighting broke out in the ground" - the Sunday Sun reported the following day. More like 29 Geordies were lifted for attacking Sheffield fans inside and outside, before, during and after the match. After the match there was a noisy victory march through the Town as hundreds of Newcastle fans ran riot through the streets. The mob smashed windows and threw paint over a car. This was one of the first post match marches which would become a regular feature over the next few years. Bobby Shinton scored the only goal of the game and actually beat us into the Black and White pub after the match as he quite often did as he knew the owner. Sometimes the bar would open at 4.30pm to regulars but if it didn't open until the legally licensed time of 5.30pm then more often than not Shinton would be standing with his pint at the bar.

Paul Younger
Newcastle

United Fans Fined £1000

Seven soccer fans were fined more than £1,000 between them after offences on the day of the Newcastle United v Sheffield Wednesday match. Offences included threatening behaviour, abusive behaviour and behaviour likely to cause a breach of the peace. Police standing in the wing paddock of the old stand at the stadium saw a group of people near them jumping up and down, chanting obscenely at the visiting fans, he said. "The words of the chant were: "We are the Geordies, the Geordie boot boys, Oh, we are mental, oh, we are mad, We are the loyalist supporters the world has ever had." One fan John Spence (18), of Benwell, Newcastle was fined £150 for using threatening behaviour. After the match Spence saw a large group of Sheffield supporters passing. He told police: "I hurled the bottle at them, though I never hit anyone." The court heard of various other offences including reports of Newcastle fans charging towards Sheffield fans, inside and outside of the ground.

v WREXHAM
ST JAMES' PARK
ATT; 15,941

SAT 22ND NOVEMBER 1980
SECOND DIVISION
LOST 0-1

We went into the match with more points than goals. After 18 games we were ninth with 19 points scoring a mere 16 goals in the process. Wrexham had lost at home to Chelsea 0-4 the previous week so we were expecting a home win, but that welsh twat Dixie McNeill scored against us yet again and Dai Davies saved an Alan Shoulder penalty. I remember one Newcastle fan that'd seen enough so he marched onto the pitch whilst play was in progress and sat down on the centre spot in protest, before being led away as boos echoed around the ground. Chants of "What a load of Rubbish," filled the air echoing around the ground. At the time on television Dallas fans were asking "Who Shot JR?" The Sunday Sun ran with the headline the following day; "Shoot JR?" They'd probably miss.

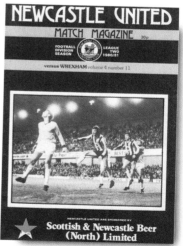

Mick Edmondson
Walker, Newcastle

The year 1980 was Newcastle's 900th anniversary and there were a number of concerts and shows at the Eldon Square Recreation centre as part of the cities 900 celebrations. That night was teenybopper idol David Essex - he actually mentioned the match during the concert. As usual for a show we were set up with two lads either side of the stage, the rest around the exits and aisles. The audience was about 99% lasses aged between 14 & 24. Two songs into the concert one of the lasses ran towards the stage trying to get to David Essex. Luckily one of the lads by the stage stopped her but it took the other lad by the stage to help him get her away and back to her seat. On seeing this, our gaffer realised what might happen if a few more tried at the same time so he hastily got more of us to be placed in front of the stage with orders to stop anyone getting on stage any way we could. Now imagine being me, I'm 16 and my gaffer has just told me that for the next two hours my job is to grab a hold of any nubile young lass who runs towards me - wahey. Except it turned out to be a night mare, sure enough there were loads more attempts as the night went on and some of these girls were determined not to be denied, we all ended up with cuts and bruises, some with torn shirts. My abiding memory of that night is hanging on to this little dark lass for grim death whilst Mr Essex sang "Hold me Close, Don't Let me Go."

Chris Ramshaw
West Denton, Newcastle

v LEYTON ORIENT
BRISBANE ROAD
ATT; 5,800

SAT 29TH NOVEMBER 1980
SECOND DIVISION
DREW 1-1

It only cost £6.50 return with the Supporters Club or in my case £6.50 to get to the capital as I decided to meet up with a Cockney lass I'd met in Benidorm earlier that summer, stay at hers and catch the national express home the next day. Bobby Shinton gave us a second half lead with his 7th goal of the season (he wouldn't score again all season, yet would still end up as top scorer!). But a shit back pass by Stuart Boam let in Peter Taylor to equalise 7 minutes from time. So after the game I dejectedly got the tube to Kings Cross where I'd arranged to meet my holiday romance. I arrived twenty minutes late. I waited and waited but she never showed and with no mobiles in those days I couldn't get in touch with her. I tried ringing her place but there was not even an answering machine. After giving her the benefit of the doubt I waited for over an hour before retiring to the nearest pub. After a few beers I decided to jump the train, buying a platform ticket before sneaking on. I managed to dodge the ticket inspectors in the early stages of the journey and after a while I must have fallen asleep. The next thing I know I was woken up by railway staff in Edinburgh Station, 120 miles past my destination. To my horror there were no more trains until Sunday morning, but luckily I hadn't been asked about my ticket. I managed to get a cheap bed in the YMCA just up from the station on the other side of Princess Street, before purchasing a single ticket to Newcastle the next day arriving home just in time to catch a pint at the club. But it wasn't all bad news as I had actually witnessed Billy Rafferty's last ever Newcastle game before his move to Portsmouth for £80,000 (plus a bag of Tudor crisps) a financial loss of £95,000 in just over a year. He managed 8 goals in 42 appearances.

Steve Anderson,
Chester-le-Street

v BLACKBURN ROVERS
ST. JAMES PARK
ATT; N/A

This game was called off at dinnertime, announced by Frank Bough on Grandstand just before Football Focus. As I looked out of the window a snow blizzard covered the street and I loved it as for the first time my garden looked just as good as 'green fingers' garden did next door. I met my mate in town as I couldn't catch him at home as he'd already left. We looked at the fixtures and after ringing Brunton Park we jumped on a train to Cumbria to watch Carlisle United v Colchester United. I saw an amazing young Geordie lad score 2 and set up another as Carlisle won 4-0. Peter Beardsley aged 20 was unbelievable, a future star. Much better than anything I would have seen at St James' Park.

Phil Morrisson
Seaton Deleval, Tyneside

Newcastle United's new electronic scoreboard which towered over the Gallowgate End was to make its debut in this match. The introduction of the 'Scoreboard and message centre' was due to bring a touch of American razzmatazz to a dull December afternoon, but its first appearance had to be put on hold due to snow. This match was the only game to be called off in the entire league programme that day. So we just had to wait a while longer to see this amazing piece of machinery, which would give us the half-time scores, a full sports service and a time clock ticking off the minutes of play. Wow, we couldn't wait.

Mick Edmondson
Walker, Newcastle

v SWANSEA CITY
VETCH FIELD
ATT; 11.672

This trip has personnel memories for me as I had to sneak home from school every day for two weeks so that I could save up my 50p a day 'Dinner Money' to raise the £8 for my travel. I even remember going to the old supporter's office on Leazes Terrace. A midnight departure from Morden Street, we had our usual stop at Ferrybridge services before continuing the long overnight journey arriving in Port Talbot at 7am, all half asleep yet desperately trying to find a drink. On our arrival in Swansea at midday we were put straight into the ground by the local plod, with a three hour wait without any food or drink available! We were terrible and the Match of the Day cameras were there to capture Peter Cartwright wearing our famous number nine shirt, whilst Gary Nicholson came on as a sub for what would be his final appearance before being sold to Mansfield for £25,000. A local lad and former apprentice he'd only made eleven starts spread over three seasons. He replaced Frans Koenan who was also playing his final game for Newcastle after scoring once in 14 appearances. The biggest cheer of the afternoon came when Leighton James who'd ripped us apart was replaced by former Toon player Tommy Craig. Swansea completed the double over us. We managed to arrive back at Byker Depot not long after midnight - twenty four hours since we'd left - and thankfully there were no video players in those days so we didn't have to suffer the defeat again. Arthur Cox said after the match "I don't think we played too badly!"

Dave Drape
Walker, Newcastle

On the train we were standing in the old luggage compartment which was a carriage on its own in the middle of the train. We had stopped at a station near Swansea when the guard got off to do his flag waving job, when after a while I decided to press the big button next to the door. Within seconds we were off leaving the station and the guard behind. The Transport Police eventually came aboard further down the line but after threats of not letting us go until somebody owned up they eventually let us go, which in hindsight didn't really do us any favours.

Deka
Gateshead, Tyneside

v BRISTOL CITY **ST JAMES' PARK** **ATT; 14,131**	**SAT 20TH DECEMBER 1980** **SECOND DIVISION** **DREW 0-0**

The last Saturday before Christmas saw Newcastle United receive an early present from Scottish & Newcastle Breweries (via a sponsorship deal). The first ever electronic scoreboard was unveiled at St James' Park at a cost of £66,000 replacing the ancient old 'Pigeon Cree' effort at the back of the Gallowgate End terracing. Arthur Cox commented on the new scoreboard saying "I hope we can light it up with a few goals." Unfortunately it was our third 0-0 draw of the season already at SJP. Also making his debut was our new record signing John Trewick who had arrived for £250,000 from West Bromwich Albion. The midfielder was a Geordie whose dad had played for Gateshead when they were in the Football League. A familiar story of letting youngsters leave the area before eventually either paying a fortune to bring them home or not being able to afford or attract them back. Bristol City who had been relegated from the top flight were lying second bottom and come May would be relegated along with their rivals Bristol Rovers. We were awful the only thing that kept us amused and awake was our new present - electronic not human. All of a sudden "Did you see that?" and other American type crap would flash up, although the updates of Nottingham Forest's 3-1 victory over Sunderland kept the crowd awake. Ten minutes from the end the state of the art scoreboard showed 90 minutes was up - wishful thinking. They must have forgotten to stop it at half time. Nevertheless both teams were eventually booed off the pitch when the whistle did go.

Mick Edmondson
Walker, Newcastle

This story had nothing to do with Newcastle's match against Bristol, but appeared in Saturdays Evening Chronicle which I read when leaving the ground. The headline read: 'Fan hit on head with plank.' It went on to say: A youth was hit on the head with a plank when he admitted to a Newcastle United fan that he came from Sunderland a court heard. The 18 year old was working on a building site when a Newcastle fan asked if he came from Sunderland. When he said "Yes" he received a blow to the face with a 4ft plank. A brick was also thrown, but that missed. The Newcastle fan pleaded guilty but said he had been provoked as he had previously had a dumper truck driven over his foot. I cut this out of the paper and when I show people they can't believe it.

Kev Drew
Leam Lane, Tyneside

NEWCASTLE UNITED
ELECTRONIC SCOREBOARD

This excellent piece of gadgetry is designed not only to make money for the Club, but also to keep the spectator informed and, dare I say it, amused. The scoreboard is an integral part of our sponsorship deal with Scottish and Newcastle Breweries and the Club is most grateful to them, for providing it.

Basically, the messages which appear are typed out on a central console which transmits them, either through a computer memory, or direct, to the board. A number of artistic graphics have also been fed into the computer and jumping men, winking eyes and footballs flying into nets will soon become familiar parts of the match day scene.

A fair proportion of the message centre's time is, naturally enough, given over to advertising but a number of ideas are being considered, such as pre-match bingo games, personalised birthday and anniversary requests and so on. Also, we intend to keep you up to date with racing results as well as the up to the minute football and sports news. I was given to understand that working these mighty machines was easier than falling off a log..... well I've had a go and it's a lot harder than everyone would have me believe. So if there's just the odd hiccup then it will be full marks to the girl who's in charge of the controller.

v GRIMSBY TOWN
BLUNDELL PARK
ATT; 17,623

FRI 26TH DECEMBER 1980
SECOND DIVISION
DREW 0-0

A Boxing Day trip to sunny Cleethorpes we travelled in our thousands (over 7,000 Geordies) watched, got steaming and came back. Nothing really to report apart from maybe mentioning our new signing, a 22 year old centre forward making his debut who at the time was the most expensive player to ever come out of the Fourth Division, as we paid Lincoln City £216,000 for his services. So Mick Harford 'Sunderland daft as a kid' became the 7th player to wear our supposed famous number 9 shirt already this season and it wasn't even New

GRIMSBY TOWN FOOTBALL CLUB LTD.

Blundell Park, Cleethorpes, DN35 7PY.

GRIMSBY TOWN v.
NEWCASTLE UNITED

Friday, 26th December, 1980   Kick-off 3-00 p.m.

ADMIT ONE TO
OSMOND STAND
Enter off Harrington Street

N<u>o</u>   5003   £1.50

Year! Yes already before Christmas, it had been worn by Clarke, Rafferty, Shinton, Waddle, Cartwright and Shoulder and it was even suggested that the shirt should be given to a defender until Harford was ready for it! At least he nearly broke the cross bar in half when his header smashed against it, but apart from that we were a disgrace totally nondescript. We were 13th in the table, the epitome of mediocrity but in fact it was a lot worse than that. There wasn't a single sign of light at the end of the tunnel it was frightening.

Mick Edmondson
Walker, Newcastle

Away games were now being travelled too by some "private coaches" or vans, the majority of which were crammed with beer. Fancy dress of some sort was usually the order of the day, anything to add a bit of humour and fun. Our Boxing Day fixture at Grimsby was no exception and the pantomime season was certainly encouraged. Making his debut for Newcastle that day was Mick Harford. So much festive ale and cheer had been consumed that when Harford hit the bar in the second half, many of us packed behind the goal thought it was 1-0. Remember, no mobiles or things then, it was not until the next day's papers that I realised the game ended 0-0.

Anth Nicholson
North Shields, Tyneside

v DERBY COUNTY
ST JAMES' PARK
ATT; 20,886

SAT 27TH DECEMBER 1980
SECOND DIVISION
LOST 0-2

We started the year at the top and now 12 months on we found ourselves near the bottom. A winless December meant we slipped to 14th place with only 7 victories in 24 league games the last of which was mid November, the natives were becoming restless and the blame was being directed at the Board whose choice of manager from the Third Division wasn't showing much promise. Kenny Mitchell suffered bad ligament damage for the third time in his career as he was stretchered off for the final time after 73 appearances and 2 goals for the club. Replacing Mitchell was Terry Hibbitt (His only appearance as a sub) who was also playing his final game, after 18 goals in 292 appearances in two spells at the club. He had to retire from professional football due to injury. The league was of such poor standard that Notts County hadn't won in a dozen games yet somehow were still in third place! I attended the match with my brother Eddie and we still talk now about the classic slogan written on a bed sheet which was unveiled in the Gallowgate End which read 'Westwood Hang Up Your Patch!'

Gary Wilson
Birtley, Tyneside

v SHEFFIELD WEDNESDAY   **SAT 3RD JANUARY 1981**
ST JAMES' PARK   **FA CUP 3RD ROUND**
ATT; 22,458   **WON 2-1**

We had failed to score in our previous four games and had only registered 1 goal in our last six matches. Chris Waddle gave us a glimpse of what was to come as he was class. He produced magic the like never seen, since the day when Paul Daniels the poisoned dwarf was set on fire. Gangly and unorthodox 'Waddler' scored a brace - his first senior goals in a man of the match performance. *"Tell Me Ma Me Ma, I Won't Be Home For Tea, We're Going To Wemberlee, Tell Me Ma, Me Ma"* After repeating excitedly 15 times, *a chorus of Wemberlee, Wemberlee, There's Only One United And We're Going To Wemberlee, Wemberlee, Wemberlee."* would circle the ground. We were full of hope, we were full of drink. At least jumping about kept us warm. England manager Ron Greenwood was in the stands as Bones (Kenny Wharton) along with Waddle were the best Englishman on the day.

Mick Edmondson
Walker, Newcastle

"Lucky bastards, they'll never get away with that again."

Jackie Charlton
Sheffield Wednesday Manager

United Fans go on the Rampage

Hundreds of Newcastle United soccer fans ran riot in a city back lane last night. The mob smashed windows and threw paint over a car after United's cup tie against Sheffield Wednesday. Most of the damage was caused to shops in Pudding Chare, off the Bigg Market. One eye witness cabinet maker Robert Wooster, described the mob as "a human tidal wave." "They ran pell-mell down the lane. If one of the youths had of fallen the rest would have trampled him to death in the surge." "I was in my shop when I heard a massive roar and saw the mob converging down the lane." "I switched the lights off so my premises would not attract their attention, but they were smashing windows on their way down the lane." The mob smashed the window of a paint shop and poured a tin of white paint over a car parked in the lane. They threw a crate of empty bottles through a car windscreen. Last night Police were guarding shops which had their windows smashed. Police said a number of arrests had been made following disturbances during and after the match.

"I know we are always hearing about crowds being worth a goal start at home. Until I came here I never really believed that but it's so true at Newcastle."

Mick Martin
Newcastle United

Newcastle United were in trouble with the FA, as they had mistakenly wore their sponsored shirts (Blue Star) for this FA Cup tie which meant that they were in breach of the rules regarding sponsorship. United along with Notttingham Forest and Bolton dropped a clanger and wore their blue star shirts.

Mick Edmondson
Walker, Newcastle

v WREXHAM	**SAT 10TH JANUARY 1981**
RACECOURSE GROUND	**SECOND DIVISION**
ATT; 6,437	**DREW 0-0**

Had problems filling our transit van for the journey to North Wales as only 15 of us made the trip! We arrived early but found more Pet Shops than Pubs, what a horribly boring place. We failed to score for the fifth consecutive league match and in our last ten league matches nobody had scored apart from Bobby Shinton. Today against his old club he missed three golden opportunities. We hadn't won in seven and had dropped to fifteenth place only 2 points off a relegation place. I should've bought a budgie and named it after our team 'Fucking Useless.' Already this was our sixth 0-0 of the season.

Charlie
Wallsend, Tyneside

I didn't make the trip down to north Wales but instead went along to St James' Park to watch the reserves run riot against Coventry City reserves winning 5-0. This win kept them on course for the title with a line up full of experience; Hardwick, Brownlie, Davies, Suggett, Barton, Haddock, Clarke, Pugh, Shoulder, Walker, Koenan. In those days if you were dropped or were returning from injury you would play in the reserves with no exceptions. Not like in the modern day game where prima donnas think their too good to play for the second team. Instead of continually playing youth players the arseholes should be forced to play.

Mick Edmondson
Walker, Newcastle

v LUTON TOWN	**SAT 17TH JANUARY 1981**
KENILWORTH ROAD	**SECOND DIVISION**
ATT; 10,774	**WON 1-0**

This was our first league goal for 491 minutes of football as our unbeaten start to the New Year continued. Little did we know at the time that it would be our last away goal of the season! It was scored by Mick Harford his first goal for the club to go with his yellow card as we completed the double over 'The Hatters.' Along with Steve Carney, Harford became the last Newcastle player to be shown the yellow card for a while as the FA decided to discard them and return to the notebook method due to an increase in cautions since they're introduction. Anyway this game will go down in the annals of history for another totally different reason, as the only game where we all got lifted twice in one day! Before the match we were drinking in a pub with Luton lads without it going off, but when we got outside we had company over the road that slightly outnumbered us and they proceeded to throw bottles at us. They obviously expected us to leg it, which of course we did, but towards them and after a few exchanges they didn't want to know. The next thing the coppers turned up and we're all nicked. We were released without charge just after the match so went to a pub for a few beers. As we left we noticed two huge brass Cannons either side of the pub door, so decided to put them in our Luton Van (Coincidence), which was a struggle as they were some size and weighed a ton. Unknown to us the manager was aware and called the Police who were there before we had a chance to get away. Although we pleaded innocent once the Van doors were opened we were nicked again. As we returned to the police station it was already full of Geordies so we were put into the staff changing area until they could sort out the charges. Dicka deciding he was hungry proceeded to search the lockers for food and finally hit the jackpot. He took a bite out of a couple of sandwiches and then put them back into the bait box, then ate an apple and put the core back! Half an hour or so later the owner of the now depleted lunch came in to collect his food and went off quite happily to the canteen. Two minutes later however he returned and asked at considerable volume "Which of you Geordie Bastards ate my lunch?" The scene that followed was straight out of Spartacus as one by one, we all claimed responsibility. We did have a whip round to buy him a pie though!

Davey T
Gateshead, Tyneside

v LUTON TOWN
ST JAMES' PARK
ATT; 29,211

SAT 24TH JANUARY 1981
FA CUP 4TH ROUND
WON 2-1

A Star is Born: I was no youngster back then having already been brought up watching some heady days of the Sixties and the Supermac era of the Seventies, but by the time the Eighties arrived, the Toon were in the doldrums…mediocrity in the Second Division (now the Championship). We all longed for something or someone to put a smile on our faces. Newcastle United need star players and hero figures and during that 1980-81 season a gangling, raw youth called Chris Waddle first arrived on the scene. He had recently made headlines scoring two goals against Sheffield Wednesday in the Third Round of the FA Cup. Next up was this game against Luton Town. Was he a one-game wonder? It was evident to me in one moment of brilliance that he wasn't. A long raking pass was fired to the touchline. It was a difficult ball to control, but in one magical piece of skill, Waddle brought the ball down perfectly then immediately galloped away down the wing. Memory fades….but I am sure it was the same scintillating run that saw him curl a vicious cross into the Luton box for skipper Mick Martin, storming in, to fire into the Leazes net. It wasn't Waddles' goals against Sheffield Wednesday that made me think we have a gem here; it was that collect-run-and cross. The youngster had something about him, a raw talent with a touch of genius. Of course Waddle developed into a star, but for too short a period in a black and white shirt. It was a great pity the Club's ambition and financial status at that time could not match others elsewhere. Waddle – like others – moved on to a world stage with Tottenham and especially Marseille – and of course England.

Paul Joannou,
Newcastle United, Club Historian

Every game I used to stand in the Gallowgate End at the back just to the left of the scoreboard behind "my barrier." This particular match stands out as I remember watching Ray Clarke jump like a salmon to head home in the cup and I ended up sitting on my arse right down at the front after being carried away by the crowd surge. Luton's manager was full of praise for the fervour of the Gallowgate crowd.

Tom Knox
Fenham, Newcastle

v BOLTON WANDERERS
ST JAMES' PARK
ATT; 19,143

SAT 31ST JANUARY 1981
SECOND DIVISION
WON 2-1

After failing to win in the month of December Arthur Cox managed to turn things around as we remained unbeaten in January and progressed to the fifth round of the FA Cup, winning four matches and drawing the other. As a result he was named the 'Bells Manager of the Month' picking up his first gallon of whiskey which was a bit of a turn around since relegated Bolton hammered us 4-0 earlier in the season which effectively finished Bill McGarry. The other winners were as follows; First Division Lawrie McMenemy (Southampton), Third Division Mike Bailey (Charlton) and in the Fourth Division Peter Morris (Peterborough). As part of the restructuring plan - more likely to save more money - Newcastle United announced that they had sacked all of their football scouts operating outside of the north-east area.

Mick Edmondson
Walker, Newcastle

v QUEENS PARK RANGERS
ST JAMES' PARK
ATT; 20,404

SAT 7TH FEBRUARY 1981
SECOND DIVISION
WON 1-0

Before kick-off we were entertained by Rangers keeper John Burridge clowning about in the penalty area. His warm up routine included him walking on his hands and standing on his head which kept the early birds happy. But once the game started he and his fellow defender Glen Roeder soon lost their cool, when they alleged that Chris Waddle had pushed the keeper as he scored the only goal of the game. From then on the match was very bad tempered as QPR boss Terry Venables, his players and staff became upset at certain decisions and went on in a ridiculous manor. As a result of the Cockney outfit's behaviour, I don't think I've ever witnessed a louder rendition of *"We Hate Cockneys And We Hate Cockneys"* anywhere ever. At one point a

Newcastle fan attacked a group of QPR players next to the tunnel - the main target a certain Glen Roeder - only to be restrained by Arthur Cox. We completed the double over them as we won for the fourth consecutive game.

Mick Edmondson
Walker, Newcastle

v EXETER CITY
ST JAMES' PARK
ATT; 36,984

SAT 14TH FEBRUARY 1981
FA CUP 5TH ROUND
DREW 1-1

My Dad had taken me to the previous two cup matches and as this was an all ticket affair asked my Mam if she would pick up a couple of tickets for the Gallowgate West Terrace. I will never forget his face when he came home from work and picked up the tickets and realised that my Mam had bought tickets for the Gallowgate East section. "The Corner!" he shouted totally irate and bemused, "You've got tickets for the bloody Corner, its

GALLOWGATE TERRACE – EAST
(GROUND)

NEWCASTLE UNITED
VERSUS
EXETER CITY
SATURDAY 14TH FEBRUARY 1981
KICK-OFF – 3:00PM

FOOTBALL ASSOCIATION CUP
5TH ROUND

STANDING ONLY

£ 1.70
(including VAT)

SECRETARY

IN THE EVENT OF A POST-PONEMENT THIS TICKET WILL BE VALID FOR THE RE-ARRANGED MATCH. NO REFUND FOR AN ABANDONED MATCH.

FOR TICKET AND MATCH INFORMATION TELEPHONE NEWCASTLE 611571

No. 02115

NEWCASTLE UNITED F.C. LTD

mad in there, full of Loonies, I can't take the lad in there!" Well he did and it was my first experience of this part of the ground and I loved every minute of it, although my Dad didn't appreciate all the swearing I think he quite enjoyed it really.

Ollie
Jarrow, Tyneside

A total sell out for this all ticket match against Third Division Exeter who just happened to have the best away record in the English leagues - although they had just lost 0-5 at Portsmouth 3 days previously. Even our local/youth football games kicked off earlier to allow players and officials to attend. Exeter had sold 2,500 tickets and had made the long trip north the majority by Football Special trains making the atmosphere electric inside a bursting SJP. Newcastle fans sang "*Arthur Cox Is Going To Wembley*" to the tune of the classic XTC song *Sgt Rock Is Going To Help Me.* Prior to kick-off there were running battles as missiles were thrown outside the ground at the back of the Leazes End where the Exeter fans were housed, as Newcastle fans fought with police, who were protecting the visitors. I remember a lad called 'Onions' who always wore a bright orange boiler suit and he was right in the thick of it, so much so that he pulled a copper off his horse. After the match a Newcastle senior Police Officer told the 'Exeter Express & Echo' that he hoped Newcastle would lose the replay 10-0 so "It will save us another cup match and make sure there is no trouble." Police made 30 arrests. Exeter forced a deserved replay with an equaliser 5 minutes from time to continue their excellent away record. Exeter's Geordie coach Malcolm Musgrave commented "Newcastle are not the team of old."

John Mooney
Newcastle

My 72 year old uncle and two of his friends travelled up to Newcastle from the south coast for this game sitting in the stands. He was really pleased that City did so well and they all really enjoyed their day, until the final whistle when a so called Newcastle supporter threw beer over one of his friends and then hit him on the back of the neck with a 'Hand Chop' knocking him to the floor, his only crime for this punishment was the fact that he was wearing a red scarf. It seems a shame that three gentleman cannot completely enjoy a day at a big game.

R.Collman
Exeter

Working every Saturday at the Eldon Square Recreation Centre meant that during this season I could only go to mid-week games. As a result I missed the start of a little cup run. Sheffield Wednesday were beaten with two Chris Waddle goals then Luton were beaten 2-0. After that game I skived up to a room at the top of the Recreation Centre and watched the 'Victory March' come down Gallowgate. I wanted to be out amongst them but by the time I finished work, clocked out and got my coat it had gone. However I was determined not to miss out again and as soon as Newcastle were drawn at home on the Monday I booked a day off and bought a ticket. On the day of the match I woke up around 6am and I couldn't get back to sleep. When Alan Shoulder scored mid-way through the second half it looked like we were into the last eight. We should have known better. Seven minutes to go and Newcastle failed to clear a bouncing ball in the box, it looped up, into the net, you knew then our chance was gone. Afterwards-Bovver….Frustration in Gallowgate as pissed off Newcastle fans kicked over the poor Keegan's Hot Dog Sellers trolley and pinched his takings…nobody touched the Hot Dogs!!!

Chris Ramshaw
West Denton, Newcastle

As we were escorted out of Newcastle with a free passage across every junction and roundabout by the superb escort of police cars and outrider, it began to sink in what had happened. We had taken on the mighty in their, own vast cauldron where hearts were heavy at the sound of the vocal opposition, let alone the enemy we had to face on the park. Everything seemed stacked against us but at the final whistle, after what must be described as a gritty performance, we had earned the right to bring the 'Magpies' back to our own St James' Park for a second bite of the cherry. We want to make the sixth round for the first time in fifty years.

Brian Godfrey
Exeter City's Manager

Youth Threw Brick

Newcastle magistrates imposed fines and costs totalling £2,400 on 14 Newcastle United football supporters. They all admitted using threatening behaviour likely to cause a breach of the peace at the FA Cup match against Exeter City. The chairman of the bench Mrs. Joan Howie, told one young offender: It's young men like you committing offences like this who have caused our city to be renowned for extremely rowdy behaviour." One fan was fined £200 for throwing a large stone at Exeter fans from the stand before the start of the match. The offences were committed at various times before, during and after the match, the court was told. Some involved abusive chants directed at the Exeter City fans and some while the Exeter fans were being escorted from the station to the ground. Others occurred when police were trying to keep the opposing fans segregated inside the ground. Proceedings against another 10 men who face similar charges were adjourned.

Soccer Fan Fined £150

Mr George Dickinson prosecuting told Newcastle magistrates that George Wright (17), of Cruddas Park, Newcastle threw a toilet roll at Exeter City fans, waved his fist, gave the V-sign and shouted obscenities. He was fined £150 with £10 costs. He denied the offence

FA Racism talks start

The Football Association and the commission for Racial Equality started talks today over complaints of racism on the terraces. "Bovver booted" teenagers are reported to have been recruited by racist groups and black players abused. Other incidents include an attack on a mosque after a match and the sale of anti-Jewish slogans.

v EXETER CITY
ST JAMES PARK (AWAY)
ATT; 17,688

WED 18TH FEBRUARY 1981
FA CUP 5TH RND REPLAY
LOST 0-4

Geordies in Evil Upset

Newcastle United supporters were last night accused of evil behavior towards officials and supporters of little Exeter. Player's wives and officials were spat at by Geordie louts. Exeter's Dave Pullar out of the side with a knee injury had to stand in front of his granny to protect her. "It was disgraceful. I come from County Durham and as a kid used to stand on the terraces at Sunderland and Newcastle. The Geordies behaved pretty badly in those days and don't appear to have changed." Exeter secretary Pat Wakeham on the receiving end of verbal abuse from home fans added: "They were an evil lot. I know soccer is life and death in the north-east, but didn't expect this." Newcastle supporters club chairman Alan Robinson said: "We deplore this. Once again the minority are dragging down the good name of the club."

An early morning midweek departure from the Haymarket with the Supporters Club travelling the length of the country only four days after a disappointing home draw, to witness this appalling humiliation at the hands of Third Division Exeter at the other St James. Despite only having a couple of days to arrange transport, time off work, not to mention cost there was still a very good following as Newcastle fans packed into this small ground, filling it to capacity, which considering they only had two home gates over 6,000 in the entire 80-81 season was quite a feat. A goal down within 13 minutes then three down at half time, the curse of John Motson - who was commentating for BBC Sportsnight - continued as he had now watched us play a total of 270 minutes already this season witnessing 14 goals hit the back of our net without reply, and to think he married a Geordie lass! That's an average of conceding every 19.2 minutes without reply! Just when you thought the nightmare was over our coach unbelievably broke down on the way back and after waiting what seemed like hours a replacement bus picked us up. After a 740 mile round trip I eventually got off at the Haymarket at 7.20am just in time to start work at 7.30am! However every cloud has a silver lining as this was Ray Clarke's last ever appearance for the club before retiring due to injury in the summer after notching 3 goals in 18 games. He wore the number nine shirt for the final time after a disastrous few months. When he arrived he did say, "I'll be judged on how many goals I score." Fair enough, he was rubbish.

Margaret Hay
Walker, Newcastle

Many of you who have followed the lad's home and away over the years will be aware of a certain supporter called Steve Hulmes, affectionately known as 'The Bloke.' He has rarely missed a Newcastle match of any description home or away for the last thirty years, however for this particular trip he had broken his ankle which was in plaster and his mother was quite adamant that it was too far for him to travel. We all had a good laugh at the 'blokes' expense but we saved the best until we got to Exeter, after finding out that the highlights were to be shown on Sportsnight' and knowing that Steve would be watching back home we hastily

84

made a banner, that we hung over the advertising barrier behind one of the goals where the Geordies were housed. The banner had a simple message that meant so much......'MAMMY 1 BLOKE 0.

Pete Langley
Forest Hall, Newcastle

In my youth if we got past the third round it was very much a case of 'Wembley here we come' and that was no more so than in the 1980-81 season when we were drawn at home to Exeter in the fifth round. We could only manage a draw at our St James' Park but remained optimistic with a small squad of us deciding to go to the replay the following Wednesday. I must confess to having no idea where Exeter was and didn't realise it was right on the south coast and a longer journey than either Southampton or Portsmouth. We were booked on a bus that left the old Gallowgate bus station at 10am for a 7.30pm kick-off. In those days there was no booze ban on football buses so we trooped on with our half a dozen cans, each thinking at the age of 19 that we had come prepared. Little did we know that we were about to embark on a trip with the biggest set of boozers I've ever encountered in my life. Every single bloke on the bus was mid thirties upwards and every single one could drink for England. Our half a dozen cans were left in the shade as lads got on with crates of brown ale all of which seemed to be supped before we got over the Tyne Bridge. We made at least three 'off-licence 'stops and I particularly remember a stop in Cheltenham. Our group of four decided to go for some chips before refueling. We then made our way into a small off-licence to get some cans only to be told that there was 'no beer left' as a 'group of mental Geordies' had just bought it all. We returned to the bus to see shopping trolleys full of cans/bottles being loaded onto the bus! We eventually got to Exeter for 7.15pm and were quickly herded into the ground only to witness a 4-0 defeat. After the match it was straight onto the bus and back home eventually arriving at Gallowgate at around 6am. We made our way to get the first bus from Worswick Street and when we got there bumped into one of the main drinkers from the trip. He was telling us how he thought he was going to be late for work as had an early start - as a bus driver!! Great trip - pity about the match!!

Colin Whittle
Jarrow, Tyneside

It took me two days to hitchhike all the way down to the south coast to witness this humiliating mauling, then three days to get back. I nearly lost my job because of it. The players don't realize or even care.

Peter Bell
Slatyford, Newcastle

I was at College in Crewe and I hitched up for the home match. Exeter equalised late on and as I came out I foolishly said to my mate (from London) that I was going to go to the replay, unfortunately he didn't want to be out done so he said he would meet me there. I hitched back to college on the Sunday and left college on the morning of the match. I was dropped on the M5 and started walking to get off the motorway. I got picked up by the police (£25 fine) and eventually

Soccer Fans revenge on Navy

A Warship sailed from the Tyne today (24th Feb) after it's sailors had come under attack-from Newcastle United fans on Saturday night after their home game with Bristol Rovers. The crew of HMS Exeter could not have chosen a worse time to make a goodwill visit to Tyneside. For the £85m guided missile destroyer berthed at Wallsend's Neptune Yard only three days after the Magpies had been thrashed in an FA Cup replay-by Exeter City. Crew members were threatened by soccer hooligans while on shore leave in Newcastle after the embittered fans had noticed their HMS Exeter cap bands. And some of the sailors left with bruises by which to remember the hostility of their hosts. Ironically, nearly 30 of the destroyers complement of 280 men are Geordies, and even some of them came in for a rough ride. One sailor said: "Some of us sought permission to go ashore in civvies to be on the safe side. Others turned their cap bands inside out to hide the name of the ship." HMS Exeter was on a four day visit to the Tyne, where she was first launched in 1978, and from where she first sailed last August. The 3,800-ton destroyer is armed with Sea Dart rockets, anti-submarine torpedoes and two 20mm cannon and carries a Lynx helicopter. It is not equipped to deal with soccer thugs!

arrived in Exeter at about 4pm. The thing I remember most was seeing a NEEB van pull up and about 10 blokes in Black and White get out. After the match we got a train back to Bristol and I can remember some Newcastle fans sleeping in the luggage racks (above the seats). I slept on my mate's cousin's floor in Bristol before hitching back to Crewe the following morning. The first person I met when I got back to college was a mate who was a Man City fan - I had bet him £5 that we would get further in the cup than them! I think they won the cup that year. My mate from London and I still both have a laugh about what was a terrible game.

Dave McPartlan
North Shields, Tyneside

This was the game when Kenny Wharton had the ball blasted in his face. As a result he lost 2 front teeth and was subbed. It was also the night that Bruce Halliday reached his true potential - absolutely shite. A notice to all supporters from the Exeter Police in the match programme read; **POLICE NOTICE. In the interest of safety, Spectators are requested not to exchange ends during the half time interval.** This summed up the size of the club who had just knocked us out of the FA Cup hammering us 4-0.

Mick Edmondson
Walker, Newcastle

v BRISTOL ROVERS
ST JAMES' PARK
ATT; 14,364

SAT 21ST FEBRUARY 1981
SECOND DIVISION
DREW 0-0

It became that desperate at times that we ended up laughing at our own players, although nobody else could of course.

Brian Hall
Heaton, Newcastle

v CARDIFF CITY
NINIAN PARK
ATT; 4,235

WED 25TH FEBRUARY 1981
SECOND DIVISION
LOST 0-1

The smallest league crowd to watch us that season witnessed a terrible encounter as Peter Johnson made his last appearance for the club after only 20 games. In a nutshell he was hopeless despite being Arthur Cox's first signing, he had failed to impress and was farmed out on loan before being given away to Doncaster Rovers, which was about his stamp. Inside the ground we seemed to be mixed in with the home fans and I was approached by a Cardiff fan who shouted "Gis your scarf," my scarf was my pride and joy and had been everywhere with me and was covered in my collection of metal badges. When I refused and took a step back he moved forward and smacked me in the face. I retaliated by hitting him across the head with the scarf which didn't go down to well but it did the trick as he backed off back into the crowd.

Deka
Gateshead, Tyneside

Not the nicest place to visit, as the locals were mad. They were throwing stones at us from the trees. Then after the match they stoned our buses. It didn't put me off travelling away though. I still haven't missed a match home or away since.

Cliffy Amhed
South Shields, Tyneside

v OLDHAM ATHLETIC
BOUNDRY PARK
ATT; 5,887

SAT 28TH FEBRUARY 1981
SECOND DIVISION
DREW 0-0

I was pissed as a fart so decided to climb over the wall just before kick-off to gain free admission to this ancient ground, only to be caught by the coppers and walked around the perimeter of the pitch. The teams were just coming out of the tunnel as I was marched past the dugouts before being thrown into the back of a Black Mariah. I was dropped off a few miles from the ground along with a handful of other Geordies who'd been lifted and after giving our details we were free to go. I didn't have a clue where I was but was soon on a bus back to the ground thanks to an old woman at a bus stop. I arrived back at the ground at half time and gained free entry via a kind steward but was chucked out ten minutes later when fighting broke out between Newcastle and the Coppers and I somehow got involved. Apparently the match was a boring 0-0 draw anyway. Stuart Boam played his last match before joining Mansfield as player/manager. He scored twice in 77 appearances in his two seasons. He did okay for us, but was well past his best when he arrived from Middlesbrough

Derek
Gateshead, Tyneside

v WEST HAM UNITED
UPTON PARK
ATT; 26,274

SAT 7TH MARCH 1981
SECOND DIVISION
LOST 0-1

As a schoolboy I travelled down to London by coach visiting Upton Park for the first time. I remember at the time everybody seemed to be talking about this match and asking "Are you going to West Ham," as it was our first visit, since the petrol bomb incident. When we arrived in East London we were given a huge police escort straight to the ground. Before kick-off the atmosphere was dodgy to say the least, but this didn't stop some of the Geordies around me singing *"He's Only A Poor Little Hammer,"* *"His Clothes Are All Tattered And Torn,"*, *"He Came For A Fight, So We Set Him Alight,"* *"And Now He Won't Come Anymore."* The song had been sung many a time over the previous months, but nobody knew whether or not it would be sung at this match. The whole Newcastle end was now in full voice giving it, its biggest airing to date. Obviously the West Ham fans were furious, they were going mental but what the Newcastle fans didn't realise was that, the Hammers' hooligans were already in our section mixed in with everybody. There was mayhem when West Ham scored to take an early lead, as the Cockneys celebrated and started laying into Geordies, punching and kicking out at anybody and everybody, I didn't know who was who, as fighting broke out around me it was terrifying. The West Ham fans gained entry into our end with ease via the infamous Chicken run', which was a neutral divide between the rival sections. The fighting continued in spasms over the next twenty minutes or so, with West Ham doing most of the damage, as the police did their best to ignore the situation, as apart from the odd eviction, the violence continued. Then the next thing we knew the doors at the back of our terrace were being forced open, but to our relief the large mob who came piling onto the terraces were 'The Geordie Bender Squad' who steamed into the Cockneys who had infiltrated the end where we were housed, it was just like being saved by the cavalry in the films. Eventually after a mass battle, the West Ham fans were sent packing battered and bruised, although there were quite a few causalities in our end. We lost the match 1-0 and now had the difficult task of walking back to our coaches, as a lot of the lads were down by train and headed off in the opposite direction. As we were herded off in the other direction we were confronted by hundreds of Cockneys who filled the street up ahead. Luckily there was a huge police presence and our escort was stopped in its tracks, while the Cockneys were moved on, as we eventually boarded our coaches to travel back home.

I. C.
Walker, Newcastle

This was our first visit to Upton Park since the petrol bomb fiasco; needless to say they weren't too happy with us!! After a session in the Viking pub, Longbenton, Billy Hunter and I in all our wisdom, decided to hitch to West Ham the following morning. On the Saturday, we found ourselves in the middle of London, not having a clue where Upton Park actually was? After finding it on the tube map, we headed off. When we got off the tube at Upton Park, we were met by a sea of West Hams finest... We retreated back into the station - where there was a mass police presence - while we waited for Geordie back up getting off the following trains. Guess what? The next tubes weren't full of back up but full of more West Ham. I was approached by a West Ham fan and asked where I was from, so remembering the previous tube stations name which was Plaistow, I gave that as my answer in my best Cockney accent. The same lad then asked my pal Billy the same question to which he replied whilst pointing "Doon there!!" After a few kicks and slaps, we took the chance of braving it through the mob and headed towards the ground. After the match we managed to jump on the supporters bus to get home which didn't go undamaged, 3 windows smashed which led to the bus only being able to travel about 40 mph all the way home, freezing cold and we didn't get back until about 3 o'clock in the morning!

Steve Reg,
Longbenton, Newcastle

Newcastle fans were originally supposed to be banned from travelling to this match, but for whatever reason we were present. The chicken run had been partly closed for this game but plenty of West Ham had infiltrated the away terrace prior to kick-off. They were quickly sorted out when the bigger lads arrived later on. The atmosphere was really dodgy and I managed to pick up £2.50 in spare change which had been thrown at us. Back home Newcastle United's Russell Cushing was happy with the response shown by fans to the clubs new season ticket offer. Over 600 fans had enquired about paying for a 1981/82 season ticket on the neva-neva.

Dave Drape
Walker, Newcastle

This was my first away game in London. I went with my 2 mates from college, Tony and Rob. We were young but had money in our pocket and wanted to spend it following the Toon, so off we went, courtesy of a Persil (2 for 1 offer) Inter-City rail voucher. Due to the Petrol Bomb attack, rumours of retribution had been festering for a while. Undeterred we boarded the 125 at 8am, me wearing my 'standard issue' Donkey Jacket and scarf. I was warned on the train to take it off and was glad I did when we disembarked at Kings Cross. I also made sure that my jacket covered the labels on my 'Geordie Jeans.' Good job too! Cos when we got across the other side of the ticket barrier half of 'Albert Square' was waiting for us. In fact it was more like the Mitchell Brothers and 200 of their mates. We managed to walk through undetected, but as we left the station a full scale brawl was developing. After this we didn't fancy going down to the tube so just got a taxi to the ground later on. But when we got on the terraces it didn't stop there. A large contingent of Londoners has infiltrated the Newcastle end and they certainly weren't there to support the Black-and-White's (One bloke had a crow bar under his jacket). The match kicked off and a rampant West Ham soon went one up. Upton Park went crazy - they were chasing promotion (And went on to win the title). A dampened roar was heard from a section in our end and our worst fears were realised. West Ham had infiltrated our section. The small, but loyal band of Newcastle supporters taunted their West Ham counterparts, over in the packed 'Chicken Run' Paddock opposite and were immediately charged by the large group of Cockney infiltrators amongst us. Mayhem

Fans Fined £50

Two Newcastle United football fans were each fined £50 at Newham magistrate's court, East London, after they admitted being involved in trouble at the Magpies away game with West Ham. Scott Smith (19), unemployed of Cullercoats admitted threatening behaviour and Ian Rutherford (17) a metal worker of Morpeth, pleaded guilty to insulting behaviour. Sergt. George Dawkins said Smith was seen kicking one of the gates at West Ham's Upton Park ground after the match on March 7th. "He ran up and kicked it with both feet and fell flat on his back. He had been drinking," he said. Rutherford was arrested when he spat over a wall at rival fans as they were leaving the ground. Neither youth had anything to say in court. Magistrates allowed them both 14 days to pay the fine.

ensued... Shortly afterwards the 'Geordie Cavalry' appeared, a group of fans who had arrived at the match late, due to some prior commitments outside. With new blood in our now swelled ranks we merged and made it quite clear that these East London trouble-makers were not welcome in our enclosure. We watched the rest of the match in relative safety as the Cockneys had been chinned and sent packing. West Ham had won their previous 15 home games and we were so close to stopping their run, before they got a winner 10 minutes from time. Their 16th consecutive home win put them top a massive 20 points above us! We made our way home and after getting attacked outside the ground, ambushed on the tube, chased all over Kings Cross, we finally caught the train home. Safely on the train we got talking to this Man U fan from Durham who had watched his adopted team lose 1-0 at Southampton. He was cursing the bloke who had scored the winning goal. Kevin Keegan. He kept saying: "Kevin Keegan the bastard, the bastard." I thought and muttered "I wish we had someone like him playing for us." as I fell asleep safely dreaming of the Fish Bar in Newcastle.

Harry Palmer
Benton, Newcastle

v PRESTON NORTH END
ST JAMES' PARK
ATT; 12,015

SAT 14TH MARCH 1981
SECOND DIVISION
WON 2-0

A new innovation, for the first time ever Newcastle United employed ball-boys for first team matches. The lads chosen came from Walker school in the cities East End a school with a great Football tradition, which was only fair I suppose because my mates Kev and Micky from Walker were ball-boys at the reserve matches every week and I was lucky enough to be first reserve so got to do it a few times also. World Cup winner and legend Nobby Stiles was Preston Knob End's boss and he must have been quietly confident of getting a result as we hadn't scored for five matches, which along with the threat of having to personally put £16,000 into the club to guarantee part of an overdraft, was a bridge to far for Newcastle Chairman Bob Rutherford and board members Lord Westwood and Dr David Salkeld. So after 20 years at the club 73 year old Pirate Westwood and Rutherford stepped down and Stan Seymour junior son of former "Mr. Newcastle United" Stan Seymour senior took over and announced "Never again will we buy old players" a dig at former boss Bill McGarry. Although £500,000 in debt the new Chairman announced "We'll bring the good times back." A low crowd saw us complete the double over relegation bound Preston as it pissed down and the lads from Middle Street, Walker, in Nylon sky blue Co-op tracksuits got soaked!! Two days earlier the transfer deadline had passed without any new faces arriving. Although the deadline existed you at least had the previous seven months to wheel and deal. A rare win as we scored for the first time in 5 matches.

Mick Edmondson
Walker, Newcastle

v SHREWSBURY TOWN
GAY MEADOW
ATT; 4,975

SAT 21ST MARCH 1981
SECOND DIVISION
LOST 0-1

After the long journey Trevor Morland, Alan Batey and I arrived at Shrewsbury's shithole but were refused entry because we were wearing pit boots, so we had to take them off and hand them over to the coppers before we were allowed in. Once inside we tied our scarves around our feet as it was canny cold before watching another dismal performance against rubbish. We never ever saw our boots again having to travel home and then around the Toon on our return in our bare feet. Their player/manager Graham Turner got the winner.

Craig Colquhoun
Killingworth, Tyneside

v CHELSEA
ST. JAMES PARK
ATT; 17,297

SAT 28TH MARCH 1981
SECOND DIVISION
WON 1-0

I was 15 years old at the time and after this 1-0 victory I spent the evening knocking about the doors, a bit of telly, then off to bed. It must have been around 3am when my older sister crept into my room and woke me up to tell me that she had scored with a footballer at Tuxedo Junction night-club. I wasn't really fully awake and must have fallen back to sleep before she had a chance to tell me who it was, for as I woke up in the morning she had already gone out for the day with him. I spent the rest of the day wondering who it could possibly be as I sat in my bedroom excited in anticipation of meeting my sister's new lad. It was around tea-time when I heard my sister return along with her escort who she had brought back to have a cup of tea and to meet my Mam and Dad. The excitement was getting too much for me, especially when my Mam shouted for me

to go downstairs. Who could it possibly be? I slowly opened the sitting room door and recognised him immediately a current Newcastle centre-forward who had worn the famous number nine shirt. My heart sunk as my sister called out to me "Come in and meet Bob, I've told him all about you," but somehow I couldn't as I had frozen to the spot. It was a nightmare as there he was sitting on our settee in front of me; I looked at my sister and shouted "Bobby Shinton, Bobby Bloody Shinton!!" "I thought you said that you'd met a footballer, he's bloody crap," and with that I turned and ran back upstairs. My sister didn't speak to me for two weeks but if she had paid to watch him play for Newcastle week after week, maybe she would have felt the same way - footballer indeed.

Jeff Jarrett
Gosforth, Newcastle

Soccer Terror as fans go on Rampage

Street battles raged as Chelsea and Newcastle fans brought terror to Tyneside. The violence was so bad that at one stage police lost control when Londoners broke away from their escorts to attack Geordies. Newcastle magistrates heard that there was trouble before, during and after the Division Two match at St James' Park. In a day-long sitting they were told of: Running street battles in the city centre, Chelsea fans being stoned as they were escorted to the ground by police, Londoners ripping light bulbs from their train at Newcastle's Central Station and hurling them across the platform, fans running back and forth across railway lines, missiles being thrown by both sets of supporters during the match-one of which struck a police officer, Newcastle fans turning on the Chelsea goalkeeper spitting on him as he retrieved the ball. These were only some of the incidents described by Mr. Leonard Coils, prosecuting. A total of 21 fans were fined more than £3,000, whilst a further 12 fans have yet to appear before Newcastle magistrates.

Clive Walker was on the wing for the Blues in the first half. As he ran past the old stand paddock, he was greeted by the three of us pulling our coats apart and screaming "Flasher!" It definitely put him off his game, as he started to move in field their Trainer/Coach kept telling him to get back out wide. Clive looks nervously at us as he returns to the wing as we resume "Flasher!" He got taken off in the second-half even though he would have been on the other side of the pitch from us. Result! Bruce Halliday got his sweet revenge after his disastrous debut at Chelsea earlier in the season when he headed home a Nigel Walker cross for his first ever goal which was enough to win it.

Marty
Newcastle

v WATFORD	SAT 4TH APRIL 1981
VICARAGE ROAD	SECOND DIVISION
ATT; 10,986	DREW 0-0

The highlight of the trip was when the travelling Newcastle fans sang in typical Geordie humour, *"He's Bent, He's Queer, He Takes It Up The Rear, Elton John, Elton John. He's Bent, He's Queer, He Takes It Up The Rear, Elton John, Elton John."*

Jenners
Gateshead, Tyneside

v CAMBRIDGE UNITED
ST JAMES' PARK
ATT; 11,013

SAT 11TH APRIL 1981
SECOND DIVISION
WON 2-1

I always wanted to be first in the ground so waited outside the Gallowgate turnstiles for them to open at 1pm. Surprisingly there were a few others waiting, but once inside I knew as I sprinted up the stairs there was no way they would catch me especially as they didn't know my intentions, the question was would anybody in any other part of the ground beat me in? Halfway up the stairs I nearly shit myself when I got the shock of my life when a couple of lads jumped out of the bushes! I found out later that they had climbed into the ground earlier and waited for the turnstiles to open before going onto the terraces as they obviously didn't want to be rumbled. Luckily I beat them onto the Gallowgate terraces and couldn't see anybody else anywhere; I was the first in the ground. It was a long boring two hours wait as our lowest home crowd of the season saw an own goal luckily win it for us in the second-half ending any relegation worries for another season.

David Bell
Byker, Newcastle

v BLACKBURN ROVERS
ST JAMES' PARK
ATT; 13,128

WED 15TH APRIL 1981
SECOND DIVISION
DREW 0-0

This was our 11th goalless draw of the season. Easter 1981, I went to watch the team training at Gibside Gardens. I had to ring St James' to ask for permission to attend and when I got to the training ground I had to report to someone to say who I was and that it was ok for me to watch. I was the only spectator present. This was the season when I think we scored 29 goals in 42 games and nil was definitely our favourite score. The players came out so did Willie McFaul who said hello, none of the players did and neither did Arthur Cox. The players did their warm up and then Cox took eleven players presumably his starting line up for the Saturday with Kevin Carr in goal and the rest of the team as the opposition! For ten minutes they practised moves against "the dustbins" with Arthur Cox spending most of his time speaking to Kenny Wharton. The back four during these ten minutes did not touch the ball and Bruce Halliday who was playing centre back at the time was doing cartwheels and somersaults. Suddenly Arthur Cox got a ball and turned and kicked it towards the defence. Unfortunately Bruce Halliday was doing a somersault at the time and the ball went straight passed him into the eighteen yard box and rolled into the empty goal. Needless to say Cox, quite rightly went berserk screaming at Halliday that he must keep his concentration at all times and sudden things like that happen in football. So to coin the phrase "dustbins could beat Newcastle" well I have actually seen it!

Bob Day
Heaton, Newcastle

v DERBY COUNTY
BASEBALL GROUND
ATT; 14,139

Some matches stick in your memory for the strangest reasons. Derby had just been relegated from the First Division the season before and this was my first visit to the Baseball Ground which was a typical pre 'Taylor Report' English football ground which became a favourite of mine - apart from the shortage of pubs. Yet there was always plenty to keep you busy around the terraced streets both before and after the match and Newcastle would always take a good following to the home of football's muddiest pitch. Derby County FC had taken it upon themselves to make this an all ticket match for Newcastle United supporters as along with Leeds, Chelsea and West Ham fans we were considered a hooligan risk. They also charged us an inflated price of £4 (Over double than other games) with no concessions aimed at preventing our 'Catogory A' thugs from travelling. It also meant that we had to buy our tickets in advance, which is the norm in this day and age but it was unheard of back then. After our club intervened it was agreed that any tickets purchased in advance would cost £2.50, but anybody turning up on the day paid £4. A huge following still travelled with many lads paying in the Derby sections resulting in a lot more trouble than they would have normally had. This was the day that I first heard the chant *"We Are The Boys In The Black & White, We Love To Sing & We Love To Fight, So Let's Fight, Lets Fight, Lets Fight."* Derby completed the double over us, we were never at the races.

Mick Edmondson
Walker, Newcastle

We were in the 'St James Tavern' Pub in Derby town centre when at about 12.30pm it went off! There were glasses flying about, fighting both inside and outside the door, as windows went through. Arrests were made and I was taken to hospital - which was full of football casualties - by the coppers, where I received immediate attention, resulting in 14 stitches to a nasty head wound. This was Derby's lowest league crowd for 14 years.

Annon
Newcastle

v GRIMSBY TOWN
ST. JAMES PARK
ATT; 13,170

I was 15 years old and was on trial at Newcastle so a few of us were given free admission to this Easter Monday match. We were taken through the main entrance and on our way to the centre paddock we were taken into a small room which had a machine which showed the turnstiles around the ground, clicking away as they totalled up, as supporters entered the ground. I took particular interest in the ones which were turned off and when I enquired was told that they weren't in use. Anyway as kick-off approached I managed to escape from the paddock and made my way to the Gallowgate End to join my mates. Just out of interest I went down to two of the turnstiles at the Gallowgate which were shown to be out of use to find that they were both in operation as fans poured through. A nice little earner or/and tax fiddle for our board, very unlike Newcastle United's board to be ripping it's own fans off eh…..

Mick Edmondson
Walker, Newcastle

v BLACKBURN ROVERS
EWOOD PARK
ATT; 10,609

SAT 25TH APRIL 1981
SECOND DIVISION
LOST 0-3

As we set off from Morden Street on the supporter's coaches for Lancashire, the weather forecast was for heavy snow (for once Michael Fish had got it right). As our convoy of coaches crawled along the motorway, we listened to Radio Two (Now Radio Five Live). Despite the weather our game was still on and after a few diversions and heavy traffic jams it was 3pm before we knew it and we were still miles from Blackburn. As we sat in traffic we listened to Radio commentary of Aston Villa on their way to beating Middlesbrough 3-0 to clinch the First Division title as we desperately listened for news from Ewood Park as and when the latest scores came through. By half-time we were informed that we were two down and still struggling miles from the ground. We eventually arrived at 4.20pm, as it happened the 'Football Special' had just got there before us and we all got in for free. The away end went from having about 500 Geordies in to almost capacity with less than twenty minutes to play. But we sang our hearts out until the end and as we spilled out onto the streets, Newcastle fans were peering through the windows of houses to find out how Sunderland had done in their bottom of the table relegation battle against fellow strugglers Brighton. The scenes of jubilation in the street had to be seen to be believed as Geordies danced and sang celebrating a last minute Brighton winner which meant that Sunderland had to win at Anfield on the last day of the season to avoid relegation and an instant return to the Second Division. An impossible task against a team, which a few weeks later would lift the European Cup beating Real Madrid. Back on the coach we listened to the final scores only to find out that we had in fact lost 3-0, Blackburn must have scored a third in-between us leaving the coach and getting into the ground. All part and parcel of following the Toon. The same day Whickham from Newcastle upon Tyne won the FA Vase beating Willenhall 3-2 at Wembley.

Kev Egan
Walker, Newcastle

To be absolutely honest there was nothing at all in this game for United and the luckiest people were the Newcastle fans who arrived 20 minutes from the end because of the snow blocked roads.

Sunday Sun Report

v LEYTON ORIENT
ST JAMES' PARK
ATT; 11,639

SAT 2ND MAY 1981
SECOND DIVISION
WON 3-1

Any long-term, long-suffering Newcastle United fan asked to nominate his or her worst-ever season of following the black-and-whites would readily suggest 1980-81. It was a season of staggering sterility … Bobby Shinton ended top scorer with a meagre seven goals whilst crowds dropped to less than 12,000 and in 23 of the 42 Second Division games United failed to score. And in none of the first 41 league games did the mid-table Magpies manage to score more than two goals. So, when it came to the final Saturday, four of us, all season ticket-holders despairing of anything better, decided to forego the tantalising prospect of Orient at home to drive to Anfield and see Sunderland, as surely they would, get stuffed by Liverpool and relegated from Division One. It felt like walking out on a sick best friend as we piled into the car and set off for Merseyside in mid-morning. Missing a home game was a heinous offence but in a dire season lightened only by the emergence of Chris Waddle and a FA Cup run that was crushed in a catastrophic fifth round replay by Exeter City, that final day was intended to bring savage entertainment for frustrated Geordies. Surely we could be excused. We discussed planting cardboard cut-outs of ourselves in the West Stand to disguise our absence: after all, most fans had stood rigid all season so the subterfuge wouldn't be easily spotted. We worked out what our apologies would consist of should our absence be spotted by stewards. But the recurring get-out clause was always going to be: Ah yes, but we saw Sunderland relegated – you didn't. At Anfield, we paid to stand on the Kop and cheer as the axe fell on the Sunderland. But, inexplicably and confusingly, Sunderland didn't let in three goals in the first five minutes. In fact, they didn't let in any goals in the whole bleeding 90 minutes. And the midget Stan Cummins stuck one in at the far end to give Sunderland a 1-0 win that you couldn't have made up on Fantasy Island. Stunned into silence, we shuffled out of the Kop and trudged back to the car. The result didn't seem to matter to the Scousers as badly as it mattered to us. Heads down and faces pale, we drove away. Five o'clock. Sports Report. Let's see how we got on against Orient, said No 1. It'll have been 0-0, muttered No 2. We might have got a lucky one, said No 3. Bet they got a hatful, said I, to bitter laughter. Radio. Results. "…Chelsea 0 Nott's County 2. Derby County 1 Preston North End 2. Newcastle United 3 Orient 1.....” AAAAAAAGGGGGGGGGG HHHHHHHHHHH! The first time we'd scored more than 2 goals at home all season and the last time we got 2 points for a win. And just for the record, Mick Harford wore the number 9 shirt in his last ever appearance scoring a meagre 4 goals in 18 appearances before he was sold to Bristol City for £160,000 over the summer.

Paul Tully
Denton Burn, Newcastle

1980-81 Season Summary

A long and proud history, Newcastle upon Tyne celebrated 900 years since Robert, Son of William I, had built a wooden fort - the "New Castle," back in 1080. However in this the FA's Centenary year, Newcastle United were boring its supporters to death, in probably the most tedious season in recent history. Although there have been worse seasons which have ended in relegation, this season was totally boring. After an abysmal start under McGarry we had nothing to play for in the league - apart from survival. The fact that our keeper Kevin Carr was named as our player of the year spoke volumes. We only managed to score a pathetic 30 goals in 42 league games, the lowest tally in our entire history. We couldn't score in Tiffany's! Not even in the fucking 'Lowther or Cats!' The fact that we had 6 different players who wore the famous number nine shirt yet our top scorer Bobby Shinton only managed a meagre 7 goals says it all. Last season's top scorer Alan Shoulder was scoring an average of 1 every 6 games, partly due to his deeper role, but was without doubt greatly missing his old partner Peter Withe, who was busy helping Aston Villa clinch the First Division title. Unbelievably and thankfully we somehow managed to keep 17 clean sheets, as we: Won 14, Drew 14 and Lost 14. Away from home we only netted 8 goals in 21 league games, of which we only managed 3 in the last 16 games. Overall we failed to score in 23 of our 42 league games! Our paper thin squad was stretched to the limit as Hardwick and Barton missed most of the season through injury. Even worse we lost Peter Kelly, Terry Hibbitt and Ray Clarke all having to retire through injury. Bill McGarry wasn't given any cash at the outset, mainly due to his incompetent signings he'd made in the previous 3 seasons. He'd only won 2 league matches in the year 1980 and he'd cluttered our squad with slow, ageing players. His sacking was inevitable although long overdue. But his replacement wasn't the big name the fans craved. Arthur Cox was strangely preferred to Clough and Robson, as he became our 5th boss in 6 years, arriving from lowly Chesterfield. Cox had to work with players who were garbage, a result of poor purchases made by the previous 3 managers. Nationally crowds were way down, football was in the doldrums due to hooliganism, the recession and TV was being looked upon as a major threat to attendances. Not surprisingly with our club being in free-fall and the season being the most boring on record the fans deserted in droves and as a result our average home attendance dropped below 20,000 for the first time since the First World War. It was our lowest since the 1901/02 season, in days before football really caught Tyneside's imagination. Our average crowd of 17,350 was still impressive considering the national circumstances and the dross being served. Cox had little money to spend, no quick fixes, so handed debuts to youngsters such as Bruce Halliday and Chris Withe (Peter's brother); one of the few bright spots though was the emergence of another youngster, local gangly striker Chris Waddle rescued from a sausage seasoning factory. He was eventually given some cash to spend and he made Peter Johnson his first signing followed by striker Mick Harford who arrived at Christmas, not the best gift, similar to wanting a purple 'Chopper Bike' but instead receiving a yellow 'Chico Bike' with stabilisers! He was bought to replace Billy Rafferty and was almost identical, absolutely rubbish. However at the same time we did spend a club record £250,000 on midfielder John Trewick, from West Brom, who although not the world's best, would prove his worth in time. All this transfer activity nearly gave our directors heart attacks as both 73 year old Pirate Lord Westwood and Bob Rutherford stepped down after 20 years at the club. They were both asked to put £16,000 in to the club to guarantee part of an overdraft, but instead disappeared into the night. Stan Seymour junior took over and announced, "Never again will we buy old players." We had struggled to score goals and spent the majority of the season in the lower half of a very average Second Division, finishing a mere 6 points off relegation. It had been yet another transitional season for the club as the new manager tried various formations with his restricted squad and it looked like it was going to be a busy summer, when at the end of the season Cox transfer listed no fewer than 15 players. European adventures and Wembley appearances had been replaced by defeats at Cambridge, Shrewsbury, Bury and Exeter, whilst once exciting quality players like Supermac, Smith and Green had been replaced by Shinton, Rafferty/Harford and Clarke. Although still a way of life travelling away in numbers with the lads, the lack of quality, hope, belief and facing our fourth consecutive season outside of the top flight was hard to take and making our lives pretty miserable. To make matters worse Sunderland unbelievably went to Anfield and beat European Champions Liverpool to avoid relegation!

Typical representative team for the season:
Kevin Carr, Steve Carney/John Brownlie, Ian Davies/Peter Johnson, Stuart Boam/David Barton, Kenny Mitchell/Bruce Halliday, Mick Martin, Kenny Wharton, Terry Hibbitt/John Trewick, Alan Shoulder, Mick Harford/Bobby Shinton, Ray Clarke/Nigel Walker.

Total Appearances: (League, FA Cup & League Cup) - 48 matches played
Carr (43), Wharton (41), Boam (37), Shoulder (36), Martin (33), Carney (32), Davies, Shinton (27), Trewick (25), Halliday (23), Walker (21), Johnson (20), Harford, Mitchell (19), Clarke, Hibbitt (18), Rafferty, Waddle (17), Barton, Brownlie (15), Koenen (14), Cartwright, Kelly (9), Hardwick (5), Nicholson (3), Withe (2), Leaver (1). *Includes all sub appearances.

Total Goals: (League, FA Cup & League Cup) - Total Scored 38 Shinton (7), Shoulder (6), Harford, Rafferty (4), Clarke, Hibbitt, Waddle (3), Martin (2), Boam, Halliday, Koenen, Trewick, Walker (1), plus Opp Own Goals (1).

Second Division							Final Table 1980-81
West Ham	42	28	10	4	79	29	66
Notts County	42	18	17	7	49	38	53
Swansea City	42	18	14	10	64	44	50
Blackburn Rovers	42	16	18	8	42	29	50
Luton Town	42	18	12	12	61	46	48
Derby County	42	15	15	12	57	52	45
Grimsby Town	42	15	15	12	44	42	45
QPR	42	15	13	14	56	46	43
Watford	42	16	11	15	50	45	43
Sheff Wed	42	17	8	17	53	51	42
Newcastle	**42**	**14**	**14**	**14**	**30**	**45**	**42**
Chelsea	42	14	12	16	46	41	40
Cambridge	42	17	6	19	53	65	40
Shrewsbury	42	11	17	14	46	47	39
Oldham Athletic	42	12	15	5	39	48	39
Wrexham	42	12	14	16	43	45	38
Orient	42	13	12	17	52	56	38
Bolton	42	14	10	18	61	66	38
Cardiff	42	12	12	18	44	60	36
Preston	42	11	14	17	41	62	36
Bristol City	42	7	16	19	29	51	30
Bristol Rovers	42	5	13	24	34	65	23

FOOTBALL SPECIALS / 3 PTS FOR A WIN / VARADI / LOAN SIGNINGS

ASTRO-TURF / MILK CUP / CHELSEA MUST DIE / SACK THE BOARD

1981-82 Season

After a summer which saw English clubs conquer Europe, as Liverpool won the European Cup with help from former 'Toon' players Terry McDermott and Alan Kennedy (he got the winner) and little Ipswich Town under Bobby Robson won the UEFA Cup, Newcastle United prepared for their fourth season in the Second Division. Summer transfer rumours linked us to Gary Rowell and Ally McCoist, but we thankfully ended up with Imre Varadi from Everton for £125,000 replacing the outgoing Mick Harford who'd worn the number 9 shirt since the previous Christmas. After only 8 months at SJP he was sold to Bristol City for £160,000, a loss of £53,000. Also arriving from Ryhope CA was Wearsider Kevin Todd who had scored 200 goals in the past 3 seasons in local non-league football. The only other new arrival at the club was new 'sponge man' - Tommy Cavanagh - who was a right character, but wasn't going to turn us into a decent side, unless of course his sponge was magic. Other departures over the summer saw Stuart Boam leave to become player/manager at Mansfield Town taking Gary Nicholson with him, Frans Koenen returned to Holland, Kenny Mitchell went to Darlington, and as aforementioned Terry Hibbitt & Peter Kelly were forced to retire due to injury. Our squad was small and we would have to depend on inexperienced youngsters and loan signings as the coffers were empty. We needed to find another 5 wins from somewhere to stand any chance of promotion, but scoring goals was a big enough problem. At least we should be able to improve on last season's points total as it was now 3 points for a win, introduced to make teams play to win and hopefully produce more exciting football which would hopefully attract the thousands of missing fans nationwide, back to the game.

v WEST BROMWICH ALBION
ST JAMES' PARK
ATT; 6,843

FRI 14TH AUGUST 1981
FRIENDLY
LOST 0-2

With only two weeks to go before our opening league match this was unbelievably our first pre-season game! Not exactly the best preparation for what was our fourth consecutive season outside the top flight. The game was originally arranged as part of the transfer deal which brought John Trewick to Tyneside. A match on a Friday night wasn't exactly ideal either, as it cocked-up our lad's night out and meant that we had to go to the match in our trousers and dress shirt as opposed to the customary jeans. In those days if you wanted to get in any decent bars where the better looking lasses would be, then you had to wear trousers and a shirt and if you wanted to go drinking after 10.30pm then you'd have to wear a tie and dress jacket! First Division West Brom's squad arrived on Tyneside including the likes of Cyrille Regis, Remi Moses and Newcastle fan and future England captain Bryan Robson. The match was poor and although Newcastle didn't look like they would score we were soon on the pull down the Bigg Market as we made sure we did.

Bri Mills
Walkergate, Newcastle

If Newcastle had a team like West Brom's then without doubt they'd get over 40,000 turning up at St James' Park every week.

Bryan Robson
West Brom player

v SUNDERLAND
ST JAMES' PARK
ATT; 9,982

TUES 18TH AUGUST 1981
FRIENDLY
DREW 1-1

What were the two clubs thinking? Two friendly matches in the space of five days between the auld enemy, was just asking for it. Obviously not a popular choice with the local constabulary, who were out in good numbers, to greet and protect the disappointing small contingent of Sunderland fans who arrived at the Central Station. I couldn't believe it when one of the lads I had seen in fancy dress two years previously at a pre-season friendly at Torquay had turned up again. (I've since found out that his name could possibly be Terence Sproat, maybe?). He loved his centurion outfit so much he still had it on and he kept charging the visiting tramps and lashing out with his plastic sword much to everyone's (including the police) amusement. Years later a mackem I worked with who was there told me it wasn't that funny as it really hurt but nobody could do owt for laughing! Not sure if they named the Centurion Bar after him as that's where the battle took place.

Marty Taylor,
Newcastle

Football Hooligans on Rampage

City shopkeepers were today counting the cost of a window smashing spree by football hooligans. Stones and bricks were hurled through the shop and pub windows after last night's friendly between Sunderland and Newcastle at St James' Park. One of the vandal's targets was the new 'Games Galore' shop in Grey Street, which opened just five weeks ago and has already had its front window smashed twice. Surveying the damage to her shop today was manageress Mrs. Alma Stewart, who found two large stones which had been hurled through the window. Other targets were the Collingwood pub, the Companions Club and the Christian Science Recreation Club both in Leazes Park Road and Carrick's the bakers in Grey Street.

v SUNDERLAND
ROKER PARK
ATT; 10,032

SAT 22ND AUGUST 1981
FRIENDLY
LOST 1-2

A friendly between north-east rivals Newcastle and Sunderland? Such a thing doesn't exist. Yet the two clubs and the local police thought it would be a good idea to let us play each other home and away within a week! These meetings didn't really attract the average football supporters, but more the hooligan element. Four days earlier Sunderland had failed to show up at St James, yet we took a few thousand down for the second leg, including plenty of the lads. One Newcastle fan actually died inside the ground falling from a height, I actually passed him as he lay on the stairs on the exit from the terraces, yet to this day I still don't know the cause of death. First Division Sunderland won with a certain Sam Allardyce grabbing the winner. After the match as we were receiving our police escort towards Seaburn Station, this mackem stood at his front door posing in his Sunderland strip arms raised in recognition of a 2-1 victory. The next thing I knew a Geordie broke the Police cordon and did what everybody in the escort wanted to do, he threw a brick straight through the mackems front window.

Everybody cheered as the mackems expression quickly changed as he remonstrated with the police.

Ken Allen
Gateshead, Tyneside

65 Derby Arrests

A young policewoman was in hospital last night - the victim of the new soccer season. WPC Ann Burn was knocked unconscious by a flying brick after being caught in the middle of a pitched battle in Roker Avenue, Sunderland. She was taken to hospital and detained overnight with head cuts and shock. Police made 65 arrests at the "friendly" derby at Roker Park between Sunderland and Newcastle United, mainly for public order offences. Four thousand Newcastle supporters travelled to Roker and fighting broke out shortly after the game began. Some youths were ejected from the ground. A Northumbrian Police spokesman said last night there were several disturbances before, during and after the game. WPC Burn who was stationed in Gateshead was knocked out by a flying brick as she was caught in the middle of fighting supporters before the match. She received a puncture wound behind her right ear. Many pubs and clubs near the ground were closed before the game to try and avoid disturbance. Letters in a pillar box in Roker Baths Road were set alight as fans made their way to the match. And windows were smashed in the streets around the ground. The police spokesman said "There was an awful lot of aggravation and disturbance at this game, considering it was a friendly."

If Newcastle can only find one or two finishers there are signs they could do well this season. One of the reasons I say that is the astonishing support and noise made by their 4,000 fans at this match. No Second Division side can match the Geordie support and it should bring them a flying start over their rivals but only if they can find a goal-scorer.

Dave Alexander
Sunday Sun (Reporter)

Soccer Fan Dies

Soccer fan Ricky Chalmers has lost his fight for life after being injured at the Sunderland and Newcastle match. Unemployed Ricky of Fairholm Road, Benwell, Newcastle, died in Newcastle General Hospital after suffering head injuries in an accidental fall down steep stairs at Roker Park during a friendly match. After receiving emergency treatment for a fractured skull, Ricky was transferred to Newcastle General Hospital for an operation to remove a blood clot from his brain. His parents said Ricky was a genuine football fan. Northumbria Police have made extensive inquiries into crowd behaviour at the match and are satisfied that his death was an accident.

v WATFORD
ST JAMES' PARK
ATT; 19,244

SAT 29TH AUGUST 1981
SECOND DIVISION
LOST 0-1

I love the first match of the season, the immaculate pitch, seeing the new signings for the first time in Black-and-White, (Imre Varadi, our £125,000 summer signing from Everton made his league debut). Also spotting any changes, however minor, with the ground and as you looked forward with high hopes that this could be our season. Then the action started.... same old same old, was it really worth cutting my holiday short for?

Chris Lamb
Fenham, Newcastle

Peace Plea to Fans

Hundreds of police officers were on duty this afternoon for the Newcastle - Watford soccer match which opened the new football season. And the man in charge of policing pleaded with the fans: Let's get the season off on a good footing - behave yourselves. Superintendent Ian Thynne made his appeal today after ugly incidents in "friendly" pre-season matches between Newcastle and Sunderland. Fans went on the rampage after both games. There were 65 arrests at Roker Park as violence broke out in the streets with gangs of rival fans fighting. Supt. Thynne said police would continue to use binoculars at St James' Park in a bid to spot troublemakers. Several hundred officers will be on duty both inside and outside St James' Park - even though only a small contingent of Watford fans are expected to travel north.

v QUEENS PARK RANGERS
LOFTUS ROAD
ATT; 14,176

SAT 5TH SEPTEMBER 1981
SECOND DIVISION
LOST 0-3

The Newcastle team travelled down on the Thursday to try out QPR's new £300,000 Omniturf pitch, a new synthetic playing surface which replaced the grass pitch which they'd dug up in the summer. More commonly known as Astro-Turf, the pitch was the first of its kind in English Football and only the second time it had been used in competitive football at the ground, the first match was for the visit of Luton Town who won the fixture taking an instant like to the plastic surface so much so in fact that they would later follow suit at Kenilworth Road becoming the second side to have it installed. For our first ever match on Astro we fielded the youngest side in our entire history. For the record our team was Kevin Carr, Peter Haddock (Former apprentice making his debut), Ian Davies, John Trewick, David Barton, Bruce Halliday, Nigel Walker, Alan Shoulder, Imre Varadi, Kenny Wharton and Chris Waddle. It was so weird watching players wearing Trainers, it just didn't look right. The acoustics in the stadium were also strange sounding as though we were indoors. After their set back against Luton, QPR became quite accustomed to the ridiculous surface and prospered with this unfair advantage. They wouldn't lose at home again until Boxing Day when neighbours Chelsea visited. As for debutant Peter Haddock aka 'Fish Cake' a Crammy lad (You could tell he hailed from Cramlington as he had no dress sense) he actually claimed that his main weakness was heading! A defender who couldn't head? Hailed by some as a future England centre half - aye that sounds likely eh! QPR's former England internationals Tony Currie and Gerry Francis were absolute class as we were ripped apart. Newcastle United's first ever competitive match on Astro-Turf is definitely best forgotten. Early days, but already we were bottom of the table.

Mick Edmondson
Walker, Newcastle

103

v CAMBRIDGE UNITED
ST JAMES' PARK
ATT; 14,666

History is made. At our third attempt we celebrated Newcastle United's first ever 3 points for a win. Meanwhile we had another star to support and adore - Tommy Cavanagh our new sponge man who'd joined us in the summer for an undisclosed fee. After he had rushed on with his bag of tricks and rubbed his magic sponge on the injured player he would always try his best to leave the field over by the East Stand. He would then walk around the shale perimeter in front of the Gallowgate End. "Tommy, Tommy Cavanagh, Tommy, Tommy Cavanagh, Tommy, Tommy Cavanagh," the crowd would chant and Tommy would lap it up and wave his cap in the air in recognition. In his column in the Match Programme, club secretary Russell Cushing asked young fans to behave themselves at Reserve matches at St James' Park. "Stop running amok!!"

Mick Edmondson
Walker, Newcastle

v NORWICH CITY
CARROW ROAD
ATT; 14,384

After dropping from the First Division the Canaries were one of the favourites for the title and most expected them to bounce straight back. We were level at half-time as Chris Waddle, now a regular in the side, scored our first goal away from home for a total of 903 minutes - over 15 hours! It also just happened to be our 5000th League goal, which was captured by the 'Match of the Day' cameras. Even though Norwich missed a penalty we still couldn't get anything out of the game as we lost for the third time, and we'd only played four games.

Mick Edmondson
Walker, Newcastle

We went down with a coach early Friday morning and arrived in time for a night out in Great Yarmouth only to end up drinking in ones and twos around the town. I can remember large groups of locals at closing time not taking to kindly to Geordies being dotted about the town and our little group getting chased down the street back to our B&B and then happily dancing the night away in our basement bar to the Sex Pistols. On the day of the game we went in the Norwich new stand behind the goal and then after the match I remember seeing hundreds of Geordies getting off the train at Yarmouth station for a Saturday night on the drink. The tables were turned and we didn't get any stick all night although a few of the locals got a few shocks.

Dave
Walker, Newcastle

v SHREWSBURY TOWN
ST JAMES' PARK
ATT; 13,783

WED 23RD SEPTEMBER 1981
SECOND DIVISION
WON 2-0

The name Shrewsbury Town is hardly synomonous with the word football is it? The worst thing about such matches as this was the fact that there was no excitement and nothing to arouse the passions of the Geordies. Even when you were struggling at the bottom of the table you knew (or at least you thought you did) that there was never any real chance of being relegated. On the other hand you knew promotion was about as likely as the Board of Directors releasing money to rebuild the ground, and that's what made our predicament so hard to stomach. Although he was to go on and finish the season as the club's leading goalscorer, I never really rated Imre Varadi one of our new signings. Yes he was quick but he lacked a good touch and, perhaps more than anything else, finesse, a quality I've always thought essential in order to be a class player. Chris Waddle who was beginning his first full season in professional football looked a class player although somewhat naive at times. He ran around with slumped shoulders and looked a bit ungainly at times but his ability to beat his man, often making a total fool of him, and deliver a quality ball into the danger area was second to none. In this most forgettable of seasons at least Waddle shone like a beacon.

Mark Hannen
Ponteland, Newcastle

This was my first goal for the first team and I remember it fondly, "I ran all over the place when I scored." Newcastle first team Coach Tommy Cavanagh said "Kenny's goal was a First Division goal if ever I've seen one."

Kenny Wharton
Blakelaw, Newcastle

105

This was the night that Imre Varadi made his mark. Kenny Wharton & Bobby Shinton may have scored the goals but it was Imre Varadi who tore the Shrewsbury defence to bits on a damp autumn night. Varadi never looked back. In the eighties the arrival of Keegan and the emergence of Waddle, Beardsley and later Gazza meant Varadi has been largely forgotten, but for me it was Imre who lit the spark for Arthur Cox's Newcastle United Football Club revival.

Chris Ramshaw
West Denton, Newcastle

v LEYTON ORIENT	SAT 26TH SEPTEMBER 1981
ST JAMES' PARK	SECOND DIVISION
ATT; 13,737	WON 1-0

As a 16 year old I had been selling match day programmes since the start of the season, in return for free admission and 1p commission per sale. For this particular match I was selling from outside the Strawberry pub at the back of the Gallowgate End. Sales were going okay, that is until I was attacked by a gang known as LBAB (Longbenton Aggro Boys), who decided to pinch my remaining couple of hundred programmes before heading off to the match. Obviously my employers weren't very happy and decided that I would basically be working for nothing for the rest of the season as repayment to them. That's where they were wrong, as I wrapped in, failing to show up at the next home match to sell. Although I made sure that I kept a hold of my free laminated pass, to enable me free entry into the centre paddock for the rest of the season. I got away with this for three consecutive seasons! The highlight of this match apart from our goal was the electric scoreboard flashing out 0-0 score line at the end?? We started to move up the table with our second consecutive league win.

John Fatkin
Forest Hall, Newcastle

v BOLTON WANDERERS	TUES 29TH SEPTEMBER 1981
BURNDEN PARK	SECOND DIVISION
ATT; 6,429	LOST 0-1

Today saw the death of football and Liverpool legend Bill Shankly aged 67 following a heart attack. "Shanks" as he was fondly known as too many retired as Liverpool manager, after beating us in the 1974 FA Cup Final. Before that he had won the Second Division title, Uefa Cup, 3 League titles and the FA Cup twice, as well as laying the foundations for Bob Paisley. On his death Kevin Keegan said "I have only ever felt like this once before and that was when my Father died, because Bill was like a second father to me." Before our match at Burnden Park there was a tannoy announcement which you couldn't hear from our position on the open terraces. It was pissing down with rain and allegedly they played 'Abide With Me' over the sound system in honour of Bill Shankly who had died earlier that day. I don't think many in the Newcastle end of the ground were aware that he was dead. The fact that a song was played instead of observing a minutes silence isn't exactly the best way to inform people either. We got slated in the papers the next day, yet you and I know that if Newcastle fans had been aware of the circumstances beforehand then a minutes silence would have been observed. Never, would the fans of Newcastle United, not respect Bill Shankly, a football legend.

Mick Edmondson
Walker, Newcastle

Fans let themselves down

There were a couple of black spots for United last night. One incident involved an unnecessary booking the other was the fans. Once again their support for United was magnificent despite the fact they were housed in an uncovered end of the ground and had to stand in the driving rain. But they really let themselves down when during the pre-match playing of 'Abide With Me' as a tribute to Bill Shankly, they kept on chanting.

v CARDIFF CITY
NINIAN PARK
ATT; 5,764

SAT 3RD OCTOBER 1981
SECOND DIVISION
WON 4-0

I was 20 years old at the time, I woke up very early on the Saturday morning totally skint, but desperate not to miss the trip to Wales. I saw my sister's purse on the fireplace and slipped an IOU into it as off I went with a £20 note for my drink and bait for the day. The thing is my mother knew that I got involved in trouble and up to no good at the matches, but she always made sure that I had money to go. Anyway it was well worth going into debt for as after a very long coach journey we were rewarded with our first away win in 9 months. Imre Varadi became the first Newcastle player for 3 years to score a hat-trick - his first goals for us - as we recorded our first win there in 60 years, failing in our previous 22 attempts. It was also our biggest away league victory since we beat Swindon 6-1 in 1964. We sang "Imre Varadi is on his way" to the tune of 'Oliver's Army' by Elvis Costello. Aye, my sister got her money back.

Deka
Gateshead, Tyneside

107

When we were inside the ground we were getting pelted by Cardiff fans that'd climbed up trees behind our end. Our coaches were also stoned after the match, although all the windows remained unaffected. Not a nice place to visit again.

Cliffy Amhed
South Shields, Tyneside

v FULHAM
ST JAMES' PARK
ATT; 20,247

WED 7TH OCTOBER 1981
(MILK) LEAGUE CUP 2ND RND 1ST LEG
LOST 1-2

Since its introduction in 1960 this competition had always been known as the League Cup but with the arrival of sponsorship it was now known as 'The Milk Cup,' as a result of a 5 year deal with the Milk Marketing Board, who became the first ever sponsors of the trophy. Well on TV and in the media it was but not in our house, it will always be known by its original name - The League Cup. Third Division outfit Fulham, with Malcolm 'Supermac' Macdonald returning as their manager not surprisingly took a lead back to London for the second-leg as we produced a terrible performance. Arthur Cox remarked: "This only proved what we already knew. These supporters are the equivalent of any in the country and probably the best of all. We realize that the fans will come flooding back once we provide the right results." No Arthur. Just a squad of players who give 100% effort every time they pull on the Black-and-White shirt and can trap and pass a ball, would be suffice.

Mick Edmondson
Walker, Newcastle

v DERBY COUNTY
ST JAMES' PARK
ATT; 17,224

SAT 10TH OCTOBER 1981
SECOND DIVISION
WON 3-0

In the eighties match-day stewarding usually consisted of several hundred police officers stationed at various points around the ground and justice was often meted out summarily, without recourse to judge, magistrate or jury. Indeed, back in its previous incarnation, the Gallowgate South-East corner was one of the most populous areas of St. James Park - the easternmost section of the vast open Gallowgate End, comprising a ninety degree turn in the terracing that radiated out from the corner flag. The uppermost steps here were higher than any other part of the Gallowgate and this was home to many of the less well-behaved elements of the home support. It also just so happened, given that it was only a fifty yard stagger up the steps from the bar in The Strawberry, that its inhabitants were usually the most inebriated come 3pm on Saturday afternoon! Needless to say, disturbances here were frequent - in fact they usually occurred several times every game - and to assist with their arduous task, the coppers eventually ordered the club to install an iron fenced gangway allowing them access to the trouble spot without having to wade through crowds further down the terrace. Not surprisingly, the gangway saw an almost constant to-ing and fro-ing on most match-days, but it would be all too easy to simply blame the pissheads for every confrontation. On the contrary, fracas between over-excitable fans and police were more often the result of a heavy handed response: minor disturbances that would usually have come to nothing if they'd just been left alone. One favourite - usually on warmer days - was for one of the resident drunks to perform a full-monty-esque striptease - the sort of thing that even the few female supporters present the packed terraces until one fan was standing proudly in the nude atop a crush barrier. This would invariably be the cue for another SAS-style raid by Northumbria's finest and all-too-often the next object flying down towards the pitch would be a police helmet! Kevin Todd a new signing from Ryhope C.A came on as a sub.

Anth
North Shields, Tyneside

v BARNSLEY
OAKWELL
ATT; 18,477

SAT 17TH OCTOBER 1981
SECOND DIVISION
LOST 0-1

A massive away following travelled down to Yorkshire, to watch a mid-table Newcastle take on the newly promoted Tykes' from Barnsley. This was the first league meeting between the two clubs, since 1948. The Geordie invasion descended on Barnsley town centre as dozens of coaches, transit vans and cars headed down the motorway, whilst hundreds also travelled by train. The locals were definitely up for bother, as street battles took place all afternoon from midday. There was trouble in every pub from the town centre all the way down to the ground. Police injured, windows smashed, pubs forced to close as Barnsley became a battlefield. On reaching the ground it was mayhem trying to gain entry to the away terraces, due to the lack of turnstiles, too many Geordies and the coppers on horseback getting in the way. Then something I shall never forget happened, this bloke we've called Man Mountain' ever since, put his full 25 stone body weight into a punch, hitting the horse which was obstructing him. I couldn't believe my eyes as the horse collapsed to the ground. I had never seen 'Man Mountain' before and I've never seen him since.

I.C.
Walker, Newcastle

A van load of us from North Shields and Walker were enjoying a pre-match drink in a bar in Barnsley called 'The Ring of Bells.' I was playing pool with my mate Dave when we were attacked out of the blue by irate local hooligans. Quite a few of them were trying to get at us inside and pool cues and balls were our preferred weapons of choice as we were totally outnumbered. We managed to hold our own and beat off the Yorkshire Contingent but my great memory from this battle is of my mate Dave trying to get more pool balls out of the table forgetting in the excitement that there is not an unlimited supply stuck up there. The Police arrived in numbers and moved in on us, the Landlord pipes up in his broad Yorkshire accent "These lads didn't start the trouble," and we were left in peace. The Sunday Sun the next day on the front page UNITED FANS IN WILD WEST BATTLE - that was us.

Jimmy
North Shields, Tyneside

We were queuing up outside the ground just having a bit harmless banter with the adjacent Barnsley queue, nothing too bad, when a mounted copper came surging through the Barnsley supporters on his horse waving his stick, unnecessarily hitting innocent people and continued towards us causing total mayhem. It got quite nasty as both sets of fans understandably weren't happy and turned on the Police shouting and complaining to the reinforcements that then landed. The end result more arrests and for what? I know there was a lot of trouble all over Barnsley that day and Newcastle fans were no angels but this attack was unprovoked and just made things worse as more than 7,000 Geordies (paying £1.70) packed onto the open terraced Spoin Kop and many more like us went into the main stand. As you can imagine the Referees decision late on in the game to disallow Kenny Wharton's header didn't go down to well.

Unknown
Newcastle

My first away trip of the season was to Barnsley which was a shocking foretaste of things to come in the football world as South Yorkshire's Boys in Blue, obviously in training for the miners strike, decided it was a terrific idea to try and force 7,000 Newcastle fans down a small back alley with three turnstiles (all operated by octogenarians, bless 'em). I was with my dad, then well into his sixties, who'd been going to Newcastle away matches since the 1940s and that was, a couple of trips to Middlesbrough aside, the last time he ever went. The aggro had simply got too much for him. But the crush down that back alley, seeing a bunch of kids so desperate to get out of it that they were trying to kick the doors in, the feeling of being tossed about from pillar to post has never left me and, eight years later when Hillsborough happened, I couldn't help casting my mind back to a perfectly horrible day I'd spent ten miles away from there. The match? We lost, 1-0, sort of summed it up, really.

Keith Topping
Walker, Newcastle

We left for Barnsley early one Saturday morning in an old ambulance borrowed from a mate in Benton who used to use it to get his drum kit around for the band they were in, he used to drum in the labour club on a Sunday morning for the strippers and hated it. Anyway there were about 10 of us landed in Barnsley for the pubs opening, parked the ambulance and settled into a quiet little bar called 'The Ring O Bells' playing pool and talking football. The pub gradually filled up and before we knew it we were surrounded by a mob of Barnsley hooligans eyeing us up. They eventually kicked off and started by throwing glass at us, we were stuck behind the pool table with no where to hide so we retaliated with a swift volley of pool balls, cues, chairs, tables and our dinner plates that we conveniently had ready after sensing being attacked. Those that weren't knocked out ran out with a few left for hand to hand combat, who were quickly seen off in shock! The cowards that ran out proceeded to put every window through in the bar before they disappeared. When the dust settled the bar was devastated with no windows left, every table, chair, picture, glass, plate, broke. Eventually after a few more beers we collected our wounded and left. The next mornings Sunday Sun insinuated that it was all us with their 'Geordies wreck bar!' slant.

Dave Emmerson,
Walker, Newcastle

110

United Fans in Wild West battle

Newcastle fans went on the rampage in Barnsley last night in one of the worst cases of mob violence the pit town has ever seen. More than 5,000 United fans arrived by rail, coach and cars for the match and trouble broke out even before the kick-off. They marauded through the town centre and wrecked a pub so badly it had to close. During the match coins were hurled on to the pitch and several policemen and a linesman were hurt. Afterwards the fans went 'berserk.' About 30 people were arrested and last night a special court was set up to deal with the offenders. Earlier in the day fans wrecked a public house. In only four minutes the yobs Smashed windows, Kicked-in doors and panels, Broke tables, Threw pool cues and balls, Shattered glass, Overturned a billiard table. And last night landlord Frank Carnevale who was forced to shut up shop told the Sunday Sun: "There's blood all over the walls. It's like an abattoir in here." "It was just like a riot. It was terrifying. If it had been a cowboy movie it would have to have a double X film rating." The aggro continued at the match. Barnsley keeper Bobby Horn was hit by a brick as Newcastle fans crammed behind his goal. Coins were also hurled at him. Horn said afterwards: "The brick wasn't very big, but it's not the sort of thing you want to face during a game."

United Fan butted policeman in face

A Newcastle supporter who climbed a wall covered in barbed wire to get into the Oakwell ground and then assaulted a police officer was given a three month suspended prison sentence when he appeared before Barnsley magistrates. The fan Mr. Brown from Jarrow was caught trying to gain entry via the wall at 3.30pm. When approached by the police he struggled with one whilst head-butting the other. A senior Barnsley police officer said that he just wished United would sink to the Fourth Division.

The Invasion of Barnsley

United say sorry

Newcastle United have apoligised both publicly and privately to Barnsley about the actions of some of their fans. Over 6,000 fans travelled to Barnsley and at one stage the town was under siege. There were countless arrests by the police which led to a special late-night court sitting. United's secretary Russell Cushing said: "These people mascarade as United supporters but we don't want them. They are a disgrace to football and some of the tales I've been told by Barnsley F.C. are frightening. "It's one thing to have to have good away support but quite another to terrorise towns."

111

v ROTHERHAM UNITED
ST JAMES' PARK
ATT; 19,052

SAT 24TH OCTOBER 1981
SECOND DIVISION
DREW 1-1

After earlier warnings falling on deaf ears and an escalation in the problems concerning the behaviour of youngsters at Reserve team games at St James' Park the club released the following statement and final warning in the match programme; "I am afraid if there is a continuation of this behaviour the club will have to seriously consider withdrawing the concession for youngsters attending reserve fixtures." Former Sunderland cup final hero Ian Porterfield was Rotherham's manager and had led them to promotion from the Third Division the previous season. The Yorkshire outfit took the lead after 71 minutes when Walker lad and Newcastle supporter Mick Gooding scored. His sister Sarah worked as a busty barmaid at 'The County Pub' on Walker Road my local for many a year. I wish I had a quid for every time…………………a Geordie or an ex-player scored against us. Booby, eh sorry I mean Bobby Shinton got the equaliser six minutes from the end.

Mick Edmondson
Walker, Newcastle

v FULHAM
CRAVEN COTTAGE
ATT; 7,210

WED 28TH OCTOBER 1981
(MILK) LEAGUE CUP 2ND RND 2ND LEG
LOST 0-2 (Agg; 1-4)

It was a long journey down to London especially with us trailing from the first leg knowing that we were up against it. But it was an even longer return trip up the A1 after an unacceptable display. For the fifth consecutive season we were dumped out of the League Cup at the first hurdle. It was now known as the Milk Cup, so you could say that we bottled it yet again when really we should've progressed. Since we entered the competition 22 years earlier, this was unbelievably the 11th time that we had been knocked out by sides from a lower division. The previous clubs to embarrass us were Colchester, Bournemouth, Peterborough, Lincoln, Sheffield United, Bristol Rovers, Blackpool, Chester, Millwall, Bury and now Fulham.

Mick Edmondson
Walker, Newcastle

v OLDHAM ATHLETIC
BOUNDRY PARK
ATT; 9,010

SAT 31ST OCTOBER 1981
SECOND DIVISION
LOST 1-3

I joined the Newcastle United Supporters Club as a youngster for this trip as all my mates were booked on. On turning up for the coach I was stopped by the Steward and informed that unless I took off my steel cap boots I wouldn't be allowed to travel. I didn't really have a choice so much to the amusement of my mates my boots were put in the hold and I travelled in my socks. Once in Oldham we had to jump on a bus to find a pub and after a few pints made our way to the ground by taxi. We were dropped off by some houses as the Taxi driver said he couldn't get any nearer, so I was forced to walk over this large area of rough ground adjacent to the ground in my bare feet as my socks were knackered. My feet were freezing and I didn't take to kindly when this bloke stood on them. I wasn't best pleased and verbally told the culprit. There were only four of us and plenty of them! The next thing I knew it went off and before I had a chance to finish the idiot off, I was face down on the deck, hands up my back and under arrest. I was taken to the Police station where I was detained until midnight then released after being charged. The coppers gave me a pair of sandshoes for my feet and dropped me off at the local doss house. I then decided that I'd rather sleep rough for a few hours before making my way to the motorway the next morning. I waited for about an hour before hitching a lift to Ferrybridge services, where I then got a lift up the A1 back home. I was reunited with my boots on the Monday, before then being thrown out of the Supporters Club.

Dave Steele
Fawdon, Newcastle

There were continuous chants of "Sack The Board" from the large Newcastle following behind the goal throughout the second half. At the end of the game a clearly disillusioned Newcastle fan raced on to the pitch and deposited his Black and White scarf on the centre circle. He threw it with obvious disgust. Back in the early eighties travelling by train was totally different. In those days you couldn't just walk freely around station platforms unless of course you had a valid train ticket. If you were either seeing somebody onto their train or going to meet somebody arriving then you needed a 'Platform ticket' which cost about 5p. Some fans would buy a platform ticket then jump on a train and try their luck travelling all over England for free. Then came the arrival of 'The Football Special' which was a very popular form of cheap rail travel, but unfortunately they were only used for certain football excursions throughout the season. The trains resembled cattle trucks and were packed to the brim, standing room only, pissing where you stood. When you arrived back at Newcastle Central the 'Checkys' would be waiting by the exit gates so more often than not everyone used to storm into them, as many hadn't paid. When returning from Oldham dozens of fans actually jumped from the train when it slowed down and stopped, as it came over the bridge, before escaping by running along the tracks.

Mick Edmondson
Walker, Newcastle

We got the train to York after our fifth league defeat on our travels in what was only our sixth league away game. We had a canny night in York before catching the midnight train. We were sitting in one of the carriages with some Chinese tourists who were joining in with our songs and beer. Their favourite seemed to be "One Bobby Shinton, There's Only One Bobby Shinton." Picture the scene as they sang "One Bobby Tin Tin, There's Only One Bobby Tin Tin." as they raised their cans of Ace lager.

Piper
Felling, Tyneside

v BERWICK RANGERS
SHEILFIELD PARK
ATT; 1,167

Two of us knocked off Benfield school in the city's east end at 2pm and caught a couple of buses to the A1 Cramlington junction, where we managed to hitch a lift up to the borders. All that trouble to see a defence which included Haddock, Hedworth and Saunders, crackers we were. Once inside we managed our usual trick and scrounged a lift home.

> **Dave Drape**
> **Walker, Newcastle**

The day before CB (Citizens band radio) had become legal in the UK. After 10 years in America 'people's radio' had hit the streets of Newcastle. My mate Keith had just paid £90 for a set, so we tuned into 934FM and joined the craze that was sweeping the country. We were officially 'breakers' as we gave it the big 10-4 up the A1 to the border town of Berwick for a few pints before popping over the river to Spittal to watch the match. We ended up getting in touch with these Berwick lasses but when they turned up they had a couple of strange looking blokes with them. Actually come to think of it, my mate Keith was a bit strange. How times have changed, we've all got mobiles now.

> **Simon Walker**
> **Dunston, Tyneside**

v CHELSEA
STAMFORD BRIDGE
ATT; 16,509

SAT 7TH NOVEMBER 1981
SECOND DIVISION
LOST 1-2

As we travelled in a convoy away from the ground on the Supporters Club buses feeling depressed after another defeat, we got stuck in traffic as we approached Wandsworth Bridge. Then without warning we were ambushed by a mob of Chelsea Hooligans who attacked our 4 coaches throwing stones and bricks. It was dark but there seemed to be plenty of them as our coach driver mounted the centre reservation to try and escape only to cause the coach to stall!! It was horrendous and very terrifying as we became a sitting target. The missiles smashed numerous windows as everyone tried to escape the glass diving to the floor in the aisle. I wasn't so fortunate as a brick hit me straight in the head and eventually when the police got things under control I ended up in an ambulance along with others as we were whisked away to St James Hospital in Balham. In the end there were 3 of us who required treatment, I had six stitches put in my head, a Gentleman broke his finger protecting his face and another Fella had glass removed from his eye. We were eventually released from hospital at 6am where our fellow passengers picked us up in a replacement bus, eventually arriving home in time for Sunday dinner. I was asked to appear as a witness at the Old Bailey but declined the offer, however gladly some of the Chelsea thugs were found guilty based on Police evidence. As for the Armstrong Galley coach it was sent to the transport graveyard in the sky, the damage was so bad.

> **Margaret Hay,**
> **Walker Newcastle**

A week earlier Chelsea had been hammered 5-0 at Rotherham. Imre Varadi went off injured after half an hour and was replaced by Kevin Pugh making his only ever appearance for the first team. Debuts for Wesley Saunders, and Alan Brown on loan from Sunderland, as Nigel Walker from Whickham played his final game after 74 appearances and 3 goals. The once promising youngster was loaned out to Plymouth before eventually signing for San Diego in the USA the following summer. After the match we had a night out in London but I missed the NUSC midnight bus back home so went to sleep in Euston station as from previous experiences I knew that this was the warmest place available. When I was woken by the police I lied and said that I was waiting for a train to Manchester but was thrown out as there were no more trains. I ended up in Kings Cross station which was freezing and the prostitutes kept approaching me, "£30 for a good time?" I replied "I haven't seen £30 for a long time pet." I then moved into the Gents as it was warmer but eventually settled in the Ladies toilets which was even better, before jumping the train the next morning.

Piper
Felling, Tyneside

United Fans trapped on bridge - Coaches Ambushed

Newcastle soccer fans came under fire when rival supporters ambushed their coaches last night. Chelsea fans brought London traffic to a standstill as they attacked two buses on busy Wandsworth Bridge. Geordies dived for cover as their vehicles were bombarded with bricks and bottles. Three Magpie fans were taken to hospital for minor cuts and injuries said a police spokesman. The rampaging Chelsea fans smashed all the windows of one coach and three windows in the coach behind. The battle began as the buses were bringing United supporters home after their teams 2-1 defeat by Chelsea at Stamford Bridge. A police spokesman said: "Two Newcastle coaches were ambushed by Chelsea supporters hurling stones and bottles. "Three passengers were slightly injured and we arrested four of the gang who attacked the coaches." "It wasn't a very friendly game. There was fighting before and during the match." "We made another 12 arrests and there were 150 ground evictions." he added. Six of the arrested were Newcastle supporters. The attacked coaches belong to Newcastle firm Armstrong Galley. Their spokesman said: "Everyone on our 53 seater buses were members of Newcastle United Supporters Club - they were not hooligans, just normal loyal fans. They've been an innocent party.

After we got ambushed, all the Chelsea fans managed to get away from the scene, that is apart from one of them who somehow managed to get himself hit by our bus driver Jimmy Campbell who accidently knocked him over on the pavement, breaking his legs!

Mala Pegg
Gateshead, Tyneside

Fans stoned coaches

Four coaches carrying Newcastle United fans were ambushed by Chelsea supporters, causing £3,500 worth of damage, an Old Bailey jury was told. The rampaging Chelsea fans hurling a hail of bricks, knew exactly where to stage the attack, it was alleged. The violence happened minutes after police had left the coaches after escorting them as far as Wandsworth Bridge - in London. Several fans inside the coaches were injured, as more than 100 Chelsea fans attacked the coaches. Charged with taking part in an affray, unlawful assembly and causing criminal damage were Michael Power (20) a labourer of Brixton, South London and Paul Wadham (18), a toolmaker of Edenbridge, Kent. Police said the youths were throwing bricks and were alleged to have said: "The idea was to get away from the game quietly and meet down at the bridge. Told about the damage and the injured fans, Power said: "That's what it's all about. It happens every week doesn't it." He was also said to have said: "A load of us met down by the roundabout to do the Newcastle lot. We were going to have a go at them and cause a bit of a ruck." (Proceeding)

v CHARLTON ATHLETIC
ST JAMES' PARK
ATT; 15,254

SAT 14TH NOVEMBER 1981
SECOND DIVISION
WON 4-1

Loan signing Alan Brown scored on his home debut against 10-man Charlton, but the goal everybody was talking about was Imre Varadi's second goal, an early contender for goal of the season. He ran from inside his own half, he just seemed to run through everybody before slotting the ball past the keeper. I can just remember being amazed by his sheer speed, so fast. He was our new hero and if we could manage to buy Alan Brown then we could have the ideal partnership, the early signs were very promising. Also the club announced that Jim Holton the once big strapping Man Utd centre half was on Tyneside for talks. *"Six Foot Two, Eyes Of Blue, Big Jim Holton's After You!"* Well somebody else must have been after him as we never heard of him again? That's fat Jim Holton the former Sunderland and Sheff Wed, red & white below average twat! Meanwhile self confessed Sunderland celebrity fan Steve Cram, had joined the Newcastle 'Buy a player fund.' Organiser Malcolm Dix was hoping that a fun run would be similar to the Great North Run, but on a slightly smaller scale!" The organisation behind the fund also had a talk-in with Jackie Milburn.

Mick Edmondson
Walker, Newcastle

v LUTON TOWN
ST JAMES' PARK
ATT; 21,084

SAT 21ST NOVEMBER 1981
SECOND DIVISION
WON 3-2

The dark days of Division Two and yet we still had a hero to worship. Having been brought up on names like Malcolm, Frank, David and thinking Wyn was exotic, now we had a name some couldn't even pronounce. Imre Varadi was the man signed by Arthur Cox for £125,000 and he would be worth at least 5 million pounds today. From the misery of 7 goals Bobby Shinton being our highest scorer the previous season, Ray scored goals for fun and his 20 in season 1981-82 would help lift the gloom of our 4th season in Division Two. This period of my support found me taking my place on the Gallowgate terraces for each home game. The Leazes End was long gone, but we still had 3 sets of floodlights. Oh and a scoreboard. Yes the famous scoreboard. I used to stand to the right of it, half way down in line with the right hand post. Four barriers along from where Tommy from the Grainger Market used to be propped up on the concrete barrier before each game and give us his version of "Little White Bull." Today would be interesting though as we had Alan Brown on loan from the mackems. *"We've Got Alan Broon, He's Playing For The Toon"* was the chant of the day. After a good few beers in the Darn Crook (now Rosies) and wondering whether to opt for the Human League, Queen and Bowie or Olivia Newton John!! on the juke box, at least it was an easy one to remember. Over 21,000 were at the game even though we were a miserable 12th in the table. Watching any Newcastle game through beer goggles is always recommended but in this era it was mandatory so my version of the match is short, sweet and haphazard to say the least. I do know Alan Brown with his pace and wing play on the right notched two. A young kid called Waddle was also having a fine game on the left. Ray Varadi though spent most of the game missing his chances and as usual opinion was divided on the merits of the new centre forward. For younger readers, Ray was a sort of Mickey Quinn or Oba Martins - needed ten chances to score one goal, but I was confident he looked like he could do a job for us. Suffice to say we all thought that at 2-2 a point was a fair result when the ball broke. I have stood corrected over the years, but in my mind it will always be like this - from where I was, Imre looked like he ran from at least the half way line towards the Leazes goal and after what seemed a life time, notched to make it 3-2. As usual the place went up. Actually, there was more than enough space to leap about! Two points and as Luton would actually go on to win the league, it was a glimmer of hope in yet another awful season. I always had a soft spot for Imre after this game and sadly his 22 goals the next season alongside Keegan, Waddle etc was his Newcastle swansong. Imagine that - 42 goals in two seasons and we sell him. Typical eh!

Tony Fiddes
Gosforth, Newcastle

Two days earlier former Newcastle legend Malcolm 'Supermac' MacDonald became the first paid Director of a football club, within minutes of an FA decision to approve the innovation at an extraordinary general meeting. Fulham Chairman Ernie Clay remarked, "He will have responsibility for controlling the football side of the clubs activities." After only 14 games Luton were top of the table 15 points ahead of us, but you wouldn't believe it as we led 2-0 at the interval, before we let them back into it as 'The Hatters' pulled it back to 2-2. Then Varadi sent the crowd wild with a last minute winner which striker Alan Brown who had been replaced by sub Alan Shoulder described, "I heard the cheers as I came back down the tunnel and when I saw the crowd on the pitch I knew we'd won it." Could this be the turning point of our season? After the match Ground staff started the monumental task of repainting the Orange barriers and steelwork around the ground Black-And-White.

Mick Edmondson
Walker, Newcastle

My son and I travelled by coach from Luton to support our team. Whilst the coach was stationary in traffic outside the Magpie, a ……… threw a stone which broke a window and struck me on the side of the head. I was being stitched up in hospital when the game started. I would like to thank the policeman who looked after me until I was back in the ground for the second half, and has since gone to the trouble of obtaining a copy of the match magazine for my son and posted it to me. This kindness has almost restored my "shattered" liking for Geordies. It would be fully restored if one of your many supporters who witnessed this act of insanity could point out the ………to the police.

Alan McPherson
Luton, Beds

v LEYTON ORIENT   **TUES 24TH NOVEMBER 1981**
BRISBANE ROAD   **SECOND DIVISION**
ATT; 4,026   **LOST 0-1**

The lowest crowd to watch us all season even with a canny following from Newcastle witnessed one of my all time lows as a supporter. We were terrible against a team who would struggle all season and go on to be relegated in May. After a mini revival of two consecutive wins, including beating the league leaders four days earlier, we had now failed to win 5 of our last 7 league games and we were way off the pace. Our away record was abysmal with 7 defeats out of 8 so far. Without Varadi's goals we would go down ourselves. A defeat on a cold night in London at Highbury, or White Hart Lane would have been a lot easier to take than this. The club couldn't get anything right from top to bottom which was made evident as our Dutch U21 international Frans Koenon signed only 15 months earlier as part of our bigger future was on trial at Exeter City!! Because of the economic climate at the club, the players travelled by coach straight back to Tyneside after the game. Hopefully it gave them a taste of what we did every season, week in week out. Terrible times but we still had a laugh and went in numbers.

Ray O'Brien
Forest Hall, Newcastle

v GRIMSBY TOWN   **SAT 28TH NOVEMBER 1981**
BLUNDELL PARK   **SECOND DIVISION**
ATT; 9,256   **DREW 1-1**

You start to realise that you're no longer in the big time when Grimsby Town, away from home, becomes a regular trip. Sunny Cleethorpes was anything but, for this cold winter's afternoon trip to the seaside. Another large following from the north-east, considering our position of mid-table obscurity yet again, were housed in the cow shed in the corner. Actually it was quite exciting in a way travelling to some of the smaller grounds, as we always seemed to get a roof over our heads, which was ideal for creating a better atmosphere and also an experience for us, as St. James Park didn't have any covered standing areas. We drew 1-1 on this occasion but although I have no recollection of Kenny Wharton's first half goal, I can remember an incident which took place in the second half when Grimsby were kicking towards us. One of their midfield players, who I believe was called Bob Cumming, was a funny looking character with a beard and a bald head, so obviously he got loads of stick from our section. *"Where's Your Hair, Where's Your Hair"* was the chant every time he came near us, especially when he came over to take a corner. As he placed the ball by the corner flag and took a few steps back and leaned back against the fence, a hand reached through the fence and patted him on the head a few times just like Benny Hill used too do. Because the ball was in his possession nearly everybody was looking his way including players and officials, but he saw the funny side and to his credit he even returned to take another corner later, joining in the fun by patting his own head as he walked over. Not so popular was ex-Sunderland man Bob Mitchell, who scored a magnificent 30 yard screamer for the Mariners.

> **Andy Graham**
> **Denton Burn, Newcastle**

A lad called Dicka' from Winlaton had done the usual and got down to the match early and hit the drink, then lost his mates he'd been with all day, as you do. Officially over 4,000 Geordies had made the trip, (which later Russell Cushing the clubs secretary thanked for behaving), and he eventually got in to the ground and stood amongst all the others in black and white shirts and thought nothing of it until Kenny Wharton scored and he started to jump up and down! He soon sobered up when he realised he was in the Grimsby end and was chased out of the stand, successfully avoiding a beating! I remember a Newcastle song from this game which was directed towards the Findus Stand *"Sing When Your Fishing, You Only Sing When Your Fishing."*

> **Davey**
> **Walker, Newcastle**

v BLACKBURN ROVERS
ST JAMES' PARK
ATT; 18,775

SAT 5TH DECEMBER 1981
SECOND DIVISION
DREW 0-0

A couple of weeks earlier the club announced an annual loss of £877,381 which in those days was colossal. This now meant that our club Newcastle United were now nearly £1 million in debt, didn't own their ground, had no saleable assets, a decrepit half knocked down ground, were a struggling Second Division side and with attendances falling, the future looked bleak. Just to cheer us up we had to watch this match which was pile of shite. Before the match we visited the Magpie Club on Barrack Road. Two days

previously it had been officially opened as the 'Newcastle United Supporters Social Club' although also retaining it's original name 'The Magpie.' You had to be a member which cost £2 to join and then an annual £1 fee thereafter. Once inside you had the choice of Darts, Pool, Video machine games, but no jukebox. The highlight though was a colour television (Not that there was owt to watch). On a match day it was open 11am - 2.30pm, then from the earlier time of 5pm after the match. (Other pubs were 5.30pm).

Jimmy Good
Walker, Newcastle

v WREXHAM	**SAT 12TH DECEMBER 1981**
RACECOURSE GROUND	**SECOND DIVISION**
ATT; N/A	**POSTPONED**

This like many games over the next few weeks was postponed due to the horrendous weather. Struggling side Wrexham were 19th in the table and we were 10th yet the Pools panel decided that our result would be a home win. Mind you this was proved to be the case when it was eventually played later in the season.

Graham Kirby
Cowgate, Newcastle

v LEICESTER CITY	**SAT 26TH DECEMBER 1981**
FILBERT STREET	**SECOND DIVISION**
ATT; N/A	**POSTPONED**

As a 15 year old this was the worst Christmas Day in my entire life, in fact the only one I haven't enjoyed in its entirety ever. To find out that our 11.30am Boxing Day trip to Leicester - they had an away end with a roof - had been postponed due to snow and ice on Christmas morning wasn't exactly what I wanted off Santa. My £2 Leicester ticket on the mantel piece, Turkey has never tasted so bad, I was gutted. You can stick your White Christmas's up your arse. Adjudged to be a home-win for Leicester City by the pools panel, which former Newcastle legend Tony Green was a member.

Mick Edmondson
Walker, Newcastle

v COLCHESTER UNITED	**MON 4TH JANUARY 1982**
ST JAMES' PARK	**FA CUP 3RD ROUND**
ATT; 16,977	**DREW 1-1**

A new year - a new start. Fourth Division Colchester United arrived as lambs to the slaughter on a rain soaked night. Then I remembered that we were Newcastle United and watched nervously as we struggled against the minnows. This was our idea of fun, getting soaked to the skin standing on open terraces in the freezing cold watching garbage week in week out struggle against other poor sides. Was this actually true loyalty, or just absolute madness? A bit of both I suspect. So all things considered this was quite an amazing turn-out to watch a club in crisis against Colchester on a Monday night, in atrocious conditions. But we wouldn't have it any other way as it's in our blood. The club was in such a state. We had no funds to buy and no players of any worth to sell. The Newcastle United Supporters Association had hoped to raise £100,000 with their 'Buy A Player Fund,' which they launched in October 1981, but their spokesperson Malcolm Dix announced that "It won't be enough for a new player, but it might be enough for a new set of strips."

Mick Edmondson
Walker, Newcastle

v WATFORD	**SAT 16TH JANUARY 1982**
VICARAGE ROAD	**SECOND DIVISION**
ATT; 12,333	**WON 3-2**

This was our first league game since 5th December so I pushed the boat out and went on the Newcastle United Supporters Club 'Stop over package' staying at the Ladbroke Mercury Hotel on the Saturday night. The fee was £11.50 and included return coach travel, a seat ticket for the match and Bed & Breakfast and the hotel was only a ten minutes away from the ground. Kevin Todd scored twice as he started his first game! His only previous appearance was his debut as a sub earlier in the season. The former Sunderland shipyard lagger aged 23 was on the dole 8 months earlier and only found out he was playing 2 hours before kick-off. Only nine minutes from time Watford had gone 2-1 up and somehow we still went on to win with 2 very late goals. The win rounded off a fantastic weekend which left their chairman Elton John rocking.

Steve McCormack
Sandyford, Newcastle

v COLCHESTER UNITED	**MON 18TH JANUARY 1982**
LAYER ROAD	**FA CUP 3RD RND REPLAY**
ATT; 7,505	**WON 4-3**

We had already attempted to travel to Colchester on the previous Wednesday, but had got as far as Yorkshire when we heard that the match had been postponed. Considering we were drawn at home to our Fourth Division opposition this tie was becoming a nightmare, after a 1-1 draw on Tyneside and then the postponement. We left at 8am for this Monday night match, but after a terrible journey we didn't arrive until 5pm. On arrival we found a supermarket where the lads helped themselves to some alcoholic freebies, which we consumed outside the ground. As we sat drinking we noticed a couple of lads climbing over a 6ft wall by the ground, so we later followed and we were pleasantly surprised to find ourselves inside the actual ground! We were able to walk around to where the Newcastle fans were housed and watch a match full of action and goals as Newcastle went on to win 4-3. We didn't get back to Newcastle until 7am the next morning, which meant only two hours sleep before my job interview at 9.30. I managed to get the job, but after the lengths we all went to and the nightmare which was Colchester, Newcastle would unbelievably yet not surprisingly get knocked out in the next round at home to a very poor side!

I.C.
Walker, Newcastle

A long journey which in the end was worth the hassle as United recorded a memorable extra-time away win - there second in 2 days - in a match where Chris Waddle scored a spectacular goal and Wes Saunders crossed the ball from the halfway line and it somehow ended up in the back of the net!! It took a replay and extra time to beat the Fourth Division side and I ended up on the pitch at one point celebrating in the goalmouth with Chris Waddle. What a weekend, we conceded 5 goals yet scored 7! A lot was later made of the fact that the players who'd travelled by coach got back at 5am after 6 hours on the road. As for us - we got back in Newcastle just in time for the 4th Round!!

Dave Drape
Walker, Newcastle

v GRIMSBY TOWN
ST JAMES' PARK
ATT; 25,632

SAT 23RD JANUARY 1982
FA CUP 4TH ROUND
LOST 1-2

An excellent atmosphere and an excellent chance to progress into the fifth round where we would've been away to Second Division QPR who went on to beat Grimsby, Crystal Palace, then West Brom in the Semi-Finals before taking Spurs to a replay in the Final. Not exactly an impossible road to Wembley, we blew it. Although Grimsby had somehow won away to Millwall 6-1 in the last round they were bottom of the Second Division without a manager, had numerous players missing through injury and were relegation favourites. They were a very poor side. The problem was so were we. We were 0-2 down and even our consolation goal was scored by a Grimsby player! The highlight of the afternoon was a pre-match Geordie streaker and their keeper's dodgy beard which came in for some stick, things were really desperate now.

Mick Edmondson
Walker, Newcastle

Hooligans injure P.C. Pagan

Football hooligans took their fury out on a police horse when Newcastle were knocked out of the cup this weekend. Pagan who has served Newcastle police for many years, suffered a nasty cut and swelling when fans hurled bricks at him. The trouble started at the end of the match when some disgruntled Newcastle supporters got into the Leazes Park area and put a volley of missiles over towards the visiting supporters and police vehicles parked there. It was dark at the time and Pagan was struck by two bricks - one hit his neck and the other his hind leg which started to bleed. In spite of his injuries the horse hardly flinched. The windscreen of a horsebox was also smashed during the attack. There were 16 people arrested and 9 were also thrown out of the ground during the game.

v NORWICH CITY
ST JAMES' PARK
ATT; 14,492

Let's face it Republic of Ireland international Mick Martin wasn't really a very good player after his long lay-off through injury. In layman's terms he was shite. Against Norwich he was booed throughout by the Newcastle fans. Afterwards he said "They pay their money and have a right to say what they think." Star of the show was David Mills who scored on his debut whilst on loan from West Bromwich Albion. Meanwhile the Newcastle United Supporters Association fronted by rebel supporter Malcolm Dix hoped to raise £100,000 with their buy a player fund. This crazy and absolutely ridiculous idea was launched 4 months earlier and had been a disaster. Dix didn't reveal the amount raised but did say, "It won't be enough for a new player, but it might be enough for a new set of strips."

Clive Turnbull
Throckley, Newcastle

Fan swore at police

A Newcastle soccer fan who screamed obscenities at a police officer was fined £100 with £20 costs by City magistrates. Mr. William McMenemy presiding told 17 year old Gary Hewitson; "There is absolutely nothing that condones trouble at football matches. Hewitson, unemployed of Newbiggin-by-the-sea shouted and swore at police officers at the Gallowgate end of St James' Park. Hewitson denied behavior likely to cause a breach of the peace but was found guilty. Mr. Lawson, defending claimed it was a case of mistaken identity.

v BOLTON WANDERERS
ST JAMES' PARK
ATT; 14,714

Fan threw tights at goalie

A United supporter, who ran on to the pitch at St James' Park, threw a pair of women's tights at the Bolton Wanderers goalkeeper. When arrested he said: "It was only the Bolton keeper. He is not much good. He is only an old woman and he needs them," Newcastle magistrates were told by Mr. George Dickinson prosecuting. Raymond James Balmain a 22 year old welder of Walker, Newcastle admitted insulting behaviour and was fined £100 with £10 costs. Balmain said he was on tablets which made him act "a bit funny."

I would regularly visit my local Sports Shop in Campbeltown, Argyle and ask for a Newcastle United football top. As usual I would be told that they couldn't get one. I'd say "Believe me you just wait one day you'll have them in pride of place in your window." Sure enough for the last 15 years the window has been full of Black-and-White shirts.

Charles
Campbeltown, Scotland

v CAMBRIDGE UNITED
ABBEY STADIUM
ATT; 5,092

Got down there early and had a couple of pints in their supporters club at the back of the home end, before my mates Carl, Davey Gunn and I went onto the away terrace at 2pm. The reason for going in early was Carl's brother Keith Lockhart from Wallsend was on Cambridge's books and he had arranged for us to go into the changing rooms. Maybe we shouldn't have worn our Doc Martin boots and standard issue Donkey jackets! Back on the terraces it gave us a rare opportunity to watch the teams get an early feel of the playing surface and we watched as Bobby Shinton whilst warming the keeper up, sent a ball way over the bar and straight through a greenhouse window in the allotments behind our end! It was one of his last contributions for the club, as he made his last appearance coming on as a sub before joining Millwall, in a United career in which he scored 10 goals in 49 appearances. This defeat ended any promotion hopes we had.

Mick Edmondson
Walker, Newcastle

v CARDIFF CITY
ST JAMES' PARK
ATT; 15,129

Remember the Gallowgate End toilets? The stink of piss from the previous match a fortnight earlier even though they were open air Nettie's! At times when it was dark you would unknowingly walk in and would be ankle deep in piss, they were without doubt never cleaned and the shithouse at the end had never seen a bog roll. Next to the toilets there were numerous trees and bushes on the bank, many just used them instead obviously. We did the double over the Welsh side then watched it all again on Tyne Tees programme 'Shoot' at 2.30pm Sunday.

Brian Hall
Heaton, Newcastle

v SHREWSBURY TOWN
GAY MEADOW
ATT; 4,636

SAT 20TH FEBRUARY 1982
SECOND DIVISION
DREW 0-0

A Mini-Bus of us arrived in Shrewsbury Town centre at midday but struggled to get in anywhere for a beer. Although we didn't lose it was one of the worst games in memory. Less than 5,000 at the match and one of the worst, if not the worst Toon team I can remember. For the record it was; Carr, Brownlie, Saunders, Trewick, Carney, Haddock, Mills, Martin, Varadi, Wharton & Waddle.

Paul Wardle
Wallsend, Tyneside

v SHEFFIELD WEDNESDAY
ST JAMES' PARK
ATT; 19,174

WED 24TH FEBRUARY 1982
SECOND DIVISION
WON 1-0

I remember travelling to the delights of Grimsby, Sheff Wed & Barnsley etc with the Supporters Club. The buses would leave from the rickety old Supporters Shop which was in fact a prefab style portacabin, right opposite the Farmer Rest pub in the Haymarket. I've still got my Membership Card! The shop itself left a lot to be desired looking back and the merchandise in those days matched our team - absolute shit! As I was around 13 most of the lads on the buses were a lot older than me and absolutely pissed at 8am in the morning when travelling to the likes of Hillsborough. We would travel everywhere in our thousands yet the likes of Sheff Wed would only bring a handful of fans, today was no exception.

Hendy
Kenton Bar, Newcastle

Arthur Cox's pre-match battle cry seemed to have some effect: "You're a bunch of north-east lads playing with your own behind you. So get on with the job." he told his team. Out of the 13 players on duty including sub Alan Shoulder and 13th man Bruce Halliday, there were only 2 not from the north-east - Brownlie and Varadi. He continued, "If these lads can't play for their own, well there is something wrong with them."

Arthur Cox
Newcastle Manager

v DERBY COUNTY
BASEBALL GROUND
ATT; 12,257

SAT 27TH FEBRUARY 1982
SECOND DIVISION
DREW 2-2

POPULAR-COLOMBO   T/S50-55
(GROUND)

NEWCASTLE
UNITED

SATURDAY FEBRUARY 27TH 82
KICK-OFF - 3:00PM

FOOTBALL LEAGUE DIVISION TWO

STANDING
ONLY

Michael Dunford
Secretary

This ticket is issued
subject to the Rules
& Regulations of the
Football Association.

£ 2.50

For ticket and match information:
Telephone Derby 364458
(24 hour service)

No. 01192

DERBY COUNTY F.C. LTD.
BASEBALL GROUND, DERBY

Derby County had won the First Division title twice in the 1970's, yet less than 7 years after their last triumph they faced the threat of closure. The Inland Revenue had given them 5 days to cough up the £100,000 that they owed. "If you don't meet the deadline you will have to fold." So at the time we all thought that this could be their last ever match! I've never missed for years and in the eighties I always travelled with the Supporters Club. We were on our way back when we stopped at Selby Services as a lad on the bus was really drunk and needed the toilet. (No toilets on board in those days). The driver wasn't too happy as he wanted to get back to his wife as it was his anniversary, so we were only given a 10 minute toilet break. Quite a few got off. When we returned the coach had disappeared, about ten of us had been left behind! Eventually when it became apparent that we were 100% stranded my mate rang his uncle who came to pick us up, whilst others tried thumbing a lift. It was the drivers fault.

Cliffy Ahmed
South Shields, Tyneside

Arthur Cox was angry at Derby trying to cash in on United fans as they charged £2.50 for advance tickets and £4 at the turnstiles on the day. The idea was supposedly to cut down on hooliganism but Cox rapped, "I don't like to see our faithful being abused. When they are prepared to turn up in their numbers this isn't the way to treat them. They deserve to be hammered if they misbehave, but it's wrong to see the loyal and well disciplined suffer.

Arthur Cox
Newcastle Manager

Derby make Newcastle pay

Derby have blacklisted Newcastle United fans. After consultation with local police, Derby have come down hard on soccer's hooligans. They have banned Chelsea fans from the Baseball ground for life after they caused £2,500 worth of damage recently. And they have taken positive action against fans from four other clubs - Newcastle, Sheff Wed, Barnsley and Rotherham. Fans will have to pay £4 nearly double the price of home fans.

v LEICESTER CITY
FILBERT STREET
ATT; 12,497

WED 3RD MARCH 1982
SECOND DIVISION
LOST 0-3

This was a real kick in the knackers for our promotion hopes. Originally due to be played at 11.30am on Boxing Day but called off due to ice and snow we were ripped apart with a certain Gary Lineker grabbing a brace, one in each half as we were hammered by a Leicester team who'd been relegated along with Norwich and Crystal Palace months earlier from the top flight. Off the pitch there was trouble before, during and after the match as rival fans clashed all night. The worst incident was inside the ground where for most of the game both sets of fans had been throwing missiles at each other, which horrifically nearly cost a Leicester supporter his eye.

Dave Drape
Walker, Newcastle

I boarded an early National Express bus from Gallowgate with 16 cans of Lager in a crate, and half a bottle of Rum. Supped the lot and got there in time for a good drink, which luckily helped make a 3-0 defeat less painful.

Derek Webster
Gateshead, Tyneside

v BARNSLEY
ST JAMES' PARK
ATT; 18,784

SAT 6TH MARCH 1982
SECOND DIVISION
WON 1-0

Fight to save fans eye after bottle attack

Police were today hunting for a Newcastle United 'super grass' - in a bid to catch a soccer thug. They mingled with Geordie fans at the home game with Barnsley - while a teenage Leicester boy fought to regain the sight in one eye. The boy, just 13, was hit by flying glass after a Newcastle supporter hurled a bottle towards Leicester fans during the Magpies midweek promotion game. The bottle shattered against a fence and a fragment of glass flew into the boy's eye.

Still unbeaten at home in the league since the opening day of the season as we won our fifth consecutive home game, a record of only 1 defeat in 14 games. We climbed to 8th only 5 points off 3rd with 2 games in hand and with the comfort that 3 of next 4 games were at home. We still had an outside chance of promotion. A Varadi goal won it, but unfortunately all the talk afterwards was of the racial abuse Barnsley's black player Winston Campbell received. Monkey chants and racist songs filled the air from various sections of the ground. Many saw Newcastle as the UK's worst offenders and we were at the top of many racist league tables published at the time. It was a huge national social problem but not the kind of trophy you wanted your club to win.

Tony Robson
Newcastle

Fan gets suspended jail

A Barnsley supporter whose abusive taunts and gestures to a section of the Newcastle crowd during the match caused an angry reaction was given a suspended prison sentence by Newcastle magistrates. He had taken out a Newcastle scarf, held it aloft and shouted obscenities to provoke the Newcastle fans. In his defence in court he said that he went to the ground to watch the match, not to cause trouble. He had taken the scarf to the match in case he got chased by Newcastle fans and he would have jumped into the crowd, mingling in, if necessary.

Search for soccer thug draws a blank

The search for a Newcastle thug who could have blinded a young Leicester fan is being stepped up by Northumbria Police. The quizzing of fans at Saturday's home game with Barnsley has turned up no new evidence, said a spokesman.

v ROTHERHAM UNITED
MILLMOOR
ATT; 16,905

SAT 13TH MARCH 1982
SECOND DIVISION
DREW 0-0

The following season's corresponding fixture where we won 5-1 with Keegan scoring four is the Rotherham away match most people remember, I got more satisfaction from this game. Rotherham had won 10 on the trot and would break some sort of record if they won. We played well, we should have won. They had a winger called Tony Towner who spent the whole game falling over. Deep into injury time he fell once again in the box, the referee pointed to the spot "Oh Dear" or words to that effect groaned us Geordies. Keeper Kevin Carr was having a great season the Chronicle even reckoned he was in the running for a place in the England World Cup squad, and he pulled off a great save. Thousands of Geordies in Rotherham's dilapidated stand celebrated a 0-0 at Rotherham as though we had just won the World Cup, the Ashes and the Grand National all at once.

Chris Ramshaw
West Denton, Newcastle

At full time for some unknown reason police on horseback actually came into the packed Newcastle End, causing fans to panic as the horses went wild. The whole situation was totally unnecessary and unprovoked yet fans were squashed, knocked to the floor, some even climbed up the floodlight pylons to safety. As far as I remember by some minor miracle nobody was seriously hurt, how I don't know.

Sean Glen
North Shields, Tyneside

Another character from the 1980's was Tommy, a middle aged bloke, possibly with some learning difficulties, who worked in the Green Market and liked a drink of beer. Encouraged by the chants of "Tommy, Tommy", this red-faced bloke would appear on a barrier in the Gallowgate End, usually the middle section or corner. Once steadied on the concrete barrier, he would then sing a few verses of the old Tommy Steele song; "A Little White Bull." The crowd would listen as Tommy rambled through the verses then join in with a huge echo of "A Little White Bull." Seemed and sounded really good at the time, poor bloke. When we played at Millmoor in 1982 it was billed a big game as Rotherham were above us and heading for promotion, under the guidance of Emlyn Hughes. We drew 0-0, with Kevin Carr saving a penalty in the final minutes. Hundreds of us had travelled down on the old soccer special trains. These were like cattle trucks, with very few facilities and people would cram in as much drink as possible from Yates, opposite the station, before getting on. Tommy was on this train and was passing through the many carriages, running a domino card. It was one of those big cards with about fifty numbers on each side, so there were plenty takers for 50p a number. After about an hour had passed someone seen Tommy and enquired about who had won the card. "Er, lad a couple of carriages down mate" was Tommy's reply, not once or twice, but every time. Cannot beat a bit of enterprise eh? I don't think anyone begrudged Tommy his beer money, but he could be a little overpowering.

Anth Nicholson
North Shields, Tyneside

After the match I along with thousands of other Geordies started to make my way out of the ground which isn't exactly pleasant due to the terrible design of this typical old Yorkshire ground. I was approaching the first exit which is a terrible bottle neck situation at the best of times as you then have to turn left into a very long thin lane, which has two very high walls on either side of it. As I tried to turn into the lane I found myself being squashed as the crowd in front had come to a standstill whilst the ones behind unaware of the situation kept on pushing, as I now started to fear for my life as I no longer had control over my body as my feet weren't touching the ground and my hands were stuck down by my side. The main reason for this unnecessary situation was that two unbelievably thick coppers on horseback were at the top of the lane keeping us all back, as around 7,000 travelling fans attempted to leave the ground in a sensible manner. Eventually after non-stop abuse and the crowd pushing forward the horses were forced to move and miraculously as far as I'm aware nobody was seriously hurt.

Mark Risi
Benton, Newcastle

This was a popular trip as it was a new ground for most and our end had a roof (unlike the St James' Park terraces which had been roofless for four years since the famous Leazes End had been needlessly bulldozed), which meant that our every song would be heard by all. Before the match I had been handed a leaflet which read 'Chelsea Must Die, On the Pitch at 3.30' referring to the upcoming visit of Chelsea to St James' Park in two weeks time. As the match got underway the chants rang around the ground *"On The Pitch At Half Past Three, On The Pitch*

At Half Past Three." Yorkshire Police who had been stretched all afternoon panicked and almost immediately formed a human barrier the full length of our end behind the goal. The chants got louder which quite amused us all as it now became a 'wind-up' which resulted in many at the front having obscured views which wasn't such a bad thing as the match ended boringly 0-0.

Mick Edmondson
Walker, Newcastle

Two fans fined for assault on police

Rotherham magistrates have fined two Newcastle United supporters £300 each for assaulting two police officers before the trouble-torn match at Millmoor. The magistrates were told that the two best friends were fighting each other on the terraces. When two police officers moved in to break up the fight, the fans then turned on the officers knocking one to the ground and then began kicking the officer before attacking the second officer. Both accused men were unable to be interviewed until Sunday because they were so drunk. One of the accused could be sent to prison as he is in breach of a suspended sentence. Another 40 fans have been bailed to appear before the town's magistrates later this month for offences committed before, during and after the game. More than 6,000 Newcastle fans travelled to the match to support their team. Rotherham United secretary Jim Bennison said the Newcastle fans caused a substantial amount of damage in the stadium. Seats were ripped out, wall panels kicked in and bricks thrown through shop windows at the supporters shop. "Not all the visitors behaved badly but some were a disgrace. "This sort of behaviour only ruins the image of Newcastle United."

Just the ticket for fans

Three Newcastle supporters proved not all soccer fans are as black as they are painted. Alan Dormer Consett travelled to the Magpies away match at Rotherham with two of his workmates. But when they arrived at Millmoor they were told that the stand they wanted to enter was already full, as most of the 6,000 Newcastle fans who had made the away trip had already arrived. "We were just looking for another entrance when Rotherham's chief executive, John Adams, came over and offered us three tickets," said Alan. "He took us through the directors entrance and showed us to our seats." Even though they didn't have enough money to pay between them to pay Mr. Adams, he said they could just send the money on to him later. "We were all very surprised and highly delighted by the treatment we received," said Alan a dedicated Newcastle follower who never misses a home match and travels to many away games. Alan and his friends Kevin Steele both Gateshead and Paul Elliott from Jarrow have duly returned the £7.20 that they owed Mr. Adams. "This is the nicer side of football," said Mr. Adams. "I never expected to see that money again. Police arrested 42 Newcastle fans at the match.

v OLDHAM ATHLETIC
ST JAMES' PARK
ATT; 18,531

SAT 20TH MARCH 1982
SECOND DIVISION
WON 2-0

Terraces... I miss them so much. The good old days when you could stand wherever you wanted. You could pick just about any turnstile, then pay a pittance to stand wherever you fancied. If you weren't bothered about actually watching the match and liked a sing song, being pushed about, pissed on, elbowed, and educated in Geordie life then the 'Gallowgate End Scoreboard' terracing or the 'Gallowgate End Corner' terracing depending on age, is where you needed to be. You could learn swear words and crack that even Chubby Brown wouldn't have heard! If you wanted to see the match in slightly more civil surroundings then you could stand on the Gallowgate West Terrace, or if you were feeling flush you could join the raincoats and flasks in the Centre Paddock. The 'A' Wing Paddock was where you could go and read a book - as we called it the Library, where there wasn't any singing unless it was a big match. The 'E' Wing and North Benches and Leazes End were areas for the thugs and more vocal fans, enabling them to be as close as possible to the away fans. The seats in the stands were for the older generation and folk with plenty wedge. Ten minutes before full time out would come the Coppers who would walk around the perimeter of the pitch, the crowd would hum *"Der Du Der Du, Der Du Der Du, Derudle Du Derudle Du."* Then chants of *"F Troop F Troop."* They would then stand and face the crowd for the remaining ten minutes, which would automatically crank the noise levels up. "United, United, United." How I miss the Terraces.

Mick Edmondson
Walker, Newcastle

v CHELSEA
ST JAMES' PARK
ATT; 26,994

SAT 27TH MARCH 1982
SECOND DIVISION
WON 1-0

Leaflet urges trouble at Chelsea match

Leaflets urging Newcastle United supporters to seek a confrontation with Chelsea's fans before Saturday's key Second Division match at St James' Park are being circulated in city centre pubs. The typewritten leaflets, which give meeting points and plans of campaign, first began circulating at Rotherham nine days ago when over 6,000 United fans travelled to support their team. And the official Newcastle United supporters club, whose headquarters are at 'The Magpie' overlooking St James' Park, have received threatening calls from supposed Chelsea fans warning of attacks on Saturday. Extra police will be on duty because of the additional risk of trouble and will escort the Chelsea fans to and from the station. The letters which urge United fans to go after the Chelsea fans are thought to be in retaliation to Newcastle supporter's clubs coaches being bombarded with bricks earlier in the season, resulting in three fans in hospital and £6,000 of damage.

This fixture attracted the weekend's third largest crowd in England. More than there was at Highbury to watch Arsenal v League Champions and European Champions elect Aston Villa! More than there was at West Ham who entertained recent European champions Nottingham Forest! Not bad for a Second Division match. Where were we when we were shit eh? Our recent good form and the fact that every hooligan in Newcastle wanted to get at the 800 Chelsea fans had a lot to do with the large attendance. It was pay back time for the Chelsea thugs who had attacked and smashed two coaches carrying normal Newcastle fans in London earlier in the season. The rumour was that there was to be a mass pitch invasion at 3.30pm so with this in mind the police were out in force around the perimeter of the pitch. Geordies wound the police up singing: *"Remember Nottingham Forest, "Remember Nottingham Forest."* (Reminding them of a mass pitch invasion in 1974 when Newcastle fans invaded the pitch, before attacking the Forest fans resulting in the referee taking the teams off the pitch). Bang on 3.30pm there were numerous crowd surges at the packed Gallowgate End which resulted in some arrests as police and fans fought. Only one nutter managed to get onto the pitch but was rugby tackled before he had a chance to reach the half-way line. The atmosphere was very hostile and the songs quite passionate and straight to the point: *"Burn Like The Hammers, You're Gonna Burn Like The Hammers."* And *"We'll See You All Outside, We'll See You All Outside,"* and *Can You Run, Can You Run."* Plus the all-time classic: *"You're Gonna Get Your Fucking Heads Kicked In."* After the match thousands went on the rampage through town towards Manors railway station but the Chelsea fans were kept in the ground for well over an hour maybe two, even though Newspaper reports said otherwise. If it hadn't of been for the police and their dogs and horses and Chelsea bottling it, then we could have been talking about Britain's worst ever football violence. The hatred and violent atmosphere that day had to be witnessed to be believed. A total of 65 fans were eventually arrested and all but one were Newcastle fans. There were 3 police cars stoned and damaged. On the pitch this was our seventh consecutive home league victory which put us up to sixth place.

Mick Edmondson
Walker, Newcastle

132

An FA decision back in December had made all Chelsea away matches all-ticket affairs, due to the behaviour of their fans. As a compensation gesture Chelsea had to pay all home clubs £1,000 to offset losses and expenses. Chelsea fans were also banned from travelling, but this ban was lifted a couple of weeks earlier after pressure from Newcastle and Chelsea as well as others. Chelsea had lost 6 of their last 7 games and had fallen down the table. Whilst living in exile in Leeds I returned to Newcastle for the weekend which included taking in the home match against Chelsea. About half a dozen of us were standing in the east corner of the Gallowgate in a relatively sparse crowd. Behind were a similar bunch of lads having a laugh, half watching the game, one of whom decided to have a piss on the terrace. Not wishing to have a shower we kept a close eye on where he was splashing. The nearest of our group, Little Dave, was obviously concerned about getting soaked, and when the lad shouted "this ones looking at my cock," Dave didn't need any further excuse to lamp him. All hell broke loose as a dozen kids got stuck in to each other, then stepped back; words were exchanged then it all started again with more kicking and punching. As we broke up at the end of the second round having given as good as we got, I was quite happy that I remained unmarked by the melee. More insults thrown and up it went again, round three. By this time the Police had began to take notice and made their way towards us. Not paying attention to the fight and taking more notice of the approaching coppers' I felt bang, bang two punches smack in the face. We all separated and scarpered. By the time we got to the old Post Office pub I had two shiners. There was no way I was going back to my Mam's, instead I thought it would be better that I gave Sunday dinner a miss, clean washing etc and return to Leeds early. One of the lads Marty drove to my parent's house whilst I hid in the back of the car, "I have come for Chris's bags he is in town with a girl and is heading straight back to Leeds tonight." He got my bag and we left for a night on the town. Back in Leeds with two cracking black eyes my face began to ache. After a visit to the doctors I was sent to the hospital for surgery as one of the punches had broken the roots of my two front teeth. Months of agony and dental appointments later I came to the conclusion, that if any one questions your mate's sexuality let him sort it out and only fight with the away supporters.

Chris Emmerson
Walker, Newcastle

Magpie fan threw stone

An elated Newcastle United fan was caught up in the mass hysteria after the game against Chelsea. He joined in throwing stones outside St James' Park after the match which attracted the biggest gate of the season. James Burns (17) admitted threatening behaviour likely to provoke a breach of the peace. He was fined £200 with £15 costs. Mr. Paul Grieveson prosecuting said more than 300 Newcastle supporters were outside the ground after the match. Mr. Carr defending said the police were trying to keep the Newcastle and Chelsea fans apart and Burns had got caught up with a group throwing stones. He said Burns had thrown the stone at the Chelsea fans and not the policeman and as far as he was aware had not hit anyone. "It was mass hysteria and it seems he wanted to be one of the lads." Mr. Carr said. He said Burns father had now banned him from going to matches and he'd taken up jogging instead.

Rival gangs clash

Five youths were taken to hospital after trouble flared on a train carrying football fans. They were taken to Tynemouth Infirmary after the north bound train was stopped for half an hour at Cramlington, Northumberland. Rival gangs from Cramlington and Widdrington clashed on the return journey from the Newcastle match. Two youths were arrested in connection with the incident on the train. All the supporters involved were Newcastle United fans.

Motorway Madness ...

Five policemen were hurt as 60 arrests were made as thousands of soccer fans went on the rampage yesterday. But for once the notorious Chelsea supporters were the innocent party - the troublemakers were the Geordies. They were after a blood bath, but Northumbria's crafty coppers saved the day. Unfortunately five officers were injured doing so. The police successfully kept rival fans apart - and last night the arrest score line read Newcastle 59 Chelsea 1. There was trouble before, during and after the match which Newcastle won 1-0 at their St James' Park ground. The final damage toll was more than 30 broken windows and several badly damaged cars. The match attendance was 26,994 the biggest of the season at Newcastle. At the final whistle Newcastle supporters were herded out of the ground while police held the 800 Chelsea crowd behind. The police intended the local lads to disperse before they escorted the visiting fans to Manors station. But the Geordies had a different idea. Thousands of them teemed through the city centre chanting "We hate Cockney's" whilst smashing shop and pub windows. They ran towards Manors station but the police blocked their path, so they leapt like lemmings over the wall of the central motorway, falling 18 feet to the motorway below. Several rolled directly in front of fast lane traffic and cars had to swerve and brake to avoid hitting them. Then they launched a missile attack of bricks and stones at the police standing outside Manors on the other side of the motorway. Chelsea FC Steward Brian Greig said "They're worse than animals." "They were the same last year, pelting us with bricks and bottles in the car park next to the station." People slander Chelsea, but Newcastle aren't any better." When the horde realised Chelsea supporters weren't at Manors, they changed course for the Newcastle Central Station, smashing more windows on the way. In fact Chelsea fans were still under police guard at St James' Park. More than 30 minutes later they were walked under heavy escort to Manors which was by now deserted and sent home on waiting trains. Chief Insp. Dennis England said; "The trouble was caused wholly by Newcastle supporters, Chelsea were very well conducted. A lot of officers, who seldom get a pat on the back, did a very good days work." "They prevented what could have been an even more calamitous situation," he added. One of the injured policeman was last night detained in Newcastle's RVI with chest injuries.

£2400 penalty for Lions den fans

Ten football fans had to pay a total of £2,400 in fines and costs for offences at St James' Park. But Newcastle court was told that the ground is 'like a lion's den' where fans are arrested for opening their mouths. Stephen Turnbull of Durham was arrested after trying to prevent police from arresting his mate, Stephen Brown. The police had two leaflets, one saying there would be a pitch invasion at 3.30pm and one saying Chelsea must die - which they took seriously. Brown was heard shouting, "Invade the pitch, Chelsea fans must die....I'm going to kill a cockney" and was arrested Brown accepted that he shouted "Chelsea Bastards," with other Newcastle supporters. But he had no knowledge of these two leaflets the police had. But Mr. Swinburne for Turnbull said, "My advice to clients charged with offences at St James' Park is not to go and see Newcastle United because it's like walking into a lion's den on a Saturday afternoon.

Hooligans pay penalty

Fines ranging from £50 to £300 were handed out by magistrates as they started dealing with the people arrested for various crimes committed including possession of weapons, assault on police, conduct likely to cause a breach of the peace and drunk and disorderly. Mr. Derek Brown prosecuting said the soccer disturbances were the worst in memory. He said a leaflet had been distributed and circulated at a previous match. It called for a mass pitch invasion at 3.30pm. He quoted from the document which he said was circulating at the Rotherham v Newcastle match. The leaflet read: Chelsea must die. O.K. It must happen. There will be a pitch invasion at 3.30pm. This is not a joke. Bring your petrol bombs. Kill them. Those accused included Newcastle hooligans who had infiltrated the Chelsea police escort as it made its way to the match. They were spotted in the Leazes End amongst the Chelsea fans making obscene gestures whilst shouting obscenities.

135

Soccer fan is cleared

Soccer fan Gary Short was cleared yesterday of taking part in a riot after a Newcastle match. Short was caught up in a mob of 200 supporters pelting police with missiles. He was arrested after a police baton charge for throwing a piece of concrete. The Leazes Terrace area outside the ground had been "the scene of some of the worst fighting and rioting seen in Newcastle that day. Short was found not guilty on grounds of mistaken identity.

Ugly Rituals,
Northumbria police 5, injured,
So-called fans arrested 63

That ugly result from Saturday's battle of St James' Park cannot help overshadowing Newcastle United's 1-0 victory over Chelsea - we fear. Throw in the wreckage of a train carriage, the smashing of dozens of city centre windows, the bashing up of a police car and we have the nearly complete picture of the rituals that show so regularly the ugly face of enthusiasm supposed to be connected with soccer. The final touches have to be made by the doctors who take care of the policemen and the 'fans' injured, and by the magistrates dealing with the participants guilty of a variety of nasty offences. In the light of the Newcastle troublemakers for a record-setting punch up with the Londoners, the bloodshed and wreckage could have been a lot worse. Instead the well prepared policemen - who must be able to think of far better ways of spending their Saturday afternoons - did a good job of protecting the Chelsea visitors from their 'Geordie hosts' while bearing the brunt of the latter's fighting spirit.

Hoodlum Jailed

A Newcastle soccer hoodlum was jailed for six months at the City Crown Court for his part in the disturbances at the Chelsea match. Nixon claimed that his offence was a result of impulse and drink. Nixon from Newburn, Newcastle was seen standing up in his seat in the East Stand shouting: "Chelsea supporters must die." A policeman had a half eaten meat pie thrown at him as Nixon yelled: "Take that." The pie hit the officer.

v CRYSTAL PALACE
ST JAMES' PARK
ATT; 22,151

WED 31ST MARCH 1982
SECOND DIVISION
DREW 0-0

Every Newcastle supporter has their "worst ever top 10" players. Some of the older generation could probably muster a legitimate "top 100". One name sure to feature amongst many of a certain vintage would be Peter Cartwright. Signed from North Shields, this man was charged with supplying the bullets for the likes of Peter Withe, Mick Harford and, erm, Billy Bloody Rafferty. Purely by coincidence, during one of the thankfully few seasons he spent with us, we managed to win the un-converted "lowest scorers in the entire football league" award. By the age of eleven I had progressed to going to the games without me fatha.' I wasn't yet brave enough to stand in the Scoreboard so me and my mates used to stand in the Gallowgate west section adjacent. In this particular match Cartwright was sent clear between the full back and centre half, looks up, sees someone in the middle, slices his cross straight into my unsuspecting face, much to the delight of my mates and people standing around me. The next home game we're standing in the same spot. Cartwright's played in again, as he's shaping to cross, still bitter from my previous humiliation, I comment loudly, "he's shit, him" before fending off another sliced cross destined for my face. The useless twat! To this day I maintain I was on the end of more Peter Cartwright crosses than any of the centre forwards unlucky enough to play with him. We missed this great opportunity to go third.

Graham
Rowland's Gill, Tyneside

Kevin Carr created history by becoming the first Newcastle United goalkeeper to keep 5 clean sheets in a row in the league! "I would have preferred if we'd won 2-1" he said afterwards. This draw just about ended any realistic chance we had of gaining promotion and everybody in the ground realised this. The crowd and the players knew that come August, we would be playing Second Division football for the 5th consecutive season.

Mick Edmondson
Walker, Newcastle

Soccer fans disrupt Metro

Soccer hooligans caused havoc for Gateshead metro passengers last night. Fans swarmed up escalators in a race to reach the top of Gateshead station then pressed the emergency stop button. Furious metro controllers made loudspeaker announcements telling passengers "football yobbos caused the trouble." The trouble flared after Newcastle's match with Crystal Palace.

v CHARLTON ATHLETIC   **SAT 3RD APRIL 1982**
THE VALLEY   **SECOND DIVISION**
ATT; 6,357   **WON 1-0**

It was my engagement party on the Saturday night at the Honeysuckle pub on Coatsworth Road, Gateshead, but unfortunately I had gone down to London to watch the Toon so missed it not arriving home until the Sunday afternoon. The Falkland's war which had started the day before with the Argentine invasion and occupation of the Falkland Islands and South Georgia wasn't the only war that weekend!! The Falklands war lasted 74 days with the sad loss of 255 Brits. The war when I got home started and finished within an hour. The end of a two year romance and as a result of going AWOL, the wedding was cancelled. Never mind it mustn't have been meant to be. We did the double over 'the Addicks' as Chris Waddle got the all important goal while at the other end our 23 year old keeper

Kevin Carr set a club record as he kept his sixth consecutive clean sheet in the league.

This was my first away game in London and Chris Waddle's goal put us to the heady heights of fourth, it looked like we were hitting promotion form at the right time. I even made myself a little chart titled 'Nine games to go can we do it?' With a table showing our next nine opponents with space for score, points and league position - what a saddo eh? I filled it in for the next three games then gave up as our season imploded.

Chris Ramshaw
West Denton, Newcastle

v WREXHAM	**TUES 6TH APRIL 1982**
RACECOURSE GROUND	**SECOND DIVISION**
ATT; 4,517	**LOST 2-4**

I travelled down with the lads arriving in North Wales nice and early at 11am. As our coach trawled the streets of Wrexham searching for a bar we were stopped by a police car. They boarded the bus and informed us that we had to follow them to the ground where we would all be put straight onto the away terrace. The copper hadn't finished his sentence when the emergency exit back door was opened and loads of us jumped ship and legged it. We ended up split up in dribs and drabs but at least we were able to enjoy a pre-match drink. This defeat put a huge dent in our late promotion push. Meanwhile back on Tyneside, Newcastle United announced that they had already sold 10% of all available season tickets for the 1982/83 season.

Deka
Gateshead, Tyneside

v LEICESTER CITY	**SAT 10TH APRIL 1982**
ST JAMES' PARK	**SECOND DIVISION**
ATT; 25,777	**DREW 0-0**

Easter Saturday and we were 5th in the league only a point off a promotion place and with 8 games remaining and now with 24 points to play for, due to the new three points for a win ruling, we were somehow still in with a chance. This was a match we had to win if we still had any hopes of promotion. Along with QPR, Jock Wallace's Leicester were promotion favourites but were down in the dumps after losing a week earlier to Spurs in the FA Cup Semi-Final at Villa Park. We got off to a great start when just before half-time Leicester went down to ten men when Kevin MacDonald was sent off. We would never have a better chance. *"All We Are Singing, Is Give Us A Goal, All We Are Singing, Is Give Us A Goal."* As usual we blew it.

Mick Edmondson
Walker, Newcastle

Supporters on the march

On a recent Saturday enjoying an afternoons shopping with my wife and family in the centre of Newcastle at about 2.45pm I was surprised to see so many extra police lining Blackett Street with police dogs. Crowds began to line the pavements and the traffic came to a standstill and then the precession came into sight: Approximately 200 so called football supporters from Leicester being police escorted by patrol cars and mounted police to the football ground. The whole spectacle was like something from the past when prisoners were led through the streets on their way to the gallows and having to walk the gauntlet, ducking objects thrown from the jeering crowds. This is a waste of taxpayer's money especially when the whole scenario is repeated at 5pm. Either ban away fans or move the ground to the outskirts of the city so that Newcastle can become a safer city for shoppers.

v SHEFFIELD WEDNESDAY
HILLSBOROUGH
ATT; 29,917

MON 12TH APRIL 1982
SECOND DIVISION
LOST 1-2

Always a huge following travelled down to Sheff Wed they must have hated the annual mass Geordie invasion, especially on a Bank Holiday Monday. The Football Special resembled cattle trucks and herded us to exotic places like Carlisle, Rotherham and the now disused Wadsley Bridge, Sheffield. Once off the 'Special' and on foot you felt as safe as houses being part of the largest travelling army of football supporters anywhere, as you looked up the hill at the amazing sight of coach after coach, too many to count. There were so many characters in the crowd; many couldn't care less, they were out for the day with their mates for a good drink and to support the Toon. As usual we were packed onto the Leppings Lane terrace where there was a flag pole which flew a Sheffield related flag. The roars went up as a Geordie climbed up to reach the ropes and duly pulled the flag down into the Newcastle End. Then within seconds the rope was hoisted back up with a pair of dirty shitty undercrackers attached, which was greeted with mass hysterical laughter, from the thousands down below. After a while the process was repeated and the kegs replaced by a Newcastle scarf to mass cheers. As usual we had a great day, apart from the match and result.

Mick Edmondson
Walker, Newcastle

v LUTON TOWN	**SAT 17TH APRIL 1982**
KENILWORTH ROAD	**SECOND DIVISION**
ATT; 13,041	**LOST 2-3**

It was the now typical, end of season, sunny day, with a good hard-core following, travelling a long way to watch a match which meant nothing - as far as our promotion was concerned, although our hosts were up there challenging. However early in the second-half we scored a second to go 2-0 up, which added to our first half strike. We were as happy as pigs in shit, well apart from the fact that missiles were being thrown by the Cockney tosspots (It's near enough London), who were situated in the paddock to our left. An object just missed my head, instead hitting the lad standing in front, before landing at my feet. I reached down to pick it up only to find that it was greasy, before realising it was half a tin of Germolene and as a result my fingers stunk all the way back to Newcastle on the coach. Obviously it goes without saying that Luton went on to win scoring three goals in the second-half. With 8 minutes remaining we were well on our way to victory until Luton scored 2 penalties. More bad news for the Newcastle players when they got back to the changing room to find that £600 had been stolen from various players' trouser pockets. Then our assistant manager Tommy Cavanagh was informed that after his daughter's 24th birthday celebrations, that 3 of his family had been injured in a head on smash. In the mysterious death crash in Northumberland, in which another man had died, the two Ford Escorts were both written off in the head on collision. Not a very good day at the office, but put things into perspective.

Mick Edmondson
Walker, Newcastle

Mills disciplined

Mills takes the rap for punch-up with Donaghy

Newcastle striker David Mills, involved in a post match punch-up with Luton defender Mal Donaghy will be disciplined by the club. Mills who had earlier been booked was left nursing a cut on the chin after his clash with Donaghy after the two players exchanged punches in the corridor outside the players changing room.

Luton repays United stars

Luton Town will compensate Newcastle players and officials, who lost cash and valuables to a dressing room thief. Key-holders at Luton Town's Kenilworth Road ground were being quizzed by detectives today after Saturday's theft from the Magpies. The haul from United has now been put at £720. This includes a £200 quartz watch belonging to Mick Martin. Other robbed players were John Trewick, Peter Haddock, David Barton, Kevin Carr, David Mills, Wesley Saunders, John Brownlie and Imre Varadi. Youngster John Carver and manager Arthur Cox and assistant manager Tommy Cavanagh were also victims of the dressing room raid. Detectives at Luton said today the system for ensuring the dressing room door is locked is usually made on the basis of "last one out locks the door." It is understood the door was open when David Barton returned to the dressing room early - and found his discarded wallet on the floor. Police say he did not immediately realise the significance of the dropped wallet and it was not until later that the theft was discovered. The team helped detectives with their enquiries for two hours after the game.

v GRIMSBY TOWN
ST JAMES PARK
ATT; 14,065

SAT 24TH APRIL 1982
SECOND DIVISION
LOST 0-1

Pre-match drinks at the Portland, Burton House, George & the Dragon, the Adelaide and the 'Canny Lad' before enduring 90 minutes of shite as we lose at home to the mighty Grimsby Town, who were second bottom of the league. Happy Days? We'd only taken a single point from the last 15. Maybe not.

Dennis Prior
Byker, Newcastle

v BLACKBURN ROVERS
EWOOD PARK
ATT; 5,207

SAT 1ST MAY 1982
SECOND DIVISION
LOST 1-4

The lengths some fans will go to when following Newcastle United away is at times unbelievable, totally crazy and on the rare occasion out of order. I overheard two kids who had pinched a car to get down and then as they had no money had robbed a programme seller to get into the match and were going to nick another car to get back home, mental.

Brian
Low Fell, Tyneside

Even a decent following from Newcastle considering it was an end of season meaningless Second Division mid-table clash, couldn't help Rovers get a half decent crowd. They've always had appalling support right throughout history which made the performance and hammering all the harder to take for the loyal fans from Tyneside. This was a low point. Half way through the first half there was a bit of entertainment behind the goal where the home support were congregated, as a small squad of Newcastle hooligans who'd infiltrated the terraces made themselves known. Only a couple of punches were thrown if any as the sparse Blackburn crowd quickly got out of the way, escaping to either side as the Newcastle lads were escorted around the pitch. The violence wasn't just confined to the terraces as United's John Brownlie was sent off for striking an opponent. Local lad Derek Bell made his debut and was our top player. Paul Ferris came on as a sub to become the youngest ever player to play in the football league for Newcastle United, aged 16 years and 294 days. The match itself was shite.

Mick Edmondson
Walker, Newcastle

After the game we headed straight for Blackpool to drown our sorrows. In the early hours we travelled up the M6 and eventually along the A69 to Haydon Bridge, where our van ended up in a Farmer's field upside down! Somehow the driver (who was sober) managed to fall asleep at the wheel. Some of the lads were also asleep as the van rolled over. Our first reaction was to look for the door and crawl out. Luckily we all escaped with minor injuries, I had a sprained ankle. It was 6am and we ended up in a nearby farmhouse whose occupants had heard the crash. They were brilliant and we phoned the AA and all had tea and toast. At 10am we got the first bus to Newcastle all knackered but all lucky to be alive.

Piper
Felling, Tyneside

v QUEENS PARK RANGERS
ST JAMES' PARK
ATT; 10,748

WED 5TH MAY 1982
SECOND DIVISION
LOST 0-4

One of the matches that sticks in my mind is this humiliating end of season red hot summer Wednesday night, when we were an absolute disgrace as FA Cup finalists QPR hammered us 4-0 in front of the long suffering but loyal hardcore. I was amongst the few thousand at the Gallowgate End who out of frustration and boredom decided to sit down on the terraces in some kind of silent protest. Things were bad.

Bob
Ashington, Northumberland

We reached the depths in this game as a Glenn Roeder inspired QPR hammered us, completed the double over us and to rub it in they even had to wear our change strip due to a colour clash. QPR would return three months later but by then we would be led by one Joseph Kevin Keegan.

Chris Ramshaw
West Denton, Newcastle

It has often been said over the years that: "If you put 11 Monkeys in Black-and-White shirts that 20,000 would turn up at St James' Park to watch Newcastle play!" Well we now know that this isn't the case. More like 10,748 would turn up. Yet as we struggled and headed towards possible oblivion the club announced that the response to their deal for 1982-83 season tickets had been magnificent with over two-thirds of current season ticket holders renewing their tickets before the 17th of April expiry date. The offer - only a price freeze.

Mick Edmondson
Walker, Newcastle

v WREXHAM
ST JAMES' PARK
ATT; 9,419

SAT 8TH MAY 1982
SECOND DIVISION
WON 4-2

Since getting thrashed-coincidently by the same score - only a month earlier, we had fallen from fourth to eleventh place after six defeats and a draw in seven games. So not surprisingly our lowest crowd of the season, nearly half of our average attendance turned up for our final home game of yet another disappointing season against the already relegated team from North Wales. The attendance wasn't boosted that much by the handful of Welshman, thirty six to be precise but my memory of this game wasn't one of the goals as they were insignificant but of the 36 Wrexham fans doing the Conga non-stop for ages in their segregated paddock.

Bob
Ashington, Northumberland

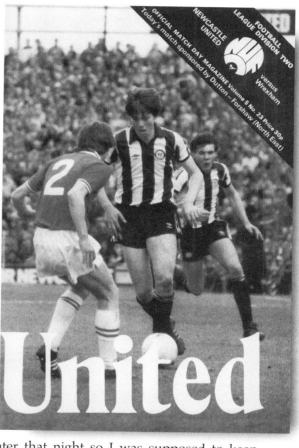

A lovely hot day on the Hippy Green (Old Eldon Square) as me and my mate spent the afternoon drinking Asti and playing football. It was my girlfriend's 18th birthday party at Palmersville, Forest Hall later that night so I was supposed to keep myself half sensible. We decided not to go into the match as we were too pissed so instead went around the back of the Leazes End where we saw student types carrying fences into the ground so we picked up a fence and followed them in, ending up in the Wrexham end. I was wearing a union jack t-shirt under my burgundy Cardy.' The Welsh were worried as there were only about 20 of them and we were singing Newcastle songs, until the stewards came in and moved us into the E-wing paddock, before the coppers then threw me out for singing (I think). I must have decided to wait for my mate outside (no mobile phones) and ended up falling asleep on a wall, missing my Girlfriends party in the process. Or should I say ex-girlfriend as she soon chucked me.

Arn
Benton, Newcastle

v CRYSTAL PALACE
SELHURST PARK
ATT; 8,453

SAT 15TH MAY 1982
SECOND DIVISION
WON 2-1

It was a red hot day as our supporters club coach crawled through South London on the final day of the 1981-82 season, as I sneaked another mouthful of beer from my secret supply. Although kick-off was still over two hours away the back seat 'choir' were in full voice as they rattled through all the old classics from 'Wyn the leap' to 'Terry Hibbitt on the wing.' Little did we know history was in the making, as somebody had the cheek to change the classic Alan Gowling song, replacing the gang-ling strikers name with none other than Mick Martin's, well sort of. Everybody on the coach burst out laughing as the song went from strength to strength, *"La la la la, la la la la, Hey Hey Zico Martin"* to the tune of the Rock Band 'Steam's' top ten hit 'Na Na Hey Hey Kiss Him Goodbye.' Once inside the ground the song soon caught on and Mick Martin couldn't believe his ears, as he kicked in' just before kick-off, probably a moment beyond his wildest dreams especially as he thought it was for real, not realising we were taking the piss. From that afternoon onwards he was called 'Zico' unfortunately he didn't play anything like him, but then who did in those days? Well the real Zico I suppose. A defender, David 'Dick' Barton played his last game after appearing 110 times scoring 6 goals. He would later join Darlington in July 1983 on a free transfer. Also saying farewell was fellow defender Bruce Halliday who signed for Bury after 38 appearances and 1 goal. Two defenders who simply were never good enough.

Mick Edmondson
Walker, Newcastle

We'd just left school and this was the game when we used the Scout Camp in Sheffield as our base for getting to and from the match and as our alibi so that our parents believed that we were tying knots and camping all weekend in the safety of a Forest. The weekend started with one of our earliest hitch hiking experiences as we were picked up from Birtley services on the Friday morning. The driver was kind enough to offer to put our rucksacks in the back of his van, but we were shocked when he opened the door to come face to face with about 15 empty coffins! Anyway off we went the driver obviously quite amused with our reaction, now looking after us in the front cab, thankfully. Up at 5am Saturday morning and after a short walk from our base alongside the M1 we were picked up almost immediately on the hard shoulder arriving on the outskirts of London at 9am. The match although meaningless sprung into life in the last couple of minutes when an equalising David Mills penalty was quickly followed by a Chris Waddle header to snatch a last gasp win which consolidated our final position in the top half of the table. Central defenders Dick Barton and Bruce Halliday played their final games before leaving for the mighty Darlington and Bury respectively. On the open terraces one of the regular away travellers was taken away by police, sporting a plastic set of tits, whilst some Geordies wearing NCB donkey jackets kicked off to our left in the Palace paddocks. Our return journey started with a lift from some Newcastle lads in a mini bus which stopped off in Hemel Hempstead for a drink before eventually everybody decided to jump into a lake fully clothed before getting back on the bus and heading north. I eventually got back home on the Sunday only to find out that my friend Vince had been knocked down on the coast road and ended up in hospital unconscious, with my home telephone number in his pocket, which I had given him at the previous Monday nights speedway meeting. The police thinking that it was me had rang my Mam and Dad who had to rush to the hospital only to be relieved that it wasn't me, especially after getting in touch with the Scout camp and finding out I wasn't there! As you can imagine, I was not a popular lad for a while.

Davey
Walker, Newcastle

v HARTLEPOOL UNITED   TUES 18TH MAY 1982
VICTORIA PARK   FRIENDLY
ATT; 1,037   WON 6-2

Left school and made my way up to the town and stood alone on the A167 slip road, trying to hitch a lift. After about 15 minutes a bloke picked me up and took me down the A1 dropping me off at Bowburn. I then eventually managed to get a lift all the way to Hartlepool, even getting dropped off at the ground and I still had an hour to kill before kick-off. Once inside I just asked about on the terraces and was lucky enough to eventually manage to scrounge a lift back to the toon. The game was arranged to raise funds for our north east cash-strapped neighbours - Hartlepool. (Not that we were particularly rolling in it ourselves). We used the game to give a trial to Gateshead defender Peter Harrison and to also put the likes of Shoulder, Pugh, Davies and Walker in the shop window.

Dave Drape
Walker, Newcastle

1981-82 Season Summary

We started badly spending the start of the season at rock bottom before our new hero Imre Varadi (Ray to friends) found his scoring touch, which helped us into the top half of the table before the horrendous winter which saw temperatures plummet and football become more or less non-existent. We didn't play a single league match between December 5th and January 16th as the very cold weather took hold. Also featuring on the score sheet and helping with our revival was Alan Brown on a loan from Sunderland. Unfortunately after his 8 week loan period was hit by the Siberian conditions he only managed 5 starts scoring an impressive 3 goals. We were sure to buy him as he was a great partner for Varadi, but we controversially sent him back to 'Beirut on Wear' claiming he had hamstring and back injury problems, but no mention that we were skint and couldn't afford him. Once the weather improved and we got playing again we signed another player on an extended loan David Mills who joined us from West Brom, who had made him Britain's most expensive player when they signed him from Middlesbrough for £516,720 only 3 years earlier. He scored 4 goals in 23 games as an attacking midfielder and helped us into fourth position with 9 games to play. Unfortunately we just collapsed failing to win any of our next 7 matches conceding 18 goals, picking up a solitary point from a possible 21, as we crashed to 11th place! Because of the introduction of 3 points for a win we actually finished with 62 points our largest total in our history. The cups as usual brought no joy as we yet again lost to poor sides. Our top performers were also our 3 ever present players Carr, Varadi and Waddle. Kevin Carr actually won Granada TV's 'Save of the Season' and received an oil painting of himself! The season also saw the end of 'The Reserves' playing on a Saturday afternoon. Due to a total lack of funds David Mills was as expected reluctantly sent back to the Midlands by Cox, who was fighting a losing battle, thanks to our board. Even so, he had still made some bad decisions in the transfer market when given a few quid here and there. We needed a miracle and quick. When John Brownlie left for Middlesbrough for £30,000 in July 1982 it was the first time in our entire history that we had been devoid of any Scottish players and would stay this way until George Reilly signed in 1985. Alan Shoulder who only actually started 3 league games as his Newcastle career came to an end, did get 20 goals for the reserves when he wasn't appearing as a sub for the first team.

Typical representative team for the season:
Kevin Carr, John Brownlie, Ian Davies/Wesley Saunders, David Barton/Steve Carney, Peter Haddock/Bruce Halliday, John Trewick, David Mills, Mick Martin, Imre Varadi, Kenny Wharton, Chris Waddle.

Total Appearances: (League, FA Cup & League Cup) - 47 matches played
Carr, Varadi, Waddle (47), Trewick (45), Martin (44), Brownlie (43), Wharton (38), Haddock (33), Saunders (32), Carney (31), Mills (23), Barton (22), Cartwright (17), Davies, Halliday (15), Shoulder (13), Shinton (12), Brown, Todd, Walker (5), Bell, Ferris (2), Pugh (1).
*Includes all sub appearances.

Total Goals: (League, FA Cup & League Cup) - Total Scored 58.
Varadi 20, Waddle (8), Trewick (6), Wharton (5), Mills (4), Brownlie, Brown (3),
Barton, Davies, Shinton, Todd (2), Saunders (1), plus Opp Own goals (1).

Second Division Final Table 81-82						
Luton	42	25	13	4	86	46	88
Watford	42	23	11	8	76	42	80
Norwich City	42	22	5	15	64	50	71
Sheff Wed	42	20	10	12	55	51	70
QPR	42	21	6	15	65	43	69
Barnsley	42	19	10	13	59	41	67
Rotherham	42	20	7	15	66	54	67
Leicester	42	18	12	12	56	48	66
Newcastle	**42**	**18**	**8**	**16**	**52**	**50**	**62**
Blackburn	42	16	11	15	47	43	59
Oldham	42	15	14	13	50	51	59
Chelsea	42	15	12	15	60	60	57
Charlton	42	13	12	17	50	65	51
Cambridge	42	13	9	20	48	53	48
Crystal Palace	42	13	9	20	34	45	48
Derby	42	12	12	18	53	68	48
Grimsby	42	11	13	18	53	65	46
Shrewsbury	42	11	13	18	37	57	46
Bolton	42	13	7	22	39	61	46
Cardiff	42	12	8	22	45	61	44
Wrexham	42	11	11	20	40	56	44
Orient	42	10	9	23	36	61	39

NEWCASTLE UNITED MATCH DAY MAGAZINE Football League Division 2
V QUEENS PARK RANGERS Volume 6 No. 1
Match Day Sponsors
THE NEWCASTLE BREWERIES LIMITED

We've Got Kevin!

35p

1982-83 Season

Since the departure of McKeag and co, new Chairman Stan Seymour Junior and his board hadn't wasted any time with their plans to put Newcastle United back on the footballing map. In the summer much needed funds were raised when for the first time ever, St James' Park played host to a live music concert as the Rolling Stones came to town. One of the worlds biggest and most famous rock bands of all time, performed on a stage erected in the Leazes End goalmouth as fans packed onto the hallowed turf, terraces and stands. The gig which also featured 'The J.Geils Band' on June 23rd was a huge success as drunken arseholes from all over the UK descended on our patch. As a teenage Newcastle fan it was horrible but if it was going to help us get back into the First Division, you had to welcome it. But this was nowt compared to the forthcoming news which would take us from footballs wilderness to the national spotlight almost overnight. That summer we were a very average Second Division side, going nowhere fast, with no money, fans living on past glories and memories. The rest of the country and the footballing world took little if any notice of Newcastle United and our neighbours Sunderland were playing in the First Division. Aston Villa had just won the 1982 European Cup (Peter Withe our former striker scoring the only goal), the third English side in as many years to do so, as the trophy stayed in England for the fourth consecutive year. July saw very little transfer activity and by mid-August the local press were reporting that we were looking at Fourth Division Hull City's Les Mutrie. However we did have a few new faces, John Anderson a free transfer from Preston, Jeff Clarke a free transfer from Sunderland and John Craggs a free transfer from Middlesbrough - not exactly what we were hoping for. These players replaced John Brownlie who'd joined Middlesbrough for £30,000, Dick Barton and Bruce Halliday who'd both gone on season long loans to Darlington, Ian Davies on a free to Man City, Alan Shoulder on a free to Carlisle and Nigel Walker on a free to San Deigo (USA). Then a couple of days later on 19th August it happened. Newcastle United shocked the football world. Footballs first millionaire, the current England Captain, twice European footballer of the year and last season's top scorer in the First Division, had signed for Newcastle United! Yes Kevin Keegan had signed for us from Southampton for a mere £100,000, (Rafferty had cost £175,000!!). Dozens of top clubs were after him, but he only spoke to Man Utd and us! Transit van sales on Tyneside immediately went through the roof. The local press were still chasing Les Mutrie when Keegan landed at Newcastle airport. This transfer shocked football never mind Tyneside. 'Wor Kev' who'd recently been awarded the OBE would earn

£3,000 a week which was tied in with crowd increases a salary which might not sound fantastic in this day and age, but at the time it was several times the salary of then Prime Minister Maggie Thatcher. The transfer was made possible by the newly decentralised S&N, who were now known as Newcastle Breweries – A star is reborn. At a press conference at the Gosforth Park Hotel United's Russell Cushing (Mr. Miserable himself) announced to the world's media, "Were in heaven, we've got Kevin." Season ticket sales went bananas as fans queued round the clock and the clubs car park. Suddenly out of nowhere the good auld days had returned as we found ourselves plastered all over the papers, magazines and we were on every TV and radio station. We were now hot favourites for promotion, but we all knew deep down that we still needed more quality through the door; hopefully Keegan would attract the best bargains about, as we still weren't flush. A perfect example of this was that before we could sign Keegan the football league insisted that United had to first complete their hire purchase payments to West Brom for the services of John Trewick who cost £250,000 over 20 months ago. Meanwhile ground improvements included new dividing fences which would allow away fans to now be housed in the west section of the Leazes End, so that home fans could now fill the centre of the Leazes terrace. As for away matches they would never be the same for the travelling hordes from Tyneside as the majority of our away matches would now be all-ticket affairs. But who cared, we couldn't wait for the season to start. *"United Are Back, United Are Back, Hello, Hello."*

Season Ticket Prices (Juniors in brackets)
West Stand Centre Paddock £37.00 (£16.00),
Seating; East Stand Centre £65.00 (£25.00),
East Stand Wing seats £55.00 (£25.00) **West Stand Centre** £60.00 (£25.00)
West Stand 'A' & 'E' Wing seats £50.00 (£25.00)
East Stand Paddock seat £42.00 (£25.00).

v GREENOCK MORTON
CAPPIELOW PARK
ATT; 2,000

SAT 7TH AUGUST 1982
FRIENDLY
WON 3-1

In years gone by I always eagerly awaited the pre-season friendly announcements. Odd fixtures, bizarre games and one-off trips to footballing hot-spots such as Gayfield Park, Palmerston or Feethams. It was a complete change of scenery to the likes of Goodison, Old Trafford or Stamford Bridge. Usually it was back to ground-roots football. And Newcastle United were a big attraction in the late summer sun. Scotland was a favourite destination and the contest with Scottish Premier League side Greenock Morton was typical and just before the headlining news that saw England skipper Kevin Keegan arrive on Tyneside to such spectacular effect. The few hundred or so United fans in the 2,000 crowd had no idea what was to follow……Kevin Keegan-mania Mark I. No-one could have dreamed what was to unfold in a matter of days. I always wanted to see Cappielow and stand on the famous "Cowshed Terrace." For football anoraks, this is *real* football. It was what I envisaged; gritty, somewhat primal yet incredibly humorous - assuming you could understand the West of Scotland accent and footi-slang! Imre Varadi was everyone's favourite back then in the No. 9 shirt; fast, elusive and erratic. He scored United's second in a convincing victory - lashing the ball home from close-in. And new signing Jeff Clarke - even though he was an ex-Sunderland player - looked the part at centre-half. Even trialist Steve Doyle was impressive, scoring with a power-packed shot. But Special K was to soon overshadow all and everything. These days friendlies are not nearly the same, almost a waste of time; especially with the profusion of substitutes on both sides which make the actual contest on the field almost meaningless. Oh for a trip back to basics at Tynecastle, Boghead Park, the old Bootham Crescent or Brunton Park.

Paul Joannou,
Club Historian, Newcastle United

v KILMARNOCK
RUGBY PARK
ATT; 1,500

MON 9TH AUGUST 1982
FRIENDLY
DREW 0-0

We caught a train up to Glasgow via Edinburgh, then a train out to Kilmarnock just south-west, towards the coast. Then after the match a few beers and a B&B before trekking back on the Tuesday morning. Two days off graft, a pain in the arse of a place to get to by train and all for a boring game without a single goal. Nevertheless a great trip, well worth it, it's what we do, it's what we know. Unknown to us our loyalty would be rewarded in stunning fashion within 10 days! As for friendlies in Scotland, us Mags obviously always find the ground, we always work out how to get there which was to come in handy for future European adventures. Unfortunately yet absolutely hysterical is the true story of a van load of Sunderland fans that went to watch their side play St Johnstone arriving just in time for kick-off! The only problem was that instead of travelling to Perth they had instead drove to Johnstone near Paisley, Glasgow 72 miles away. Daft Pillicks.

Brian Hall, Heaton,
Newcastle

v PARTICK THISTLE
FIRHILL STADIUM
ATT; 1,500

WED 11TH AUGUST 1982
FRIENDLY
WON 2-0

Two goals from Imre Varadi were enough to beat Glasgow's third club in this match which was part of our pre-season tour of Scotland. I learnt a little ditty that afternoon from an old Jags' fan, and I've remembered it ever since: *"There's A Well-Known Glasgow Football Team, They Don't Play In Blue And They Don't Play In Green, Partick Thistle The Best Team You've Ever Seen."* Unfortunately they'd just been relegated from the Scottish Premier League.

Deka
Gateshead, Tyneside

v NACIONAL
ESTADIO DOS BARREIR
ATT; 1,000

THURS 19TH AUGUST 1982
MADEIRA TOURNAMENT
DREW 0-0

Earlier in the week I was at Newcastle airport with my mates before we flew to Spain for our holidays. I bumped into Ken Mullen from Newcastle United Supporters Club who was off to watch the team play in the Madeira Tournament. Madeira is a small tropical island which is just off the coast of Morocco, 350 miles off the north-east coast of Africa. To the south are the Canary Islands. Madeira is a Portuguese colony and three years later would be the birthplace of Cristiano Ronaldo, a puffy bloke who used to play for Man Utd. There wouldn't have been many Newcastle fans able to make the pilgrimage for the two friendlies as it was an expensive yet low-key trip. Hats off to supporters like Ken Mullen. The 17 man squad which flew out on the Wednesday to Madeira: Carr, Hardwick, Craggs, Clarke, Saunders, Haddock, Martin, Trewick, Carney, Cartwright, Anderson, Doyle, Wharton, Varadi, Todd, Waddle and Ferris.

Dave Drape
Walker, Newcastle

As Newcastle played a friendly on the island of Madeira Tyneside was alive and buzzing with Keegan mania as one of the world's best players signed for the toon. Barbers all over Newcastle were preparing themselves for an outbreak of 'perm-mania' and 'beans on toast' mullets. The new season was only 9 days away, yet I was working in Bolton for the next couple of weeks so it would be an expensive journey back for his debut. I went out straight from work and got hammered before reversing the charges back home so that my Dad could read the Chronicle from back to front down the phone as I sang and shouted in Bolton town centre. I just wanted to be home.

Mick Edmondson
Walker, Newcastle

v MARITIMO
ESTADIO DOS BARREIR
ATT; 1,000

SAT 21ST AUGUST 1982
MADEIRA TOURNAMENT
WON 1-0

Situated in the capitol, Funchal, the ground was built in a hillside and we got outstanding views of the bay, across the city and the rising Madeiran Mountains. Definitely a change from Oldham. The pitch was in poor condition for the start of the new season had a running track around it. The fact that 3 different clubs all used it may have had something to do with the state of the surface. The stadium was actually built into the ground and we entered by climbing down stairs at the back of the terraces which were at street level. Chris Waddle got the only goal of the game. As Keegan mania swept Tyneside, United had a major problem as they flew into Newcastle landing at midnight on the Wednesday - with just over 48 hours to prepare for the opening match. Goalkeeper Kevin Carr who was an ever present the previous season and had been named as player of the year for the past two seasons was to miss the big kick-off. He had allegedly injured himself whilst all the players and directors were having a cup of coffee after their evening meal. Suddenly everybody heard an almighty crash as Kevin had accidentally walked through a glass door, literally crashing through it. Meanwhile back on Tyneside Kevin Keegan was house hunting with manager Arthur Cox and their starting price was an amazing £70,000 upwards!

Jonesy
Whitley Bay, Tyneside

v QUEENS PARK RANGERS
ST JAMES' PARK
ATT; 35,718

SAT 28TH AUGUST 1982
SECOND DIVISION
WON 1-0

The atmosphere in and around the pubs on the Friday night was electric, the Bigg Market was like a human fire work display as everybody was going potty, because Kevin Keegan was about too make his debut for Newcastle United. Saturday morning arrived, a bright hot summer's day it was just a perfect start to what we all hoped would be a perfect day. Although the match had caught the whole countries attention it wasn't an all-ticket affair, so you could just pay on the gate. I arrived at the ground just after 8am, with the kick-off 7 hours away, yet the queues were already taking shape, so I joined one at the centre of the Gallowgate End. Everybody was obviously excited and had been for days since he signed, the crack in the queue was excellent and as the hours passed the crowds got bigger and noisier. By 11am the police were having difficulties containing the crowd, yet the turnstiles didn't actually open until 1pm! At exactly 12pm midday Concorde made a very rare Tyneside appearance actually flying over the ground, although not many seemed to notice. St. James Park was full to the brim by 1.30pm; the atmosphere was electric as the new Keegan songs were given their first airing. Eventually the moment arrived just before 3 o'clock, something we thought we'd never witness at St. James Park, Kevin Keegan the living legend, twice European footballer of the year and England captain, leading out the Black n' Whites. I've never witnessed noise like it as everyone in the ground pointed towards him singing simply "Keegan, Keegan." A fan ran on and lifted Keegan aloft in the centre circle. But this was nothing though to the noise and scenes later which occurred when Varadi passed the ball to Keegan, who headed forward before running on to slot the ball past the keeper, before disappearing into the Gallowgate crowd. The whole place went mental, I could hardly breath there seemed to be 35,000 in the Gallowgate End alone, never mind the whole ground. Actually when I look back at video footage of the match there probably was.

Julian Brannigan
Gosforth, Newcastle

As we queued outside the old west stand with thousands of others, in the ensuing melee, my mate Tim Lamb was hoofed in the balls by a copper horse as it did a back flick. He was taken to hospital immediately in agony and as a result missed the whole match. He was absolutely gutted.

Andy Macinlay
Montagu, Newcastle

What a way to celebrate my 21st Birthday. Kevin Keegan scores the winner on his debut for Newcastle United! I had an unbelievable day and then my birthday party celebrations on the Saturday night, class. A day I will never forget as long as I live. Nineteen years later and I had my 40th birthday party on Saturday 1st September 2001, as my guests arrived early to watch England beat Germany 5-1 in Munich in front of 63,000 as Michael Owen grabbed a hat-trick. That was another canny party I tell you. Roll on my 75th birthday we might win at Wigan for the first time!!

Keith Patterson
Durham

Just before kick-off Kevin Keegan was standing in the centre circle, when just after winning the toss, a lad ran on to the pitch and approached him. He wore black half mast sta-press, white socks, loafers and a bowler hat and managed to lift Keegan aloft to huge cheers. Welcome to Newcastle Kev.

Kev Drew
Wardley Tyneside

Two weeks earlier I was getting changed for the first Sunday League game of the season. One of the lads mentions a piece in the Sunday Mirror which said Man

U and Newcastle were battling it out for the signature of Kevin Keegan. "Ha, we know where he'll go then," was the unanimous verdict of the rest of us (It wasn't Newcastle). The following Thursday unbelievably it is announced on Metro Radio that Kevin Keegan was jetting in to sign for Newcastle United that afternoon. Keegan mania breaks out. A week later and were on the town on the Friday night, the place is jumping. I've rarely been part of a better atmosphere in Town. All the talk is about Keegan's debut the next day. On the bus home there is a song which I never heard again more's the pity. To the tune of Hava Nagila it went *"With Imre And Kevin Keegan We'll Win This Season La La La La La La."* The big day arrives and I'm just pulling myself round when the phone goes at 11am. It's Dave one of the lads. "Me Mam's just come back from the Town and the queue at St James' is a mile long we better get away now." A few calls later and were on our way. It's like the old Winalot advert when it started with one dog running through a field and it got joined by more and more dogs as one by one the lads join me on the way to the bus stop at Denton Square. Cheesy is the last to join, he lives opposite the bus stop and hops across the wall with a paper bag filled with his Mam's home made chips. He doesn't get many as the greedy guts all dip in. We get off the bus and join the queue, its red hot and the gates aren't open. New signing Jeff Clarke arrives and gets generous applause and a few handshakes from the fans. We are all secretly worried that we won't get in due to the crowds. The queue moves slowly but eventually to our relief we climb the stairs and we are in to the Gallowgate End. The players warm up all except Keegan. Finally the referee leads the teams out and there he is in the jazzy new white training kit. There is an almighty roar followed by chants of *"Keegan, Keegan."* The match passes in a blur but just on the hour I am one of those who Keegan says sucked the ball into the net as he slips it past Rangers keeper Hucker.

Chris Ramshaw
West Denton, Newcastle

The summer of 1982 saw probably the most important event in my life up to that point....my first season ticket for Newcastle United Football Club, something I have held continuously to this day. I believe the cost was £25 for a junior seat ticket in the old West Stand. A small price to pay for the pain and suffering a 14 year old was about to embark upon...Thanks Dad! Sparked by Keegan mania, I can still vividly picture the ground full as the great man made his debut against QPR.

Pete Grieves
North Seaton, Northumberland

"Today was the proudest day of my life. It was the fans who sucked the ball in to the net. They are far and away the best supporters in the land. I've enjoyed the roar of the Liverpool Kop, but I've never heard anything like that today. It was stereo with four speakers."

Kevin Keegan
Newcastle United

As Newcastle led by Kevin Keegan ran down the open tunnel (Aye, ran) in their white tracksuit tops to take to the field a lad in a black t-shirt sporting a blond Walker-wedge-haircut leant over the wall and touched Kev's head, ruffling his perm hair-do. Step forward Dave Emmerson of Walker. Check out your videos and DVDs and you'll see him leaning over from the Centre Paddock, (aye had money did Dave).

Mick Edmondson
Walker, Newcastle

"The crowd was boisterous but good natured. There were a few arrests, nothing out of the ordinary. But there were one or two things which disappointed me. A number of fans ran onto the pitch despite being asked not to. And supporters at the Gallowgate End were sitting perched on the hoardings at the back of the terracing. This is an extremely dangerous practice which will have to stop."

Supt. Barry Redfearn
Deputy Commander, Ncle Division

"I queued for five hours at the Gallowgate End to watch Keegan's first match."

Alan Shearer
Gosforth, Newcastle

Just after half-time as the teams lined up to kick-off Kevin Keegan was near the half-way line when a bloke wearing nothing but his birthday suit and a pair of bright lime green fluorescent terry-towelling socks, with a black-and-white scarf around his neck ran on the pitch. When he reached Keegan he presented him with the scarf putting it around the legends neck to massive cheers and laughter, *"Were Geordies Were Mental Were Off Weh Fucking Heads"* before being escorted away, detained, and later charged - obviously missing the great occasion. The lad was Davey Dickas from Newcastle's West End and his socks were raffled in the Darnell pub at Spittal Tongues to raise money to pay for his fine.

Mick
Newcastle

A throw in on the right, Keegan and Varadi linking up before Varadi squeezed the ball through. Keegan reacted like lightening and was clear of the defenders before steadying himself to slot the ball past the advancing keeper. Ecstatic crowd scenes followed. A Newcastle legend was born. Also making their debuts were Jeff Clarke a free transfer from Sunderland who actually won the man of the match award. Also returning for his second spell at the club was another free transfer signing - John Craggs, who became the only player to play for us in the 1960's, 70's & 80's. He originally made his debut back in October 1966 against Everton and was a member of our victorious Fairs Cup winning squad in the 1968/69 season. QPR had just lost the FA Cup final and had hammered us 4-0 at SJP months earlier, so were quite rightly the bookies favourites for the title and promotion. After the match Rangers manager Terry Venables moaned calling his team his 'reserves' as he had 5 players missing including a certain Glen Roeder. On the same day it went totally unnoticed that Sunderland beat Aston Villa the European champions 3-1 on their own patch, Villa Park. Nobody on Tyneside cared as Keegan mania gripped Newcastle. This crowd was the largest to watch a Second Division match all season and I'm sure that everybody who was there would agree with me, in that there were actually thousands more inside than the official attendance indicates. The scenes and reaction since his arrival had been tumultuous and far more dramatic than they would have been if he'd signed for any other club. No other town or city in the land would have had the same impact. When he signed for Southampton there was only a ripple compared to the tidal wave of euphoria which swept Tyneside. Football in Newcastle is like nowhere else, total fanatics. Always has been always will be.

Mick Edmondson
Walker, Newcastle

"It was pure theatre if you sat down to write the story, you couldn't have come up with a better ending."

Arthur Cox
Newcastle United Manager

v BLACKBURN ROVERS   WED 1ST SEPTEMBER 1982
EWOOD PARK   SECOND DIVISION
ATT; 14,421   WON 2-1

I'd just left school and was working in nearby Bolton, Lancashire where I'd spent the summer serving my apprenticeship as a dental technician. The job meant that I'd had to spend 8 weeks living and training in Bolton before heading back to Newcastle. For Keegan's debut I'd had to pay £26 train fare for a home match which was nearly a week's wages! But it had been worth it and this short trip along with Newcastle's impending visit to Bolton on Saturday, in what was my final week before returning home, worked out perfectly. After the match I had to return to the train station along with only a handful of other Geordies. The walk was a long one and it soon became apparent that we were being followed by a large group of Blackburn 'hoolies.' Our average age was only 16/17 and their older mob outnumbered us considerably. The 2 coppers who were walking nearby didn't seem keen and to be honest either were we, but we weren't going to let our farewell committee know. Verbals were exchanged throughout the walk and our shouts of "Come on then any 5 of you" didn't seem to interest them. The road was dimly lit and we seemed to go under numerous bridges, but the expected attack never took place and before we knew it we were at the station where there were more Blackburn tits. The police at the station came running towards us as Blackburn fans all of a sudden became aggressive. We laughed at them and shouted that if they couldn't even chin the kids they had no chance with the blokes. It was quite a frightening experience for a 16 year old but at the same time a canny buzz. The win meant that we had bridged a 22 year gap, as it was the first time we had won our first 2 league games of the campaign since 1960.

Mick Edmondson
Walker, Newcastle

Billy and Teka travelled down for the match and as usual by the time they arrived, Teka needed to be fed. On requesting a Hot Dog from a street vendor he was told that they cost 50p each for home fans and £1 each for away fans! On politely suggesting that this was taking the piss a bit, he was told that he knew what he could do if he didn't like it! So he did, as he and Billy proceeded to tip the cart over. The streets of Blackburn were certainly well fed that day even if the fans weren't.

Davey
Gateshead, Tyneside

Keegan's first away match saw the birth of Magpie Travel as Newcastle United launched their new official coach trips to all away games. For this maiden voyage the cost was £4.25 which they sold as 'most competitive' and advertised the fact that you'd be financially helping the club. No thanks, we were the 'Sarnie Squad' and it was the Supporters club everytime for us.

Tony James
Byker, Newcastle

United fan smelt of glue

A Newcastle United football fan, seen throwing water from an ornamental fountain in Blackburn smelled of drink and glue. But when a policeman went to speak to him he threw a tin of glue at the officer and threatened to kick his teeth in. The youth from Wallsend pleaded guilty and was fined £100 with £5 costs.

v BOLTON WANDERERS
BURNDEN PARK
ATT; 17,707

SAT 4TH SEPTEMBER 1982
SECOND DIVISION
LOST 1-3

Tradition had it that on away trips everything was up for grabs and helping yourself was always part of the trip. Whether eating everything on your tray at the service station as you queued before getting to the till, or as a mate of mine often did when visiting the off-license - picking up a couple of slabs of beer whilst handing over 50p and gleefully telling them to keep the change. However an off-license in Bolton turned out to be more prepared, because when a number of us entered the shop we were welcomed with the shopkeeper shouting "Rashid, get the dog," shortly followed by a young boy being dragged out of the back of the shop by the biggest and angriest Alsatian I've ever seen. Needless to say we gladly paid for our purchases and left as quickly and quietly as possible. However not to be totally beaten on the day, entry to the ground consisted of climbing over the turnstiles, paying to get in was for mugs.

Millie
Rosies Bar, Newcastle

There were thousands of Geordies all over Bolton town centre before the match taking over the pubs, as if it was a home match. When I tried to gain entry to the visitors section just before kick-off, it seemed as though they were refusing fans entry as it was full up. I decided to try the paddock, the next turnstile along to make sure I saw the match. Once inside I realised that I wasn't the only Geordie amongst the home supporters and as the match kicked off, I was arguing with this Bolton fan who beckoned me towards him for a fight. As I approached him I suddenly realised, that I was surrounded by his mates. Then this lad came over the fence from the Newcastle section, shouting "its alreet, I'm from Scotswood," he then nutted this kid, and the whole paddock went up. More Geordies came piling over the fence as the match continued as the police arrested people at random. I managed to get onto the side of the pitch where I decided to stay, sitting down next to a cameraman, posing as his colleague, where I remained until I told John Craggs that he was shite as he ran past me. The police then moved me to the Newcastle section, where I had originally wanted to stand. The non-stop violence between rival fans continued throughout the first half, then at half-time whilst we were trailing 3-0, I saw a lad who was a joiner, who I worked with at the time down the shipyards. There he was along with others ripping the metal adverts down from the back of our open terrace, before passing them above people's heads across the crowd. Do you know in all the time I knew him it's the only time I ever actually saw him doing any work!

Micky Carr
Walker, Newcastle

There was mayhem outside the ground as hundreds of queuing Newcastle fans started pushing through the turnstiles resulting in many gaining free entry. An old fella on the turnstile panicked and picked up his cash and tried to run through the melee, but somebody mischievously tripped him up sending his cash float flying. It was snowing pound notes along with various coins rolling round the dirty floor. Once inside the Bolton fans were pelting us with rocks from their decaying terraces, only for Newcastle to reply with a vast amount of 10p pieces. On the pitch the only positive thing was that Kevin Keegan became the first player in our history to score in his first 3 games for Newcastle.

Marty Taylor
Newcastle

162

Myself and ten mates including Eric our driver, decided to travel to Bolton in an old Post Office van basically because it was cheap. We set off through Gateshead when almost immediately the van started to move from side to side along the road, with us thinking Eric was just pissing about, that is until he told us the steering had gone. Cue blind panic and a sudden stop against the kerb. We locked the death-trap up and found a phone box (oh for a mobile phone). Eric rang ACE Van Hire and managed to sort transport out, but by this time it was 10.30am and we were still in Gateshead! Eventually down the A1 we headed fast as possible trying to make up time. At 1.30pm we were still 10 miles from Bolton but stuck in traffic and were at a standstill, the clock was ticking away and we we're moving so slow we knew we wouldn't make the kick-off. We'd already passed an exit from the motorway and were now next to the motorway entrance slip road, when quick thinking Eric dropped the van in reverse and started to back up the slip road, gradually until he got to the very top! Luckily we got out of the traffic and bombed it to the ground, parked the van and legged it. For those who have been to the old Burnden Park ground there is a pub next to the railway bridge beside the ground, it was just emptying as we got outside, when they clocked us we had to run that little bit faster in order to get away from our Bolton welcome. We made the kick-off (just).

John
Gateshead, Tyneside

As we drove along the M62 in my Austin Allegro the tyres were going flat near Oldham. So we stopped at a cafe and put on our spare on the worst one and just blew the other one up. We got talking to a local who said that if we followed him he would show us where there was a garage which would be open to repair our punctures. So we followed him to the garage and got a remould and he even waited until we were all sorted before he so kindly showed us back to the main road. Unfortunately as he stopped at the junction we smashed straight into the back of him. Our front end was smashed in and we agreed to pay for the damage to the back end of his. We eventually said our goodbyes and continued on to Bolton with our window stuck down and a lad in the back keeping the drivers seat upright. Not only did we not get a pint we also missed the first ten minutes.

Bill Gibbs
Wallsend, Tyneside

Soccer hooligans on rampage

In Bolton where more than 8,000 Newcastle United fans invaded the town, a policeman was hit on the head with a brick. Angry fans also tore down advertising hoardings at the back of the terraces as United slid to defeat and damaged cars after the match. Last night as Bolton police were collating the statistics of shame an officer described it as "bloody murder!" Nearly 60 United fans were arrested and 50 thrown out of the ground. United were beaten 3-1 but the fans blotted their copy book even before the game started. With kick off over 30 minutes away the police had to move into the United end of the ground to break up several fights. There was more aggro at 3pm with United supporters trying to climb the railings into the Bolton section.

United may face aggro rap

Newcastle United may be fined following the violent behavior of some of their fans at Bolton at the weekend. Four policemen were injured and 75 people arrested – three quarters of them United fans. One policeman was knocked unconscious by a flying brick. The FA's disciplinary department was today waiting to receive written reports from the officials and two clubs. Trouble flared before the match, continued on the terraces for the majority of the game and for one and a half hours after the final whistle.

Sick! That's how I felt on Saturday as I witnessed some of our so-called fans introducing the people of Bolton to Geordie Finesse. Apart from the usual loutish behaviour that again reared its ugly head it didn't really please the people out Saturday shopping to see several of our personage, for want of a better word, urinating over the flowers and plants in the main square - not ten yards from a gents toilet. I must add: nor did the gentlemen who leapt out of the van brandishing socks filled with bricks and the like. The Bolton Police fortunately were on the spot to sort that out.

Russell Cushing
Club Secretary, Newcastle United

v MIDDLESBROUGH	**WED 8TH SEPTEMBER 1982**
ST JAMES' PARK	**SECOND DIVISION**
ATT; 27,984	**DREW 1-1**

WE'LL FENCE YOU IN

Behave yourself - or we'll fence you in. That was the stark warning to Newcastle fans today from club chairman Stan Seymour. The warning comes in the wake of Saturdays disturbances at Bolton and is directed at tonight's match v Middlesbrough.

It could only happen at Newcastle United. I along with hundreds of others queued from 5am on the Monday morning for my ticket against recently relegated Boro. Unfortunately we were all still waiting at 11am long after the ticket office was supposed to have opened, as the staff couldn't get the safe open to get the tickets out! As for this being billed as a local-derby match, it always did my head in and still does. Middlesbrough used to be in Yorkshire, then Cleveland before they invented Teesside. We only have one derby and that is with Sunderland, end of. I'd consider playing about 30 other English clubs being more attractive and of bigger stature than this fixture against Boro. I mean for this match they received 5,000 tickets yet only sold 1,100 sending 3,900 back!! One Newcastle fan obviously didn't listen to all the pre-match warnings about encroachment of the pitch area, as he performed a one man pitch invasion and mini riot. On loan former England international Mick Channon made his debut scoring our goal, while John Cragg's played against the side he'd just left. Peter Cartwright who'd started all four games so far made his last appearance of 69 (including sub appearances) scoring 4 goals along the way. He was a fully committed player, who was a bargain at £2,000 from North Shields FC. But Newcastle were now going places and were no longer looking for cheap non-league bargains, but instead players with international pedigree - or so we hoped.

Mick Edmondson
Walker, Newcastle

v CHELSEA
ST JAMES' PARK
ATT; 29,136

SAT 11TH SEPTEMBER 1982
SECOND DIVISION
DREW 1-1

I was unable to get to the match due to work commitments because at the time I was working in Top Shop / Top Man, Eldon Square only two minutes walk from the ground. In the early eighties Top Shop was the number one fashion store in the city for both male and females and was jam packed on a Saturday afternoon. It was about 5pm on a Saturday just after the match had finished when all hell broke loose as a Chelsea fan ran into the store being chased by a small group of Newcastle fans. He ran across the shop floor then jumped over the cash desk sending the female cashier's into screaming fits but at the same time thinking that he was safe from the chasing pack. It was then that the chasing pack set about him punching and kicking him to the ground. Ever since that day the Top Shop doors which also act as a main entrance to the Eldon Square shopping complex have remained locked on match days from 4.30pm onwards.

Graeme Preston
Gosforth, Newcastle

On the Saturday night after the match Steve Cram was the toast of Tyneside as he won the 1,500 metres gold medal in the European Championships in Athens. The next morning the Sunday Sun's front page headline read; 'Geordie Gold-Steve Cram. No mention of mackem back then! Sunderland fans loved being known as Geordies back then, even though they have never been and never will be. Let them keep dreaming.

Mick Edmondson,
Walker, Newcastle

Police act to save soccer peace

A MASSIVE police presence prevented a repeat of last season's bloody skirmishes between Newcastle United and Chelsea supporters. Mounted police and dog handlers escorted 1,500 followers of the London club to and from the ground yesterday, keeping them clear of Newcastle supporters. Only some first-class policing prevented a pitched battle in Westgate Road, Newcastle before the game, as a crowd of chanting Newcastle supporters converged on a small group of rival fans who were being escorted from the Central station. Police with dogs kept the fans apart. After the game, a long crocodile of visiting fans was marched by police through Newcastle city centre to Manors station, as shoppers fled to the protection of Eldon Square. When the fans reached Manors safely, it was discovered most of them were catching trains from Newcastle Central. So police then had to march them to the Central, as traffic approaching the Tyne Bridge was halted. Last night, a police spokesman said that about 50 Newcastle Supporters were arrested before, during and after the match. "It is quite obvious hundreds of Newcastle supporters have no interest in football, their behaviour leaves a lot to be desired. "But the Chelsea supporters were well behaved. We managed to escort them safely to and from the ground." Last season after the Newcastle - Chelsea match five policemen were injured as rival fans battled.

Youth stoned soccer train

A gang of 15 youths stoned a football special full of Chelsea fans as it left Newcastle, city magistrates were told. The hooligans were throwing missiles at the train as it passed over the viaduct near the All Saints office centre, the court was told.

SOCCER FANS SENT TO PRISON

A Newcastle football fan was sent to jail for three months by City magistrates. John Bolam was seen by police hurling an opened can of liquid at Chelsea fans from the Leazes End in St James' Park. Bolam of Felling was also shouting obscenities at the Chelsea fans in the neighbouring enclosure said Mr. John Cooper, prosecuting. Bolam told the court he did throw the liquid but had not used bad language. Another fan was banned from 12 home matches after admitting behaviour likely to cause a breach of the peace. Another fan was ordered to go to an attendance centre for two hours on alternate Saturday afternoons for a total of 24 hours as punishment for shouting racial abuse at coloured Chelsea fans whilst jumping up and down. Another Newcastle fan was also jailed for jumping up and down whilst shouting abusive comments at the Chelsea fans. Police arrested more than 40 fans and fines totalled over £3,000.

166

v SHREWSBURY TOWN
GAY MEADOW
ATT; 7,907

SAT 18TH SEPTEMBER 1982
SECOND DIVISION
LOST 1-2

It seemed to take forever to get there by coach as the traffic was terrible. With only seven days notice this match was made all-ticket, which was such short notice that it definitely put fans off travelling. It was £2 to stand behind the goal in the cow shed and £3.50 in the seats. I wonder how Kevin Keegan felt playing and losing in a tiny old fashioned ground like this in a week, when new England manager Bobby Robson omitted him from his first England Squad for the European Championship match against Denmark. Dereck Bell made his third and last appearance for us before retiring due to injury in November. We took the lead on what was a boiling hot day, but Alan Brown who had scored twice for us whilst on loan the previous season got their late winner, giving them their first win of the season. Our league record at Gay Meadow now read 3 defeats and a draw in our 4 visits. It may have taken forever to get there, but the journey home was even longer.

Mick Edmondson,
Walker, Newcastle

v BARNSLEY
ST JAMES' PARK
ATT; 24,522

SAT 25TH SEPTEMBER 1982
SECOND DIVISION
LOST 1-2

Since winning our first two matches Keegan mania had calmed down slightly as we had failed to win any of our next five. Keegan himself had received a bombshell when new England manager Bobby Robson left him out of his first ever squad. The strange thing was the squad only contained nineteen players? Also dropped was Mick Mills who Robson had managed for years at Ipswich. On Keegan's absence Robson said "Although it is possible for a Second Division player to be capped, it is more difficult." Neil McDonald became the youngest ever player to play for Newcastle United making his debut at the tender age of 16 years and 326 days. Neil was a very close friend of mine as we played together at Wallsend Boys Club for five years as well as Northumberland County Boys. Newcastle signed him from Carlisle United for a fee of £10,000 a month earlier and he was thrown straight into the starting line-up. After six years many fans scapegoat Steve Hardwick made his 101st and last ever appearance before leaving for Oxford. Also departing was Mick Channon who played his fourth and final game for us. We were desperate for some midfield talent to compliment Keegan. This defeat was hard to take but you can always count on our friends from down south on Wearside to cheer us up when we are vexed. When we purchased our customary Football Pink newspaper the street seller informed us that Sunderland had lost 8-0 at Watford, which equalled their worst ever defeat in their entire history!! It didn't exactly help our poor start to the season but nevertheless it helped cheer up our miserable Saturday night. Sunderland's manager Alan Durban said, "We were pathetic, we were lucky to lose by only 8-0!!"

Mick Edmondson,
Walker, Newcastle

Unruly fans rapped

A Newcastle magistrate has slammed unruly football fans for bringing the sport and the city into disrepute. We cannot allow this sort of behaviour here for which there can be no excuse.

Soccer fan fined £100

A Newcastle fan was so shocked by a rival supporter's obscene gesture that he did one back, city magistrates heard. "They're just Barnsley" he told a policeman. Colin Lochart, 18 of Jubilee Street, Wallsend admitted using threatening words and behaviour at Newcastle s home game with Barnsley.

Top Twenty in the NorthEast, Supplied by HMV

1. There it is...Shalamar
2. The Bitterest Pill...The Jam
3. WOR KEV... Don Juans
4. The Message...............................Grandmaster Flash
5. Pass The Dutchie...............................Musical Youth

---

v ROTHERHAM UNITED
MILLMOOR
ATT; 12,436

SAT 2ND OCTOBER 1982
SECOND DIVISION
WON 5-1

An all-ticket affair against 'Emlyn Hughes' Rotherham, the former Liverpool and England captain was player-manager at Millmoor. 'Crazy Horse' as he was known throughout his career - after an illegal Rugby tackle on Newcastle United winger Albert Bennett - had always been a thorn in our side. His first goal for Liverpool was in a 6-0 win over us in 1967 and he then lifted the FA Cup for Liverpool when they beat us in 1974. So it was a joy to watch him run around like a headless chicken as Kevin Keegan became the first Newcastle player to score a quartet since Vic Keeble did the trick at Huddersfield in 1955. The Match of the Day cameras were there on what was a very rare visit to a game outside the top flight and captured a rampant Newcastle United with a huge, noisy and ecstatic following. Rotherham had increased the admission prices of the seats by a £1 to help pay for the huge police presence inside and outside the stadium. The Social Club which was situated at the back of our end was unfortunately smashed up before the match when a game of Bingo got slightly out of hand resulting in Bingo balls being launched around the room. Terry McDermott made his debut on his welcome return to the club - this being his second spell. We originally sold him to Liverpool in November 1974 for £170,000 (a profit of £145,000) after nearly 2 years service since his arrival from Bury. He went to Anfield to win things and came back with 3 European Cups, a UEFA Cup, 4 Charity Shields, 4 First Division Titles, 2 League Cups and a Super Cup. He made 328 appearances scoring an amazing 80 goals from midfield in 8 seasons on Merseyside, he also collected 25 England caps and scored 3 times as well as being named PFA Players' Player of the Year. In that same period we had won a few corners, a few matches, lost a League Cup final, qualified for Europe and been relegated. He was a snip at £100,000 and he lined up with his ex-team mate Keegan who had made himself unavailable for future England squads as a result of Bobby Robson failing to give him a courtesy call when dropping the England skipper. The Geordies crammed into the ground, let the nation know that he'd made a big mistake as his goals flew in. *"Bobby Robson, Bobby Robson, Are You Watching On The Box, Are You Watching On The Box?"* Terry McDermott remarked "I already get the feeling that everybody is still as Newcastle daft as ever."

Mick Edmondson
Walker, Newcastle

On our way down the Motorway a car hit our coach beside Wentbridge Services and spun off the main A1 towards the cafe area and plate glass windows. Our supporters assisted in helping causalities both in car and on the coach. All you ever here is bad news whenever Football fans are mentioned in the media whilst all the good things go unreported.

Unknown
Newcastle

On the Monday after the game Bobby Robson was due to announce his England squad to play West Germany at Wembley. The squad he picked for the previous game was missing a certain Kevin Keegan who had since made his intentions clear. After scoring 4 against Rotherham he announced, "This doesn't change anything. I don't regret having said I won't play for England again. I had to make a decision. My challenge is now here with Newcastle. You saw the fans followed us here and with fans like this you need to do well. They are a different breed."

Kevin Keegan
Newcastle United

v LEEDS UNITED
ELLAND ROAD
ATT; 24,012

WED 6TH OCTOBER 1982
(MILK) LEAGUE CUP 2ND RND 1ST LEG
WON 1-0

We had the whole of the Lowfield Road stand both the seats upstairs and the terraces below, as a huge mid-week following descended on Elland Road for what was David McCreery's debut after his £75,000 move from Tulsa Roughnecks. Yet for some unknown reason one Newcastle fan ended up in the Leeds end and just prior to the match was escorted from their end after getting a kicking and put in the Newcastle terrace. It just so happened, that he was wearing all white clothing and was absolutely covered in blood. After the match it was kicking off every where as groups of Leeds thugs tried picking off Newcastle fans returning to their transport. As we had arrived late we had just abandoned our car, driven by my new boss who'd just moved to the North East from Bolton - so had just literally dumped it at the end of the dual carriageway.

We got attacked but the four of us soon had the six or seven Leeds knackers on the back foot as two were decked straightaway. Then as we got to the car not only did we have a parking ticket but also a mob waiting, but along with a few other Geordies we chased the Leeds fans up the stairs, over a foot-bridge and down the other side and into a housing estate, stragglers and slow coaches getting it as we chased, there only retaliation being the use of bricks. Once back at the car we were surrounded by Copper Cars before we had a chance to pull away and were asked to all get out and were searched and then the police found bricks under the seats in our car. We were just about to pay for our actions even though we had just defended ourselves when their radios started going mental, and they were off like a shot saying we were so lucky that it was going-off big time elsewhere.

Mick Edmondson
Walker, Newcastle

David McCreery made his debut for us that night, a great favourite of mine for his guts and tenacity; he gave his all for the cause. We came away with a 1-0 win, thanks to a Varadi goal, the Wetherby Whaler chip shop making huge profits, though the pubs stayed closed on the way back home.

Anth Nicholson
North Shields, Tyneside

Four of us travelled down in my mate's mother's brand new car, parking a short walk from the ground. After the match as we returned to the car we were sussed and our car was attacked and smashed to *fucking* bits with us inside! The two side doors were completely kicked in, the back window was smashed with a brick as well as various other bits of damage. We feared for our lives and had no choice but to drive through the bastards knocking them flying, luckily escaping and eventually getting home frozen to the bone. There was over £2,500 worth of damage which just about wrote the car off, obviously his Mother went through the roof and never let him forget it for months, and we never got to use any of her cars ever again.

Kev Milburn
Gosforth, Newcastle

My first visit to Leeds what a night it was as I saw United win away for the first time in what was my 19th away match. After the match we were herded onto Double Decker buses which were parked outside at this bus terminus type place. As we pulled away from Elland Road towards the train station we were expecting to be bricked and weren't to be let down as the windows duly came in. Our bus emptied but our attackers were well away. Just another mad trip, following Newcastle in the eighties. Thousands of Newcastle fans had made the journey and we were packed into the Lowfield's Road stand, filling the terraces and seats above. On the same night Manchester United only had 22,091 at Old Trafford for their League Cup tie. Even though we were both Second Division clubs both ties in this fixture easily topped the Mancs! Where were we when we were shite eh? Following our club in the thousands that's where we were.

Graham Parker
Ashington, Northumberland

Fans pelt Keegan with Missiles

A human shield of marshals and policemen protected soccer superstar Kevin Keegan from a barrage of lethal missiles last night. They formed the barricade after Keegan was injured in a tackle near the goal line. As Keegan waited for attention a hail of coins and two three-quarter inch nuts were thrown at him.

Eyewitnesses said as soon as the police and Marshals saw what was happening they rushed to protect Keegan. United physiotherapist Ian Liversedge, who dashed on to the field to assist Keegan, was struck by one flying missile.

v OLDHAM ATHLETIC
BOUNDARY PARK
ATT; 9,000

SAT 9TH OCTOBER 1982
SECOND DIVISION
DREW 2-2

Chris Waddle was an ever present the season before playing 42 league games and had started the first four games of this campaign, but had found himself dropped. Our fleet of coaches stopped at the service station on the way down and the news soon got round that Waddle was half pissed with loads of lads who'd travelled in the back of a transit van. I didn't see him myself but when inside the ground I saw him with my own eyes climbing on the fence down the front with his Donkey Jacket on. This was the match when Terry McDermott and Steve Carney were sent off in a minute of each other and there was nearly a full scale riot as missiles were thrown and travelling fans fought with police. The scenes were amongst the worst I've ever witnessed inside a football ground, although it didn't put me off travelling as unfortunately it was all part and parcel of football back then. The game was held up for 4 minutes as police fought with angry United fans behind the goal. Years later when Waddle went on to play in European Finals and World Cups I couldn't help but think back to the normal drunken Geordie lad on the terraces supporting Newcastle United. Unbelievable to hear a few years later that he actually confessed to being a Sunderland fan!!

John Reid
Gateshead, Tyneside

RIOT STOPS GAME

Furious Newcastle football fans stopped play when they tried to invade the pitch yesterday. Their anger was sparked off when two United players - Steve Carney and Terry McDermott were sent off within seconds of each other. Geordie supporters spilled down the terraces at the Oldham ground and started to climb over the safety barriers. There were ugly scenes and they pelted police and players on the pitch with coins. The game was stopped for five minutes while policemen fought to hold back the yobs. There were 42 arrests - most of them made during the disruption. Supt. Walter Elder of Oldham police said: "The Newcastle fans were incensed at their men being sent off. They made their way down the terraces and tried to get on to the pitch. "They wanted to get hold of the referee. "There were a lot of coins thrown at the police and the officials on the ground. We had 140 officers at the match and we managed to keep them off the pitch," he said.

UNITED TO FENCE IN FANS

Newcastle United are to fence in their fans at St James' Park. This news was released today in the wake of Saturday's disgraceful scenes at Oldham.

v FULHAM
ST JAMES' PARK
ATT; 29,647

SAT 16TH OCTOBER 1982
SECOND DIVISION
LOST 1-4

I went to see the Damned at the Mayfair on the Thursday night, exactly a week after I'd seen the 'Beat' there. This match was exactly 17 years to the day since we lost to Liverpool at Anfield, on the day I was born. My 17th birthday and nothing was going to spoil it. Not the rain, not the return of Supermac with his newly promoted Fulham side, not the fact that we'd only won one of our last seven league games, not a Keegan penalty miss, no nothing was going to spoil my birthday. That was until I found out that the BBC 'Match of the Day' cameras were present with bloody John Motson. The first ever game he covered for the BBC was our embarrassing FA Cup defeat against non-league Hereford ten years earlier. He'd been a jinx ever since; Swansea 0-4, Exeter 0-4 and Chelsea 0-6. Today was no different as we were 0-3 down by half-time as the returning Terry McDermott and David McCreery made their first home appearances. Only the Liverpool v Man Utd game had a larger attendance as the second highest crowd in England watched us turn in a terrible performance. Supermac got a great reception then his team gave us a great hiding. Meanwhile only 5,521 turned up to watch Boro at Ayresome Park! Saturday night was spent around the town with my mates visiting the Whistle Stop, Cordwainers, Fish Bar, Market Tavern, The Lowther and the Canny Lad. After drinking Cider for England like an Olympian I decided to continuously fall down across town as I went to catch the number 12 bus back home. The rest is a blur, as my mates headed off for their buses, Fawdon and Kenton bound, but luckily a lass I knew managed to somehow carry me home from the bus stop, even allowing for the fact that I got off the bus at the wrong stop! I awoke to have two really bad black eyes which was a result of me stotting my wobbly head off the metal rail at the front of the bus upstairs. Keegan missed a penalty and I missed playing for the Prince of Wales pub in Byker on the Sunday - totally ill.

Mick Edmondson
Walker, Newcastle

"Unfortunately the pressures upon the club created by those morons amongst us who appear more interested in a punch up than watching a good game of football can no longer be ignored so fencing it's got to be" An announcement that was made in the matchday programme, explaining that fences are to be erected in the near future.

The Directors
Newcastle United

Policeman kicked as fan arrested

Policemen were kicked and spat at as they struggled to break up a gang of chanting football fans during the Newcastle-Fulham match. The fans all from North Shields were accused of jostling, kicking, spitting and verbally abusing the officers who went into the crowd to arrest the ringleader who was on the barrier, inciting the crowd to attack the police.

v CRYSTAL PALACE
ST JAMES' PARK
ATT; 22,616

SAT 23RD OCTOBER 1982
SECOND DIVISION
WON 1-0

"That was an exceptional atmosphere not only for the Second Division but for anywhere, quite remarkable"

Alan Mullery
Crystal Palace, Manager

I used to love standing in the Gallowgate End on a cold afternoon watching the Black and Whites with the beautiful smell of the breweries filling the air. That was when I was at my most happiest, enjoying the two passions in my life

Kenny McMaster
Walker, Newcastle

v LEEDS UNITED
ST JAMES' PARK
ATT; 24,984

WED 27TH OCTOBER 1982
(MILK) LEAGUE CUP 2ND RND 2ND LEG
LOST 1-4 (AFTER EXTRA-TIME)

Police to isolate
Leeds supporters

Strict segregation of Leeds and Newcastle United fans will be in operation as the two teams meet tonight. Only 1,500 Leeds fans are expected to travel on a special train and will be escorted to and from the ground. After scenes in the first leg at Elland Road police are anxious to ensure that this game isn't ruined by trouble on the terraces. A large crowd is expected but thousands of tickets for the all-ticket tie have been returned by Leeds. A spokesperson for Northumbria police said; "We want to keep the fans well apart. The Leeds fans have a reputation for being the one of the hardest sets of fans in the country. Their bad behaviour can only be matched by the hooligan element of the Newcastle fans. It looks as though many Leeds fans have chosen not to travel up to Tyneside for this clash."

Just fewer than 50,000 watched this two legged tie between the two Second Division sides. Already 1-0 up from the first leg Jeff Clarke scored within 2 minutes which gave us a 2-0 aggregate lead. Yet in front of the rounds biggest attendance we collapsed and lost 4-1 after extra-time, our sixth consecutive season exiting from the competition at the first hurdle. Newcastle United build you up only to knock you down again. I couldn't believe it at the time and was gutted, yet over the years have come to expect it and the club have unfortunately time and time again obliged. The only predictable thing about Newcastle United is their unpredictability, which is all part and parcel of being in love with Newcastle United.

Mick Edmondson
Walker, Newcastle

"Oooooh Wanky Wanky, Wanky Wanky Wanky Wanky Worthington." Water off a Ducks back, but if I had to offer a prize for the best rendition of the chant that followed me throughout my career then it must surely go to the supporters of Newcastle United.

Frank Worthington
Leeds United & England

Arthur Graham in particular tore us apart on the flanks, and yet another League Cup campaign was over at the first hurdle. On the terraces a handful of Leeds supporters had managed to find their way into the Gallowgate End. Whether this had been planned or whether inadvertent they were quickly identified, and I distinctly remember seeing them being thrown out over the wall at the back of the terrace with the obligatory kicking to help send them on their way. The drop over the wall must have been at least 10 feet, and the fate that befell them was seen, by those who were involved, as retribution for what we had suffered at Elland Road in the first leg a fortnight earlier.

Mark Hannen,
Ponteland, Newcastle

v LEEDS UNITED
ELLAND ROAD
ATT; 26,570

SAT 30TH OCTOBER 1982
SECOND DIVISION
LOST 1-3

Due to the volume of Geordies who made this trip the Police for some crazy reason decided to put about a thousand of us - who'd been put straight into the ground early - into a section behind the goal which usually housed the home fans. Because the section was adjacent to the away terrace this was an area which the Leeds hooligans frequented and today they were right behind us, almost within touching distance. There were some of Leeds main firm the 'Service Crew' all wearing pastel colour jumpers and the latest sports gear; they looked like an army of puffs in their Pinks, Baby Blues, Yellows and Bright Greens, whilst our end was full of Donkey Jackets, Doc Martins and skinhead haircuts and Harrington Jackets. The atmosphere between the two sets of fans was at boiling point and it was only a matter of time before it kicked off. Sure enough the trouble started well before kick-off when the Leeds fans threw a seat into our section followed by coins and anything else they could get their hands on. The teams weren't even on the pitch and it was absolute bedlam behind the goal as the police tried to keep rival fans apart. The trouble kept flaring up and continued throughout the first half as rival fans battled, as dozens of seats were hurled, coins and bricks, you name it. Then after about 20 minutes things got really out of hand when Kevin Keegan was felled by a missile thrown from the 'Gelder Kop.' The police again struggled to restore order as fighting broke out between rival fans and eventually the teams were taken off the field, whilst we were forced towards the already overflowing Newcastle section by riot police wielding batons. Newcastle fans had the whole of the side of the pitch including the seats behind. To escape the police brutality I scaled the perimeter fence but as I jumped down I landed on a 'St John's medical stretcher' and nearly broke my neck as I was sent flying - as the thing did a wheelie. I ended up on the side of the pitch dodging the police before managing to jump over the fence and into our end. The trouble continued sporadically and at one point the police came in to the middle of the main Newcastle terrace in numbers only for their hats to be knocked off and thrown onto the pitch, and for them to leave covered in hockle from head to toe, even losing the fans they'd come in and arrested in the melee. The trouble continued outside the ground and my lasting memory is the pitch battle which took place on the hill with the police horses trying to restore order. Local lad and former apprentice Chris Hedworth came on as a sub for Varadi to make his Newcastle debut but unfortunately for him this match will always be remembered for different reasons. In the early eighties I had spent numerous school holidays training whilst on trial with Newcastle United at the old Benwell Training ground. We used to get changed at St James' Park in the first teams dressing room then transported to Benwell in a mini bus where we would train on pitches next to the first team. At the end of one particular week I was standing at the bus stop with fellow Walker lad Chris Hedworth who was slightly older than me. "You'll be alright Mick, I can see you playing for Newcastle in a few years time." I smiled embarrassingly and replied "Aye whatever Chris," thinking to myself I hope he's right, it's my dream, but only time will tell, and thinking 'poor sod he's a canny lad but hasn't really got a chance.' So here I was (a Sunday league player) with my Doc Martins, jeans and customary scarf on the terraces watching with disbelieving eyes as Chris 'bloody' Hedworth came on as sub making his debut for Newcastle United!! I saw him at the auctions a few years later and when I reminded him he laughed and said "Aye and I was shite!" Aye Chris you were kidda, but you did it so you mustn't have been that bad, you wore the shirt and you're a smashing lad.

Mick Edmondson
Walker, Newcastle

It went off big time inside the ground as Leeds and Newcastle fans battled in the seated area behind the goal and it got quite naughty as seats were thrown and the coppers struggled to stop the mayhem. Fans were just getting dragged out randomly and used as scapegoats and just as luck would have it I was one of the unlucky ones. I hadn't asked to be put in an area with Leeds fans but once it went up Newcastle's lads gave as good as they got and it wasn't as though it was our top lads in there, but just a mixture from the coaches who had arrived early which the police had decided to put in there. I was arrested marched around the pitch and thrown in a cell, then charged before being released the following morning. I had allegedly according to the police thrown a seat into the Leeds fans causing injury to a one of their fans and damage to the property of Leeds United Football Club. I was totally innocent and this was proved when I produced one of the seats in court I was alleged to have thrown quite a distance. The judge could hardly pick it up so the case was thrown out.

Paul
Gateshead, Tyneside

Not sure why, but Elland Road has never been a pleasant place to visit, its miles away from the train station, has poor parking and irritating fans. Of course, what irritated them even more was the fact that at a distance of 90 miles, they were the next nearest rivals to the North East, and what a noisy, unruly rabble used to congregate from NE1 4ST, on our trips to *"Leeds Leeds Leeds."* European Cup finalists only seven years previously the Yorkshire outfit had been relegated in the summer and this was the third time we had met in October, this game was hyped up. All away buses were guided to a large field near the ground to be "safely parked" and fans would be escorted (herded) in an orderly fashion (I think not) to the ground. Some bloke after an obvious quick profit was selling Newcastle flags for just £1 and

they were selling like hotcakes as we prepared for the short walk to the ground. And so, upon the instruction of the Police, in full Billy Elliot type precision, we were all marched forward. An amazing sight of us all walking down, waving the flags and singing. It was only by chance a lad I was with noticed his flag had a "C" missing. Indeed, we all had a "C" missing, and we were in fact all waving "Newastle United FC" flags!!!! Not sure if the Leeds fans or indeed half the Newcastle fans noticed and when I did look back, the seller was gone! By the time we reached the turnstiles, 'the Law' had now decided that no flags should be on sticks, so they were all removed and binned as we gained entry to the ground. Inside the flags were waved by hand, like an enormous hankie, or made into a variation of hats, hoods, masks. Shame they had not been so vigilant with the home fans, Keegan was struck by a missile, which required treatment. A miserable day was complete with a 3-1 defeat, Anderson (he seemed to enjoy Elland Road) scoring for us, and the short journey home took forever, and we weren't even allowed in to Wetherby at all this time!

Anth Nicholson
North Shields, Tyneside

I can remember that there was continuous battling between rival fans inside the ground. Keegan got felled by a coin by Leeds supporters then a few minutes later United's John Anderson was struck by a coin thrown from his own fans. It was intended for a Leeds player. One Newcastle fan was actually jailed for 28 days after being found guilty of swearing but was later released on bail pending an appeal against the sentence, meaning he could be reunited with his pregnant wife who was due.

Kev Drew
Leam Lane, Tyneside

Missile Madness

Fan violence held up Newcastle United's match at Leeds for six minutes yesterday after the referee led the teams off the field for their own safety. Trouble erupted at Elland Road in the 20th minute when Kevin Keegan was felled by a missile thrown from the Leeds section of the crowd. Within three minutes, Newcastle team mate John Anderson went down after being struck by a coin. There were 45 arrests - mainly Newcastle fans - and three policemen were injured by missiles. Two officers were taken to Leeds General Infirmary, one with a broken arm and the other suffering from a broken cheekbone. Supporters broke up seats and hurled them onto the pitch. A police spokesman said: "Some of the fans just went wild." Now both clubs, whose crowds have bad reputations, will probably face an inquiry by the Football Association. This is the second away game in a row that Newcastle fans have been in trouble. Three weeks ago they tried to climb the fences at Oldham and clashed with police after United players Terry McDermott and Steve Carney were sent off. Keegan who was pelted with coins and nuts and bolts in the Milk Cup match at Elland Road earlier this month, said last night: "I don't know what hit me bit I think it could have been a ball bearing. I wasn't knocked out but I was stunned for a couple of minutes." However the Newcastle skipper managed to joke: "I never saw it coming or I would have headed it into the net." It seemed that Anderson was hit by a coin thrown as a reprisal by the Newcastle section of the crowd and intended for Leeds Eddie Gray. Anderson who went on to score his first goal for the club said: "It may have only been a coin but I thought I had been hit by a bullet." During the sixth minute delay, referee Mr. Malcolm Heath, who had earlier warned the crowd that he would finish the game with or without them, made a broadcast over the public address system. He said: "I have brought the players off for their own safety. But this game is not going to be abandoned. We will finish it but I need your total co-operation." Newcastle chairman Stan Seymour then appealed to the visiting fans "for commonsense."

Courts Jail United Fans

Two Newcastle United supporters were jailed and another two were sent to detention centres for offences during the game at Elland Road. Magistrate Ian Boyd sitting at Leeds said; in cases like this the time has come to say enough. These offences are like a disease. The public must be protected.

Fans may face away BAN!

Newcastle United's horde of fans, face a ban on travelling to away matches for the rest of the season. This could be the outcome of Saturday's disgraceful scenes at Elland Road and following in the wake of the trouble involving Newcastle fans on previous trips to Bolton and Oldham this season.

Its so sad ..
Day of shame leaves fans in danger

Trouble is looming for Newcastle and Leeds after another unhappy day for football. Crowd trouble at Elland Road during the Yorkshire clubs victory is certain to lead to an FA inquiry. It is the second away game in succession where Newcastle supporters have clashed with police and rival fans. Now they could face being banned from all away games, as happened to Chelsea last season.

v BURNLEY
ST JAMES' PARK
ATT; 20,961

SAT 6TH NOVEMBER 1982
SECOND DIVISION
WON 3-0

As you can well imagine my name would never be taken in the same vain again, now that we had signed the England Legend. Heads would turn in Doctors waiting rooms, companies would think I was taking the piss when asked for my name and details over the phone and I'd obviously get some friendly stick. Yet I could think of worse names to be called such as Bobby Hinton or Chris Edworth!

Kevin Egan
Walker, Newcastle

Chris Waddle was class, he ran rings around Burnley. Yet it was rumoured that he was to be leaving Newcastle as part of an exchange deal. Waddle joked "I've read all the stories in the papers. There's been so much talk of swaps that I'm thinking of getting in touch with Noel Edmonds on Swap Shop!"

Chris Waddle
Newcastle United

Fans fall foul of the bench

Fines totaling £1,100 were slapped on soccer fans for crowd trouble during Saturdays match between Newcastle and Burnley at St James' Park. Eleven fans all admitted using threatening, abusive and insulting words and behavior likely to cause a breach of the peace in separate cases. One of the guilty was a Burnley fan who had travelled up to the match in a mini-bus containing both Burnley and Newcastle fans said the defence. The 'V' signs he was making were directed towards friends among the Newcastle crowd!

v LEICESTER CITY
FILBERT STREET
ATT; 15,044

SAT 13TH NOVEMBER 1982
SECOND DIVISION
DREW 2-2

On the way back I stopped off in York for a few beers. I was quite drunk when I got on the train to go home. Somehow I woke up in Carlisle? Don't ask, as I haven't got a clue. In fact ever since that day I've tried to work out how? Did I get on wrong train? Did the train do a detour? Did the train continue on to Carlisle from Newcastle? I will never know. What I do know though, is the reason why - I was blotto. I slept in Carlisle railway station; it was freezing and got the train back at 11am.

Piper
Felling, Tyneside

v CARLISLE UNITED
BRUNTON PARK
ATT; 16,276

SAT 20TH NOVEMBER 1982
SECOND DIVISION
LOST 0-2

Due to injury we had no Mick Martin or Kevin Keegan. Keegan had picked up an eye injury whilst appearing as a special guest at Ayresome Park for John Craggs testimonial days earlier. So today we had Peter Haddock in midfield! We

179

were awful. In the closing stages as we trailed without any hope the 6,000 travelling fans chanted *"There's Only One United."* Eventually after a very disappointing 2-0 defeat we were herded back to the station like cattle to catch our 'Football Special' for the short journey home across the country. On arriving at the Train Station we were then made to wait down a side street with a huge posh hotel next to us. The coppers were well out of order as they made us stand there in the cold for what seemed like hours which resulted in arguments between supporters and police followed by scuffles which led to arrests. This sent a lot of fans up a height and the next thing I knew was that the hotel windows opposite were being smashed as dozens started throwing stones. The police horses charged in, along with the dogs to try and sort out the riot as we were then quickly moved into the station and onto our waiting train. What should have been a quick trip home still wasn't over as the train was stopped on several occasions by people pulling the emergency cords. My first pint in Yates' bar opposite the Central station never touched the sides as I tried to drown the memory of this rather long crap day.

Mick Edmondson
Walker, Newcastle

Security tight at big game

Carlisle was a city under siege this afternoon as thousands of Newcastle United fans swarmed in for the derby match at Brunton Park. Alcohol was banned on the two football special trains for supporters who were met at the Citadel Station by police and escorted to the ground. Thousands more travelled by road as police warned those without tickets not to go to Cumbria, in a bid to prevent trouble, especially as the FA Disciplinary committee is due to deliver its verdict on the Leeds v Newcastle crowd riots.

The pre-match entertainment at the time was joining the masses and taking over the nearest pub to the Railway Station. Carlisle was no exception, however no one obviously warned the landlord what to expect when the Toon turned up in town. He and his only other member of staff just couldn't cope with the couple of hundred Newcastle fans who had packed into the pub, making self service a necessary requirement. Within half an hour the landlord decided he'd had enough and throwing down his apron on the floor left the premises with the welcome words of "help your fucking selves, I've had enough." And of course we did.

Millie
Kenton, Newcastle

A late start for an away game for the short trip along the A69 to Carlisle. We travelled with Magpie Travel. I decided to buy myself a cap for the trip one with the NUFC round Magpie badge. For some reason everybody used to buy their bait for the trips at Greggs. The match was one to forget, Carlisle were good value for their win. Newcastle supporters with nothing to cheer about decided to amuse themselves by dismantling the greyhound scoreboard at the Petrill End, and somehow some of it ended up on our bus.

Chris Ramshaw
West Denton, Newcastle

Now this was a bad defeat. I got a lift over to Carlisle by my Mam as I was only young. Then she looked around the shops in Carlisle while my mate and I went to the match. I was practically sitting on the pitch and the match was crap. My Mam bought some shoes.....probably.

Gavin Haigh
Newton Hall, Durham

United fans wreck Hotel

Newcastle United's notorious away match wreckers went on the rampage at Carlisle. Geordie supporters hit the city centre's Cumbrian Hotel with a barrage of bricks and bottles - smashing 27 windows. Police arrested 15 fans for public disorder offences before the derby match against Carlisle and many others were ejected from the ground after kick-off. The final whistle was the signal for Newcastle fans to smash a door and windows at a house under construction near Brunton Park.

v DYNAMO KIEV
ST JAMES' PARK
ATT; 12,572

TUES 23RD NOVEMBER 1982
FRIENDLY
WON 2-1

Visiting St James' Park in the early eighties was a total different experience to what it is these days. You could just stroll up to the turnstile at 2.45pm on a Saturday and more or less just walk in. You'd sometimes have to queue as the police/fascists on horseback would somehow manage to get there horses between each queue causing more hassle than necessary. Calamity Jane a fat bird used to ride one of the horses for years. Then if you'd escaped being crushed or bitten by the beasts you'd be body searched just inside the turnstile to make sure you had no ammunition before climbing the 'north-face' aka the Gallowgate steps. The amount of police needed and used at a match back then was unbelievable. No chance of the Russians getting any nuclear war heads into this match. This match was a change to the norm, but at the end of the day friendlies are a waste of time, although I always seem to attend them. I mean a total of 36 players actually took part in this friendly and their squad included 8 World Cup players. The game was arranged as a practice game for Kiev who were in the middle of their winter break and wanted to play against English opposition as there was a chance that they could meet Aston Villa or Liverpool later in the season in the European Cup. Yes we had 2 English clubs in the competition as Villa qualified as holders. Kiev also played Hearts and Hull. The match was played in atrocious conditions, a constant downpour making it a rain soaked evening for all who braved the elements. Arthur Cox commented, "There is nowhere else in the world where so many people would turn up on such a night for a friendly match. And if Kevin Keegan had of been on view there would have been over 20,000 in the ground."

Mick Edmondson
Walker, Newcastle

**V CAMBRIDGE UNITED
ST JAMES' PARK
ATT; 20,385**

**SAT 27TH NOVEMBER 1982
SECOND DIVISION
WON 2-0**

Howard Gayle made his Newcastle debut after joining us on loan from Liverpool as cover for the injured Kevin Keegan. I hate racism but there was a song which went, *"He's Black, He's Broon, He's Playing For The Toon, Howard Gayle, Howard Gayle."* The 12 (Yes twelve) Cambridge supporters who had made the trip laughed whilst huddled together on this freezing cold day. In the stands watching were the Dynamo Kiev players and officials who had stayed on Tyneside after their match against us.

**Brian Hall
Heaton, Newcastle**

**v CHARLTON ATHLETIC
THE VALLEY
ATT; 10,381**

**SAT 4TH DECEMBER 1982
SECOND DIVISION
LOST 0-2**

A visit to the old Valley in South London which could house 75,000 yet just over 10,000 turned up for this match with a good following from the Toon to witness two former 'European Footballers of the Year' go head to head. Charlton had

new signing Allan Simonsen the Danish international who'd only arrived 3 weeks earlier and was on a reported £82,000 a season! He scored and ran the show, whilst our former 'European Footballer of the Year' Kevin Keegan had unfortunately failed to recover from his eye injury. I can remember drinking pints of lager on the big massive side terrace only yards away from the late great Brian Moore who was covering the game for London Weekend Television. Wearing Keegan's famous number seven shirt was a young Irishman making his first ever start in a Newcastle first team game Paul Ferris - the next George Best? Another one of our great young hopes, so great he never ever started another league match for us.

Paul Wardle
Wallsend, Tyneside

v WOLVES
ST JAMES' PARK
ATT; 19,595

SAT 11TH DECEMBER 1982
SECOND DIVISION
DREW 1-1

An Open letter to all Newcastle United Supporters.
At a Football Association Disciplinary Committee Meeting held on November 22nd the Newcastle United Football Club was found guilty of a breach of FA Rule 33(a), following the misbehaviour of its supporters at the Leeds United v Newcastle United Football league match played at Leeds on October 30th. Newcastle United Football Club was severely warned as to its future conduct. Under Football Association Regulations, clubs have an absolute responsibility to the Football Association Council for the conduct of their supporters. Spectators are only permitted to attend matches on condition that they observe the rules and regulations of the Association. The Football Association have wide ranging powers to impose very severe penalties, including heavy fines and closing a ground either permanently or for an extended period. It is imperative to your club that no further incidents of misbehaviour occur. The consequences would most certainly considerably affect the Club's progress both in financial and playing terms. The reputation of the club and the City of Newcastle upon Tyne are at stake. Every supporter has a part to play by acting in a responsible manner both at St James' Park and while travelling to, and attending away fixtures. The club appreciate that it is only a minority of supporters that cause trouble but the effect reflects on everyone. It is the responsibility of supporters not only to keep out of trouble themselves but to ensure that others around them do so as well. Please give Newcastle United your full support and co-operation.

Stan Seymour
Newcastle United Chairman
(Match Programme)

An open letter to all Newcastle United supporters is included in today's programme and we trust that ALL supporters will take time out to read, digest and, most of all, remember the contents. If any further incidents of misbehaviour occur in the future the club will almost certainly be disciplined. That could mean a heavy fine or even the closure of St James' Park. We don't want that, and we are sure that the majority of supporters feel the same way. Let's have a trouble free remainder or the season. It's in your hands. The match against Sheffield Wednesday on the 18th December is not all ticket and the Leppings Lane end of Hillsborough has been allocated in it's entirety to Newcastle United supporters. This section holds around 10,000 spectators. It's always an entertaining fixture and sure to be well supported. PLEASE REMEMBER OUR EARLIER WARNING REGARDING CROWD BEHAVIOUR.

Russell Cushing
Newcastle United Secretary
(Match Programme)

When travelling anywhere with work I would always wear my black-and-white shirt on the way home and one time in 1983 (before the wall came down) I was coming through the Airport in Hamburg when I noticed that a couple of heavily armed policemen, you know the type - grimfaced, moustachioed, shoulders back, chest out, sub-machine gun held across the chest, sneeze and they'll shoot you type. Well, one of them was giving me the evil eye and I was thinking, "oh no! Here comes a strip search for the football hooligan!!!" As I got closer I saw him nudge his colleague with his elbow and nod my way. The second policeman turned and said "Ve know Kevin Keegan" in a broad German accent and the pair gave me a salute as I walked passed. Unfortunately Kevin Keegan didn't play today, in front of the third largest crowd in the country.

Davy Gregson
Durham

v SHEFFIELD WEDNESDAY	SAT 18TH DECEMBER 1982
HILLSBOROUGH	SECOND DIVISION
ATT; 16,310	DREW 1-1

The Saturday before Christmas a cold miserable day and although an impressive following from Tyneside, and still larger than any other clubs would take, it was the least I've ever seen at Hillsborough. Before the match in an off-license there was a large queue of Geordies purchasing cans of pop whilst each concealing a bottle of spirits under their coats! After the match which saw us drop to 15th, I was in a Bakers shop getting some scoff for the trip home when unbelievably in through the shop door came a copper on a horse. It's not exactly an ideal situation being trapped in a small shop by a giant horse but never the less it was quite funny when the beast started eating the cakes to the embarrassment of the overreacting tit on its back and the not too pleased Shopkeeper.

Deka
Gateshead, Tyneside

v DERBY COUNTY	MON 27TH DECEMBER 1982
ST JAMES' PARK	SECOND DIVISION
ATT; 30,558	WON 1-0

Norman Egg loved Newcastle, though sadly he died before his 30th birthday, through his own sad addiction to alcohol. Norman worked on the North Shields

fish quay and rarely missed a game. In order to get a bit more money, he would often sell fresh fish and seafood's in some of the pubs in Shields before a game, and then jump on the train to Newcastle. We were once in the White Hart pub and in came Norman, loud and jovial. He approached an older lady and said; "Here Mrs do you want some fresh fish?" "No thank you son" replied the lady rather timidly; "I had fish for my tea last night". "That's nowt man Mrs" came Norman, "I had twelve pints of Ex' last night, but I'm having another twelve tonight." The place erupted in laughter, though Norman was deadly serious. A fashion of the early 80's had been sheepskin coats, everyone had one. Norman wore his one day for a match near Christmas; he had got his from a mate in the trade, allegedly. We were playing Derby and we won 1-0 thanks to a late goal by Howard Gayle. When Newcastle scored, the crowd went crazy and someone went to hug Norman and pulled the sleeve of his new coat. It was a cold day on the Gallowgate terraces, but so as not to look odd, Norman pulled the other sleeve off and told everyone that sheepskin waistcoats were the "new fashion."

Football League Division Two
NEWCASTLE UNITED
versus
DERBY COUNTY
Official Matchday Magazine
Volume 6 No. 11 Price 35p

Anth Nicholson
North Shields, Tyneside

v GRIMSBY TOWN
BLUNDELL PARK
ATT; 14,983

TUES 28TH DECEMBER 1982
SECOND DIVISION
DREW 2-2

There was loads of us went down for the match, but one of the pubs near the ground wouldn't let us in and locked the doors, so we all went around the side of the pub and climbed in through the windows.

Sean Glen
North Shields, Tyneside

v CARLISLE UNITED
ST JAMES' PARK
ATT; 28,578

SAT 1ST JANUARY 1983
SECOND DIVISION
DREW 2-2

I can recall not feeling totally comfortable, but unable to stop laughing on first hearing Howard Gayle being referred to as "Blackie Milburn" and singing along to *"He's Black, He's Broon, He's Playing For The Toon, Howard Gayle, Howard Gayle"* and then being amused but unconvinced by *"He's Broon, He's Black And We've Sent The Bastard Back, Howard Gayle, Howard Gayle"* when his loan spell came to an end.

185

The Geordie dilemma - At times the most open welcoming of people, but the flip side, the most insular and closed ranks.

Tom Knox
Fenham, Newcastle

v BOLTON WANDERERS
ST JAMES' PARK
ATT; 23,533

MON 3RD JANUARY 1983
SECOND DIVISION
DREW 2-2

After slipping up at home to Carlisle two days earlier it was important that we got back to winning ways against eventual bottom of the table Bolton. Howard Gayle played his final loan game before returning to Liverpool with two goals in eight starts. With Terry McDermott receiving his marching orders for the second time in two months and Davey Mac picking up a horrific leg wound which needed sixty stitches and kept him out for the next two months, things didn't look to promising as we entered the final minute, trailing 0-1 to a first half goal. With it being a public holiday quite a few of the fans left before the end as all transport was running a skeleton service, thinking they'd witnessed a disappointing defeat. Then in the final minute Chris Waddle grabbed an equaliser but when we were still jumping about like nutters celebrating, Wanderers went straight up the other end and scored. However we weren't finished as unbelievably well into injury time Mick Martin got a very late second equaliser. Fans that had left the ground early would have maybe heard the roars and moans across the city but would have probably had to wait until they got home (no mobile phones) to find out the result. Once home unless you rang somebody at home then it still wasn't an easy task finding out the result as there was no sky sports news, not even teletext! You'd maybe catch the local sports news featuring the latest technology, a photo of Sunderland fan Doug Wetheral on your screen holding a telephone whilst his badly recorded muffled voice gave a brief summary of the match. As it was a Monday there wasn't even a 'Football Pink,' so many would wake up on the Tuesday morning believing we had lost. One rule to remember especially when watching Newcastle United, never ever leave before the end.

Mick Edmondson
Walker, Newcastle

v BRIGHTON & HOVE ALBION
GOLDSTONE GROUND
ATT; 17,711

SAT 8TH JANUARY 1983
FA CUP 3RD ROUND
DREW 1-1

A couple of memorable moments from our long trek to the south coast will stay with me for ever. The game of sixty-a-side football on the beach early on the Saturday morning would normally take some beating. But earlier after stopping off at the services on the way down in the middle of the night, was the scene of the biggest food fight ever to be staged in this country. You name it, it was thrown. Eggs, sausages, chips, mushrooms and beans as a couple of hundred drunken 'Mags' had a choice to either join in or take cover.

Mick Edmondson
Walker, Newcastle

We travelled down on the Friday night arriving on the south coast in the early hours. I never stopped drinking, so can't remember much about it apart from when I fell down a grass bank at the back of our terracing, rolling down from the top and smashing through the toilet roof, which luckily broke my fall before landing at the feet of startled fellow Geordies. Amazingly apart from the roof nothing else was broken.

Chillo
Walker, Newcastle

After a midnight departure and journey through the night me and my mate Davey were walking along the sea front at 8am when we bumped into Imre Varadi and 'Spotty McDonald.' "Do you think they'll be many down today?" enquired Varadi just as we were passing dozens of Mags sleeping it off on the beach in those beach shelter jobbies. We wished them well as we went in search of a drink as we were dying for a pint and hadn't walked far when we saw a lass sneaking into a nearby bar, could it be the cleaner? We slowly sneak a look round the door, fuck me it was like Heaton Buffs on a Sunday afternoon, Jukebox blaring, Pool games, Darts, & Doms, wall to wall Black n' White and it wasn't even 9am!! Only Newcastle could do this man, over 300 miles from home, unbelievable.

Jimmy King
North Shields, Tyneside

The Brighton fans taunted us with "England, England" trying to insinuate that we were Scottish. Then in London as we had a few pints before we caught our connection I was asked "Which part of Wales are you from?" I'm Geordie, English and proud. Clueless Southerners - French Bastards the lot of them.

Piper
Felling, Tyneside

v BRIGHTON & HOVE ALBION	WED 12TH JANUARY 1983
ST JAMES' PARK	FA CUP 3RD RND REPLAY
ATT; 32,687	LOST 0-1

On their last visit to Gallowgate 'The Seagulls' won promotion to the top flight at the expense of Sunderland who finished fourth. This would be their fourth and final season in the First Division as they'd finish bottom come May. Already they were in trouble and hadn't won away all season and we hadn't lost an FA Cup replay at St James' Park since World War Two. What could possibly go wrong? Trelford 'Bloody' Mills, that's what. Mills who had refereed Keegan's debut a few months earlier turned in the worst ever refereeing display ever. As I stood on the Gallowgate I and thousands of others couldn't believe our eyes when in the last five minutes he disallowed two perfect legitimate goals at our end (as proved by TV footage), turned down two definite penalties and chested away a Varadi shot!! The goals from Varadi, and a Keegan header which beat Graham Moseley, without question should have stood so much so that Keegan, Carney and Varadi went absolutely mental with Mills. *"Who's Ye Father, Who's Ye Father, Who's Ye*

Father Referee, You Haven't Got One You're a Bastard, You're A Bastard Referee" reverberated around the ground. Brighton unbelievably went on to reach the final and should have beaten Man Utd when Gordon Smith missed a gilt edged chance your Granny could have scored, in the final minutes at Wembley. Their luck had run out and they went and lost the replay 4-0. As for Trelford Mills could he ever dare set foot in Newcastle again? Well, that's what we thought...

Mick Edmondson
Walker, Newcastle

v QUEENS PARK RANGERS   **SAT 15TH JANUARY 1983**
LOFTUS ROAD   **SECOND DIVISION**
ATT; 13,972   **LOST 0-2**

Short of cash I decided to hitch down to London in the middle of the night. Luckily I didn't have to wait long as I was picked up on the south side of the Tyne Bridge by two lads in their van who were also on their way to the match. The crack was canny and they seemed like good lads although a bit mad. As we approached London we were pulled over by the police who searched the van and questioned all three of us. I couldn't believe it when the police told me that the van was stolen and that we were to be arrested. However I was allowed to leave the scene with a warning from the police when the two lads explained what had happened. So they were lifted as I made my way to the match and I've never ever seen them again. As for the match we lost to the eventual runaway champions, a team who we'd memorably beaten on Keegan's debut. Afterwards I eventually made my return journey by Lorry.

Unknown

v SHREWSBURY TOWN
ST JAMES' PARK
ATT; 19,333

SAT 22ND JANUARY 1983
SECOND DIVISION
WON 4-0

Just a few months out of school we thought we were the dog's bollocks with our new 'Newcastle United Union Jack flag' as we stood proudly on the concrete barrier showing it off for the first time to all below. Then a much older and bigger skinhead and his ugly skinhead bird pinched it off us, escaping through the crowd as they told us what would happen if we went near them. I hate bullying but it was all part and parcel of the 80's match experience, gutted but the 4-0 win helped cheer us up, although after 24 games we were a massive 14 points off the 3rd automatic promotion place.

Kev
Walker, Newcastle

v MIDDLESBROUGH
AYRESOME PARK
ATT; 25,184

SAT 5TH FEBRUARY 1983
SECOND DIVISION
DREW 1-1

Who would want to live at the back of Ayresome Park? The fortnightly visit of away fans saw the wardrobes strategically placed in front of the windows and with a ready supply of broken concrete at the back of the away fans end, what else was there to do while locked in waiting to be released onto the streets? However this year was memorable for another incident, while leaving the ground an overzealous officer on horseback persisted in riding his horse into fans until a mate had had enough, punching the horse smack on the nose and knocking it out.

Millie
Kenton, Newcastle

I had travelled by train and was in the police escort, walking from the ground back to the station after the match. Eventually we arrived at the railway station and the police were herding us around like cattle, as hundreds of us were pushed against the wall, without choice as mounted police and dog handlers forced us back. We were trying to stand still but it was impossible as everybody was getting squashed, I managed to grab hold of a little lad who couldn't breath, lifting him up. In the commotion I was pushed around and fell out of the crowd. A copper shouted at me, "Get back in there you fat bag of shit." I replied, "Hey, there's nee need for that," "You don't speak to people like that." He came towards me and when he went to grab me his dog latched onto my arm, sinking it's teeth into my forearm. I was in agony and before I knew what was happening I was handcuffed and on my way to hospital, where I received an injection and numerous stitches. Believe it or not, I was then charged and asked to appear in court at a later date. In court the copper whose dog attacked me lied through his back teeth, saying that I supposedly ran out of the police escort, shouting "I'll kill you and your fucking dog." Well apart from that being totally out of character, I'm a big lad and anybody who knows me will tell you, there is no way that I can run! I was fined £75 for nowt' and still have the dog bite scar on my arm, but the worst thing about it is that it put me off travelling away as much as I would have liked.

Micky Carr
Walker, Newcastle

I had my first date with Wendy (whom I went onto marry) arranged for the Saturday night in town. I was meeting her in the Canny Lad pub and then we were going to a wedding do at the Rainbow Rooms (inside the co-op building), but beforehand I spent the day with the lads going to Boro' away. So there I was standing on the terraces at Ayresome Park on the coldest day in living memory getting all the usual shite off the 'Smoggies' when all of a sudden out of nowhere a fuckin' half-brick hit me in the nose. I'm not kidding you my fuckin' bugle was all over me face, claret everywhere. As the game went on I could literally feel my eyes narrowing. Of course when I eventually met her I didn't quite look my best with my face looking like I'd gone 10 rounds with Muhammad Ali and my powder blue Pringle v-neck looking like a tie & dye, its a wonder we ever had a second date never mind walked down the aisle together.

Terry O'Donnell
Kenton, Newcastle

Soccer battle terrorises residents

Soccer yobs went on the rampage yesterday before, during and after the derby game between Middlesbrough and Newcastle United. The hooligans: Fought a pitched battle outside the Ayresome Park ground. Threw bricks and bottles at houses near the ground. Clashed during the game. Pelted an injured soccer player with coins. Battled in three public houses on their way to the match. Twenty-seven people including four police officers - one of them a woman - received hospital treatment. A Cleveland Police spokeswoman said last night 40 arrests had been made. "It was the largest crowd of the season at Ayresome Park and there was certainly a lot of trouble. Newcastle supporters are becoming notorious for aggro." she said. Last night, angry residents living near the ground visited Ayresome Park to ask for compensation for the damage to their homes. And last night Middlesbrough chairman Mike McCullagh said: "I visited the houses in Ayresome Park Road after the game and told the people the club would repair the windows on Monday morning. The police spokeswoman said: "Four police officers were injured. The most serious injury was a broken nose. We also had a number of police vehicles damaged." Rival fans fought a pitched street battle outside Middlesbrough football ground after the game. Using bricks and bottles, they clashed in Ayresome Park Road. Terrified householders cowered behind the curtains as bricks rained through the air. At least three houses had their windows smashed by flying missiles. Mrs Jean Welch, who lives in Ayresome Park Road said: "I have lived here 10 years and this is the worst trouble I have witnessed. "We have lived here when Leeds United, Chelsea and Manchester United have all been playing. But this was worse. It was terrifying. Anybody who doesn't live near a football ground can't begin to imagine what it is like to have a pitched battle outside your house." Another resident Paul Gittens, who had a front door window broken, said: A lot of Newcastle supporters were kept inside the ground for about 15 minutes after the match. "They were throwing bricks and rubble over the wall into the street. "Other Newcastle fans and Middlesbrough supporters were outside fighting, it was mayhem. Police on horseback tried to separate the fighting fans while missiles were hurled over the wall onto them from inside the ground. Police on horseback tried to separate the fighting fans in Ayresome Park Road and nearby streets. It was estimated that 8,000 Newcastle fans were in the 25,000 crowd.

v OLDHAM ATHLETIC
ST JAMES' PARK
ATT; 20,689

SAT 19TH FEBRUARY 1983
SECOND DIVISION
WON 1-0

Before the match we got talking to a couple of Oldham fans in 'The Darn Crook' pub. We were slating Steve Hardwick who'd finally lost his battle with the Boo Boys and had been sold to Oxford a couple of days earlier. 'The Latics' fans were bemoaning their captain Ged Keegan a previous player of the year at Boundary Park, "Keegan, he's not the player he used to be, he's a wanker, and he's shit!!" Not realising they were talking about Ged but instead thinking they were slating 'Wor Kev' a Geordie passing us on the way to the bogs just planted the nut on this Oldham lad. After jumping in between them and an explanation it was complete embarrassment and apologies. "Sorry mate I'm on a mission because I've just been told, that bastard Trelford Mills is back again today."

Graham Evans
Whickham, Newcastle

v FULHAM
CRAVEN COTTAGE
ATT; 14,277

SAT 26TH FEBRUARY 1983
SECOND DIVISION
DREW 2-2

I travelled down with the supporters club arriving in London a couple of hours before kick-off. We were dropped off at Craven Cottage and after a visit to the off-license about fifty of us went into the park, which was just behind our end. One of the lads had made a DIY football on the coach, made out of newspaper and sellotape just like they did in the old days, only this one didn't last very long. This didn't really matter as we now had a proper ball the legendary 'Wembley trophy', which was the next best thing to a 'caser' (Case-ball). The kids we pinched it off, although offered weren't very keen on joining in, which didn't surprise me as a full scale twenty-five a side match kicked off. The West End (made up of Kenton, West Denton, Blakelaw, Scotswood and Cowgate lads) v The East End (Lads from Walker, Byker, Heaton, Benton, Wallsend and North Shields). The match was a bit crazy at times as waist high tackles by half pissed blokes were a regular occurrence, on the more skilful cider drinking youths. For goals we just used jumpers although The East End had an advantage as their goal was up on the bandstand, which was almost waist high. A public footpath ran diagonally right across our pitch which was normally used by the Fulham supporters walking to the match. As kick-off approached the park was becoming busy and before long we had an audience, who seemed to be totally bewildered by this huge Edwardian type football match with no throw-ins, free-kicks and definitely no rules. Players being sick, objects being thrown, plenty of swearing and men in Kilts seemed to make the Cockneys miss out on their normal short cut. I can't actually remember the final score I think it was a 2-2 draw, with goals from McDermott and Varadi !! As for our match it was 12-7 to the East End but we went on to win as the shout went up "next goal the winner."

Stevas
West Denton, Newcastle

v CRYSTAL PALACE
SELHURST PARK
ATT; 10,239

SAT 5TH MARCH 1983
SECOND DIVISION
WON 2-0

Excellent organization by the powers that be, as we made our second trip to London in eight days, thanks to the FA's piss taking computer. Waddle scored here again repeating his feat from last season's victory as we did the league double over them this time round. Unbelievably this was our first away win since we won at Rotherham in the first week of October! Meanwhile outspoken Nottingham Forest manager Brian Clough announced to the world that "Football should be banned from TV for the next three years."

Mick Edmondson
Walker, Newcastle

v LEEDS UNITED
ST JAMES' PARK
ATT; 24,543

SAT 12TH MARCH 1983
SECOND DIVISION
WON 2-1

This was the day when the E-Wing Paddock in the old West Stand was full to capacity at 2pm. The reason being it was situated right next to the travelling Leeds fans in the corner of the Leazes End. A lot of hooligans, wannabe hooligans and 'Singers' frequented this terracing back then taking over from the older more sensible type of supporter who'd made it their home for years. As soon as Leeds

finest showed they were greeted with various chants; *"Can You Run Can You Run Can You Run, Can You Run Can You Run Can You Ruuunnn, Can You Run Can You Run Can You Run, Can You Run Can You Run."* And *"We'll See You All Outside, We'll See You All Outside, We'll See You All, We'll See You All Outside."* As well as; *"You Can Stick Your Yorkshire Puddings Up Your Arse,"* And the old favourite *"You're Gonna Get Your Fucking Head Kicked In."* By kick-off the whole paddock was hoarse. The Leeds section looked like a massive oblong Battenberg Cake, with all the pastel coloured Yellow and Pink Jumpers and casual attire. The majority of the Leeds following were Dressers/Casuals whereas the majority of the Newcastle fans were still into Donkey Jackets and Doc Martins. Although we did have a casual scene which was growing quickly and was bigger than what others thought. The match which was very entertaining was played in the most intimidating atmosphere of the season. David Harvey saved a Kevin Keegan penalty only for the Newcastle skipper to score with the rebound.

Mick Edmondson
Walker, Newcastle

"Kevin Keegan's Performance is the best individual display I have ever seen."
Brian Murphy
Leeds United Coach

v BURNLEY   **SAT 19TH MARCH 1983**
TURF MOOR   **SECOND DIVISION**
ATT; 13,900   **LOST 0-1**

We were lying in mid-table our promotion hopes in tatters, yet we still had our usual large loyal following for the visit to this typical Lancashire town. Once inside the ground there was talk of various scuffles and incidents, that had took place in and around the pubs before the match. We were housed on a covered terrace at the side of the pitch adjacent to the Burnley nutter's who were too our left. I spent the majority of the ninety minutes with one eye on the match, whilst the other watched out for the barrage of missiles being constantly thrown at us. The Coppers were useless as very few arrests were made yet dozens of fans from either side needed treatment; as a result tempers were at boiling point. At half-time at the back of the terraces a Hamburger seller was attacked and covered in his own sources from head to toe, as his trolley was kicked down the stairs from top to bottom. Then Newcastle fans charged the fence around the back some got into the home section by scaling it, others by storming the gate as Burnley fans quickly retreated. Fighting broke out and the coppers waded in with their truncheons drawn making the odd arrest whilst at the bottom of the stairs a bloke in a white coat covered in red tomato sauce was trying to salvage his handcart... Meanwhile on Wearside Sunderland fans were incensed after earlier in the week, their very own chairman Tom Cowie had announced I wish we had supporters like Newcastle United did!" While we travelled to Burnley, a crowd of only 17,445 at Roker Park for Sunderland's game against Swansea sang *"Cowie Out, Cowie Out* and *"Cowie Is A Magpie."*

Mick Edmondson
Walker, Newcastle

v LEICESTER CITY
ST JAMES' PARK
ATT; 22,692

SAT 26TH MARCH 1983
SECOND DIVISION
DREW 2-2

Played on the same day as the League Cup Final between Liverpool and Man United at Wembley, we had the biggest League gate in England. Not bad for a Second Division match! City's Gary Lineker was class, scoring twice for the FA Cup semi-finalists. We should have signed him, he would have been perfect. Instead keeper Martin Thomas arrived on loan, oh well never mind.

Mick Edmondson
Walker, Newcastle

v GRIMSBY TOWN
ST JAMES' PARK
ATT; 20,202

SAT 2ND APRIL 1983
SECOND DIVISION
WON 4-0

Grimsby only brought 17 fans up with them!! There was more in the disabled dugout in front of them. They'd conceded 25 goals in their last 8 away matches. We couldn't fail and surprisingly we didn't.

Mick Edmondson
Walker, Newcastle

v DERBY COUNTY
BASEBALL GROUND
ATT; 19,779

MON 4TH APRIL 1983
SECOND DIVISION
LOST 1-2

Easter weekend and yet another fantastic following, the usual pushing and shoving getting into the game after being in a local pub nearby and after the match fighting to get out onto the narrow terraced streets, with the police doing their best to make the situation worse. Nothing better than looking back and seeing the thousands of Newcastle fans flooding the streets with their huge support!

Dave Drape
Walker, Newcastle

If you wanted bother you could nearly always get it at the Baseball ground. I remember they used to have a squad of lads who used to wear green berets - I can also remember a small group of Newcastle lads who used to wear bright red berets and would always infiltrate the away enclosure at SJP. We had picked up some complimentary tickets from one of the players, so were sitting amongst the player's wives and club officials in the main stand at the opposite end of the ground to where the Newcastle fans were congregated. We were bored and wanted to move and got our chance when some Geordies who had infiltrated the Derby home end behind the goal to our right had been spotted by the police who moved in quickly to stop the ensuing battle. There were about twenty of them and we were soon down there joining them pitch side, as the police started to escort us around the perimeter of the pitch. Newcastle hooligans would quite often invade enemy territory then be led around the pitch and put into the away supporters section, greeted with cheers like heroes returning from battle. *"Geordies Here, Geordies There, Geordies Every F***ing Where, Lalalalalalalalalala."*

Mick Edmondson
Walker, Newcastle

v BLACKBURN ROVERS   **SAT 9TH APRIL 1983**
ST JAMES' PARK   **SECOND DIVISION**
ATT; 17,839   **WON 3-2**

Our lowest home crowd of the season witnessed a bizarre match as we completed the double over Rovers. A candidate for goal of the season opened the scoring for United as Blackburn's Metcalf juggled the ball on the edge of his own area, before unbelievably lobbing his own keeper as well as a penalty area full of players! Then when we were 2-0 up former United defender and boo-boy Glen Keeley, came on as a sub and scored with a half-volley. We then went 3-1 up before Keeley got a second which prompted the Gallowgate End to chant "Geordie Reject" to which Keeley responded to by turning with his arms raised as a champion, which was actually quite funny. Paul Ferris made his last appearance; he actually only ever started one game for us but also made twelve appearances as a sub scoring a solitary goal whilst on Tyneside. He was highly rated when we signed him from Lisburn Juniors in November 1981, but as often was the case he just wasn't good enough.

Mick Edmondson
Walker, Newcastle

A really boring end-of-season drag, despite the five goals (one of which was a magically silly own goal by one of the Blackburn lads). The match was so boring, in fact, that a bunch of us in the benches were listening to the National on the radio and getting quite excited. Particularly my mate John (who'd borrowed my dad's ticket that day) who had two quid on the winner at 12-1. A few minutes later, the ball went out for a throw-in directly in front of us. Terry Mac comes over to take it. "Who won?" he asks. "Corbiere" a bunch of us shout back. "Aw, bugger" he says giving a rather exaggerated "pah!" gesture with his hand and returning his attention to the match that he was playing in. You can't keep a good gambler down.

Keith Topping
Walker, Newcastle

v CHELSEA   **SAT 16TH APRIL 1983**
STAMFORD BRIDGE   **SECOND DIVISION**
ATT; 13,446   **WON 2-0**

Probably Chelsea biggest league match of the season at the Bridge. Yet even with Keegan, Waddle, McCreery and McDermott in town, Chelsea yet again proved what fickle part time supporters they are, I bet the likes of John Major, David Mellor (Probably at Fulham), Seb Coe and all the other toffee nosed glory hunting celebrities weren't there. There probably wasn't even ten thousand cockneys in the ground because as usual there were plenty of fans down from the North East. Anyway I was still at school - 15 years old, yet I travelled to every single match that season, home and away. After the match we drank wherever we could get in around the west end, my dodgy tash' did come in handy sometimes. We eventually caught the midnight coach back to Newcastle, but all I can remember is waking up in the early hours naked apart from my kegs, carrying a bag full of clothes covered in spew. After all it was our first victory at Stamford Bridge for 29 years.

Eddie Snowdon
Byker, Newcastle

As a canny teenage lad from the east end of Newcastle I had my eyes opened by various other fans as I travelled away with lads from different parts of the city. For this particular match I was told to meet at the Deckham pub for a few drinks before an overnight journey. It was the usual scenario of too many lads in a small transit van, which obviously worked out a lot cheaper so I never complained about being squashed or the continuous farting. Just before arrival at Stamford Bridge I remember one of the Deckham lads whilst tightening his Doc Martens announcing that if anyone runs today you'll get this boot in your face! It's the way it was back then.

Dave
Walker, Newcastle

v ROTHERHAM UNITED   **WED 20TH APRIL 1983**
ST JAMES' PARK   **SECOND DIVISION**
ATT; 18,523   **WON 4-0**

The reality of playing in the Second Division is when shit teams such as Rotherham and the like turn up and it's pissing down on a cold night. It isn't so bad when you visit their places as it's a day out, a drink in another town and another ground for the list. But at home it's bloody Rotherham and not Man Utd, Liverpool or Arsenal. Our third consecutive win put us 5th after completing the double over them.   We still had an outside chance of promotion with 5 games to go. Before the match there was an under-13 football tournament on the pitch between Newcastle schoolboys, Sunderland, Middlesbrough and Blyth.   The Newcastle side featured a certain youngster by the name of Alan Shearer. The semi-finals were at 6.30pm with the final at 7pm. The winners of the North Eastern Co-op trophy were Newcastle managed by Ted Hayes of Walker school and captained by Gosforth's Alan Shearer.

Mick Edmondson
Walker, Newcastle

"Kevin Keegan is by far the best player I have ever seen - and he seems to be getting even better."

David McCreery
Newcastle United

v CHARLTON ATHLETIC
ST JAMES' PARK
ATT; 20,567

SAT 23RD APRIL 1983
SECOND DIVISION
WON 4-2

Our 4th win on the trot and we were fifth with 3 away games and 1 at home to play. QPR who we beat on the opening day of the season as Keegan mania hit Gallowgate, clinched promotion today. Back then at St James' Park there used to be a flag pole in the South East corner of the Gallowgate End (The Corner) and with 10 minutes remaining the 'Black-and-White 10 Minute Flag' would be taken down. This would be closely followed by dozens upon dozens of Coppers marching around the perimeter of the pitch which would cause an instant reaction amongst the Geordie ranks *"Der Du Der Du, Der Du Der Du, Derudle Du Derudle Du!"* And chants of *"F-Troop, F-Troop, F-Troop!"* After the match as usual hundreds stayed on the Gallowgate terrace singing the names of all the players as they left the field. Then it was down the stairs everyone singing as we turned left onto Strawberry Place, past the Strawberry Pub then turned right down Leazes Park Road and past Carrick's bakery shop at the bottom. This what we called the Geordie March used to take place after every home match for years and on big matches could be over 2,000 strong. Once on Percy Street it would continue left along Blackett Street where the singing would reach a crescendo as it would bounce off Blackett Street Bridge and the walls of Eldon Square shopping centre. When we were playing the likes of Chelsea, West Ham, Leeds and Boro then it would continue right the way along as far as Manors Train Station, although thinning out as it progressed, many turning right at Greys Monument and heading for the Central Station, whilst others just randomly walked off to catch a bus. As for us we always stopped at the 'Milk Maid Cafe' where we would get served from the street through the hatch by our former school pal, the large breasted Vivienne G' with our free Chips. Tittytastic memories.

Mick Edmondson
Walker, Newcastle

v CAMBRIDGE UNITED
ABBEY STADIUM
ATT; 7,591

SAT 30TH APRIL 1983
SECOND DIVISION
LOST 0-1

Won our previous four matches and were making a late push for promotion when we came up against the mighty Cambridge! In typical Newcastle fashion we lost to a club we should have easily beaten. The coaches parked in a grass field adjacent to the river banks and you then had to walk past numerous cows grazing to get to the small decrepit ground. Not exactly Old Trafford or Anfield, very depressing especially getting back on the coach and listening to Radio 2 sports report going around the top flight grounds. We'd be lucky to even get a mention. If you're not in the top flight then you are nobody. Even more depressing were the results from the Second Division as all of our promotion rivals results had gone our way - but really they were immaterial due to our defeat. Cambridge however had broken a football league record which had stood since 1921, by going 12 consecutive home matches without conceding a goal.

Phil Miller
Jesmond, Newcastle

v BARNSLEY   **MON 2ND MAY 1983**
OAKWELL   **SECOND DIVISION**
ATT; N/A   **POSTPONED**

A bank holiday trip down to Yorkshire started on the Sunday with a van load of us travelling down to York for a good session. Had a great time chatting to the locals and my mate Frankie ended up scoring with this bird and staying at her house. The next morning he had arranged to meet us back at our hotel, but didn't show up even though we waited an extra hour. It was the day's long before mobile phones so we had no way of contacting each other but knew that he would try and get to the match himself by either catching a train or hitching a lift. The weather was atrocious as we drove south and by the time we arrived in Barnsley there was flooding everywhere. We were all gutted when at about 1.30pm we were told that the match had been called off, so after a few more beers we left at closing time (3pm) and decided to travel back to Newcastle ready for the pubs opening again at 6pm. Before we left we drove down to the ground to see if we could see Frankie anywhere, then via the train station before giving up all hope. Unknown to us Frankie had gone on another bender with his new chic taking her down to Barnsley arriving just before 3pm not knowing that the match was off. He had then planned for us to drop her back in York on the way back after the match. Down to his last few quid and no cash card (not many had them at the time) he was a bit stuck so decided to try and hitch to York, not wanting to leave his new found love alone. He had a problem though, what would he tell his wife!! Anyway he eventually arrived in York at 11pm only to be told he couldn't stay at his new bird's house as her boyfriend was back from his weekend away and he might pop around when the pubs shut. He was skint, bombed out, soaking wet, tired and feeling rough with nowhere to stay and 100 miles from his wife who would be wondering where he was. He decided to make up a story to cover his own arse so rang her up reversing the charges to save the few pennies he had left. "Hello I have a call from your husband in York, can I put it through" the operator asked his wife. "York? Are you sure, it's definitely York" replied his wife. The operator assured her that it was before putting Frankie through. "Hey, what a day I've had, me and a couple of the lads got caught up in a mass battle at half time and got wrongly arrested and have just been let out" Frankie moaned. He continued "And the three of us are stuck in Barnsley without any money but the good news is at least we haven't been charged love and I should be home by dinnertime tomorrow." "So can you explain to me what the f**k you are doing in a phone box in bastard York" she screamed, "And which match you got arrested at because the young laddie over the road was back from Barnsley at 5pm his Dad explaining that the match didn't even start you wanker" Another one bites the dust.

T.S
Newcastle

v BARNSLEY
OAKWELL
ATT; 10,958

WED 4TH MAY 1983
SECOND DIVISION
WON 5-0

A hastily re-arranged fixture - this match had been postponed two days earlier - so it was another trip back down to Yorkshire to see Martin Thomas on loan from Bristol Rovers make his debut between the sticks. If we ever got to the away grounds early we occasionally used to approach the players getting off the coach and ask if they had any spare tickets. As we'd had to pay twice within three days to travel here we thought it would be a good way to recoup some cash. Although we only did this a few times, the times we did we were always lucky. The few players I remember who used to always oblige were Terry McDermott and Mick Martin. They used to send the young apprentices out with the tickets which we then sold - made a profit- then paid into the terracing and it left us with a few pennies to spend on a beer, which went down well on what was a great Toon performance played on a lovely sunny evening. This was Barnsley's heaviest home defeat for more than 40 years in what was our first ever win at their ground. It also meant that no team was able to do the double over us. Elsewhere it was confirmed that Wolves were already promoted.

Dave
Walker, Newcastle

v SHEFFIELD WEDNESDAY
ST JAMES' PARK
ATT; 29,874

SAT 7TH MAY 1983
SECOND DIVISION
WON 2-1

I will always remember the great false score scandal! Could we sneak promotion? With two games left we were in fifth only three points behind Leicester and Fulham who were directly above us, with our superior goal difference any slip up from them could let us in. Varadi scored his 20th of the season, a goal which maintained and completed our record of scoring in every home league fixture, before future magpie Pat Heard equalised, then an own goal (I think by Mel Sterland) put us back in front. Then there was a buzz around the ground. Fans in the East Stand then started jumping up and down. The commotion spread as word was coming through that both Leicester and Fulham were apparently losing we would be in a promotion place with just one game left. The crowd were now going mental. Now a common sight at matches in those days was the bloke with a transistor radio pinned to his lug who would shout out scores as they came in. There was one just beside us and amid all the noise he shouted out "What's the matter with everybody?" "Leicester and Fulham are both winning man" "Are you sure man?" said somebody. "Whey aye I'm the one with the wireless aren't I" he replied. Unfortunately he was right and we would have to wait another year, possibly without Keegan who still hadn't decided to take up the offer of a second season and was rumoured to be joining Portsmouth. However fans stayed behind afterwards, many invading the pitch, creating amazing scenes as they begged Keegan to stay chanting *"Keegan Must Stay, Keegan Must Stay"* The scenes were as though we'd been promoted and not of a team who had failed to live up to their expectations. This was the final game to be played at St James' Park before perimeter fences were installed.

Chris Ramshaw
West Denton, Newcastle

I STAY - KEEGAN

Newcastle United have missed out on promotion to the First Division....but Kevin Keegan will definitely be staying to lead the club next season. Emotional scenes involving thousands of Geordie fans followed yesterdays 2-1 win over Sheffield Wednesday at St James' Park. And the clubs 32 year old skipper emerged from the dressing room to say: "You don't leave people like this. I want to stay here. I'll be here again next season all right." The former England star had just witnessed an astonishing demonstration of support by thousands of fans who refused to leave the ground after the last home match of the season. Eventually they were allowed on to the pitch by police and several thousand were still shouting and chanting for Keegan almost 30 minutes after the match had finished. Thousands more were being held back off the pitch by a cordon of police. Two or three times six mounted policemen attempted to clear the supporters off the pitch without success. The fans refused to move until Keegan appeared. At one stage the situation

became uneasy as police horses were moved into the crowd and fans started to throw mud at them, but the police drew back and defused the situation. At last Keegan appeared in the stand in response to the crowd, which gradually dispersed about 45 minutes after the game finished. Then Keegan - who took his shirt off after the game and handed it to a small fan in the player's tunnel - gave his assurance that he would not be leaving the club, as he hinted last week. "I'm so sorry that we have not won anything for them" he said, referring to Newcastle's unique army of supporters. I've won European cups at Liverpool, and championships at Hamburg, but I'm lost for words.....it's embarrassing for us because we've got nothing to give them. They've got plenty to give to us though. "All season they have encouraged and supported us, home and away. They have been patient a long time, the Geordies. But I swear they won't have to wait more than another 12 months before we have something for them, because we are going places."

v HULL CITY
BOOTHFERRY PARK
ATT; 5,431

MON 9TH MAY 1983
FRIENDLY
LOST 2-3

"Where were they when honouring some loyalty?" Monday night on Humberside for Les Mutrie's testimonial. Most of our usual group - otherwise known as the Supporters Club 'sarnie squad' - made the trip down on a half empty coach. On arriving at a deserted Boothferry Park we decided - as sometimes we were inclined - to go in the seats. As it was we were able to take up position within spitting distance of the director's box due to the lack of a crowd. As usual though it was not long before those around us knew we were Newcastle mainly due to Peter's repertoire of songs and it wasn't long before the Hull 'lads'- all two of them - wanted a go. Common sense prevailed though mainly due to the imbalance of numbers on either side and none of our lot were bullies. Moments later an old commissioner bloke, all kitted up, came wandering up to us. He informed us that Don Robinson - the Owner - was well impressed with us and had requested our company in the director's lounge at half-time for beer and bait. How could we refuse? The old timer dished out passes to us which, ahemm, consisted of a piece of scrap paper with a signature on it. Half-time came and we headed into the depths of the stand, Don personally introduced himself to us, shook hands and thanked us for making the trip "all the way from Newcastle" (a piece of piss trip actually compared to midnight set off's for the south coast etc) and had a bit crack then left us to pillage predominantly the free beer (naturally). We hung in there as long as we could 'dipping' little souvenirs like team sheets off the wall and stuff, nowt serious good lads us were. We were told that we were very welcome to return at full-time too and some of the lads thought long and hard about 'fuck the coach home.' We watched the second half in peace, our two mates hadn't returned. At full-time given we felt we had the freedom of Kingston upon Hull we took it on ourselves to walk across the pitch to the Supermarket End and out into the car park via the away section. Once in the car park we noticed a bit of a carry on at our coach doors with the two lads who had become known as the 'red berets' and a couple of others having a bit of a ding dong with some Hull lads. They were seen off pretty sharpish and the coach was able to leave the car park. We got about half a mile up the road at a set of traffic lights and fuck knows where they'd come from but a mob of Hull stoned the coach putting out the back window and a side window. The driver put his foot down before things could escalate, but we had to pull over as a lad sitting next to the smashed window half way up the bus had felt the full impact and had a quite horrific injury to his face, which needed urgent hospital treatment. After waiting for the ambulance we were off, fucking freezing all the way home. Aye Don mate 'all the way to Newcastle.' Hull, Happiness and Hell.

Stephen Brennan
Walker, Newcastle

I went down by coach and was one of the 89 die-hards supporting the toon. The Newcastle contingent were on the away terrace, but about 12 of us decided to go in their main stand. As a result of our singing and shouting we eventually attracted the attention of some locals and as a result ended up in the players lounge at half-time, courtesy of the Hull Chairman. After a few free beers about 4 of us walked out and took up a seat in the Directors box, sitting in the seat directly behind Arthur Cox. During the second half a cooper tapped the Newcastle boss on the shoulder and after a whisper in his ear; Cox followed him down the stairs. We later found out that the reason for his early departure was him being told of the very sad news that Newcastle Scout Brain Watson had sadly passed away. The players were informed after the game. Brian Watson was the man behind Peter Beardsley signing for his first league club - Carlisle United. I knew him from my days playing for Wallsend Boys club and he was a real character and well liked and respected in the game. Sadly Brian never lived to see Peter Beardsley as a Newcastle United and England player. It would have made him so proud.

Mick Edmondson
Walker, Newcastle

Brain Watson Newcastle United youth development manager was found dead at his home in Wallsend aged 41. He was the man who originally took Peter Beardsley and Neil McDonald to his then employer Carlisle United and was also instrumental in McDonalds return to Tyneside. "Brian is a big loss to the football club and the area. For me I have not only lost a good worker but a good friend. The schoolboys we've got on associated forms thought the world of him. "I was sitting at the front of the director's box at Hull last night when a policeman put his hand on my shoulder and said I must go with him. It was to get me to phone the club about Brian. I never saw the last 20 minutes of the match as a result, but afterwards I got the players together and broke the news. Neil McDonald was in tears because Brian meant so much to him and his dad."

Arthur Cox
Newcastle United Manager

v WOLVES	**SAT 14TH MAY 1983**
MOLINEUX	**SECOND DIVISION**
ATT; 22,446	**DREW 2-2**

This was our last match of the season and we were well numbered. Straight off the train and we piled into a bar next to the station. For some reason or another things got a bit rowdy, one thing led to another, it kicked off and some Newcastle lads went and smashed up the bar. The Police turned up and a police horse stuck its head through the boozer door and somebody through a bottle off its napper, then the Police Riot Squad came in and chucked us all out. We were then given a Police escort all the way to the ground where about twenty of us managed to get into the Wolves main stand seats. The estimated 4,000 travelling Geordies were housed behind the goal fenced in on the huge roofed terrace and were in fine voice throughout the afternoon, especially when after being two goals down we pulled it back just before the interval with goals from Varadi and a 30 yard thunderbolt from Neil McDonald. At the final whistle the home fans invaded the pitch in their thousands to celebrate promotion and an immediate return to the First Division, and many walked towards the Newcastle fans taunting them, as we came on from the side at first unnoticed. Then the Wolves fans attacked a couple of lads wearing Toon shirts who were somehow on the pitch. This caused absolute mayhem in the Newcastle End, as our little mob grouped and confronted them only to be forced back due to the sheer volume coming at us. Then we went for it backs up against the fence, as many more Newcastle fans managed to scale the fences, having to fight with the coppers to reach us. As we fought on the pitch I was hit over the head with a copper truncheon then we were forced back up a steep muddy hill adjacent to our end by the huge Police presence. My mate Goff was all alone handcuffed to one of the advert hoardings which were in no-man's-land between the pitch and the main stand! Then I was pounced on and handcuffed and later accused and charged with breaking a coppers shoulder? The case eventually went to crown court where after a 3 day trial I was found not guilty as a result of Police lies which were highlighted and proven by video evidence.

Arn
Benton, Newcastle

Only 3 defeats in the last 18 games had propelled us up the table from 14th to 5th place, just missing out on a promotion place. After 155 starts and 6 goals Mick 'Zico' Martin made his final appearance leaving his boots in the changing room after the match as he signed on a free for Wolves within weeks. Also unknowingly playing his final game for us was fans favourite Imri Varadi who had worn the number 9 shirt all season only missing three matches. In two seasons he had twice finished top scorer scoring a very impressive 42 goals in 90 games. One of my schoolboy dreams was to watch a full season of every single Newcastle United home and away matches in all competitions. Here I was on the number 12 bus as an unemployed seventeen year old about to fulfill my dream on the last day of a very exciting season. It was Keegan's first now it was going to be mine, only I had a slight problem, the Supporters bus was leaving Morden

Street at 9am and I was stuck on the number 12 bus on Shields Road, Byker as they changed drivers with the clock striking the hour! Totally pissed off and panicking I arrived nearly twenty minutes late to find that my coach had thankfully waited and I would complete my ambition, however the only seat left was next to this Punk/Skinhead bird who although canny would have came in handy a few nights earlier when we were at Hull. Once down there this was a great trip which had everything which typified the 1980's.

Mick Edmondson
Walker, Newcastle

Last game of the season, another large support in one half of their big covered end, remembered for the scuffles on the pitch after the game as Wolves boys picked off the tiny groups of ones and two's of Newcastle fans who were not looking for trouble after the game. I won't forgive them for that!

Dave Drape
Walker, Newcastle

Just before half-time Neil McDonald scored a raker, right in the top corner, at our end. At half-time a Kids Jazz Band marched around the field of play but didn't resemble our local band the 'Meadow Well Dragoons.' This lot were multi cultural, represented by every colour and creed, one even had ginger hair. I'd never seen anything like it before in my life and I'm not on about 'Spotty McDonalds' goal.

Sean Glen
North Shields, Tyneside

1982-83 FAR EAST TOUR & THE JAPAN CUP
WED 18th MAY - TUES 7th JUNE 1983

At the end of the 1982-83 season and with Kevin Keegan the big attraction, the Keegan bandwagon headed for first, Thailand where they won four exhibition

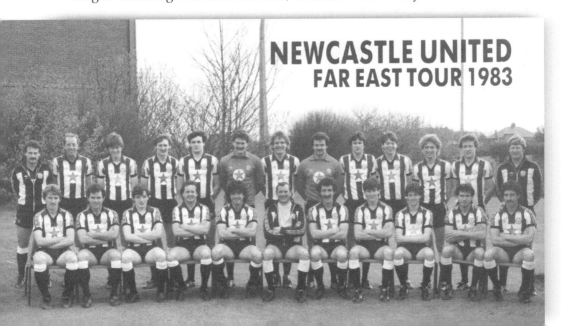

games. Then it was off to Tokyo for the Japan Cup, a five-club mini-league competition. Defeating Yamaha and a Japan XI, then forcing a draw with Syria, United lifted the trophy – a glorious jade vase – after securing a point in a 0-0 draw with Brazilian side Botafogo in front of around 30,000 in the Olympic Stadium. Then it was a gruelling 26 hour trip home.

TOUR OF THE FAR EAST

18TH MAY	v SELECT X1 (MALAYA)	5-2	ATT; UNKNOWN
20TH MAY	v SELECT X1 (MALAYA)	1-0	ATT; UNKNOWN
22ND MAY	v SELECT X1 (THAILAND)	1-0	ATT; UNKNOWN
25TH MAY	v SELECT X1 (THAILAND)	3-0	ATT; 10,000

THE JAPAN CUP TOURNAMENT

29TH MAY	v JAPAN X1	4-0	ATT; UNKNOWN
31ST MAY	v SYRIA	1-1	ATT; UNKNOWN
4TH JUNE	v YAMAHA X1	1-0	ATT; UNKNOWN
7TH JUNE	v BOTAFOGO (BRAZIL)	0-0	ATT; 30,000

Paul Joannou
Club Historian

1982-83 Season Summery

Keegan mania hit Tyneside and after years of being a laughing stock we were in dreamland, it was an amazing time. But after winning our first two games we were all brought down to earth as we then pushed the self-destruct button and quickly fell to 12th place. An injury picked up by John Trewick in the season's opener went almost unnoticed, but resulted in him missing the rest of the campaign which put a big dent in any hopes we had of promotion. Although we managed to score in every home match our form was poor and we found ourselves as low as 15th in December and by mid January had only managed to climb one place. But after a late run which saw us lose only 4 of our final 23 matches we just missed out on promotion by 3 points. If only we had grabbed a few more points early on! There were a lot of ifs and buts as to why we didn't go up; the fact that we could only manage two draws against third placed Leicester City, somehow little Carlisle took 4 points off us and Kevin Keegan missed 5 league matches through injury as we only took 5 out of a possible 15 points. But in the end our squad was to small and we needed more quality and more strength in depth, although there were signs that Cox and Keegan were starting to get things right. Keegan had not only been a great signing for what he personally gave us, but also in the way he became a magnet to help persuade other players such as McDermott, McCreery and Channon, not forgetting the inspirational qualities he showed to others helping their careers immensely. Although disappointed with our final league position and being knocked out of both cups at the first hurdle, after doing all the hard work away from home, the football was a joy at times, compared to the previous crap we'd endured over the last 5 seasons. Our average home crowd was 24,573 which may not seem impressive these days but it was the 5th largest in England only bettered by Man Utd, Liverpool, Man City and Spurs all of whom played in the First Division. The likes of so called big clubs Arsenal, Aston Villa (European Champions) & Everton couldn't match our attendances even though we spent the majority of the season in the lower half of the league below – the Second Division. Sunderland who at the time were boasting of their First Division status whilst we struggled in the second tier (a rare occurrence) were once and for all embarrassed beyond repair as their highest crowd at home was less than our worst at home!! With results improving and Keegan pledging his future to Newcastle we now had a great opportunity to strengthen over the summer and to mount a realistic promotion assault.

Typical representative team for the season:
Kevin Carr, John Anderson, Kenny Wharton, Jeff Clarke, Peter Haddock/Steve Carney, Mick Martin/Neil McDonald, Kevin Keegan, David McCreery, Imre Varadi, Terry McDermott, Chris Waddle.

Total Appearances: (League, FA Cup & League Cup) - 46 matches played.
Wharton (45), Clarke, Varadi (43), Keegan (41), Waddle (40), Martin (39), Anderson (37), Carr (36), McDermott (35), Carney (32), McCreery (28), McDonald (26), Haddock (18), Saunders (15), Craggs (13), Gayle (8), Hardwick (7), Todd (6), Ferris (5), Cartwright, Channon, Hedworth (4), Thomas (3), Bell (2), Trewick (1).
*Includes all sub appearances.

Total Goals: (League, FA Cup & League Cup) - Total Scored 78. Varadi (22), Keegan (21), McDermott, Waddle (7), Wharton (5), McDonald (4), Martin (3), Clarke, Gayle (2), Anderson, Channon, Todd (1), plus Opp Own Goals (2).

Second Division	Final Table 82-83						
QPR	42	26	7	9	77	36	85
Wolves	42	20	15	7	68	44	75
Leicester	42	20	10	12	72	44	70
Fulham	42	20	9	13	64	47	69
Newcastle	**42**	**18**	**13**	**11**	**75**	**53**	**67**
Sheff Wed	42	16	15	11	60	47	63
Oldham	42	14	19	9	64	47	61
Leeds	42	13	21	8	51	46	60
Shrewsbury	42	15	14	13	48	48	59
Barnsley	42	14	15	13	57	55	57
Blackburn	42	15	12	15	58	58	57
Cambridge	42	13	12	17	42	60	51
Derby	42	10	19	13	49	58	49
Carlisle	42	12	12	18	68	70	48
Crystal Palace	42	12	12	18	43	52	48
Middlesbrough	42	11	15	16	46	67	48
Charlton	42	13	9	20	63	86	48
Chelsea	42	11	14	17	51	61	47
Grimsby	42	12	11	19	45	70	47
Rotherham	42	10	15	17	45	68	45
Burnley	42	12	8	22	56	66	44
Bolton	42	11	11	20	42	61	44

BEARDSLEY, KEEGAN & WADDLE / CAGED IN / GOIN UP
INVASION OF ANFIELD / SUNDAY FOOTBALL / HELICOPTERS
HILLSBOROUGH FIASCO / AUF WEIDERSEHEN KEV

1983-84 Season

Our sixth consecutive season in the Second Division, cups weren't important, just a top 3 finish and automatic promotion, nothing else mattered. No excuses we had to go up. Over the summer we were strongly linked with Scottish footballer & young footballer of the year Charlie Nicholas who'd scored 50 goals for Celtic the previous season, yet we ended up with two full backs! We signed Huddersfield's Malcolm Brown for £100,000 and we paid Oldham Athletic £225,000 for England Under-21 left-back John Ryan. Brown who hadn't missed a fixture for his former club in 259 games (five years) sustained an Achilles tendon injury in pre-season training and unbelievably missed the whole season! We also signed keeper Martin Thomas from Bristol Rovers for £50,000 after his impressive loan period. As for 'Champagne Charlie' he turned down Liverpool and Man Utd and signed for Arsenal for £800,000 – never believe the papers. Our squad which was found wanting last season needed to be strengthened, yet in typical

Newcastle style we lost more players than we actually brought in. From last season's squad we had lost Derek Bell to injury, John Craggs on a free to Darlington, Stave Hardwick to Oxford United £15,000, Mick Martin to join Wolves, Kevin Todd to Darlington £5,000, while Peter Cartwright and Paul Ferris, were totally out of favour and would not feature. To make matters worse, the unbelievable happened only one week before the season actually started. The season started in controversy when our top scorer for the past two seasons with 18 and 21 goals - crowd favourite Imre Varadi - was sold to promotion rivals Sheffield Wednesday in a cash exchange deal, where we got £150,000 along with David Mills returning on a permanent basis. Realistically our first team squad only consisted of 16 players as we opened our account at Elland Road as the bookies title favourites. Rumours were rife that Cox wanted George Reilly as Varadi's replacement, but he thankfully signed for Watford instead. In a summer which saw Aberdeen beat Real Madrid in the European Cup Winners Cup Final, competitive bidding for the rights to show football highlight programmes on TV between BBC and ITV raised the income entering the game from Television. But it was the arrival of live games which led to the biggest changes. At first clubs were worried that live games would hit already declining attendances and saw television income merely as a compensation for the loss of gate receipts. However increasing revenue from successive TV deals created an increasingly important source of income, especially for those clubs regularly featured. It was now vital that we didn't miss the promotion boat, as financially football's top flight was changing rapidly and if we weren't careful we would get left behind. We actually had a new silver kit for our travels but still needed some quality players as we chased gold, silver or bronze position.

1983-84 TOUR OF WEST GERMANY & GREECE
WED 10TH AUG - WED 17TH AUG 1983

It was a return to the Hamburg region for Kevin Keegan, such a popular player when he played for the HSV club and reached the European Cup final. Newcastle played Hamburg's second club, Altona 93, and won easily by 6-1 with new signing at left-back John Ryan scoring the opener. But everyone wanted to see Special K, although John Anderson caught the eye too, netting an unlikely hat-trick. Against SC Drochtersen, a lower division German club, near to the city of Hamburg, United cruised to another victory, by 5-0. All this after Keegan had been lowered onto the pitch by helicopter! Newcastle then flew to Athens to face AEK managed by Geordie John Barnwell. That was a much tougher contest after the stroll in Germany. A 0-0 draw was the outcome, and had been another great PR exercise for the Keegan inspired Newcastle United.

10TH AUG	v HANBURG ALTONA	6-1	ATT; 4,500
11TH AUG	v SC DROCHTERSEN	5-0	ATT; 3,000
17TH AUG	v AEK ATHENS	0-0	ATT; 15,000

Paul Joannou
Club Historian

v LEAGUE OF IRELAND
ST JAMES' PARK
ATT; 7,739

A horrible new perimeter security fence greeted the few (yet still impressive considering the opposition) who turned up for the St James' curtain raiser. Installed at a cost of £15,000 to comply with UEFA legislation it would become a viewing hazard for thousands for the next few seasons. The 7ft 6in wire fence surrounded 3 sides of the pitch. The benches in front of the East Stand were excused as the monstrosity was only erected in front of terracing where fans were standing. Just as we were trying to come to terms with the new obstruction, we got a further shock when rumours began to sweep the terraces that United were set to sell last season's leading scorer and crowd favourite Imre Varadi. He was down at Hillsborough talking to Sheff Wed. Just when you thought that we were starting to get things right, we look to sell our top goalscorer! As for the match, why we played an Ireland select side and were actually charged to watch it was an absolute disgrace. Their team wouldn't have been good enough to play in the Fourth Division.

Mick Edmondson
Walker, Newcastle

That morning I had actually split up with my girlfriend and decided to leave her, before making my way to the match. Goalkeeper Kevin Carr who was on the bench actually had a two minute spell as substitute linesman when the match official Ken Lipton from Sunderland was injured! As it emerged later on that night, Newcastle had agreed a fee with Sheffield Wednesday for 24 year old Varadi and he was away down reluctantly to talk personnel terms with their boss Howard Wilkinson. As for me I had nowhere to go as I didn't want my family to know I'd left home so I spent the night at the Salvation Army hostel on City Road. The bloke who was captain (in charge) told me that it was his Grandfather who rode the White Horse in the 1923 FA Cup Final at Wembley.

John Allen
Shiremoor, Newcastle

v LEEDS UNITED
ELLAND ROAD
ATT; 30,806

SAT 27TH AUGUST 1983
SECOND DIVISION
WON 1-0

The football special left the Central Station jam packed with lads aged 16 to 30, including a lot of nutter's who were looking forward to their afternoon in Leeds city centre. It was a boiling hot day as we headed off towards Yorkshire for the league seasons curtain raiser against the other big club from the east of England. We weren't far from our destination when the train came to a complete standstill seemingly in the middle of nowhere, apart from a small housing estate to our left. At first we thought it was a signal stopping us but as time passed the news made its way down the carriages that we had broken down. Here we were nearly one thousand of us stuck without drink watching the afternoon tick away, not knowing when or how we would get to the match. To make matters worse some low life, was continually playing a Man Utd record in his bedroom which didn't go down very well. Everybody was convinced that the police had pre-planned this stoppage keeping us away from Leeds until the last minute. Then as if by magic our knackered train eventually made tracks, arriving at the station to be greeted by a massive police presence including dogs and mounted coppers. After our escort which many fans managed to escape from we eventually arrived at the ground missing the first fifteen minutes and a rare John Anderson goal - a grass cutter - which turned out to be the winner. Inside the ground about 8,000 of us were packed onto the Lowfield Road Terrace and fighting broke out all afternoon between Geordies and the coppers as they tried to enter the terraces to make arrests only for them to be attacked and spat at, as well as losing their hats which were in turn thrown over the fences and onto the pitch, which was greeted by huge cheers. We managed to hold onto our slender lead, even though we lost Kevin Carr just after half-time when he fell heavily breaking a bone in his left arm, an injury which would keep him out until after Christmas. Chris Waddle deputised in goal for 42 minutes without conceding whilst John Ryan a current England U21 who cost £225,000 from Oldham made his debut. Also arriving in the summer and wearing the number 9 shirt today was the returning David Mills only this time on a permanent basis. After the final whistle we were kept inside the ground by the police in a massive sort of court yard as the Leeds fans threw missiles over the high walls, in retaliation a Newcastle fan stood on top of the toilet block in the corner and threw a ceramic toilet at the Leeds fans outside before jumping down and risking his life, but at the same time escaping arrest. Everybody wanted to be outside and got their wish when Geordies to our left set fire to the grass embankment next to the Lowfield Road stand, causing a dodgy situation as flames shot up in the air, just below the stand. The sound of Fire Engines could be heard as Newcastle fans forced the gates open and charged forward into the street. There was absolute mayhem outside as rival fans battled; Newcastle forced Leeds away from the ground as the majority of Leeds didn't want to know although some didn't have a choice as fights broke out regardless, but the ones who remained, put on a show before also being forced back. Luckily nobody was injured as a result of the fire and the main stand didn't become engulfed and eventually we were all rounded up and escorted back to the train station and put back on our train which funnily enough didn't break down on the return journey.

Mark Risi
Benton, Newcastle

My Leeds connection started years before this fixture with my earliest memory of going to the match, which was leaving St James' Park on Christmas Eve 1966, having just watched us get beat off Leeds 1-2, it was bitterly cold and as we piled out of the ground the snow started to fall and it was a white Christmas. Two days later on Boxing Day and Leeds stuffed us 5-1, a white Christmas in more than one way. Years later whilst still at school and following Newcastle around the country, we stopped of in Leeds for a pint, pie and punch up on the long usually miserable journey back to Walker. Then in September 1979, I left home to live and study in Leeds. Why Leeds? It was the nearest course to Newcastle which meant I could get home as often as possible. At the time we were in the Second Division but unfortunately there were no Yorkshire teams in our league. But by the 83-84 season Leeds, Barnsley, Huddersfield and Sheff Wed had all joined us and Leeds away was the first game of a memorable season. I met my brother and a van full of mates in Headingley before the game for a few drinks and a carefree ride in their van to the match. It was lovely sunny day and in the car park around the ground it was a party atmosphere, ice-cream vans, hot-dog vans, people hanging around, and black and whites everywhere. The party atmosphere didn't last long with fights breaking out all over the car park, the ice-cream and hot-dog vans were turned over it was mayhem getting into the ground but worth it as we beat them. It was even worse trying to get out knowing that the Leeds supporters were waiting for us. Then someone set fire to the grass embankment behind the away supporters stand, and with smoke billowing back into the ground the Leeds supporters thought the Geordies had set fire to the Elland Road and not just an area of dry grass. Hell reigned for quite some time until the police managed to separate the supporters and get everyone back on their buses etc. I made my way back to the van, only to be told "we're not going back into Leeds, we're going straight onto the motorway back to Newcastle!" Concerned I asked "But how the fuck do I get away from here?" "Dunno, not my problem." came the reply - that's brotherly love for you. At least I would be safe walking past the line of Newcastle coaches – wrong. Coaches each carrying 45 testosterone and alcohol fuelled Geordies pressed against the window, screaming death threats at me as I walked passed. Whilst not wanting to attract the attention of the Leeds hooligans, I tried to let the animals in the coaches know I was also a Geordie which of course they mistakenly took for me offering them all out. I was pelted with bricks, had truncheons on string thrown at me not to mention the bucket and a half of phlegm. Once, safely past the coaches which were now streaming out of the coach park on their way to the M62 I made my way to the bus stop to go into Leeds, followed by a couple of Leeds supporters who spoke the words all away supporters dread; "Got the time mate?"

Chris Emmerson
Walker, Newcastle

I was working at Terry's Hairdressers on the coast road (Home of the famous Walker/Wallsend Wedge) as a young lad of 22 with my work mate Ray aged 18. We had arranged to go down to Leeds for the match but we had to open the shop on the Saturday morning as it was the gaffers' day off. So we spread the word and opened at 5.30am so that we could hit target before getting off to a flyer. Happy days.

Keith Errington
Cochrane Park, Newcastle

It was my first ever trip by myself up to Elland Road to see my beloved Leeds United, it was a massive game with Newcastle the visitors. My family all come from the Leeds area, but we moved down to London when I was young. On the train up I was reading an article in the newspaper, the rise of hooliganism. The main protagonists were in there Chelsea, Millwall and of course Leeds United & Newcastle. What struck me about the Newcastle article was the name of the firm - 'The Kenton Bar Boys,' described as skinheads, Doc Martins, no tops and Kilts!!!!! They got that wrong, they just had a picture of lads scuffing but no-one with kilts. Once at Elland Road, I was in the Kop, the atmosphere was cracking and of course Newcastle had brought a big following for the opening game of the season. Waiting for the two teams to come out, I just stared at the Newcastle fans and right at the front, saw four lads, Doc Martins, skinheads, no tops and kilts. The Kenton Bar Boys were in town!!!!!

Paul Brace
Enfield, London

I used to run a bus from the Trafalgar Pub in Gateshead and as usual it was full as we set off early to enable us to be down in Yorkshire for opening time. We stopped off in a village called Scarcroft on the outskirts of Leeds which consisted of about ten houses, a golf course, a Spar shop and a pub. We had a great bunch of lads on the coach, some right characters and some who were not scared of lifting a few things off the shelf of any establishment you could mention. So after three hours drinking we decided to make tracks to Elland Road via the Spar shop as the lads were still thirsty. A mass case of sticky fingers ensued prior to getting on the bus and heading into Leeds I got up and asked what loot we had on board. The snatch ranged from cans of lager, Tetley's etc, Whiskey, cigs you name it, but when I got to the back of the bus my mate Paddy was sitting there laughing. When I asked him what he had got he showed me; Two loafs of bread, half a pound of ham and a tub of butter! He made a small fortune selling sandwiches at the back of the bus.

Paul
Winlaton, Tyneside

We got down there nice and early drinking in a pub called 'The Peacock' right next to ground. As time was getting on a group of about 15 Leeds lads tried to get in not realising the place was full of Mags! They were singing *"There's Only One United"* as they pushed there way in, once in the bar they were offended that we had taken there pub and promptly kicked off only to get the hiding of their lives. The Coppers piled in and told us to leave which we duly did singing *"There's Only One United"* the Leeds boys could only look on in their bruised and battered state, a treasured memory, dead funny on the day.

Archie
Wallsend, Tyneside

Following Newcastle United in the 80's was more of a passionate and exciting buzz, than my Grandad, my uncle, my brother, my mother, my favourite school teacher, or the messiah himself Johnny Weissmuller could instill into a lad. I lived in, and was brought up in the "Sunderland stronghold" town of Peterlee, and running the gauntlet of enemy lines just to go to home games, was a tense enough affair to say the least. Not to mention getting off the bus in Peterlee town centre when returning from home games, when there would be plenty of red'n'whiter's about (mainly because they didn't really travel well!) A few close magpie mates and I started going away the season Keegan signed for us as a player. I was decked out in black-and-white stripes and scarf everywhere I went, and the sense of unity and passion of what it was to be a real home and away follower soon set in! We would use local transit vans with rickety wooden benches in the back and whoever sat near the back doors usually got soaked with leakage from the rain if it was hoying down or sunburnt on one side of our faces if it was canny bright! Whether we got wet, sunburnt, or had backsides shaped like kit-kats off the uncomfortable seats, it didn't matter or phase any of us one iota, it was all about going to the game and exploring new and massive expanses of cities and towns. The big wide world was out there for us to find, and find it we did, as long as it involved watching Newcastle. Booze, food, and tabs for those who smoked were the priorities for all of us before heading off anywhere. The crowds back then, in the early to mid 80's, were made up 99% of lads and blokes, and football grounds and stadiums were cold, damp, uninviting and intimidating hostile places to go. Football was a very physical full on contact affair, on and off the field, not the family game it is today. I first saw how confrontational things were when we visited Leeds the previous season, Keegan was decked by a ball bearing off his heed and John Anderson was hit in the knackers by a coin or object. There were no real full on fights but some running across seats and goading from the Leeds fans. This was met by a hail of seats, missiles, bangers, rockets and other stuff from the Newcastle fans below. Today was another fun day out for all.

Tomahawk (NME)
Peterlee, Durham

50 United fans charged

Fifty Newcastle United fans were today said to have been charged after Saturday's game at Leeds. West Yorkshire police said about 50 of the 67 people arrested in the city during and after the match were Magpie followers. Most have been charged with public disorder offences and will have to return next month to answer the charges. Supporters are said to have been responsible for setting fire to waste ground inside the Elland Road football ground.

Fireman were sent to put out the blaze, but a Leeds United spokesman said luckily there was no major damage to the stadium. A 29 year old female Newcastle fan said. "The police held all the Newcastle fans in the ground after the game to let all the Leeds fans get away first. "Some people got impatient and set fire to the grass, so the police had to let everybody out."

The two sets of fans always clashed down there, but this time there was hell on. There was a little hill near the ground and it was like a scene out of the American Civil War. Police horses the lot and the Mag's gallantly fought on, very much part of those days of course.

Brian Hall
Heaton, Newcastle

It's fair to say I've never liked Leeds, in fact you could say I hate them and I take great delight in their plight today. First match of the season and we wore the Silver Grey away kit. I loved that kit, it was a boiling hot day and we looked like eleven Space Men! Mind you when it was dull and Grey and pissing down with Rain (like it does for 10 months in this country) it didn't look so hot. We went 1-0 up early on thanks to a John Anderson goal. Kevin Carr went off injured and Chris Waddle went in goal but I don't recall him having to touch the ball! The thing that sticks out though about this match was the bother at the end. Leeds fans hurling rocks over the gates at Newcastle fans locked in and Newcastle fans setting the grass banks behind the main stand on fire and over turning a food van and Wagon Wheel fights every where! Hundreds of Wagon Wheels thrown like Frisbees in the air! - That really takes the Biscuit! Groan!

Hendy
Kenton Bar, Newcastle

v SHREWSBURY TOWN
ST JAMES' PARK
ATT; 29,140

MON 29TH AUGUST 1983
SECOND DIVISION
LOST 0-1

Watching football at St James' Park wouldn't be the same for some time as this was the first league match we had to watch through the newly erected perimeter fence, which just happened to be one of the most obstructive in the Country. It was an ugly thing which seemed a lot thicker than others I saw on my travels. It was erected on three side of the ground, with the Benches (East Stand Paddock Seats) escaping because it was a seated area. Tickets for this area were now like gold dust. After our excellent opening day win at Leeds a bumper Bank Holiday Monday afternoon crowd saw former United loan signing Alan Brown score the winner yet again. This was Shrewsbury's first ever win on Tyneside.

Mick Edmondson
Walker, Newcastle

v OLDHAM ATHLETIC
ST JAMES' PARK
ATT; 22,573

SAT 3RD SEPTEMBER 1983
SECOND DIVISION
WON 3-0

One of the things I miss most about going to the match before all-seater stadiums arrived is the fact that you could just pay at the turnstile on the day. Or better still you could pay at the under 16's turnstile which I did on numerous occasions even when I was in my early twenties, cross eyed, wobbling from side to side and stinking of drink, with three days growth. Some blokes even older than I could often be seen on their knees going through the kid's entrance with their 'football-tashes' (Five-a-side) and their CIU club card sticking out of their top pocket. Coppers would turn a blind eye at times, but others without a sense of humour would frog march the culprits out of the ground. After 3 games the first league tables were published and we were third with 2 wins from our first 3 matches, in a promotion place exactly where we hoped we'd be come May 12th.

Mick Edmondson
Walker, Newcastle

I was standing in the Gallowgate End and was desperate for the toilet. So off I went in search of the Ladies. I had no joy so then tried looking for a steward to ask. Eventually when I found one I was told that there wasn't any!! So a steward went into the Gents and once he'd cleared it I was able to paddle through the ankle deep piss to the comfort of a dark smelly room with a cracked toilet without a seat. The urinals which although were open air, still stunk. The steward kept toot but couldn't stop the lads banging on the corrugated iron roof, *"Get Your Tits*

Out For The Lads, Get Your Tits Out For The Lads." "I haven't got any!" I replied.

Debra Gunn (nae Fairley)
Battlehill, Tyneside

v MIDDLESBROUGH   **TUES 6TH SEPTEMBER 1983**
AYRESOME PARK   **SECOND DIVISION**
ATT; 19,648   **LOST 2-3**

Not exactly the best of starts to the new season as our promotion hopes took another knock as we gifted Boro 3 goals including a late winner in the last few minutes, which didn't go down to well with the 8,000 Geordies in the all-ticket crowd. There was intense battling before and after the match all the way down Linthorpe Road and the surrounding back streets. I got a lift back from this particular match with lads from Deckham in a works carpet van and they made a big effort to chase any boys they came across with carpet rails with the nails on them, thankfully Boro were too fast!

Dave
Walker, Newcastle

Our 'Football Special' arrived in Middlesbrough then we had a huge escort from the station down through the town centre. There was so many of us that some were squashed up against the shop windows and a kid ended up accidently going through a shop window! It was a long walk, a right laugh. Inside the ground seats being thrown out of the back of our stand and at Boro fans in the streets. You always got some action down there.

Unknown
Newcastle, Tyneside

We went down to this match by transit van and parked up at 6pm next to a pub up by the bus station. After a few beers we started to walk down through the shopping centre then through the dozens of back streets. There were 15 of us and we literally had to battle our way through the streets to reach the ground. Then at the end of the match we were kept in for what seemed like ages. Some Newcastle fans had managed to get out and you could hear the chaos in the street at the back of our end. Newcastle fans were desperate to get out, but police on horseback and with dogs kept the Geordies away from the large closed exit gates. Hundreds of seats were ripped out and used as missiles in reply to the stones and missiles being thrown at us from the streets. It was bedlam, but frustrating as we couldn't get out on the street to get Boro. Eventually we were let out and it was like a war zone outside, windows smashed, bricks and seats all over the place. You'd think a bomb had gone off. Our mob took a right and went to the far end of the ground where we ended up battling with Boro next to a hospital - which was quite handy. In fact a lot of the older grounds were situated next to hospitals-Newcastle being right next to the RVI is a prime example. Luckily apart from a few black eyes, cuts and bruises we got back to the van and headed home. Without doubt Boro was one of the worst/best grounds to visit for trouble in the 1980's depending on what your view was on football violence.

Vince,
Newcastle

Fans chief slams match lunatics

Newcastle Supporters Association chairman Malcolm Dix today branded Tyneside fans who went on a wrecking spree after last night's derby match at Middlesbrough a "lunatic mob." But he praised police handling of violence which erupted after United went down 2-3 at the Ayresome Park ground. He said damage - ripped out seats in the stadium, and broken windows in nearby houses - could have been a lot worse. "This sort of thing is almost always going to happen where you get this kind of unfortunate supporter penned in after the match. If their team has lost - they take it out on the seats." said Mr. Dix. There is no other way of dealing with the situation, if they are to be kept penned in until the Middlesbrough supporters leave the ground. About 2,000 seats were ripped up and hurled onto the pitch and out of the stadium into the streets after the game.

v GRIMSBY TOWN
BLUNDELL PARK
ATT; 9,000

SAT 10TH SEPTEMBER 1983
SECOND DIVISION
DREW 1-1

I travelled down with the clubs official Magpie Travel with a few of my mates. The driver wouldn't stop on the way down and as the coaches didn't have toilets in those days, I was pretty desperate when we arrived in Cleethorpes. I was first off the bus jumping from the stairs and straight to the nearest fence not arsed who was watching as you know what it's like when your bursting for a piss. It seemed to last for ages and when I'd eventually finished I turned round only to find that I'd been left on my own. No mobiles either in those days so I set off down the street looking for the first pub where I was sure to find my mates. Problem was I couldn't find a pub so nipped into a corner shop to ask for directions. There was a Pakistani bloke behind the counter so I asked him "Where can I get a drink?" He looked at me puzzled so I slowly repeated my question this time accompanied with a right handed drinking action. He smiled then disappeared into the back, maybe to get somebody who could help me or so I hoped. I waited a while and just as I was about to disappear myself he returned carrying a wooden chair, "Just sit down" he said. Before I had a chance to reply he vanished again quickly returning with a mug of tea!! Which, by the way, was honking of curry. I smiled and thanked him as I looked around for a plant pot to pour it in to. Once the biscuits arrived I knew I was stuck there, I was there for ages. Too nice me.

Kev Drew
Wardley, Tyneside

As we attempted to enter the away turnstiles the organisation or to be precise the lack of it was an absolute disgrace. The whole of Newcastle had seemed to turn up at the same time and the small badly designed entrance couldn't cope as hundreds struggled to stay upright with the Police nowhere to be seen. Of course we weren't Leeds United so as per usual the kick-off wasn't delayed, yet the vast majority of travelling fans missed the start. Once inside it was clearly visible that we had a lot more fans than Grimsby yet we were packed in like sardines whilst they had acres of room. Without a doubt there was a lot more than the fictitious crowd of 9,000 in the ground.

Mick Edmondson
Walker, Newcastle

v CRYSTAL PALACE
ST JAMES' PARK
ATT; 22,869

Goals from Waddle, Keegan and Ryan! It just doesn't sound right does it? Nevertheless a cracking goal from defender John Ryan his only one for the club helped us on our way to a comfortable win. Later on at the end of the season in June 1984, Dave Bassett resigned as manager of Wimbledon and agreed to take charge of Crystal Palace but never signed the contract. Within 72 hours after accepting Palace's offer, he changed his mind and returned to Wimbledon. Not many people know that!

Mick Edmondson
Walker, Newcastle

v BARNSLEY   SAT 24TH SEPTEMBER 1983
OAKWELL   SECOND DIVISION
ATT; 14,085   DREW 1-1

Arthur Cox was beginning to mould Newcastle into quite a force. And this match saw a substitute debut for Peter Beardsley, in my opinion possibly one of our greatest ever players. Waddle equalised for us and as he went to celebrate with the Newcastle fans massed behind the goal, he jumped on the fence, though soon jumped off as it nearly collapsed. It was only the weight and pushing of our fans that kept the Waddler safe. Fences – what were they all about? They added to the problem.

Anth Nicholson
North Shields, Tyneside

One trip that sticks out was this trip to Yorkshire. To get to the away end you had to climb a large hill that then steeply dropped towards the ground. Some local Barnsley Nutters were hanging around looking for bother then all of a sudden loads of drunken Geordies in Black-and-White Kilts came marauding down the bank. God knows what the Barnsley lot thought of that but they didn't hang around! Mind you I've seen the women in Barnsley, perhaps they thought it was their wives coming! In the 80`s at the height of Football Hooliganism the Sun newspaper did a huge article on various Hooligan Firms and their titles and attire etc. You had the likes of Chelsea Headhunters, Leeds Service Crew and Millwall Bushwhackers. What did they have for Newcastle? The Kenton Bar Bootboys! God knows where they got that from but anyone who lives over this neck of the woods will tell you that it was a fucking ridiculous statement!

Hendy
Kenton, Newcastle

There was hell on after the match in the streets surrounding the ground. Rocks, stones, missiles of every shape and size. My mate Charlie climbed on a fence and got a rock off his head. He was covered in claret and had a nasty wound. He wasn't happy so went and bought an aspirin.

Ken Allen
Gateshead, Tyneside

v PORTSMOUTH
ST JAMES' PARK
ATT; 25,488

SAT 1ST OCTOBER 1983
SECOND DIVISION
WON 4-2

I was in the old Adelaide pub on Newgate Street having a pre-match pint minding my own business when I couldn't help but notice some commotion in the street outside. It appeared that a squad of about 50 Pompey' fans were kicking off, hitting out at anybody in the street who got in their way, as they then tried to entice the Geordies inside the Canny Lad (now known as Sinners), out onto the street. The Doorman at the Canny Lad had locked the doors preventing the Newcastle fans inside, getting out at the Portsmouth fans who were now bouncing around outside dressed like a bunch of Dick Emery's with their Kagool's and umbrellas as a couple of them even took photos. Before I knew it the few of us who had been in the Adelaide were in amongst it in the middle of the road as Big Harvey the Doorman from the Canny Lad was knocking them up a height protecting his pub, as all hell broke loose I ended up rolling about the floor in the middle of the road as a bus just missed us as the traffic surrounding us came to a standstill. I was dragged off the Portsmouth fan by a copper who declared that I was nicked and the next thing I remember was being thrown into the back of a police van, where I met up with Harvey and a Pompey lad who didn't seem to enjoy his journey back to Market Street? I was charged and appeared in court on the Monday morning receiving a £180 fine, but to make matters worse I missed the match an excellent 4-2 victory, and didn't manage to finish my pint in the Adelaide. Arthur Cox in his own typical style hauled off Waddle who'd scored twice, five minutes from the end because "he didn't show me that he was hungry for a hat-trick."

Terry Mann
Longbenton, Newcastle

The 6.57 Crew came out of the station at about 1.30pm, about a 100 of them. Unusually there was no welcoming committee waiting for them (I later found out the NME were over at Manors and no-one else was expecting them). Only two coppers were standing around and they walked with Pompey as they crossed Neville Street and headed up Bewick Street and round onto Clayton Street. I followed behind as they crossed Westgate Road and headed along Clayton Street and turned onto Newgate Street. Having not been challenged they were obviously full of it and once they saw The Adelaide pub, they ran at it. No-one got out the pub but the lads in there battled at the entrance to keep Pompey out. The huge window of the bar was cracked in the incident (not smashed and was left like that for a week or so) and one or two lads from Mr Smiths bar (Canny Lad) over the road got involved in the street but the minor battle was over very quickly as Police backup arrived and Portsmouth were shepherded passed the Co-op. That was as I saw it. It certainly was not the battle - 'result' that a certain hoolie publication claims. However, it is worthy of note, because rarely did any other mob turn up as impressively as the 6.57 did that day and fair play to them for that.

Stephen
Byker, Newcastle

Terror Soccer Fans Fined

Rampaging soccer fans terrorised children and an elderly woman as they clashed in a Newcastle street full of shoppers, a court was told. Rival gangs of Newcastle and Portsmouth supporters clashed before Saturday's fixture. A half brick was thrown through a pub window, striking an elderly woman on the leg. Magistrates slapped fines of more than £1,200 on eight men for using threatening words and behaviour.

v OXFORD UNITED	WED 5TH OCTOBER 1983
ST JAMES' PARK	(MILK) LEAGUE CUP 2nd RND 1st LEG
ATT; 21,184	DREW 1-1

We drew the largest crowd for the second round of the competition which is quite astonishing considering that it was a Second Division side against a Third Division side. Even more remarkable was the fact that this was one of three home games we had in a week. This was the first time we had ever played Oxford in any competitive match and a second-half McDermott equaliser saved our blushes. Oxford were managed by a certain Jim Smith and had old Newcastle goalkeeping scapegoat Steve Hardwick between the posts as well as Andy Thomas and Kevin Brock in their side.

Mick Edmondson
Walker, Newcastle

v CHARLTON ATHLETIC	SAT 8TH OCTOBER 1983
ST JAMES' PARK	SECOND DIVISION
ATT; 23,329	WON 2-1

After eight matches we were in 4th place behind Sheff Wed, Man City and Chelsea. Charlton had lost 7-0 against Brighton the previous week but it took two late Keegan goals to win it. The last gasp victory in monsoon conditions, in front of the MOTD cameras was enough to keep the pressure on our promotion rivals. As the Gallowgate End was totally open, it led to the song, whenever it was pissin' it down…"Singing In The Rain, I'm Singing In The Rain, Happy Again"….and we would probably be losing, but it was an act of defiance. Some even used to sit down on the terraces during this song taking shelter. Today the thunderstorm seemed to act as a stimulant and a drenched crowd went home happy.

Brian Hall
Heaton, Newcastle

It absolutely peed it down. The game was shown on Match of the Day with Kevin Keegan scoring two late goals to win it. After the second goal the camera panned on to the Gallowgate and you could see the steam rising off the celebrating fans. Apparently the TV weather wife Wincey Willis had predicted it was going to be a bright, bright, bright sunshiny day! This prompted a one off song amongst part of the Gallowgate End, *"Wincey Willis Is A Liar Is A Liar, Wincey Willis Is A Liar Is A Liar."*

Chris Ramshaw
West Denton, Newcastle

v SWANSEA CITY
VETCH FIELD
ATT; 9,807

SUN 16TH OCTOBER 1983
SECOND DIVISION
WON 2-1

The coaches left at midnight from the ground and most of the occupants were mortal from a heavy Friday night session. I was only 14 at the time and distressingly sober. We arrived in Wales's second city at about 9am and everyone piled off, most shaking off hangovers and working out where to get a fried breakfast before going on the drink again. Almost immediately it began to rain, sheets of it, incessantly. I went down with a mate and it was clear no pub was going to let us in so we wandered the streets getting wetter and wetter, and more and more miserable. Eventually, we discovered their club shop. You went through a door and at the bottom of a long corridor there it was, bit like our old one at the Haymarket, selling all sorts of things of interest staffed by a couple of lovely old dears. After spending time cracking on the with a few locals, getting warm and trying to dry out, we left. By the front door was a trolley with some packages in it. I casually opened one to find the match programmes inside. I don't know why, since I am to the criminal fraternity what Nick Leeson is to independent financial advisers, i.e.

NEWCASTLE UNITED
SUPPORTERS' CLUB

(Affiliated to the National Federation of Football Supporters' Clubs)

Season 1983-84

useless. But we calmly picked up a couple of the packets each and legged it. Demonstrating a lack of business acumen which has served me so badly well into alleged adulthood, I gave them away to any passing Toon fan rather than, say, charge a nominal fee to make some cash. Never mind, the programme was to become obsolete very quickly because at about 1.30, after several hours of roaming the drenched streets, the game was called off. I remember the coaches not being able to leave the place till about 3ish – either some law about drivers' hours or they were trying to round up all the Toon fans busy getting mortal. We eventually left soaking wet and highly pissed off but there was one final cherry on the cake. Some fat obnoxious twat who'd obviously spent the day getting legless - and keeping warm and dry-decided he was going to sleep in the bus isle next to me. Very shortly into the journey I noticed the horrible git had emptied the contents of his fat, flatulent gut - an apparent heady mixture of snake bite, bile and fried breakfast - all around my feet. The stench remained all journey and took an age to clear from my nostrils. I've never back to the miserable hole that is the Vetch Field, Swansea since. Either have Newcastle United, in fact that was the last time we ever played there before it was demolished.

Graham
Rowlands Gill, Tyneside

Following Newcastle United to the extremes of the country has never been easy - but when Welsh Wales became Wet Wales it was even harder. When the Keegan-Waddle-Beardsley combo had just come together, United were scheduled to play Swansea City and Cardiff City away in the space of four days. It was too good an opportunity to miss - two new grounds, two Newcastle matches, and a few days' holiday in the principality with the added bonus of Newport County v Lincoln City on the Tuesday. I took in a Tranmere Rovers home game on the Friday night, stayed on Merseyside overnight, and set off good and early on the Saturday morning to drive through the heart of Wales and down to Swansea. But it rained. And then it poured. And then it hammered down. And it flooded the hills and valleys of central Wales. I ploughed on down the A493 through places like Llandrindod Wells. Five times the road was axle-high in water, but I pressed on, finally arriving in Swansea at two o'clock. There had been no news on the car radio of a postponement - but as soon as I came within view of the Vetch Field, I could see the 'Match Off' signs going up and disappointed fans of both Swans and United turning away from the turnstiles. Numbed by the apparently wasted journey, I drove on into the town centre and found a café for a bite to eat. Then I set off, disconsolate, for the hotel on the cliff top at Mumbles Bay, to the west of Swansea that would be my base for that Saturday night. Knowing the team was staying down in Wales, I hoped against hope that they might manage to squeeze a quick rearrangement in - and my prayers were answered when, on a local radio bulletin that evening, they said they would try to get the game played on the Sunday - weather permitting. However, when I looked outside, the rain was still lashing down and it was still lashing down when I turned in at 2.00am. In fact, so bad was the wind and rain that the hotel receptionist advised me to turn the car around so it faced away from the sea, as the sand it was blowing up the cliff from the beach would have clogged the engine! Amazingly, I woke on the Sunday morning to brilliant sunshine. A quick phone call - and, yes, the game was on, with a 2pm kick-off! Joy!! The journey hadn't been wasted after all. I had an hour on the seafront then drove into Swansea, and found numerous United fans wandering around looking dishevelled and tired. It turned out they had refused to come home on the buses that had had to return to Tyneside on the Saturday evening, and now they had been rewarded by the weather gods. Newcastle United, having heard of the fans' bravery, actually sent free transport from Tyneside on the Sunday to bring the several dozen die-hards home, but so many more missed the game. I was then a news reporter on The Northern Echo, and when I let it be known I'd been down in South Wales for the week, I got a kicking for not having tramped the streets of Swansea interviewing Geordies sleeping in doorways for the Monday morning paper! But, Ed, I was on holiday!!

Anyway, endeavours were rewarded. United beat Swansea 2-1 with goals from Kenny Wharton and, after a second-half Swansea equaliser, David Mills got the winner. Dinner tasted good that Sunday evening. I was staying for the next three nights in Monmouth, and duly ticked off Newport's Somerton Park on the Tuesday (they beat Lincoln 1-0) then on the Wednesday, weather by now dry, watched the lads beat Cardiff City 2-0 at Ninian Park when newly-signed Peter Beardsley scored his first goal for United and Keegan added the second. Then home - setting off from Cardiff at 10.00pm and arriving back in Newcastle at four o'clock on the Thursday morning exhausted, happy, and with the three South Wales grounds safely in the bag on the way to the 92, not to mention six points safely in the bag on the way to promotion to the First Division.

Paul Tully
Newcastle

This turned out to be the only game I missed all season. Me and my pal travelled on the old Magpie Travel coaches, anybody who travelled with them would confirm how shit they really were. With our smuggled drink on board we travelled down to Wales waking on arrival at 9.30am, but it was hoying it down. I've never seen rain like it. After sheltering in some arcade shopping centre waiting for the pubs to open we found a bar - settling in looking forward to the match. We watched Football Focus on Grandstand as the pub actually had a TV hoping that we would get a mention as we were flying high. We got a mention alright….Swansea v Newcastle game off due to a waterlogged pitch, what an absolute sickener! After drowning our sorrows we visited the ground where there was a rumour that the game could be played the next day. My mate had to return home for graft the next day, but I was undecided what to do? Then we saw Swansea Manager John Toshack and after going out of his way to say how sorry he felt for us, we asked him, "What were the chances of the match being played the next day?" He replied, "No chance whatsoever" Big John replied, "The pitch is underwater." We made our way back to the coach and after a nightmare six hour journey home missed out on a beer in the town. On the Sunday I had a long lie in before I walked into the Battle Hill social club at 1pm to be greeted by, "Hey Paul what's the matter with the match?" "What you on about?" I asked. "Kenny Wharton's just scored, the Toon's winning 1-0!! I've hated John Toshack ever since. Two days later I was back on Magpie Travel travelling down to Cardiff, fantastic memories from a fantastic season.

Paul Wardle
Wallsend, Tyneside

Drenched fans were involved in angry scenes after the lunchtime postponement outside of the ground. Although the bus drivers were up for accepting a bung to stay down an extra 24 hours their bosses at the various coach companies wouldn't allow it. As it was rumoured that the game would be played the next day many fans stayed regardless. Some stayed in beach huts, some rough whilst the lucky ones found lodgings with the kind locals. However Swansea police branded Newcastle fans actions as "Foolish." One officer said "They will be soaking wet, freezing, tired and hungry and will only end up in trouble." How wrong he was.

Kev Drew
Wardley, Tyneside

We went down with Magpie Travel. About 7 coaches left St James' Park at Midnight after a Friday night around the Toon. About 90% of the people travelling were very drunk. The long overnight journey soon passed and we arrived in South Wales to a torrential downpour. The pubs were open from 10.30am and the usual faces started to appear - Cockney Dave, Monty, Ray "Thin on top" etc, etc, and more. The rain was persistent and at 12.15pm our worst fears were realised when Bob Wilson announced that our match was off due to water logged pitch. We all kept drinking, making the most of the situation, then people started to drift off. Alone, I headed back to the buses when the bar shut at 3.30pm. The buses had already left over an hour earlier on police instruction. Rumour was that the match might be played on the Sunday so me, Seymour and Towla decided to stay. We went to a chip shop for leek and chips and we were just about to order when we saw Newcastle and Swansea fans squaring up to each other in the street. We ran outside when the 'boxing' started and got stuck in for our fellow Geordies. It was calmed down quite quickly with the Welsh lads getting a bit of a pasting as well as my three day old Pringle Jumper getting ripped in several places. Things calmed down and about 60 of us were wandered around the town centre until the pubs reopened. The first pub we went in the Swansea lads who we had been fighting with were in. When someone asked what had started the trouble, they said that there had been a misunderstanding. We all had a laugh about it and ended up going on a pub crawl together. Eventually later on everyone got lost and I ended up with Budgie and his mate. The days drinking had taken its toll and once the pubs were closed, we ended up in a police station asking for some advice and assistance. No joy. "No beds boyoes." After losing Budgie and his mate I met some other Geordies. One I knew as Gary Donaldson and we ended up going to a local supermarket and getting as many cardboard boxes as we could carry. Then we searched for a good dry spot to sleep. We eventually made ourselves comfortable in a doorway of a shopping forum. We awoke at about 6.30am and tidied ourselves up, asking a road sweeper where we were? He told us we were near the train station and he had already seen loads of Geordies in similar situations. I checked my pockets and realised I only had 52p and no credit cards. We exchanged stories with fellow Geordies at the station. Some lads had made it to B&B's but most had roughed it. Budgie and his mate had slept in a car they'd found open. The beach area had proved popular, where a building site had been made into a temporary open air hotel for the night. Others had slept in bus stations, bus shelters and one Geordie had slept in the shovel of a JCB. I phoned home and my uncle from Merthyr Tydfill came and gave me some cash. He came to the match with us which we won. Towards the end of the match a PA announcement informed the 200 stranded Geordies that the directors had laid on buses to take us home. Heading up the motorway somebody suggested that we stop off at 9pm and go to the nearest pub. We ended up stopping at Micklefield, Yorkshire and went to the local C.I.U club. In the concert room there was an organist playing such classics as the "Birdie Song" and other pop hits. We joined in with the lads and all had a great laugh. At 11pm we boarded our coach for the last familiar stage of our journey home. A total of 64 hours without a bed - but we'd had plenty of beer and laughs. Incidentally in the following match programme a letter from the Micklefield C.I.U club was received and printed praising our good Geordie behaviour and exemplarily manners. It was a good trip, despite the adverse weather, and the South Wales accents.

G.I.
Heaton, Newcastle

"We felt we had more supporters in the ground than Swansea, they were tremendous, magnificent."

Arthur Cox
Newcastle Manager

v CARDIFF CITY
NINIAN PARK
ATT; 9,926

WED 19TH OCTOBER 1983
SECOND DIVISION
WON 2-0

Whoever was responsible for the fixture lists wanted a good hiding as we were off to South Wales for the second time in 5 days, unbelievable and totally unfair. I had stayed down overnight for the Swansea match, when it was delayed for 24 hours, then arrived home by courtesy bus well after midnight on the Sunday night. Two days at graft then I got a bus back down on the Wednesday morning to neighbouring Cardiff for this evening kick-off. It was all worth it as we ran out easy winners taking 6 points out of 6 on the South Coast of Wales, the highlight being Peter Beardsley's first ever Newcastle goal. I eventually arrived back home at 4am just in time for a couple of hours kip before getting up for another shift. About 1,240 miles in total travelled. *"Were Geordies Were Mental Were Off We Fucking Heads."*

Paul Marshall
Killingworth, Newcastle

v OXFORD UNITED
MANOR GROUND
ATT; 13,040

WED 26TH OCTOBER 1983
(MILK) LEAGUE CUP 2nd RND 2nd LEG
LOST 1-2

I went with my mate David Holding whose brother lived in Oxford so we decided to travel down on the Tuesday and stay a couple of nights. As we were both unemployed money was tight so we decided to try hitch-hiking for the first

time, so with nothing better to do we began our trek crossing the Tyne Bridge heading south with thumbs of course hanging out. Fortunately we only had to walk a mile or so through Gateshead before a big wagon stopped and drove us all the way to Coventry. Not quite where we'd intended to finish up but we had plenty of time on our hands. From Coventry we managed two car rides to Banbury, and then on to Oxford and we'd made it. I was a little surprised at how many Newcastle supporters were already milling around the town centre before lunchtime on the day of the match. The ground was a couple of miles outside the centre of town in the Headington district, and getting into it is a tale in itself as you have to walk round the back of a row of houses, through a narrow wooded area before eventually arriving at the away terrace. Needless to say the ground was appalling and, regretfully, so was Newcastle's performance which resulted in our obligatory early round cup exit.

The following morning the journey home took us through the delights of Milton Keynes and Watford Gap Services before getting a ride all the way back to Tyneside, via Leeds, in a big juggernaut, arriving home at about 8.00 p.m.

Mark Hannan
Ponteland, Newcastle

Three weeks after the first leg we travelled to the University City to play little Third Division side Oxford United, the first time I had visited this compact little shithole. Not that my mate Chillo saw much of it as he ended up throwing a can at the Coppers which then turned into a fight, resulting in his arrest. In court his plea of "They started it by trying to take my cans off me" didn't seem to sway the judge as much as he'd hoped! Even with Keegan, Beardsley, Waddle and McDermott we couldn't beat a team from the league below who had Steve Hardwick between the sticks! Over 3,000 Geordies had made the trip as Oxford's average attendance was more than doubled. We couldn't cope with them; some blamed the slope - even though the one at St James' Park was probably worse. An example of how small a club, Oxford were, was when their defender Bobby McDonald went into the visiting changing room after the match and asked Keegan for his autograph. Since Man Utd beat us 7-2 at Old Trafford in 1976/77 we had failed to get past the first hurdle in this competition in seven seasons. Yet elsewhere Liverpool chased their fourth consecutive final. By the way, may I just add, John Ryan was shite.

Ray
Walker, Newcastle

v MANCHESTER CITY
ST JAMES' PARK
ATT; 33,675

SAT 29TH OCTOBER 1983
SECOND DIVISION
WON 5-0

I was standing in the Centre Paddock in front of the old West Stand for this top of the table clash against Man City who'd been relegated the previous summer, which was watched by another large Second Division crowd. The match itself was unforgettable as Newcastle really turned it on playing the best football seen on Tyneside for years as Keegan, Waddle and Beardsley ran riot, as all three got on the score sheet, the latter grabbing a hat-trick as we went on to win 5-0. The only thing to put a damper on my celebrations was when the fifth goal went in, I followed through' making a right mess of my Kegs!!!

Terry Mann
Longbenton, Newcastle

I was in the 'Scoreboard' for this early season promotion battle and I swear I could see a big ladder going up against the back of the Leazes End wall. I think some Mags were clambering up the ladder to get into the away section, where the Man City fans were housed. A few days earlier the mighty Liverpool had a smaller crowd for their European Cup match v Athletic Bilbao than this Second Division fixture. Where were we when we were shite eh?

Panda
Forest Hall, Newcastle

One of the memories, which will stay with me forever was standing in the Gallowgate, behind my barrier with my grandfatha' next to me, him wanting to see the toon one last time, as he'd recently been diagnosed with cancer after decades of smoking rollies. My arms around him, when needed, to protect him from the surges when we scored. Waddler was on fire as I commentated to my Grandfatha' at times because he couldn't see the pitch down the packed terraces. He sadly died a few weeks later on Christmas Day. I remember a few years later thinking how our roles all reverse when 'wor kid' bought me the Chelsea v Newcastle programme for Christmas from my first ever game.

Tommy Knox
Fenham, Newcastle

Like a lot of people my age I spent some time on the Nat King Cole during the early eighties courtesy of Mrs Thatcher and her Merry Men. Football was the one thing you looked forward to end, interrupt the boredom of having no job. Days like these kept you going. Three from Beardsley (his first on home soil), one each from Keegan and Waddle, but the whole team's performance was superb. For a long time this was my favourite game ever – it's still in my top three now.

Chris Ramshaw
West Denton, Newcastle

I was working on Ascension Island in the South Atlantic Ocean building an army station. It was after the Falklands war and they needed somewhere to stop between the UK and the Falklands. So they decided on this little volcanic island in the middle of the ocean with nothing on it except a few donkeys, sheep and a satellite tracking station. I was away for 4 months and missing football and home. Newcastle had made a great start to the season and the next big test was Man City. The only contact we had was BBC 'World Service' radio and letters; this was before satellite TV the internet or mobiles. I was working in a toilet block half way up the island with a bloke from Benton called Billy Nevin who had a little tranny. You could be in a bog with a tranny and a bloke from Benton in those days and not be gay or get nicked! What a god send that little tranny was. The BBC 'World Service' had probably not changed since the war, it was very official, but kept you up to date with the world and always covered a football match on a Saturday afternoon - we used to play on a Saturday in those days. Newcastle had made such a good start they covered us even in the Second Division and the guest commentator was fellow Geordie and Newcastle supporter Jack Charlton. His broad Ashington drawl was not quite what 'World Service' was used too. The match went great and we hammered them 5-0 with Beardsley tearing them apart all over the pitch. The rather pompous BBC presenter asked 'Big Jack' what he thought of this new lad Beardsley. Jack's reply was "he's a funny bugger," not really what the rest of the world was expecting to hear, but for us Geordies around the globe a proud moment to be one. I don't think Jack covered any more Newcastle games after that.

Dave Emmerson
Walker, Newcastle

v FULHAM   **SAT 5TH NOVEMBER 1983**
ST JAMES' PARK   **SECOND DIVISION**
ATT; 31,660   **WON 3-2**

As we made it six league wins out of six, in the stands was the recently retired legendary Liverpool boss Bob Paisley who had no doubt as to the catalyst for this. "If Newcastle do win promotion, then forget about making Kevin Keegan 'Player of the Year' - he'll deserve to be named 'Team of the Year.' They should rename Newcastle, 'Keegan United.' He took throw-ins, free kicks, doubled up as a striker and a midfield player, scored one goal and created another. He had more touches of the ball than the rest put together. Kevin is playing as well as I've ever seen him even at an age when most players are looking for a less demanding stint."

Bob Paisley,
Liverpool Manager

Bonfire Night and another 30,000 crowd were treated to a mouth watering game against Malcolm Macdonald's Fulham. With half an hour to play Fulham went into a 2-1 lead, but then Newcastle were urged on by a vociferous and passionate crowd. Chance after chance was wasted until with only 3 minutes remaining David Mills got the equaliser. Then amid scenes which could only be described as bedlam on the terraces Geordie boy Wharton unbelievably grabbed the winner sending the whole ground delirious. There were impromptu firework displays going off everywhere as United moved back into second place. Aye, remember, remember the 5th of November. Loads of fireworks were set off all afternoon. You wondered where the next rocket would land, how close the next banger would be. Imagine that happening these days! Football and society has changed an incredible amount. The Fulham players complained bitterly to the referee at the end all pointing to the scoreboard which showed the time to be 4.45pm. In those days games finished at 4.40pm. I can still see the players surrounding the ref pointing towards the electronic scoreboard.

Mick Edmondson
Walker, Newcastle

v CHELSEA
STAMFORD BRIDGE
ATT; 30,638

SAT 12TH NOVEMBER 1983
SECOND DIVISION
LOST 0-4

Our away game at Chelsea was a humiliating defeat, 4-0 as I remember, but an estimated 8,000 turned up at Chelsea - with around 400-500 N.M.E. and Benders

mixed, walking the distance from Sloane Square up to Stamford Bridge, having major confrontations with several hundred Chelsea all the way along!! The best supporters in the world, with the best team in the world, was how we felt, and nothing was going to get in our way to stop us reaching Division One again!

Tomahawk (NME)
Peterlee, Durham

My mate Steve and I climbed the stairs of Fulham Broadway tube station to be greeted by a Chelsea mob numbering over 200 strong waiting outside in the street for Geordies. Fearing for our own safety we were straight back down the stairs to be greeted by a train pulling in packed full of Newcastle lads. The first lad came towards us and we said, "You don't want to go up there mate there's hundreds of Chelsea waiting." He replied "Great," as hundreds of Newcastle's finest poured off the train and charged up the stairs, spilling into the street scattering Chelsea everywhere. We followed behind as they attacked the White Hart pub as well as others and anyone who dared get in the way, before marching along Fulham Broadway towards 'The Britannia' pub outside Stamford Bridge.

Mick
Gateshead, Tyneside

v SHEFFIELD WEDNESDAY	SAT 19TH NOVEMBER 1983
HILLSBOROUGH	SECOND DIVISION
ATT; 41,134	LOST 2-4

We were heading down the A1 in our mini-bus for this top of the table clash. Just past Scotch Corner one of the lads Watson' decided to get his dick out to entertain the passing cars, sliding the window along and letting it hang out. One particular woman passenger with a perfect view didn't look too happy as she approached, but nevertheless still had a damn good luck. But it's a good job that, she had her window closed as seconds later her husband had the windscreen wipers going like the clappers, only it wasn't water? As for the match it was good although disappointing due to a Varadi inspired 4-2 Sheffield win - so it was shit really.

Simon O'Toole
Newcastle

This game will always remain in my memory for the awful crush on the terraces. Everyone knows about the tragedy involving the Liverpool fans on the Leppings Lane terrace during the 1989 FA Cup semi-final, but many Newcastle fans would tell you it was almost pre-empted six years earlier. As usual thousands of Geordies had travelled to South Yorkshire and the queues outside Hillsborough were massive. It took almost until kick-off time to get into the ground and even then we were stuck in the tunnel leading out to the terraces unable to move with the force of people both behind and in front of you making things decidedly unpleasant. I don't know how but we eventually got onto the terraces where the crush intensified, and people were clambering up to the seats above to escape the panic. It was an obvious case of mismanagement by the home club, and it wasn't until well into the first half, when an additional part of the ground was made available to the Newcastle contingent, that matters became a little more bearable. I enjoy big crowds, packed terraces, surges and the like, but this was taking things a little too far and it could have proved fatal. It goes without saying that when I heard of the tragedy in 1989 my mind immediately flashed back to this day.

Mark Hannen
Ponteland, Newcastle

Out of all the away matches I ever attended I used to love going to Hillsborough and wasn't alone as 16,000 travelling Geordies boosted the attendance, all packed onto the Leppings Lane terrace. Every season Newcastle always took a huge following to this semi-final venue ground, but today it seemed that the whole of Tyneside was in Sheffield. Once through the turnstiles, to get to the terracing behind the goal you had to go through a very narrow tunnel which had barely enough room for two people to pass. Once at the other end of the tunnel you found yourself in the centre at the rear of the terracing, with fences on three sides and the seated stand which you had just walked under, up above behind you. As kick-off approached it was obvious that there were far to many Newcastle fans squashed into this end and panic started to set in, as dozens of fans scaled the perimeter fences, having to fight with batten wielding coppers! They just didn't get it did they? Others climbed to safety in the seats above helped and lifted to safety by fellow Geordies dangling their arms down. Luckily there weren't any really serious casualties and extra terracing was eventually opened, although we were still packed in like sardines. One of our recent favourite players Imre Varadi who'd been forced out the previous summer was playing for Sheff Wed, but he didn't read the script as he scored 2 goals. When he netted in front of the Geordie hordes at the Leppings Lane End he didn't celebrate but instead stood almost apologetically and received a sporting hand clap. Also on the score sheet for 'The Owls' was future signing Tony Cunningham. It was a very disappointing result but nevertheless a good game.

Kev Egan
Walker, Newcastle

Sitting in 'The County' pub on Walker Road on the Friday night it was decided that we would go to the match the next day. In the 80's you didn't have to apply to the club and all that nonsense, all you had to do was drive down, go to the away end and pay at the gate. I was the designated driver, I hadn't been long past my driving test and had an 850 Mini, with the spotlights on the front and sport seats, it looked the business, or at least I thought so, first car and all that, but had no poke whatsoever. We set out first thing Wor kid, Andy Ed, Davey Douglas all dressed in Black-and-White kilts and my mothers wigs. Why Geordies do this at away games is beyond me but if everybody else was up for it then why not. Once I'm onto the Tyne Bridge I haven't got a Scooby Doo where anywhere is or for that matter how to get there. Luckily since leaving the army, Wor kid was doing lorry driving and is one of these twats who always knows the short cuts everywhere, which by the way seems to take longer than the way you were going to go in the first place. In the past we'd always got the train so weren't sure where the ground was when we arrived in the steel city, so we're driving round aimlessly when Wor kid shouts out, "Those lads in the Sierra are

going to the match, because look you can see their scarves, Follow That Car!!"
Not being the brightest, I swung from the inside lane straight into the outside
lane, without indicating, or looking or even thinking about it to be totally honest,
only to hear a screech of brakes. I'd only pulled out in front of a rather irate fat
fellow driving a big Post Office truck. Now the lads in the Sierra seeing this,
obviously thought we were a crew from Sheffield trying to get to them, so they
did what any sensible chaps would do, seeing a 6 ft. ex-Para in a orange wig,
squeezed into a little red 850 mini with his head sticking out the sun roof, they
ran away, or drove away pretty fast at any rate. This Sierra went off like a bat out
of hell followed closely by a little red mini with 4 lads in various coloured wigs.
The lads in the Sierra jumped red lights, closely followed by a little red mini.
They went the wrong way down a one way street, closely followed by a little red
mini. They pulled into garage forecourts, closely followed by a little red mini.
They wheel - spun out of garage forecourts, closely followed by a wheel spinning
little red mini. "You're gonna kill us all" was the shout from Andy Ed. "Let's just
stop and ask someone for directions" whined Dougie. "What the Fuck are you
doing" screamed Wor kid. But by this stage it was personal, I could keep up with
a Sierra, no fucking problems, they couldn't outrun me, but I was Mad Max and
those sorry son's of bitches were 'The Toecutter.' They were slowing down,
speeding up, undertaking and overtaking but I was on their tail. I was Maverick
and Wor kid was Goose, I would have them no worries, later Wor kid reckoned
it was like being an extra on the Italian Job. Wor kid was trying to catch the
attention of the lads in front by showing them our colours yelling, "Slow down
for Christ's sake" out the window. I wasn't doing that bad considering I was
driving an 850 mini and these cowardly bastards had a 2.0 litre Sierra. Eventually
to my passengers delight we saw the floodlights and the plan had worked, these
lads did know where they were going after all.

Andy Farrell
Walker, Newcastle

This was the event that showed me my true vocation in life. I remember being
excited a few weeks earlier when my Dad first showed me the slip of card with
the letters SWFC boldly printed alongside the name Newcastle United FC. Little
did I realise how misguided I was when I questioned the sanity of leaving at 8am
for a match two hours down the road that started at 3pm. Nor if there was really
any need for us to stay in this smoky Working Men's Club for the intervening 4
hours (it's funny how the thought of going to watch them sober now fills me with
an abject terror!) It did however all become clear at about quarter to three on that
Saturday afternoon when I took my seat in the third from back row at the
Leppings Lane End of Hillsborough. The fact that we were sitting so far back
only helped to convey the sheer passion and enormity of the occasion. The whole
of Tyneside had decided to come and watch the match as well. At least that was
how it appeared to me. The official estimates later said that 15,000 had made the
trip and it was my first real understanding of my second family. The noise from
both the singing and the rattling of the old wooden seats; the toing and froing of
the match and the general experience of the day left me desperate for more. Not
even the fact we lost 4-2 could put me off, in fact it just gave a truer picture of life
following the 'Toon'....that of glorious failure following unbelievable highs! (We

had pulverised fellow promotion candidates Man City 5-0 just a couple of weeks earlier).

Pete Grieves
North Seaton, Northumberland

Kevin Keegan the player, 15,000 Geordies squashed on way out with the egg timer arrangement and up the hill to one of the Football Specials. Great memories and very happy days.

Duzza
Battlehill, Tyneside

We were queuing up at the Leppings Lane turnstiles along with thousands of other Geordies when a huge furniture wagon pulled up. The driver got out of his cab and went to the back of the vehicle, where he unlocked the padlocks before opening the large shutter. Dozens of bottles and cans came rolling out of the lorry, smashing on the road below. The Police looked on in disgust as dozens of Geordies who'd been packed in like sardines climbed out the back

Rob Phillips
Walker, Newcastle

Went down by Service Train and got off at Rotherham for a few beers. But the majority of the lads stayed on and when they got off at Sheffield there was a huge Police presence waiting for them. They were all forced on to special buses and told that they were being taking to a bar which had been reserved for them near the ground. But when they arrived at the ground they were all put in a special security pen for two hours in the freezing cold. Eventually when the gates were opened everyone got in to the ground free of charge.

Piper
Felling, Tyneside

v CAMBRIDGE UNITED　　　　　　**SAT 26TH NOVEMBER 1983**
ST JAMES' PARK　　　　　　　　　**SECOND DIVISION**
ATT; 25,065　　　　　　　　　　　　**WON 2-1**

Before kick-off the clubs physiotherapist Alec Mutch who had served the club for 53 years was presented with a £500 cheque from Chairman Stan Seymour. He had previously managed the Reserves to their only Central league title in our history. He came on the pitch in his white Doctors coat, waving the cheque in the air. Manager Arthur Cox was missing due to an ear infection and Bronchitis. Cambridge were rock bottom and were on a run of nine defeats, yet we struggled to just do enough to beat them. In the programme notes Chairman Stan Seymour praised the thousands who had travelled to Sheffield the previous week, "We salute you and your exemplary behaviour at Hillsborough makes you all a credit to Newcastle United." The club made 500 more season tickets available and they were all snapped up within three hours. On a less happy note Geordie lad Derek Bell was forced to retire through injury.

Mick Edmondson
Walker, Newcastle

v DERBY COUNTY
BASEBALL GROUND
ATT; 18,691

SAT 3RD DECEMBER 1983
SECOND DIVISION
LOST 2-3

Three days before the game I came off my motorbike in Northumberland wrecking my machine and was taken by ambulance to hospital where I had an operation on my badly broken right arm and dislocated shoulder. I was hospitalised for at least a week as my arm was a compound fracture and I had a Hoffman's frame attached to my bone. On the Friday night the escape committee met around my bed at the General Hospital planning the Saturday morning breakout. I hadn't missed a Keegan match for the Toon and there was no way I was going to miss the trip to Derby. It was decided that it was best not to mention anything to my family or girlfriend as it would then be a total non-starter. After breakfast early Saturday morning I waited for the doctor to do his rounds and once I'd been seen I managed to escape in my pyjamas walking along the corridor and down the stairs to a waiting car where I eventually changed into some clothes my mates had managed to get together. The bastards had been to some charity shops and bought me some bad taste gear for a total of about £3. Although in pain and discomfort and slightly embarrassed at my new attire this was all forgotten about as we led 0-2 at half time. But in typical Newcastle style we managed to lose 3-2 as McCreery who had just returned to the side, suffered a recurrence of his ankle injury and we conceded three goals in ten minutes (Two scored by South Shields born Bobby Davison)!! As you can imagine the drive home was quite stressful as I also began to worry about facing the music on my return!! To think I went to this length to watch my football team, yet Arthur Cox didn't travel with the team due to an ear infection and a touch of Bronchitis. Oh by the way the hospital forgave me and I was treated by a nurse calling at my home and as for my girlfriend I can't even remember her name.

Jimmy
Elswick, Newcastle

I was supposed to get picked up at Heworth metro-station but slept in and missed the van at 7am. I luckily made it across to the Haymarket and caught a supporters coach at 9am. After the match our 4th consecutive away defeat I just travelled back on the bus but the lads who I'd supposed to travel with originally stopped off for a night out on the outskirts of Derby. At about 10.30pm a huge fight broke out and as a result they all got locked up. For the court case a couple of weeks later they again they hired a van and travelled back down where they were all fined but just managed to get out of court in dribs and drabs before the pub next door shut at 3pm. Inside they were greeted by the landlord Billy Hughes who won the FA Cup with Sunderland in 1973. The crack started and the curtains were closed as he gave them a lock-in and after a good afternoon they stayed for the evening session eventually leaving at midnight.

Piper
Felling, Tyneside

v BRISTOL ROVERS
EASTVILLE
ATT; 4,107

TUES 6TH DECEMBER 1983
FRIENDLY
LOST 4-5

This game was arranged as part of the transfer deal which brought goalkeeper Martin Thomas to Tyneside. I went down to Bristol for this pointless friendly in Billy's car, there was only me him and my mate Paul Taylor going. We were waiting for Paul outside the RVI where he was having a check up on his dodgy heart. He eventually turned up with his bait in a shopping bag big enough for the first and second team, whilst complaining that the doctor had told him to loose another 6 stone! Paul settled into the back seat got out his sixty tabs for the journey a 3 litre bottle of coke and a family pack of pork pies saying "Av had nee breakfast!!"

Dave Emmerson
Walker, Newcastle

Two days before the transfer deadline and Birmingham City put in a £150,000 bid for Chris Waddle whose contract was up in the summer. Newcastle United turned down the offer and refused Birmingham permission to speak to the player. When asked about his thoughts Waddle said: "There was no way I wanted to move at the moment. I only got married in June and settled into a new house. We have a new bathroom suite, shower and stair carpet coming next week so you can see that I'm putting down roots rather than preparing to leave." That was unbelievably what he said. How times have changed, imagine Steven Gerard staying at Liverpool because he had a stair carpet arriving the following week!

Mick Edmondson
Walker, Newcastle

I went by train but it came to a standstill about an hour from our destination. We were informed by an announcement that the reason for our delay was that rats had eaten through the cables!

Cliffy Ahmed
South Shields, Tyneside

v HUDDERSFIELD TOWN
ST JAMES' PARK
ATT; 25,747

SAT 10TH DECEMBER 1983
SECOND DIVISION
WON 5-2

Can't remember if it was after this game but it was around this time I went to see the legendary Geordie band 'The Animals' in concert at the City Hall. Can't say it was the best concert I ever went too but it was fascinating to see the obvious friction that was present between the group members. Eric Burdon made pithy remarks, Alan Price glowered at his keyboard and the rest looked somewhat bemused by it all.
(The Animals played the City Hall on Dec 13th & 17th).

Chris Ramshaw
West Denton, Newcastle

I was with Radio Tyneside and went to the Benwell training ground on the day before the match against Huddersfield to interview David McCreery (absolutely delightful bloke). We talked about the game and when I had finished the piece I asked him if he would mind recording a Christmas message for the people who were unfortunate enough to be in hospital on Christmas Day. We used to do this with all the well known people we interviewed and played them all out on Christmas morning. "No problem," he said. "This is David McCreery of Newcastle United and to all those folk in hospital this Christmas my message is get well soon and what I always say is never say die!" Then he realised what he had said and added: "Oh shit I shouldn't have said that should I?" The whole piece went out unedited on Christmas morning!

Barry Hindson
Radio Newcastle

After 3 defeats in our previous 4 games we bounced back in style. We hung around after the match before going around town on our Christmas night out. It wasn't until we got into Julie's Nightclub that we found out that we had drawn against the current champions Liverpool at Anfield in the FA Cup third round. The draw had taken place at tea time but because there weren't any mobile phones or Sky TV then you were none the wiser, unless somebody told you. Roll on January.

Tessa B
Gosforth, Newcastle

v BRIGHTON & HOVE ALBION	SAT 17TH DECEMBER 1983
GOLDSTONE GROUND	**SECOND DIVISION**
ATT; 13,896	**WON 1-0**

A week before Christmas and we had to travel the full length of England, madness. Back then I used to be a manager at Newcastle's top nightclub Tuxedo Junction and Terry Mac was a regular and more often than not would be pissed, in fact it was round about this time that I found him sleeping like a baby on the sofa in the restaurant!! Terry was a class act and I got to know him quite well and organised a game of snooker at Supasnooker next to Madison's nightclub. I took my brother Micky along and told him we were playing Terry Mac and Kevin Keegan he just laughed, we walked into the club and Terry Mac shouts "Rob we're on now" with Keegan standing next to him, our Mick nearly shit himself with fright!!

Rob Scott
Walker, Newcastle

I travelled down for free with my mate on his rail ticket as he worked for British Rail. And with free match tickets supplied by my mate Chrissy Waddle the scorer of the only goal it was a rather cheap and enjoyable day out to the South Coast. Rumours had been flying around the terraces that there had been a bombing in London and sure enough when we arrived at Victoria Station there were Police everywhere. The station was surrounded by them and everybody seemed confused and concerned amidst all the chaos. In all the mayhem I lost my mate and never saw him again that night. Once I settled in a bar I learnt the full extent of what had happened. The IRA had planted a bomb in a side street near Harrods department store in Knightsbridge. It exploded just before 1.30pm killing six people (including three police officers) and wounded a further 90, during Christmas shopping at the West London store. The events came after a series of threats from the IRA in recent days that it was planning a pre-Christmas bombing campaign in the capital. With Police and the armed forces and thousands of people everywhere I knew that I would never make my 8pm train so I decided to have few beers and then catch a train later. When I got to Kings Cross after midnight there were loads of Geordies in the same boat, who'd missed trains. We got an old rattler, the mail train and the guards just turned a blind eye which was quite handy seeing that I didn't have a ticket.

Piper
Felling, Tyneside

At various places we visited I couldn't help but notice there were often groups of Newcastle fans who would come out of other teams home ends and not look like they'd just been hung drawn and quartered, but more jubilant and focused! Not easy to spot in a crowd as they wore no colours. As Newcastle fans always networked with each other in pubs and bars they were lucky enough to get a stop off in, and talked about where they came from, we got to know loads of lads and blokes who told us about how to get to other teams grounds and how to go for a pint in cities and where to find other Newcastle fans if we did. Magpie travel was also good and cheap, but many away days were met by police lines as soon as you got off the coaches and a tight escort straight into the ground. The rail network was a good, cheap, and free-er type of way to get around the country, and young person's rail cards, as advertised by 'Sir Jimmy Saville,' were a true godsend. Brighton away (in the league when we won 1-0) cost me a measly £19! Fantastic! There were occasions though when the rule of thumb was the only option for getting away, hitching down the motorways either early morning or through the night. I went to Crystal Palace one year with around £17 in my pocket and hitched down a freezing A1 and M1 till I got into London. The absolute fanaticism that was inside us all by this point was unbeatable and not something you could easily put into words. We soon learned the advantages of not wearing team colours, and staying together in groups and in numbers. There were various flashpoints along the way where aggro came looking for you, or because you stayed with the main group you yourself entered "enemy" territory. The lads that stayed together back then, and travelled everywhere gave themselves the nickname of The N.M.E. (The Newcastle Mainline Express). Several of us from Peterlee, and the East Durham Collieries joined the N.M.E. (purely safety in numbers you see!) even though it was never an 'official entity.' But just you try telling that to the hundreds of people involved and the story will be different! The word was around Newcastle that there were 3 main groups of who some would call mindless yobs, hooligans, scum of the earth etc etc.......The older lads "The Benders" so called because every game was like having a bender in the Bigg Market, The N.M.E., and the next Generation who got the nickname "The Gremlins." That word spread around the country to other team's gangs/firms/mobs whatever names anyone wants to give em!!! So this promotion year especially was an era where the stakes were very high for you as a Newcastle fan travelling to away games. Everywhere you went there were hundreds of lads and blokes, who wanted to do nothing else but kick your frigging heed in! I hold my hands up and admit I felt the same way about other team's lads a fair few times with the adrenalin of the day catching up with you. I did end up in some sinister scrapes, and sometimes paying the price courtesy of her majesty's forces of law and order! It didn't matter where we were playing, or where your feet took you when you landed in remote areas of other teams' territory. There was an invisible magnetism, which always drew you to where there would be faces you recognised, and help was there if you needed it. There were no heroics expected, but if you played the game you had to play your part! There were a few things I thought were baffling, mainly how some of the dressed lads would jeer and sneer at our "trees" scarfers/shirters, but if they ever saw any of them getting a hiding off other fans they would be getting stuck straight in there to help them and stick together with them, work that one out? The 80's years were what made a lot of us who we are today, in terms of experienced men who know a thing or two about what it is to be a dedicated follower of Newcastle: The fun and our passion for the team, the dangers and excitement of facing the dangers. We outgrew the hooligan phase and most of us have lived to tell the tale, but there are some lads and blokes who are sadly missed by all who knew them - Big Stevie, Simmo, Matches, Pringle, Bodsa to name a few.

If we could wind the clock back and go and do it all again we more than likely would! If we go to any games in this day and age, those days do get talked about from time to time but they don't get re-visited in the physical sense, they're all stories of days gone by, and a massive part of our 80's heyday history and heritage. The authorities may not like this one bit, but my thoughts on the state of affairs are: If you want to totally get rid of hooliganism/violence/conflict in football you have to make football into a game where it's not a case of "us and them," which as we all know is 'Never Going To Happen.' I met loads of decent lads blokes and lasses during my obsessive time following Newcastle in the 80's and I can say whether you're a Bender/N.M.E./Gremlin or any other primary group, or even just a pure fanatical supporter with a personal hatred for aggro at football, it doesn't matter one bit, as every single one of us, is a part of the big picture that is, to be a lifelong supporter of Newcastle United and proud of it.

Tomahawk (NME)
Peterlee, Durham

v BLACKBURN ROVERS　　　　　　　　**MON 26TH DECEMBER 1983**
ST JAMES' PARK　　　　　　　　　　　　　　**SECOND DIVISION**
ATT; 33,622　　　　　　　　　　　　　　　　　　**DREW 1-1**

A Boxing Day debut for Newcastle's new signing Mick McCarthy? Well it almost was but our first choice target thankfully turned us down and instead signed for Man City. So instead we luckily signed our second choice centre half from QPR for £120,000, a certain Glen Roeder who was only available because Nott's County couldn't raise the money to turn his loan period into a permanent move. The player, who had guided QPR to an FA Cup final at Wembley only 18 months earlier, forcing Spurs to a draw, with a man of the match appearance before missing the replay through suspension, was now a Newcastle player. He marked his debut with a double 'Roeder Shuffle' which made him an instant Gallowgate hero. The final piece of our promotion jigsaw was now in place.

Mick Edmondson
Walker, Newcastle

v CARLISLE UNITED
BRUNTON PARK
ATT; 14,756

TUES 27TH DECEMBER 1983
SECOND DIVISION
LOST 1-3

A trip along the Roman Wall to the west coast to play 'The Cumbrians' a short journey welcomed by many because of the festive season. We caught the train from the Central and everybody was having a sing song on the way there until someone decided to pull the emergency cord (twice), stopping the train in the middle of the Tyne Valley just past Hexham somewhere. Then the train guard going berserk when some wags got a hold of the intercom in his unlocked guard's room and made a few announcements of their own! Once inside Brunton Park Newcastle fans were housed behind the goal on an open terrace as well as the paddock to the half way line. I can remember loads of Toon fans climbing on top of the scoreboard whilst other fans shook it so they fell off, and one lad stripping down to his Keks with arms aloft on the very top declaring "The man from Del Monte, He says Yes!" to thunderous applause. Chris Waddle scored for the 5th consecutive game making it 6 goals in 5 matches, yet at the other end our keeper wasn't having the best of days at the office, as Martin Thomas let in 3 goals, in such a fashion, that a Newcastle fan ran onto the pitch and attacked him throwing punches before being dragged away. The trip home was uneventful with no guard abuse or unofficial stops.

Tom Knox
Fenham, Newcastle

Travelling along the A69 in our hired mini bus we stopped off for a pre-match piss stop just before Brampton when one of the lads noticed a circular Stop & Go temporary road sign abandoned at the side of the road. He immediately sprung into action using it to control the traffic in both directions much to our amusement. He would show the westbound traffic the green go sign then within seconds spin it round to show the red stop sign, thus causing cars which had just started to move to suddenly brake and visa versa for eastbound traffic! Eventually he had huge traffic jams and the police sirens could be heard as we decided to make a sharp exit.

Skippy
Bedlington, Northumberland

A trip of attending an away match in promotion year, oddly, is Carlisle on the day after Boxing Day. A horrible, lousy game played in foul weather that we lost 3-1, in which the goalie, Martin Thomas, had a 'mare and in which we were outplayed by a team of pit yakkas. And the reason it's so memorable? The huge argument that erupted on the supporter's club bus on the way back - with the author of this book a central figure in it - about whether Keegan (you might remember him)

241

was actually a decent player or not and if the team wouldn't be better off without him. 'I've played football, man,' said Mr Edmondson at the top of his, not inconsiderable voice, 'and I can tell you, although a class act he's still over-rated!' Seemingly, King Kev was feeling the same way - a week later, after finding himself outclassed in a cup tie at Liverpool, he announced he was going to retire.

Keith Topping
Walker, Newcastle

It was a really weird experience travelling to an away match by coach without going down the boring A1. I say boring as it is quite repetitive but more so, on the return journey when it's usually dark and it seems to take for ever. At least when your going south on the morning of an away match you tend to be full of crack and pre-match excitement. Carlisle have always received the welsh treatment from Geordies: *"Sheep Sheep Sheep Shaggers."* As well as the classic: *"Sing In The Bike Shed."* As for Kevin Keegan - in my eyes he is the messiah, always has been - always will be. I'm his biggest fan and will never forget what he did for Newcastle United twice as a player and twice as a manager, but I still think Peter Beardsley is the greatest player I have ever seen. Yet Kevin Keegan and Newcastle United is the perfect combination. The most exciting times whilst following Newcastle have always been when KK has been involved. The man's an absolute genius.

Mick Edmondson
Walker, Newcastle

v OLDHAM ATHLETIC   **SAT 31ST DECEMBER 1983**
BOUNDARY PARK   **SECOND DIVISION**
ATT; 8,518   **WON 2-1**

"Jingle Bells, Jingle Bells, Jingle All The Way, Oh What Fun It Is To See Newcastle Win Away." After we finished the year off in style completing the double over 'The Latics' a few bevvies were sunk before it was time to get home for the New Year celebrations. As 'Rento' had decided to drive home the rest of the lads settled down in the back of the van for some well earned rest. A little while later we were rudely awakened by a spectacular view of the Humber Bridge! Rento still cannot to this day explain why! He says he just followed the white lines. The real problem was that the van had only so many free miles of petrol so ended up costing us a canny bit to get home, luckily just in time for New Year.

Dave
Gateshead, Tyneside

v BARNSLEY   **MON 2ND JANUARY 1984**
ST JAMES' PARK   **SECOND DIVISION**
ATT; 29,833   **WON 1-0**

I will not be associated with negative tactics. I much prefer to concede a couple of goals if we can score three or four. We are capable of doing the hardest things in the game - creating and taking chances, we have proved many times this season that scoring goals is not a problem. Where we have been found wanting in the first half of this campaign is doing what many would term the easy part of the game - defending. I want promotion for the best supporters in the game and I want us to achieve our aim with style, flair and excitement.

Arthur Cox
Newcastle United Manager

v LIVERPOOL	**FRI 6TH JANUARY 1984**
ANFIELD	**FA CUP 3RD ROUND**
ATT; 33,566	**LOST 0-4**

Liverpool were clearly a tough draw and, as the game was being billed as Keegan's return to Anfield, the BBC moved it from its normal Saturday slot to Friday night for the benefit of live television. The Geordies like nothing better than converging on clubs such as Liverpool and Manchester United with thousands of supporters and, to all intents and purposes, taking over the ground and singing themselves hoarse for a couple of hours or more. I remember this particular night's exercising of the vocal chords beginning at least an hour before kick-off and not letting up until well after the final whistle. Although we ended up losing 4-0 it was one of those nights you'll never forget, simply because of the unique atmosphere generated by the Geordies. It made you feel so proud to be a Geordie and you can't say any better than that. The game also made up Keegan's mind to retire at the end of the season. During the match he had been up against the classy Mark Lawrenson and barely got a kick, one incident in particular when he had a head start on the defender only to be beaten to the ball made him realise that he couldn't do himself justice again at the top level if promotion was gained, so his decision to call it a day come May was a brave and logical one, although he wasn't to announce it for a while.

Mark Hannen
Ponteland, Newcastle

Friday night live on the TV, but still Anfield was the place to be. I arranged to meet two mates at the Central Station to catch the train to Lime Street. Being sensible me and one mate got the bus into town whilst another one of the lads aged 17 and who had just recently passed his driving test and acquired a battered old Ford Escort, decided to drive into town. I could not bring myself to tell him that when he parked up in the station car park that he would be charged by the hour. Some twelve hours later it cost him more to get his car out than we had collectively paid for our train fares and match tickets. Don't think he did that again.

Millie,
Kenton, Newcastle

I went into work on the Tuesday morning which was my day off. The supervisor Jackie Lowes remarked, "I know what you're doing in, it's so that you can blow your Friday shift and gan doon to the match." I replied "Aye that's right" Jackie knew the crack and was canny enough, "Well make sure you ring in," came the reply.

Deka
Gateshead, Tyneside

Before the match we had a friendly game of football in the car park with a group of 'Mickey Mousers,' when one of our lads split his trousers in the middle.   He was invited into a nearby house by an elderly couple and whilst the woman sowed his trousers the old Fella got him a beer as he sat by the open fire. At the end of the match I ended up on the pitch as I'd been in the Liverpool end, but was joined by many more from the Newcastle end.

Davey
Walker, Newcastle

We were meeting my mate who had shifted down there since he'd married a lass that he had met in Magaluf. We had arranged to meet his new Liverpool mates in the "Flat Iron" which is their boozer just along the road from the ground beside 'The Arkle.' In those days it was still quite hip to wear a scarf and we were all coloured up so when we pulled up outside the pub my mate said "listen lads it's a staunch red bar this and you may think of taking your colours off as there may be bother." Of course we ignored his advice and entered the pub to find it at least 200 Toon fans on the tables singing the Blaydon Races and his red mates sitting in the snug shitting there pants. Absolute classic, there faces were a treat honestly.

Terry O'Donnell
Kenton, Newcastle

I can still remember one of ours sticking his Newcastle flag in the centre spot before the game. We may have got hammered 4-0 but we showed the world how to support a team, I can still remember their keeper Bruce Grobbelaar applauding us during the game and shaking his head in disbelief at the noise coming from our end, proper fans not like these days and the PC tosser's that follow Newcastle. On the way home we headed up the M6 and on to the A69 through Cumbria where at after midnight the Police stopped us on suspicion of sheep rustling and insisted on searching the Van!! So they opened the back doors shining their torch into the van straight on to Flynny's big ginger mop, with the ginger chap shouting shut the fucking doors you twat. We have been accused of a few things in my time but that takes the biscuit.

Archie
Wallsend, Tyneside

As our coach left Anfield it was attacked and one of the windows was put out by a brick which hit Newcastle legend Willie McFaul's nephew in the face. Our driver Dennis Marren didn't stop and drove back to Newcastle in record time to get him medical assistance.

Mala Pegg,
Gateshead, Tyneside

Tyneside was full of optimism for an upset against the mighty reds. Teenage boys from all over the Toon were concocting tall intricate tales to be explained to parents, teachers, probation workers and any other authority figure who may stand in the way, of a free pass out on a Friday afternoon. A bout of 'boy flu' hit epidemic proportions, grandfathas' died for the third time that year, dental appointments tripled and the West Denton Wild Bunch just walked out and said they wouldn't be home til they were... I was probably wearing my blue and white Puma tracksuit top, Geordie Jeans in burgundy and my Puma Vilas trainers. We didn't need that Gok gadgie to know how to accessorise in those days! I even had some hair left, a Howard Jones style quality mullet with 'Sun-In' added blonde bits. Having recently recovered from my Fatha's efforts to save himself a few quid and give me and wor kid haircuts himself, I fully intended to flaunt what I had left. My sister never recovered from being given a number one. Anfield is nestled right among the terraced houses of that district of Liverpool and leaving the coach and entering the ground as always allowed a mix with the local scallys in the narrow streets surrounding the ground. I remember staying with the lads from school avoiding any alley ambushes and entering the ground with a mixture of anticipation, excitement and needing to pay a visit as the McEwans Export needed to be recycled. The smells of cigarette smoke, beer and Bovril mixed with the steam from the open urinals, was the smell of football. I remember the steps up to the terrace and then the explosion of light from the floodlights, the bright green of the pitch, the red of the Kop and the swell of pride and hope as I saw and heard the masses of singing, swaying Black-and-White hordes. We were invincible. Together we could take on the world. The TV cameras couldn't capture the euphoria of being there, being a Geordie with all your mates, and a few enemies, all united in a mass of passionate pride. No way could we lose this. How man, we had Keegan. The fans played a blinder and out sang the mighty Kop all night. The team meanwhile were well beaten with Keegan shackled by Lawrenson... On the trip down, I had told one of the Garcia brothers that I fancied Lorraine Barker and he had promised me he would put a word in on my behalf as he would see her at a party the next night. It might not be a wasted trip after all... As we left Anfield, I was warm, I had a cushty seat at the back and I was dozing off with impure thoughts of Lorraine Barker when BOOOSH! There was a loud smash, followed by the sound of breaking glass and numerous other thuds and smashes. I thought we had crashed, but soon realised that the front window of our coach was shattered and that windows on both sides were going out under a stream of missiles. We were still on the outskirts of Liverpool and as we drove up a slip road heading for the motorway we had been ambushed from both sides by an army of brick wielding scally hooligans. The Steward was powerless as he shouted for everyone to stay on the bus "or else." Mel Gibson would have been proud as the Black-and-White hordes spilled from doors and windows on to the tarmac. On either side of the road twelve year old Barry Grants, Sinbad's and Yosser Hughes's retreated in a mass of Fila and Sergio Tacchini, the static from their 'trackies' lighting up the night sky. Black-and-White shirts were seen to run over fields towards dodgy housing schemes in a pointless pursuit, performance jaded by excess. By this time the bus Steward had changed his ground rules and was busy leading a charge down the embankment shouting "C'mon then you Scouse Fuckers" in a final charge in the battle of

Junction 27. Despite a wide-spread lack of glass, the bus made steady progress across the wilds of the M62 only hampered by the frequent steaming up of 'Ronnie the drivers' glasses and the wind threatening to detach his winter length toupee. I soon remedied part of the problem by allowing Ronnie to borrow my black and white bobble hat to offer wig protection and to keep his heed warm. Despite having a sizeable catholic contingent on the bus the Gods were definitely not looking favourably on us as the weather turned and it started to pour with rain as we passed through Leeds. In an inspired move to cheer us all up the Steward, his bleached jeans now showing a small map of Europe around the groin area, made the suggestion that we stop at the next services on the A1. It seemed like a plan. The woman left in sole charge of the services shop had not counted on an invasion of over fifty Black-and-White savages fresh from battle. The shop door opened the hordes entered, asked where the netty was and then as members of the Kenton crew skilfully sidetracked her with requests for obscure top shelf titles, the West Denton boys skilfully and efficiently managed to clear the shop display of boxed chocolates. Back on the coach, a well organised syndicate distributed the chocolates, with a cross eyed West Denton lad sporting a number of 'homemade tattoos' in charge of supply and distribution. The rules were simple. You could take two chocolates each and then had to pass them back. There was no going to the next layer until the top one was finished and if you didn't like hazelnuts, tough shite. After a few splutters and coughs the bus engine died and we pulled in next to the A1 in the middle of nowhere. The rain had been pouring in through the broken windows and the electrics had gone. No ignition, no lights, no heaters. Ronnie would have to walk to a phone box to call for a replacement bus to come down from the town to some desolate, wild and wet part of North Yorkshire. We were stuck and would be here for hours. Some lads attempted to hitch home as cars swerved to avoid some kamikaze lads in the middle of the road. The oncoming drivers must have thought a herd of zebra had invaded North Yorkshire as drivers swerved, and blared their horns as they tried to avoid a collision. I stayed on the bus as if I died I wouldn't ever be able to snog Lorraine Barker. Outside, as the rain gave many of the lads their first bath in weeks, the fun was only beginning. Soon bored with chasing 70mph cars, some of the more creative minds saw a field of cows adjacent to the coach. If you were bovine that night, sleeping, standing up, in a field in North Yorkshire I would like to apologize on behalf of Newcastle United football club and its supporters. If you work for the RSPCA, what cows? The operation was planned with military precision. In teams of 3, under cover of darkness, the sleeping beasts were approached in a pincer movement. Big gangly lads from West Denton were joined by small weasel - like Kenton lads with bum fluff tashes and youths with stutters from B'Benwell. They moved as one. The cows had no chance. One minute dreaming of being milked and the Friesian with the big teats, the next being pushed over and biting turf. From the bus, the night air was filled with the sounds of panicked, muffled MOO's and then a loud thud as the teams did their work and the beasts hit the deck. So, if people ask me about 1984, Liverpool away, on a Friday night, in the FA Cup at Anfield, do I remember when Lawrenson caught Keegan with a ten yard start? I say no, but I do remember

'Cow Tipping' in North Yorkshire (among other things). I love the Toon, ME.

Tommy Knox
Fenham, Newcastle

We were 6-1 to actually win the match. We were a Second Division side and it was live on the tele, yet we still sold our original ticket allocation of 10,000. Liverpool then sent us another 3,000 which were snapped up immediately. The first Football Special left the Central Station at 1.50pm, followed closely by a second at 2.20pm taking a total of 2,000 fans by train. Two passengers travelling by service train were Paul Young 19, from Wallsend and his mate Paul Johnson, 18 who had earlier missed their coach from the Rising Sun pub in Battlehill. They had already paid £6.50 and now had to pay a further £14 for the train, but they weren't bothered as they had a bag load of sarnies!

Geordie
Wallsend, Tyneside

v CRYSTAL PALACE	**SAT 21ST JANUARY 1984**
SELHURST PARK	**SECOND DIVISION**
ATT; 9,464	**LOST 1-3**

I was on a train heading for Selhurst Park, when an argument broke out between some Newcastle fans and a West Ham fan, who just happened to be in the wrong place at the wrong time. The Cockney was well out of order with his snide remarks and quite fancied himself with all the latest terrace designer clobber, but was quickly put in his place by a couple of the Geordie skinheads, sporting Donkey Jackets! They striped him down to his birthday suit, threw all his branded gear out of the carriage window and on to the tracks, leaving him with just his 'Undercrackers' on! He got off at the next stop, to a barrage of laughter and wolf whistles. I can't really remember anything about the match, apart from their keeper playing an absolute blinder and our defence being shite.

Anon
Newcastle

v PORTSMOUTH	**SAT 4TH FEBRUARY 1984**
FRATTON PARK	**SECOND DIVISION**
ATT; 18,686	**WON 4-1**

I hired a coach with my mate Kev from Target travel in Cramlington and had over thirty lads on it for our weekend break to the south coast. We left the Central early on the Friday morning watching Olivia Newton John on the coach's video and every time she flashed her knickers a loud cheer went up. Eventually after a few stops on the way down we arrived at our digs, The White House Hotel in Southsea, Portsmouth early evening. We all went out on the drink around the centre of Southsea and fun was had by all as we drank ourselves silly, looking forward in anticipation to an away victory the following day. As the evening went on we slowly got split up into smaller groups, and later on a group of roughly fifty Pompey fans kicked off with a group of about fifteen of us, as all hell broke loose we were completely outnumbered as bottles, glasses and chairs were thrown at us. The scenes were horrendous, absolutely horrific as one of our mates got glassed; the whole pub resembled a battlefield. The trouble then continued outside the Coastguard Tavern as the police arrived trying to restore law and order, making arrests at random. The trouble was considered so bad that it made the front page of both the Evening Chronicle and the South Coast papers. After everything calmed down, the police moved us back to our hotel where we had a bit of a party into the early hours before crashing out into a deep sleep. The next morning we all went for a walk and as planned got the hovercraft over to the Isle of White for our pre-match session which consisted of plenty of drink, a pool competition against the locals and plenty of songs before going to Fratton Park to see the lads turn on the style as Beardsley, Waddle and Keegan ripped the Pompey defence apart winning 4-1 to keep our promotion hopes on track. Sadly though it was the night I first heard rumours that Kevin Keegan was to leave us at the end of the season, with Pompey favourites to sign him. A very eventful weekend had by all.

Arn
Longbenton, Newcastle

We left the 'Toon' on the mad bus after the pubs closed on the Friday, travelling down through the night arriving on the south coast early Saturday morning. We were looking for a certain pub where we'd all arranged to meet up but were having problems finding it. We saw what looked like one of their boys so pulled over and asked him for directions and information to which he told us quite aggressively to "Fuck off!" Not exactly the reply we wanted but not wanting to take liberties, but at the same time wanting to get the message across, one lad clipped him knocking him to the ground whilst the piss and shit bucket from our bus was poured over him. There he was with his bleached jeans, white trainers, tracksuit top all the gear on, with shit all over his head. If he had of been civil he could have even had a lift on our coach, but decided to be a shithead instead. After a quite eventful pre-match drink we witnessed an unbelievable performance and result with braces from both Peter Beardsley and Kevin Keegan which completed a double over Pompey. Peter Beardsley was out of this world scoring a wonder goal as he weaved his way from the left wing past numerous defenders with the ball seemingly stuck to his foot, before tapping the ball over the line.

Kev
Gosforth, Newcastle

United fans in Pompey pub fight

A police chief has slammed North coach operators after Newcastle fans were in a Portsmouth pub battle. Trouble flared when 30 magpie fans clashed with Pompey supporters in Portsmouth's Coastguard Tavern last night. Two people were hurt by flying beer glasses and the pub was damaged as the rival fans fought. Three men were arrested - one a Newcastle fan. Superintendent Robert West, of the Southsea sub-division said: I will be making official complaints about the number of supporters who have arrived in the city too early by coach. The government guidelines say they are not supposed to arrive more than two hours before the game.

v GRIMSBY TOWN
ST JAMES' PARK
ATT; 28,633

SAT 11TH FEBRUARY 1984
SECOND DIVISION
LOST 0-1

Our first league game at home for six weeks and only our second in nine weeks stretching back to early December. With 17 games remaining of which 10 were at home, we were joint third with a game in hand and only 6 points off the top with 3 games in hand of leaders Chelsea. Keegan nearly got sent off after verbally attacking the ref, and continuously disputing a disallowed Kenny Wharton goal. A former school Geography teacher Mr. Blevins was a Grimsby fan and we would obviously take the piss out of him over the years and I'd kept in touch so he joined me in the 'Gallowgate Corner' for this easy home win! Obviously he stayed quiet but had a big smirk on his face throughout as 'The Mariners' not only beat us but also leaped above us in the table as we fell to fifth. I hated bloody Geography anyway.......

Mick Edmondson
Walker, Newcastle

v MANCHESTER CITY
MAINE ROAD
ATT; 41,767

SAT 18TH FEBRUARY 1984
SECOND DIVISION
WON 2-1

Completed the double over our promotion rivals in front of the Division's largest crowd of the season which was swelled by the thousands of Geordies who'd made the trip. We had half the famous 'Kippax' plus another two sections of the ground and the Manchester Police had a busy afternoon as it went off all over Moss Side. It was a brilliant first half display as we went into the interval 2-0 up, Keegan grabbing his 18th league goal of the season in a week in which he announced his retirement from the game. His announcement came on Valentine's Day, his 33rd Birthday amid rumours that he was off to sign for Portsmouth. He would hang up his boots in the summer retiring as a Newcastle United player a decision he'd privately made after the Anfield Cup match a month earlier. John Trewick returned from his loan spell at Oxford and did enough to become a major player in our final promotion push. Another brilliant solo effort from Peter Beardsley which only he could execute sent the travelling hordes delirious. *"Sing In The Cow Shed"* didn't go down to well with the natives and their beloved Kippax.

Manchester City Football Club P. L. C
MAINE ROAD · MOSS SIDE · MANCHESTER
Supported by SAAB

FOOTBALL LEAGUE—DIVISION TWO

C I T Y

versus

NEWCASTLE UNITED
SATURDAY, 18th FEBRUARY, 1984
Kick-off 3.00 p.m.

BLOCK **J** ROW **7** SEAT **1 8**

North Stand £3.00

Mick Edmondson
Walker, Newcastle

I hope my announcement will prevent any further speculation about what I'll be doing after this season. I've always said I wanted to quit at the top and I really feel I'm still there. I've won a lot of things in the game, but I can honestly say I've never wanted anything more than to leave Newcastle United knowing they are looking forward to the First Division football their marvellous supporters deserve. Even though we missed out on promotion last season the reception that they gave me after our final home game against Sheff Wed made me banish any thoughts about leaving then.

Kevin Keegan
Newcastle United

Manchester City Football Club P.L.C.

FOOTBALL LEAGUE

18/2/84

Newcastle United

No. 0828

KIPPAX STAND

£1.80

Turnstiles

52 to 56b

What a season, Keegan, Beardsley, Waddle, goals galore and adventures on the road. It was really between Man City and us for the third promotion place as Chelsea and Sheffield Wednesday were well ahead in the first two places. What a trip it was to Maine Road, Moss Side, Manchester. Tensions were high amongst the locals though my mate Sean and I travelled down with a City fan, in his car, hoping his knowledge of the area would guarantee our safety. Another mate of ours had travelled by car and when their colours had been spotted at a road junction, a concrete slab was put through the windscreen, never a nice place Moss Side. Anyway, we got parked up and although very intimidating, got in the ground safely. Unusually the away fans were on both sides of the pitch that day, some in seats in a corner segment and others opposite, standing on the old Kippax. It added to a super atmosphere, though also contributed to everyone running around the ground outside. Two glorious goals from Beardsley and Keegan gave us a 2-1 away win, though all hell broke loose at the final whistle. We somehow managed to exit Maine Road from lower down the ground, meaning we casually mixed in with the home support. Much to our relief, we got back to where the car had been parked, only to discover it had gone! With mayhem occurring at the other end of the long terraced street, we began to fear the worst. Our driver, Andy had anticipated some of this nonsense, so drove the car around the block away from the gathering hordes. It seemed like an eternity, though was only minutes, before he returned and picked us up.

Anth Nicholson
North Shields, Tyneside

v CARDIFF CITY
ST JAMES' PARK
ATT; 27,964

SAT 25TH FEBRUARY 1984
SECOND DIVISION
WON 3-1

We comfortably completed the double over the 'Bluebirds' with some lovely controlled football as our side now had a settled look about it now since Keegan's announcement and the return of John Trewick. After the doom and gloom in previous seasons it was now a joy and not a chore to visit St James' Park.

Graham,
Gosforth, Newcastle

v FULHAM
CRAVEN COTTAGE
ATT; 12,290

SAT 3RD MARCH 1984
SECOND DIVISION
DREW 2-2

At the age of twenty I had started to play competitive football on a Saturday afternoon as a Goalkeeper, for Chester Le Street in the Northern League. The only problem with this was that I missed quite a few Newcastle matches as these were the days before Sky TV and England get-togethers, when we actually played on a Saturday afternoon at 3pm. So to help compensate I placed a radio in the back of my net and tuned into the local station, for updates followed by live commentary from Craven Cottage. I got some funny looks when in the middle of our match news came across that Kevin Keegan had scored a second half equaliser to make the score 2-2, as I celebrated by yelling and jumping around my penalty area like a lunatic shouting out the news. This is the match when I realised that playing football on a Saturday wasn't for me, so decided to quit what was a good standard of football. (Although the lads probably think that playing football is a major part of the weekend, it wasn't for me on a Sunday either!).

I. C.
Walker, Newcastle

There was a large mob of us down about 100 strong and we were drinking in the 'Cockney Pride' at Piccadilly Circus before the match. We were having a right laugh and one of the lads Micky was swinging from the pubs chandelier. A few of us walked outside and were standing in the street when all of a sudden loads of kids came running towards us, but continued straight past the pub. They were Leeds boys being chased by a much larger group of Chelsea. All of our lot were still inside and were oblivious to what was going on in the street, as Chelsea approached us and started shouting and threatening us, "Come on you Yorkshire Bastards." One of the lads replied "I'm not from Yorkshire and I'm not running from that." A few punches were exchanged then the next thing we were getting sprayed with tear gas and as we were cut off from those inside and totally outnumbered we retreated back into the pub, as the coppers came on top. The lads inside were gutted that they'd missed the fun. I had paid for a ticket for the match but once at the ground the lads were just picking at the diamond shaped wire fence and just sneaking in, so I followed even though I had a ticket in my pocket! Young and daft I suppose.

Harmer
Newcastle

v CHELSEA
ST JAMES' PARK
ATT; 35,544

SAT 10TH MARCH 1984
SECOND DIVISION
DREW 1-1

The eighties saw fans fenced in. Trust Newcastle United to have worst fence in the league for viewing through, as it had a thick bar on top. What that meant was that everybody got squashed up at the top of the terrace and the slightest move in the crowd could send you falling forward, the view was crap as well. With a sell out crowd for this all-ticket promotion clash between the second placed 'Pensioners' and the 'Toon' lying in third, we were hemmed in at the Gallowgate whilst latecomers were locked out. There was no blanket coverage of football then only the odd game on either Shoot or Match of the Day. Or you'd sometimes on the rare occasion have the local news present, using just a single camera to cover the highlights. This was such a game and just to the left of us Tyne Tees telly man Roger Tames resplendent in sheepskin coat accompanied by a lone cameraman were setting up on top of the turnstile building in the west corner. Part way through the game someone thought it would be funny to "borrow" Rodge's ladder and climb up on the turnstile building for a better view. Thinking this was a good idea someone else joined him then another and another until an uncomfortable looking Tames was surrounded by radgies. The police got interested and started trying to get the fans down. One of the lads Paul who could get gobby called a Copper over "It was him who got them up there" he told the Copper "Who?" asked the PC. "Him there" pointed Paul "The one with the sheepskin" Luckily the Copper had a sense of humour. We had lost away to Chelsea 0-4 earlier in the campaign and Jeff Clarke who played on after breaking his nose in a collision with David Speedie after only half an hours play showed how determined we were not to lose this particular match

Chris Ramshaw
West Denton, Newcastle

As a Chelsea fan my fiancée and I travelled up by train leaving Kings Cross at 9am. The train was full of Chelsea supporters and there were hardly any 'normal' folk on board. One thing that did surprise me was that the Newcastle Supporters' Club (London Branch) had reserved a carriage on the same train! However we never saw any of them. Just after noon we arrived at Newcastle

Central, where the train literally emptied. We decided to go it alone and spend an hour or so walking around the town, take in the sights and get a bite to eat. Now I have been all over the country supporting Chelsea and I have never experienced anything like Newcastle! To say the atmosphere and attitude of the locals was hostile would be a considerable under statement. The place oozed hostility and made us both quite nervous. Now and again a 'buzz' would go up from the natives as yet another large group of Chelsea fans were escorted to the ground. The match itself was a terrific advert for football and I have never seen the Chelsea fans react to our goal like that for years, as they went wild with joy. After the game we had to hang around for a while before making the long walk to the wrong station. Confusion followed as no one knew what was going on, including the local police (who were very friendly and sympathetic). We were eventually herded onto a slow train back to London.

Peter Fitzpatrick
Worthing, Sussex

"We've got a great chance of going up now and if we do then I hope Newcastle go up with us. I say this because of their marvellous fans. I hope they're in the First Division with or without Kevin Keegan next season. I love coming back up here, it's a bit special for me and so was the atmosphere today - the fans were tremendous."

John Neal
Chelsea Manager

We'd done our marauding passed the 'Hippy Green' Eldon Square - which had become a ritual whenever a visiting club with a reputation had turned up - and headed towards John Dobson Street, The Burton House and The Portland where

as usual a couple of Police dogs scattered everybody. Sometime later having doubled back and watched Chelsea's escort come through the town and be taken into Manors Station, me and Scotchy found ourselves on Swan House roundabout - literally - looking down Melbourne Street. To our amazement a mob of about 30 Chelsea came out of the back entrance and onto the street and headed towards us. Whether they actually saw the two of us is debatable but we legged it knowing full well they were going to head for the Central Station. Sprinting up Pilgram Street, along High Bridge , down Pudding Chare and round onto Grainger Street (Scotchy wasn't the fittest like, so the initial sprint broke into a 'fastish' walk) we turned onto Neville Street and immediately saw a few of the Bishop Auckland lads standing outside 'The Green Dolphin' (Head of Steam). Within seconds of us heading towards them, Chelsea came into view heading along Collingwood Street. "They are Chelsea" we shouted to the 'Bishop' lads. I think at that point we all froze as Chelsea saw us and started running towards us. Seven of us up against 30 Chelsea!! Oh dear, I don't think any of us would have claimed to be mad enough to get stuck into them. Suddenly, out of nowhere came the shout of "f...ing stand" and four of the 'Benders' had appeared from Grainger Street, they ran across Neville Street and straight into them with us looking on in amazement. After an initial bit of fisty cuff's Chelsea backed off from beside the bus shelters and grouped together against the wall approximately where 'The Centurion' is now and with the help of two BTP literally slid along the wall into the station making no further attempt to fight. Visits from Chelsea were never without incident I also remember their Football Special sat stationary on Manors viaduct (between Manors and The Central) with a group of Newcastle down below - at the top of Broad Chare - hurling insults and trying the impossible task of 'bricking' the train. Chelsea were hanging out the windows laughing.

Eventually Police vans turned up and everyone scattered. Also, on the grass verge of Leazes Terrace behind the East Stand I remember coming face to face with 'Hickey' and his little mob, again they were not too keen faced with some Geordie meatheads and only one police dog in attendance to keep order.

Stephen
Byker, Newcastle

81 fans held at big match

Police made about 81 arrests before, during and after yesterdays crunch match between Newcastle United and Chelsea. The Londoners brought about 4,000 fans with them. Extra police including many on horseback and some with dogs, were drafted in to escort the Chelsea supporters to their trains after the game. Shoppers watched as the long crocodile was marched through Newcastle centre to Manors station. Apart from some scuffles between rival fans outside Gallowgate coach station which were quickly broken up by police, the visitors reached there without incident. Police said there had been some clashes before the game and the arrests were for public order offences and drunkenness.

v MIDDLESBROUGH
ST JAMES' PARK
ATT; 30,421

SAT 17TH MARCH 1984
SECOND DIVISION
WON 3-1

As the Irish celebrated St Patrick's Day we celebrated being Geordie and English as England International's McDermott, Keegan and Beardsley (in waiting) scored our goals. At half-time we were entertained by the 'Police Dog Demonstration Team.' It made a change watching them from a distance as opposed to have one hanging from the arse of your jeans when we played 'Boro.'

Mick Edmondson
Walker, Newcastle

v SHREWSBURY TOWN
GAY MEADOW
ATT; 8,313

SAT 24TH MARCH 1984
SECOND DIVISION
DREW 2-2

On the same day as our supposedly big club neighbours Sunderland were watched by a mere 11,908 at Joker Park for their First Division game against recent European Champions Aston Villa, we got the train from Newcastle to Shrewsbury via Birmingham and Wolverhampton for our visit to Shrewsbury. It was on the final leg of our marathon journey between Wolverhampton and our destination when we pulled into a small station and noticed some graffiti on the station wall which read 'Codsall Mods' which had us all howling. When we got to Shrewsbury we heard that one of Newcastle's main lads had been chinned so as you can imagine there were fun and games in and around the ground. We ended up going in the home end behind the goal where it kicked off a few times before the coppers came in and confronted us, "Are you lads local?" Wor kid replied shouting at the top of his voice in a Yorkshire sounding attempt at the local accent, "Codsall." We were immediately dragged out of their end and marched around the pitch, and past an unhappy Arthur Cox sitting in the dugout. Wor Kid couldn't help himself again, acknowledging the boss with a cheeky, "Hello Arthur." Arthur Cox knew the score.

Little Hag
Kingston Park, Newcastle

v LEEDS UNITED   **WED 28TH MARCH 1984**
ST JAMES' PARK   **SECOND DIVISION**
ATT; 31,222   **WON 1-0**

Originally postponed in January due to a frozen pitch this was third time lucky as we went 17 points clear of Leeds thanks to an own goal from a very young Denis Irwin. Peter Lorimer aged 37 once the hardest shot in football just looked shot, as a young Scott Sellers stood out for the Yorkshire outfit. I have always enjoyed games against Leeds and would much rather be playing them instead of shit little clubs, especially when we do the double over them. This win put us 4 points ahead of fourth place. An excellent crowd especially considering that on the same night the Football League Cup Final replay was being broadcast live from Maine Road, Liverpool beating their local rivals Everton. The weather was naff as well, a cold wintry night as we stood in the old corner of the Leazes End paying £1.50 to get in. Leeds had the normal 'Away End' and also the centre of the Leazes. From what I remember it was a shit game and my biggest memory was at half-time, these were the days when away fans used to get a block of seats in the 'New Stand' (East Stand). At half time 8 or 9 Newcastle lads attacked the Leeds fans 'Service Crew' in the seats, one lad in particular known as Darky, about 15/16 years old was giving this Leeds bloke a good beating with an umbrella of all weapons. Leeds ran away, the police sorted it out, but this prompted missiles been thrown between the two sets of fans in the Leazes, and above all this the DJ was playing 'Run Runaway' by Slade, so all second half we sang *"See The Leeds Fans Standing There In The Snow, See The Leeds Fans Run Run Away,"* This was the first violence I'd seen inside the ground and sticks in the memory for the big Leeds hooligan getting a beating with a brolly by a lad half his size.

Mark
Birtley, Tyneside

v SWANSEA CITY   **SAT 31ST MARCH 1984**
ST JAMES' PARK   **SECOND DIVISION**
ATT; 27,329   **WON 2-0**

After staying unbeaten in March with 3 wins and 3 draws, Arthur Cox was named manager of the month. Elsewhere the First Division award went to Joe Fagin (Liverpool), Third Division to Ian Porterfield (Sheffield United) and the Fourth Division to John Newman (Hereford). Why is it whenever we play any Welsh bastards it always rains? And we are not talking about drizzle, but torrential downpours which earlier in the season caused our visit to 'The Vetch Field' to be postponed. I mean we had a fixture against Wrexham in the 1977/78 season postponed twice through torrential rain and even when it was eventually played it was pissing down. Today was touch and go and amazingly so many turned up to see us win, as we were watched by the largest and most colourful

Kagool wearing crowd of drowned rats ever seen. Thankfully this was our last league match against welsh opposition for over a quarter of a decade. Swansea were in free fall, last seasons debut in the First Division had ended in immediate relegation and they'd be playing Third Division football next season. Sadly and quite unbelievably the man who had done so much to make sure that the St James' Park playing surface was immaculate over the past few seasons passed away the same day aged 58 years old. The 1984 Grand National took place at Aintree the same afternoon. The winning horse was Hallo Dandy ridden by jockey Neale Doughty who was a Newcastle fan. He had been receiving treatment at St James' Park for the previous 6 weeks after he'd came off a mount at Sedgefield. Only minutes after winning the race he was interviewed on BBC 1. "I just want Newcastle United to get promotion now and everything will be right!!"

Mick Edmondson
Walker, Newcastle

v CHARLTON ATHLETIC
THE VALLEY
ATT; 15,289

SAT 7TH APRIL 1984
SECOND DIVISION
WON 3-1

These days television runs football, resulting in fixture changes and stupid kick off times, it won't be long before were playing Sheffield Tuesday at midnight on a Bank Holiday Thursday!! But on a more positive side there are cameras at every single league match so that every incident is recorded. Unfortunately in 1984 the few cameras that were available were busy at Anfield and Anfield and as a result missed out on what I consider to be the best goal I've ever seen, not to mention my celebrations. Those of you who visited the old Valley ground will remember the field you had to walk across between the turnstiles and terrace, as well as the largest paddock in England situated on the right hand side. Peter Beardsley picked up the ball and went on one of his jinky runs as only he can, before causing their keeper and chasing defender to collide whilst slipping the ball into the net. This goal secured a 3-1 victory which sent the travelling hordes into a frenzy, as I did a somersault underneath three Copper horses on the wasteland at the back of the terraces. Their biggest gate of the season saw us go 7 points clear of Man City in fourth place with only 7 games to go. Before the game Kevin Keegan was presented with a crystal punch bowl and a Charlton Athletic pennant from the hosts to mark the former England captain's forthcoming retirement from football at the end of the season.

Joe Carpenter
Longbenton, Newcastle

v SHEFFIELD WEDNESDAY
ST JAMES' PARK
ATT; 36,288

SAT 14TH APRIL 1984
SECOND DIVISION
LOST 0-1

A little reminder that we weren't the 'Brazil 1970 World Cup side' as Sheff Wed completed the double over us with a Gary Shelton overhead scissor - kick at the Leazes End, which in reality could have easily ended up in Leazes Park. Going

into the game we were unbeaten in nine and only 3 points behind the top placed 'Owls.' This was the game when Kevin Keegan got involved in a scuffle with a Newcastle fan who'd ran onto the pitch and tried to join in with play, tensions were running high. Our highest home crowd of the season went home unhappy; some so annoyed they decided to smash windows and destroy cars rampaging through the city centre. I've never understood why these idiots smash their own city up, their fellow Geordies property and livelihoods? Sheffield caught us offside more than 20 times in a very frustrating match as the crowd chanted *"Boring Boring Wednesday."*

Mick Edmondson
Walker, Newcastle

<table>
<tr><td>

v BLACKBURN ROVERS
EWOOD PARK
ATT; 19,196

</td><td>

FRI 20TH APRIL 1984
SECOND DIVISION
DREW 1-1

</td></tr>
</table>

Good Friday and we had been standing at the bus stop for sometime waiting for a bus to take us into town, as we were going down to Lancashire with Magpie Travel. Then it dawned on us, there were no buses on a Good Friday! Panic, quick flag someone down low & behold we are hitching a lift to Newcastle. This was the first and only time that I've ever done this and I was only 15 years old.

Gavin Haigh
Newton Hall, Durham

We travelled by mini bus early morning stocking up with the usual, cans and dirty mags obtained at the Service station. No piss stops, as we needed to be there for opening time, so it was a case of pissing out the back of the bus doors whilst motoring or trying to hit the bottle neck if you couldn't hold it any longer. A massive following from the Toon' standing on the Darwin End terraces and round into the main stand saw a late equaliser from John Trewick in a best forgotten match. After the match our bus wouldn't start and we just stood and watched as all the supporters' buses just went past and our driver tried to do a runner by hitching on one of them but we pulled him off, nevertheless - we were stuck. As it was 6pm on Good Friday we were a bit stuck, as everything was shut, so we had a few beers then started walking the streets for what seemed like hours - ending up in Darwin, spent up and boozed up. Word was getting round and we seemed to be getting a bit of notice from the locals when an advert in a house window got our attention - minibus hire. We scraped whatever cash we had left and got on the road to get home in the early hours - talk about relief.

Duzza
Battlehill, Tyneside

Another transit away trip with Arty Kirkbride and Terry Kirkbride sharing the driving. There must have been about 17 of us in the back, how the van took the weight that day is still a mystery. We were in a pub in Preston for about fifteen minutes and noticed little Joe talking to a local at the bar. Joe asked who he supported and the local replied Man U. Joe replied "you wanker" the local then called Joe a Geordie wanker which resulted in a head butt from Joe. All hell breaks loose and the manager asks us to leave as the locals start frisking things up and one lad Jimmy stood with a pool cue in his hand telling the whole bar it was going through their heads if they wanted it, but nobody wanted to play with him much to his disappointment. Off we went to Blackburn only to be stopped by a 'Jam Sandwich' because the van looked overweight, too fucking right it was. They opened the driver's door asking Arty where the weigh plate was. "It must have fell off" he replied, much to lad's amusement who knew that may have been a little white lie. "Follow me to the weigh bridge" said the Copper. Us bright sparks in the back Archie, Little Joe, Flynny, Jimmy Marchbanks, Terry Main, Mildo, Baz Ankram, Jonsey and a few others all pissed out of our heads decided that if the lightest person sat on the wheel arch it would be lighter on the weigh bridge. You should have heard the crack, "Aye good idea, what do you weigh am lighter than yee so if we change seats when the wheels gan on the bridge they wont be as heavy aye good idea." Little Joe pipes up "If I grab the ridge on the roof and lift my feet off the floor there will be nee weight on the floor when he weighs us!!" At this point the copper opens the van doors to see Joe hanging there in mid air and asks what the fuck we are doing. Joe replies "I'm trying to make the van lighter man by lifting me feet off the floor the copper could not believe what he was seeing or hearing, he just stood there and shook his head. But let me tell you at the time it made fucking good sense to us at the time!!!! As he stood there the copper was hit on back by a can thrown from some good Samaritan Geordies as they were passing on the motorway don't know who they were but what a fucking shot. The coppers went after them and caught them as we passed them further down the road. Happy Days.

Archie
Wallsend, Tyneside

Blackburn away has always been popular with 'Toon fans.' In the early 80's we travelled away in an orange transit van not at all comfortable but great crack with our regular driver Eric, Jean his lass and about 10 mates. We got to Blackburn no problem but on the way back things were different. If you know the route through Kirkby Stephen from the M6, our van ran out of petrol in the pitch dark at the bottom of a mountain of a road, so it was everyone out push the van to the top of THAT hill, (you know it if you've done the trip). Once at the top the idea was that everyone could get back into the van and freewheel into Kirkby Stephen, simple. But Eric our driver forgot to stop at the top and only 5 of us got into the van before it quickly picked up speed leaving the rest of the lads in the darkness miles from Kirkby Stephen. The van and the 5 who did get in got to Kirkby filled the van up with petrol and then we ourselves filled up in the local pub where we waited for our pissed off mates to catch up after their very long walk.

John
Gateshead, Tyneside

v CARLISLE UNITED
ST JAMES PARK
ATT; 33,458

MON 23RD APRIL 1984
SECOND DIVISION
WON 5-1

Easter Monday and a very hot sunny afternoon kick-off against little Carlisle United who had already stuffed us at their place at Christmas. After three wins on the trot we hadn't won in the last two and the pressure was on with only five matches to play. We needn't have worried as we played them off the park with some very fast and skilful football - we were on fire, no better example was when former mag Alan Shoulder had his penalty and rebound saved at the Leazes End by Kevin Carr, before the ball broke loose and within seconds had been passed beautifully through the side and into the Cumbrian's box, before ending up in the back of the net. Before the match my all time favourite player Peter Beardsley was on 14 league goals only one behind Chris Waddle who had played 8 more games. At the final whistle they were all square with 16 a piece and Beardo would go on to finish second top scorer with twenty, seven goals behind Kevin Keegan.

Mick Edmondson
Walker, Newcastle

We were leading 2-1 in the second half but were under the cosh for a while, when Carlisle were awarded a penalty at the Leazes End. We thought they were bound to score. However Kevin Carr not only saved the spot kick and the rebound but the ball then somehow went out to the right, finding John Anderson who strode forward and after a quick one - two he crossed to the back post where Kevin Keegan was arriving. We were still leaping about celebrating the double save at the other end when 'Wor Kev' scored at the Gallowgate End to put us 3-1 up, when it could have so easily been 2-2. Everybody went berserk and as we were still celebrating the save I was totally knackered and out of breath and could hardly speak, as we then went on to win 5-1.

Jeff Jarrett
Gosforth, Newcastle

v CAMBRIDGE UNITED
ABBEY STADIUM
ATT; 7,720

SAT 28TH APRIL 1984
SECOND DIVISION
LOST 0-1

We'd just thumped Carlisle at home on the bank holiday Monday five days earlier and we travelled down to face a team that hadn't won in 31 matches. (Drawing 10 and losing 21). Not even Newcastle could cock this one up! We were watched by their highest gate of the season swelled by the travelling Geordies, yet still the smallest crowd to watch us anywhere all season. In the early eighties this was probably the worst ground and the worst place to travel too. There were only four matches remaining and we were just about up if we won this near certainty, you can almost guess the rest. A twat (he was at the time) from Wallsend scored the winner, a youngster called Kevin Smith a lifelong Toon fan who had just swapped the Gallowgate terraces for a career in professional football. Their side also boasted Newcastle fan and future England international Andy Sinton. It could only happen to Newcastle United. I went to Cambridge and Shrewsbury a combined total of ten times in the early eighties, yet never won a single game. And younger supporters thought we were shit under Dalglish, Gullit and Souness eh! Never in my wildest dreams did I ever think that twenty years later I would be at the San Siro watching the Toon draw with Inter Milan in Europe's ultimate competition.

Paul Wardle
Wallsend, Tyneside

The memory I have from this match has nothing to do with the happenings on the field, but something which was said over the tannoy system. The Abbey Stadium announcer brought us the news that one of the Newcastle fans in the ground had just became a father. His wife had given birth too triplets!!! The bloke who at the time was over 200 miles away from his new family was lifted onto the crash barrier by his mates. The rest of the travelling fans started to point towards him as their cheers turned into laughter as the chanting started, *"Superspunk, Superspunk."* Geordie youngster Kevin Smith destroyed Newcastle's promotion dream and cried his heart out. The 19 year old from Wallsend, a former Wallsend Boys Club player scored a 38th minute penalty. Some Geordie mates stayed with him on the Friday night and when he mentioned that he took the penalties they asked him to miss.

Brian Sibley
Kingston Park, Newcastle

Cambridge are one of these teams who, with all due respect, shouldn't really be in the same division as us. The fact that they were was testament to the shrewd management of their limited resources and of course the bad management that had led to us being in Division Two. The Abbey Stadium is nowhere near the centre of Cambridge, which is perhaps; just as well as I'm sure the 'peaceful' people of Cambridge wouldn't have known what had hit them if the Geordies had been let loose on their University haven. Instead we eventually located it on the ring road on the outskirts of the city and even then you weren't sure if you had come to the right place because the ground was so small. We parked in a nearby field (yes a field!) and had to walk past a herd of cows to reach the ground. We all had tickets, Goggs, Macas and myself for the seats and Hally and Alan for the terraces but what we found once we'd got in to the ground was a farce. Naturally our seat tickets had been more expensive but we'd seen Hally and Alan on the terrace on the other side and they found they were able to walk round the perimeter of the ground and find a standing place right next to our seats. All that divided us was a wall about three feet high! Although you were annoyed at being ripped off you had to laugh at the situation. In a ground holding no more than 8,000 the Geordies must have had at least three quarters of it. Regretfully though there was little cheer about as we turned in an inexplicably poor display and with the car not wanting to start for about half an hour after the match it just about made our day. On the way home Macas and Alan fancied a night out so we ended up stopping at some quaint little Nottingham village called Bottesford. A good meal was the first priority and after finding a suitable place we all ordered massive platefuls of steak, chips and the works, that is with the exception of Macas! Macas, being a student still, was always claiming poverty so while the rest of us were tucking in he ordered a measly sandwich. We couldn't stop laughing at Macas afterwards when it turned out that the restaurateurs didn't produce a bill for us so we ended up with a free meal which Macas missed out on. What an irony, especially if you knew what a huge appetite he usually has. Later on Alan proceeded to fail miserably in his attempts to charm the local talent and so we just gave up after a while and headed back north to civilisation but not before Alan had taken out his frustration on some vehicles left in the car park - I've always thought Scots were mad!

Mark Hannen
Ponteland, Newcastle

I remember going to Cambridge in the back of a white transit van with a mattress thrown in, about 12 of us in the back, we left at about 5am. It was a gloriously hot and sunny day and we got bladdered beside the river. Some posh oyks were playing football on the other side of the river after their rowing session ended, when their ball went in the water. Quick as a flash one of the lads dived in and retrieved the ball on our side. The posh lads weren't happy so we invited them over for a game. T-shirts were quickly discarded and formed goal posts as the

Geordies played in skins. We kicked the shit out of them and they kept apologising if they fell on us after a scything tackle, it was hilarious. Unfortunately it was our only victory of the day as the mighty Cambridge United who hadn't won a game in months beat us 1-0. There followed my only pitch invasion as fortified by several cheap bottles of wine we stormed onto the turf to confront the obviously terrified Cambridge fans only to be forced back by a couple of plods and an over zealous Alsatian....happy days....

Frank Kirton
Kingston Park, Newcastle

v DERBY COUNTY
ST JAMES' PARK
ATT; 35,866

SAT 5TH MAY 1984
SECOND DIVISION
WON 4-0

Newcastle United proceeded to tear the visitors to shreds with the sort of football that was a joy to behold. Peter Beardsley in particular was on a different planet and the final 4-0 score line could have been doubled with ease as United almost made sure of promotion. The only dampener on a near perfect day was the head injury that Kevin Keegan suffered which would rule him out of the next and all important penultimate match of the campaign. With 15 minutes remaining and the game won a vast army of police lined all four sides of the ground to prevent the jubilant crowd encroaching on to the pitch, but the fans stayed behind after the whistle and refused to leave until the players went on a lap of honour. After the victory which almost certainly clinched promotion back to the big time Kevin Keegan claimed to have "Never felt so emotional after a victory," Chairman Stan Seymour described it as his "Proudest Moment" with the club and teetotal Arthur Cox remarked, "I might just have a glass of champagne later. And probably go to bed at 11.30pm instead of 11pm!" On our manager Stan Seymour claimed that "without doubt" Cox would be staying as manager and that he had "backed him all the way." He boasted "Our sights are raised high," although there was no promises of funds being available for new players. The Evening Chronicle later reported that after the match 'A group of Newcastle fans arrived at 5.30pm (Opening Time) at the Printers Pie pub then proceeded to force open a lock on the upstairs bar and helped themselves to dozens of bottles of spirits which were handed out downstairs as the party crowd drank the lot.'

Mick Edmondson
Walker, Newcastle

You didn't see many women at football in those days. This was the game where we pretty much clinched promotion, we decided to splash out and get tickets for the benches. One of the lads Paul got them and gave us them on Friday night saying mysteriously he would meet us inside the next day. When we got there we found there was a spare seat. The mystery was soon solved as Paul turned up with a lass! He'd only been seeing her for a week and instead of celebrating the four goals by jumping up and down mentally like the rest of us he planted a sloppy kiss on her. Around the same time my wife's mate got bombed out by a lad after she started putting make up on at a match.

Chris Ramshaw
West Denton, Newcastle

v HUDDERSFIELD TOWN
LEEDS ROAD
ATT; 25,101

MON 7TH MAY 1984
SECOND DIVISION
DREW 2-2

We only needed a draw to secure our long awaited return to our rightful place-the top flight of English football. But we had to do it without the messiah Keegan, who had injured himself two days earlier. It was certainly looking dodgy as we trailed by two goals early on, but the twenty thousand travelling hordes that packed into the three sides of the compact ground, were soon going mental as we pulled it back to 2-2 before half-time. The memories are great, I can still picture a Newcastle nutter climbing all the way to the top of one of the floodlights with a flag, as thousands below pointed at him singing *"Going up, Going up."* And we sure were, as the scores remained level thanks to two superb first half efforts by Beardsley and David Mills. As the final whistle blew I along with thousands of other Geordies scaled the perimeter fences and invaded the pitch in celebration. But one of the first fans onto the pitch was a lad wearing a black and white kilt and toon top. He did the Roeder shuffle past one plod, before coming face to face with a WPC. He dropped his shoulder once more but the WPC was as quick and dived at his waist, only to catch his kilt which came straight off in her hands. While she lay on the ground he danced a Geordie Jig half naked with his knob hanging out, before being led away from the scene.

Kirk
Kenton, Newcastle

One point was still needed from our last two matches to mathematically clinch promotion as Bank Holiday Monday's trip to Huddersfield Town came around. Once I'd got into the ground I just stood at the back by myself away from all the heaving masses of supporters and, for the first time I could remember, didn't sing or shout but just stood quietly taking it all in. The quite amazing thing about this game was the fact that the Geordies occupied three sides of the ground; behind both goals (the only time I've ever seen an away following do this) and part of the main stand to the left of where I was situated. It was such an amazing sight that if you hadn't actually witnessed it you would never have believed it - my conservative estimate of the number of supporters who made the trip down from Tyneside, by every means possible, would be 18 - 20,000, absolutely phenomenal. Keegan injured 48 hours earlier against Derby was reluctantly forced to sit out his only game of the season. It didn't matter though as we came back from a two goal defecate to earn a 2-2 draw and that was all that mattered. Very surprisingly, I don't think there were any cameras present to capture the game for posterity, as certainly I don't recall ever having seen any highlights. Apart from obviously being able to re-live the promotion celebrations, I would have loved to have seen Beardsley's goal again as all I can remember of it is seeing him smash a half volley into the net from 25 yards at the other end of the ground. This was just one of Beardsley's special goals that he scored during the season. Beardsley must have the 'quickest' feet in the game and with a footballing brain to match he could outwit defences and goalkeepers at will, making them look so silly in the process. After the summer he would be plying his trade in the First Division as Newcastle United were at long last back in the big time.

Mark Hannan
Ponteland, Newcastle

I travelled down the night before staying at a friend's of a friend's student flat. I had my favourite knitted toon' scarf hanging out of the car window on the way down and it got caught in the wheel, trashing the scarf. I still kept it for years though. I Remember Devaz climbing the floodlight pylon and pissing on the crowd below, who were all singing *"Going Up, Going Up"* to him! We had three sides of the ground and I can remember going over the fences and onto the pitch en masse at the end of the game and invading the main stand. I do remember some idiots needlessly smashing the windows of their stand and frightening the bairns, we were celebrating and there were always a few arseholes on hand to lower the tone. Great trip though, drank Yorkshire dry in my threaded scarf.

Tom Knox
Fenham, Newcastle

In the pub for an early drink while waiting for the van to take us down to Yorkshire, the place was in full swing as we played Pool and Darts, the Bandits were also going fifty to the dozen. As you can imagine when we opened the curtains the six council workers repairing the street outside were rather envious to see such revelry at 8.15am especially as it was a bank holiday, but were very appreciative at being invited in for a swift half. A few beers later and a short discussion left just two of them to do the job as the other four joined us and came to the match instead.

Dave
Gateshead, Tyneside

Fifty of us piled into the back of a removal van, with one of the lads Jeff Lawson driving. On the way down we stopped off at a service station which had a hotel attached and the Newcastle team were hanging about outside. We had a right good bit crack with Arthur Cox and Terry Mac. When we got to Huddersfield we all went in this bar which was already crammed with Geordies, so it was a nightmare to get served especially as there was only one lad serving. Due to a lack of space we were having trouble playing Pool, so the lads decided to lift the Pool table up, and carry it outside into the car park. It was a great sight to see the likes of Mad Mac and Ramma playing pool outside, Mac doing his party trick with his pint on his head.

Sean Hunter
Newbiggin Hall, Newcastle

As hundreds of us all celebrated promotion in good spirits on the pitch at full time my mate was approached by a copper on horseback wielding his truncheon. To defend himself he managed to grab the Coppers truncheon which caused him to lose balance and fall off his horse.

Kev
Gosforth, Newcastle

I remember getting a very slow train, changing trains at least twice, arriving in a time warp of a Yorkshire village and walking in a big huddle to the ground. At the final whistle a full scale "on the pitch" occurred and I lost all my mates, and vividly remember getting chased across the pitch by an enormous police horse with a baton wielding policeman on board. I must have sprinted 50 metres being pursued by the local constabulary and managed to dive into the nearest stand, eventually getting the train home on my own! Now that promotion was guaranteed me and my brother got an old bed sheet and using black paint wrote "Going Up" and hung it out of our bedroom window. I remember the whole street being woken up the next day at 5am as the bin men came along and started cheering and blasting the wagon's very loud horn!!

Paul Donaghy
Newcastle

We had three sides of the ground, behind both goals was full of Geordies, the main stand seats was half full of Newcastle fans and there was continuous fighting in the opposite terraces. We were everywhere and when Newcastle fans climbed the floodlights the chant went up *"Sing In The Floodlights!"*

Scud
Prudhoe, Tyne Valley

As I remember it, I'm sure we were 2-0 down early on. Then we managed to get the ball in the back of the net three times in the last five minutes of the first half. But the game ended 2-2. Alright, it was enough to clinch promotion but in the mayhem, I honestly thought we'd won the game 3-2 and only realised when I got back on the bus after the game and Radio two told us the final score. We had both ends behind the goal, half the seats on one side and loads more in the big 'Kippax type end' on the other side. The crowd was 25,000 and we must have had 17,000 there at least. It was at the height of the miners strike and passions were running high. I wonder how many others thought we'd won that day. Certainly some on the same bus as me did!

Chris Ramshaw
West Denton, Newcastle

One of my favourite memories comes from the promotion season down in Yorkshire and the immortal line *"Sing In The Cowshed."* The fact that one end of the old Leeds Road ground at Huddersfield not only looked like but was also called 'The Cowshed' was too good to be true.......in fact it might not have been true, merely a figment of my recollection. The sight of Newcastle fans taking over three sides of the ground (for the first but not the last time) was very real as were the multiple renditions of the above ditty!

Pete Grieves
North Seaton, Northumberland

Our final away game and curiously we had fans at either end of the ground, in fact there were that many that travelled we also had some on the side terracing as well as in the seats opposite. We opted to travel by train and it was a nightmare, *"We'll Go By Bus Next Time, British Rail"* replacing the advert of the time *"Well Take More Care Of You, British Rail"* was the song that echoed around Huddersfield station as we hurriedly made our way to the ground. We were in the uncovered end of the ground, behind the goal, packed in like sardines. On the train going down I had made a bag of confetti out of the morning papers, the journey really was that long and boring. I forgot that my apple and remaining sandwiches were in the same bag as we got into the ground just before kick-off. As the players took to the pitch, Newcastle were met with a deafening wall of noise from almost three sides of the ground, ticker tape, balloons, toilet rolls (from the train) and lots of confetti, oh and also my apple and cheese savoury sandwiches which landed on some bemused lad a couple of yards in front. One lad from Shields climbed up the floodlight, to gain a better view. He was instructed to come down by Police waiting at the bottom, but knowing that he was going to be ejected or arrested, he remained up there for most of the first half. Not sure what happened when he came down, though rumour had it he dived into the crowd, who then caught him and hid him from the hapless West Yorkshire Police. No Keegan that day, out with an eye injury, but goals from his replacement Mills and the honourable Pedro, ensured promotion and a party that was to last almost a week.

Anth Nicholson
North Shields, Tyneside

Our promotion celebrations were marred by significant crowd trouble, before, during and after the match. About 1,200 Geordies invaded the pitch at the final whistle and when they refused to leave hundreds of Police many with dogs and dozens on horseback made a charge giving the Newcastle fans little option other than to climb into the main stand. Although the pitch invasion was in the main good humoured the Police's response and tactics resulted in the fans going on a rampage, as between 300 and 400 seats were ripped out, windows were smashed and numerous people were attacked. There were over 70 arrests made and fans and police were taken to hospital. Although Newcastle fans were slaughtered by the press and media and roundly held responsible, it was the Police who incited the trouble. Outside pubs were damaged and trouble continued late into the night. Huddersfield were not totally blameless though as our train was attacked in a well renowned area where it was a common occurrence for a handful of Terriers fans to throw bricks and stones at visiting fans trains. The cowards managed to put a couple of windows out and in the process a supporter was hit by flying glass. Our Football Special arrived back at the Central hours late to chorus after chorus echoing around the old station of *"We'll Take The Bus Next Time, British Rail, British Rail,"* as a dig at their advert and slogan at the time *"We'll Take More Care Of You, British Rail, British Rail."* I heard a story whilst in the ground, that on the Sunday night a group of Newcastle lads who were staying over night had a confrontation with a group of local youths wearing turbans. As a result one of the locals had NUFC spray painted on his turban. Later that night they unbelievably slept in a police waiting room as there was nowhere else to sleep.

Davey
Fawden, Newcastle

v BRIGHTON & HOVE ALBION
ST JAMES' PARK
ATT; 36,286

SAT 12TH MAY 1984
SECOND DIVISION
WON 3-1

Our final game of the season had a carnival atmosphere. I remember this as being the game in which I witnessed one of my all time favourite goals, the magical Peter Beardsley disposing a defender with a sliding tackle then coolly lobbing that giant of a keeper Joe Corrigan, who was rooted to the spot. That was the final goal in a 3-1 victory, the pubs and Town centre were heaving that night as we danced and sang late into the evening. It was at this game that a Scot's lad, whose identity I will protect, was a student who had fell in love with Newcastle. Although it was a warm day, the lad had gone to the game and stood near the Brighton fans, in the open Leazes End, wearing a duffel coat. He must have been sweltering, packed in with everyone else and with the sun shining down. The large amount of

alcohol consumed before the game had him sweating and feeling very unwell. The combination of beer, atmosphere and heat was all too much and with about

269

five minutes to go he shit himself!! Gaps appeared around him, though he stayed for the lap of honour before returning home in disgrace, funnily enough he was able to get a great vantage point for that final encore.

Anth Nicholson
North Shields, Tyneside

"At this moment I don't know where my future lies. I know where I would like it to lie, but I also know my responsibilities to the aforesaid public and my family. The situation is as it was; the ball is still in the court of the Chairman and Directors."

Arthur Cox
Newcastle United Manager

The actual match scarcely mattered; the result had no real significance. The afternoon was all about the last competitive appearance of Kevin Keegan. On a boiling hot day Keegan didn't disappoint as he grabbed a first half goal at the Leazes End. This was without doubt one of the greatest ever 'I was there moments.' To round off a superb afternoon and an unforgettable season Waddle got a rare header and Beardsley scored with the greatest individual goal I have ever witnessed. Many recall the 1983/84 season as the Promotion season; I simply recall it as the Beardsley, Keegan and Waddle season.

Mick Edmondson
Walker, Newcastle

270

It has been my privilege to play all over the world – but I have never played in front of more loyal and caring supporters. The supporters of this club deserve success – and lasting success – more than any other."

Kevin Keegan
Newcastle United

v DARLINGTON   **SUN 13TH MAY 1984**
FEETHAMS   **FRIENDLY**
ATT; 5,000   **WON 3-0**

Still drunk from the all day party session on the Saturday we travelled down to Darlo by train and before we knew it we were back on it. What makes you bad makes you better. When we arrived at Feethams in good spirits we could hear the crowd in full voice, but were surprised that as we walked across the adjacent Cricket Pitch we were alone, not a single supporter anywhere to be seen? Once at the turnstiles we were informed that the second half was just under way, as the match had kicked off at 2pm instead of the customary 3pm!! It was all square at 0-0 as we were allowed in through a side gate in time to see 3 second half goals as Keegan scored a penalty as well as goals from Clarke and Wharton. The ground was packed an excellent turn out for ex-Newcastle player David 'Dick' Barton's Testimonial/Benefit match. He had been forced to retire due to injury, as he tore his knee ligaments at Turf Moor, Burnley in the Associate Members Cup tie two months earlier. Not only did we miss the first half but we also missed a celebrity game played prior, which included Roy Chubby Brown, Weathergirl Wincey Willis and that Teesside knob 'Me Mark Page.' Roll on the First Division.

Mick Edmondson
Walker, Newcastle

v LIVERPOOL   **THURS 17TH MAY 1984**
ST JAMES' PARK   **KEEGAN'S TESTIMONIAL**
ATT; 36,722   **LOST 1-2**

An excellent party, to celebrate the end of a long and very successful football career against champions Liverpool. (The record match receipts taken from this game actually went to the club). My re-collection from this historic match was the sheer out-pouring of emotion on a night that has forever meant the chant of *"Keeee-gan, Keeee-gan"* springs to mind whenever I see a helicopter above St James' Park. A final lap of honour finishing with a spectacular 'Topshop' sponsored firework display, as Keegan was whisked away from the centre of the pitch by helicopter, pure theatre. The fact that his testimonial against Liverpool also linked my favourite all time TV series just further enhanced the memory of that night. "Auf Wiedersehen, Kev."

Pete Grieves
North Seaton, Northumberland

271

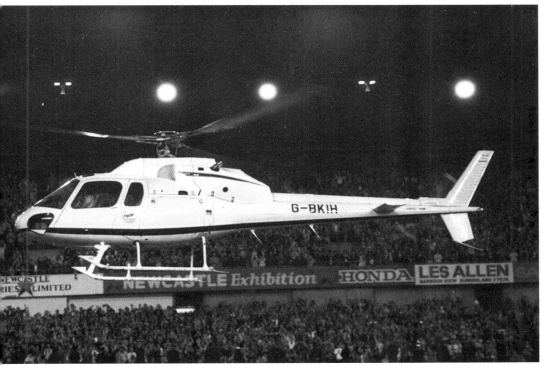

1983-84 Season Summary

At the time, it was to many, the most memorable and enjoyable season to have been a follower of Newcastle United. After the previous seasons of rubbish and heartache, we at long last at a team we could once again be proud of. Okay looking back we only finished third in the Second Division and failed to beat either of the other two promoted sides Chelsea and Sheff Wed, but it was open, exciting attacking football, as Beardsley, Keegan and Waddle ripped teams apart, both home and away. More than one million fans had watched our league home games, an average of 29,811, which was only bettered by Manchester United and Liverpool. First Division side Sunderland had an average of 16,180, which was almost half of our average even though we were in a lower league. We spent the majority of the season in the top 4, Man City our nearest rivals. Although the likes of Grimsby and Shrewsbury both took 4 points off us, we never really looked like missing out. The signing of Peter Beardsley was without doubt the difference between promotion and staying put - playing at Anfield or returning to Gay Meadow. Unfortunately many of his goals and breathtaking amazing skills weren't all captured on TV, but are imprinted in my head. It was a pleasure and a privilege to watch him play and such a relief that Charlie Nicholas and George Reilly went elsewhere as we might never have had the chance. Another great addition was Glen Roeder a Christmas present from Arthur Cox. Other players collectively played a major part in our success, such as the versatile Kenny Wharton and John Trewick who returned from injury for the final promotion push. Once again our cup results were abysmal, but the league was our priority and we kept at it collectively, continuing to bounce back after each minor hiccup. From Easter onwards it was party time as we scored for fun finishing with 85 league goals as Beardsley, Keegan and Waddle the 'Three Musketeers' turned on the style. After unbelievable scenes against Derby, which continued down at Huddersfield we had the grand finale v Brighton at SJP, when football legend Kevin Keegan played his farewell match. Then the spectacle which was his testimonial against Liverpool, which the proceeds he so kindly gave to the club, a donation which was supposed to be used on strengthening the team. Kevin Keegan said at the time; "Now is the time for this club to go into debt because they have been given a great chance. With 3 good new signings this club could not only go into the First Division and hold its own, it could challenge everyone bar Liverpool and Man Utd. Manager Arthur Cox wanted to sign the likes of Steve Bruce, Mark Wright, Mark Hateley, and Kevin Sheedy, but it wasn't to be as the board who originally only took 15 minutes to give him a 4 year contract, were now only offering him a 3 year contract after he'd won promotion? Yet again in typical Newcastle fashion, disaster struck only 12 days after the season ended when Arthur Cox resigned. He later explained; "We should have been building on all the good work and driving forward, but the place was falling to bits, we needed to go forward and continue to keep climbing." Cox would be at Derby County as their new boss within days. Did the board think that maybe he couldn't manage without Keegan? Idiots.

Typical representative team for the season:
Martin Thomas/Kevin Carr, John Anderson, John Ryan/Kenny Wharton, Jeff Clarke/Wesley Saunders, Steve Carney, David McCreery, Kevin Keegan, Peter Beardsley, Chris Waddle, Terry McDermott, John Trewick/Kenny Wharton

Total Appearances: (League, FA Cup & League Cup) - 45 matches played
McDermott, Waddle (45), Anderson, Keegan, Wharton (44), McCreery (43), Beardsley (38), Carney (35), Thomas (26), Ryan (25), Roeder (24), Carr, Saunders (19), Mills (18), Trewick (16), Clarke (14), McDonald (13), Haddock (3),

Total Goals: (League, FA Cup & League Cup) Total Scored 87.
Keegan (28), Beardsley (20), Waddle (18), McDermott (7), Mills (5), Wharton (4), Anderson, Ryan, Trewick (1) plus Opp Own Goal (2).

Second Division							
Final Table 1983-84							
Chelsea	42	25	13	4	90	40	88
Sheff Wed	42	26	10	6	72	34	88
Newcastle	42	24	8	10	85	53	80
Man City	42	20	10	12	66	48	70
Grimsby	42	19	13	10	60	47	70
Blackburn	42	17	16	9	57	46	67
Carlisle	42	16	16	10	48	41	64
Shrewsbury	42	17	10	15	49	53	61
Brighton	42	17	9	16	69	60	60
Leeds	42	16	12	14	55	56	60
Fulham	42	15	12	15	60	53	57
Huddersfield	42	14	15	13	56	49	57
Charlton	42	16	9	17	53	64	57
Barnsley	42	15	7	20	57	53	52
Cardiff	42	15	6	21	53	66	51
Portsmouth	42	14	7	21	73	64	49
Middlesbrough	42	12	13	17	41	47	49
Crystal Palace	42	12	11	19	42	52	47
Oldham	42	13	8	21	47	73	47
Derby	42	11	9	22	36	72	42
Swansea	42	7	8	27	36	85	29
Cambridge	42	4	12	26	28	77	24